Las Vegas

Also Includes Reno, Lake Tahoe, and Laughlin

ECONOGUIDE.COM | 2001

Corey Sandler

CONTEMPORARY BOOKS

This book is not authorized or endorsed by any hotel, casino, restaurant, attraction, or business decribed in its pages. All attractions, product names, or other works mentioned in this book are trademarks or registered trademarks of their respective owners or developers and are used in this book strictly for editorial purposes; no commercial claim to their use is made by the author or the publisher.

Econoguide is a registered trademark of Word Association, Inc.

Cover photograph copyright © Steve Bly/Dave Houser Stock

Published by Contemporary Books
A division of NTC/Contemporary Publishing Group, Inc.
4255 West Touhy Avenue, Lincolnwood (Chicago), Illinois 60712-1975 U.S.A.
Copyright © 2001 by Word Association, Inc.
All rights reserved. No part of this book may be reproduced, stored in a retrieval system, or transmitted in any form or by any means, electronic, mechanical, photocopying, recording, or otherwise, without the prior written permission of NTC/Contemporary Publishing Group, Inc.
Printed in the United States of America
International Standard Book Number: 0-8092-2638-3
International Standard Serial Number: 1520-0256
01 02 03 04 05 06 LB 18 17 16 15 14 13 12 11 10 9 8 7 6 5 4 3 2 1

To Janice, my fellow traveler

Contents

Acknowledgments	vii
Introduction to the Eighth Edition, 2001	ix

Part I Nevada Bound — 1
1. A Short and Irreverent History of Nevada — 1
2. How to Buy the Lowest-Cost Airline Tickets and Protect Yourself from the Uncertainties of Modern Travel — 9
3. How to Sleep for Less — 19
4. Cars, Trains, and Buses — 23

Part II Las Vegas — 27
5. Welcome, Pilgrim — 27
6. The Best of the Strip — 29
7. The Rest of the Strip — 81
8. Downtown Las Vegas — 97
9. Las Vegas Showrooms and Nightlife — 107
10. Mama Don't Allow No Gambling 'Round Here: Area Attractions — 111
11. Local Protocol: Sex, Marriage, Shopping, Comps, and Tipping — 125
12. An Index of Las Vegas Casinos, Hotels, and Motels — 141
13. Eating Your Way Across Las Vegas — 145
14. Sports and Recreation — 161
15. Journeys North of Las Vegas: Mount Charleston, Lee Canyon, Red Rock Canyon, and Valley of Fire — 167
16. Journeys South of Las Vegas: Henderson, Hoover Dam, Boulder City, Lake Mead, and Lake Mohave — 173
17. Laughlin — 183

Part III Reno, Virginia City, and Lake Tahoe — 199
18. The Biggest Little Chapter in This Book: Reno — 199
19. Eating Your Way Through Reno-Sparks — 223

20.	Reno-Sparks Area Attractions	229
21.	The Great Outdoors in Reno-Sparks	233
22.	Shopping and Getting Married	235
23.	Drive, He Said: Eight Trips from Reno and Lake Tahoe	239
24.	Virginia City: A Side Trip Back in Time	261
25.	Carson City: A Capital Before There Was a State	277
26.	Lake Tahoe: Mountain Shangri-La	283
27.	Winter Sports in the Lake Tahoe Region	303
28.	Warm Weather and Year-Round Activities in the Lake Tahoe Region	315

Special Offers to Econoguide Readers 327
Quick-Find Index to Hotels, Attractions, and Restaurants 353

Acknowledgments

Dozens of hardworking and creative people helped move my words from the keyboard to the place where you read this book now.

Among the many to thank are Editor Adam Miller of Contemporary Books for working with me as we expand the Econoguide series.

Val Elmore headed up the prodigious fact-checking effort with good humor and attention to detail, and then changed hats to polish my prose as copy editor. Collie Raye worked the Reno and Lake Tahoe beat. As always, Janice Keefe managed the Word Association office and the author superbly.

Thanks, too, to Julia Anderson and the production staff at Contemporary.

We appreciate our friends at hotels, casinos, restaurants, and attractions who opened their doors to us; special thanks to the companies that offered discount coupons to our readers.

Thanks to Olympus for the loan of their sophisticated Olympus Camedia C-2020 digital camera, used to take many of the photos credited to the author in this book.

And finally, thank you for buying this book. We all hope you find it of value; please let me know how we can improve the book in future editions. (Please enclose a stamped envelope if you'd like a reply; no calls, please.)

                        Corey Sandler
                        Econoguide Travel Books
                        P.O. Box 2779
                        Nantucket, MA 02584

You can also send electronic mail to: csandler@econoguide.com.

And check out the contents of the other books in the Econoguide series on our web page, at: www.econoguide.com. You'll also find some current links to explore and a gallery of photos.

NEVADA

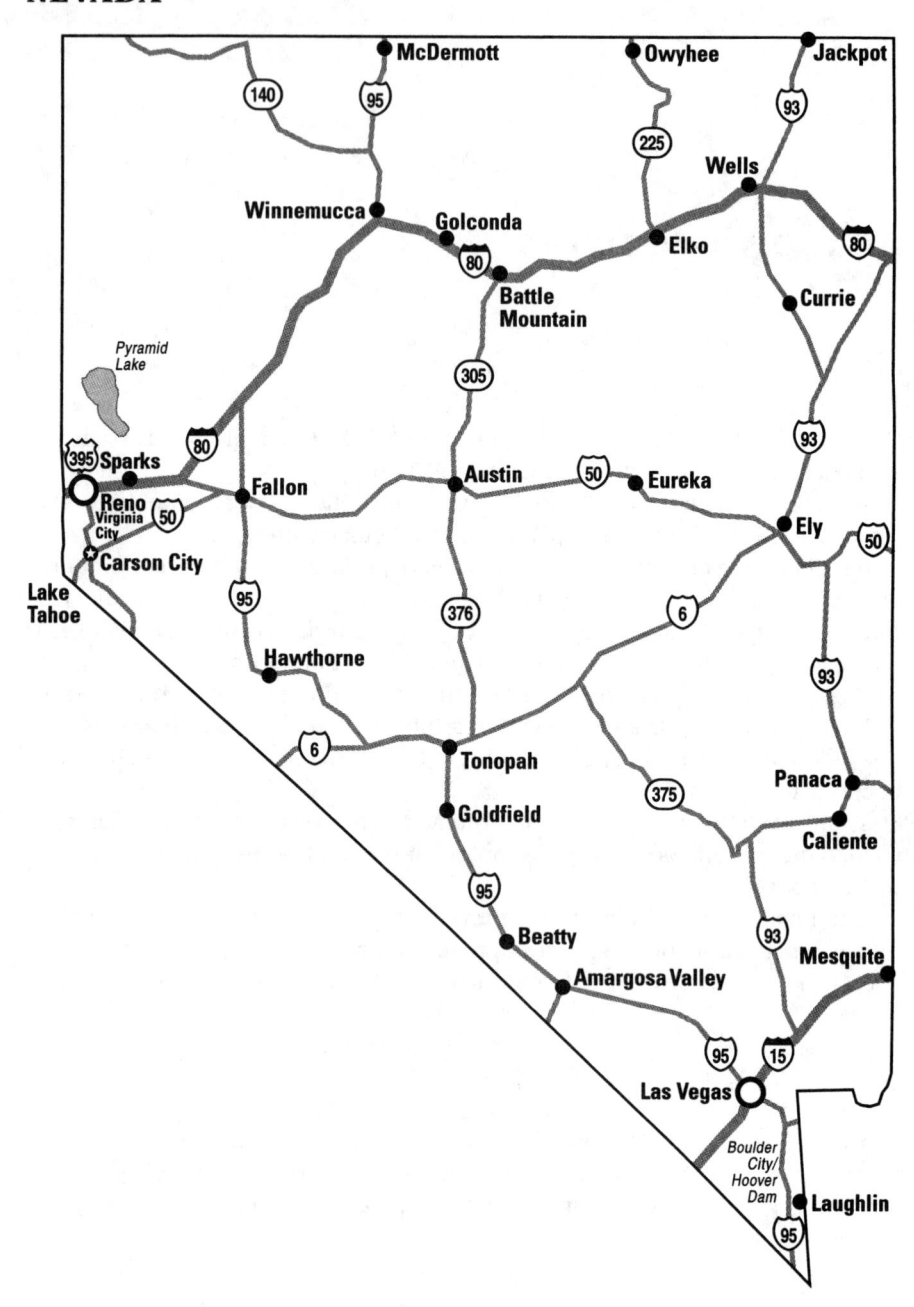

Introduction to the Eighth Edition, 2001

This is the eighth time I've put fingers to keyboard to write an introduction to a book about Las Vegas, Reno, Lake Tahoe, and Laughlin, and each time I've marveled at how much has changed in the previous year.

I worry that someday I will run out of superlatives.

In this edition, we'll explore Paris and Venice and Mandalay, a trio of fabled places reborn on the Las Vegas Strip. I'll tell you about major improvements at dozens of other hotels and casinos, and offer a preview of the next big thing: the new Aladdin.

Over on the other side of the state, the biggest little city in the world (also known as Reno) has a dramatic new downtown plaza. At the southern end of the gorgeous Lake Tahoe, Stateline is on the verge of new development among its casinos and ski resorts.

All in all, Nevada is one of the most exciting places I know, from the manmade wonders of the Las Vegas Strip and Glitter Gulch to the concrete canyon of Hoover Dam to the almost indescribably beautiful natural splendors of Lake Tahoe and the Sierra Nevada mountains.

Forever Frontier

Nevada will probably always be the frontier. It is a place where things are different, where old assumptions are challenged, and where new ideas are tried.

That is, after all, why people come to Nevada. Although gambling has begun to spread across the nation, there is still no Las Vegas in Chicago or Boston or Los Angeles. There is no Lake Mead in New Jersey. There are no snow-capped mountains with ski runs that careen down to an alpine lake in Kansas. And, although Nevada is a relatively young state, there are few places I know that are as imbued with living history as Virginia City.

Before we go too far, let's start with what this book is *not* about:

- It is *not* a rose-colored view of the world endorsed by the chamber of commerce. Not everything in Nevada is wonderful, a good value, or a worthwhile use of your vacation time. We'll try to help you get the most from your trip.
- It is *not* a guide for the cheapskate interested in sleeping in bus terminals (or motels that look like bus terminals) and eating exclusively at restaurants that use plastic forks. What we mean by "Econoguide" is this: helpful information so you can get the most out of your trip to Nevada. We'll show you how to save time and money on travel, hotels, restaurants, and entertainment. Even if you choose to go for first-class airfare, luxury hotels, and the most expensive restaurants in town, we'll help you spend your money wisely.
- It is *not* a guide to making money at the gambling tables. I will, though, offer a cautious guide to casinos, concentrating on how to have fun and not lose more money than you are prepared to donate in the name of fun.

Let's think a bit about the state of Nevada, a place of great contrasts.

The seventh-largest state in the union, it is 38th in population. It is today the fastest-growing state, though it is still very sparsely populated with 1.8 million people across 110,540 square miles—and almost all of the residents are concentrated around the urban areas of Las Vegas and Reno. Clark County, which includes Las Vegas, Henderson, Boulder City, and Laughlin, is bigger than the entire state of Massachusetts.

Winters are extremely cold in the north and west; summers in the south are oven-like. Nevada's highest point is a lofty 13,143 feet at Boundary Peak on the snowy border with California; the lowest is along the Colorado River as it enters the hot and dry desert in the southern tip of the state.

Nevada's economy is focused on mining: mining minerals out of the ground and mining gold and silver out of the pockets of tourists who come to visit in great droves. Las Vegas alone draws more than 30 million visitors annually. Fully half of the workers in the state are in the service trades, with 25 percent directly employed by a casino or hotel. In Las Vegas alone, casinos provide more than 100,000 jobs.

One of the great, uncelebrated things about Nevada's tourist centers of Las Vegas, Reno, Laughlin, and Lake Tahoe is that you can find a bathroom, telephone, change booth, or restaurant at any hour of the day or night, any day of the year. You can also find a casino open at any time. Usually in the same place, of course.

Let's head out on an exploration of all sides of Nevada, from the oasis in the desert at Laughlin to the mirage at Las Vegas to the Great Western Rest Stop at Reno to the honeycombed mountains of Virginia City and the Comstock Lode to the breathtaking beauty of Lake Tahoe.

But first, a salute to the members of the Econoguide 2001 Bests.

Introduction to the Eighth Edition, 2001

econoguide 2001 Best Casinos in Las Vegas

★★★★★ Bellagio
★★★★★ Caesars Palace
★★★★★ Mandalay Bay
★★★★★ Paris–Las Vegas
★★★★★ Rio Suite
★★★★★ The Venetian
★★★★ Aladdin
★★★★ Hard Rock Hotel
★★★★ Las Vegas Hilton
★★★★ MGM Grand
★★★★ The Mirage
★★★★ Monte Carlo
★★★★ New York–New York

econoguide 2001 Best Restaurants in Las Vegas

Casino Restaurants
★★★★ Bistro Le Montrachet. Las Vegas Hilton
★★★★ Emeril Lagasse's New Orleans Fish House. MGM Grand
★★★★ Empress Court. Caesars Palace
★★★★ Le Cirque. Bellagio
★★★★ Lutéce. Venetian
★★★★ Red Square. Mandalay Bay
★★★★ Rumjungle. Mandalay Bay
★★★★ Star Canyon. Venetian
★★★★ Zefferino. Venetian

Outside the Casinos
★★★★ Andre's French Restaurant
★★★★ Pamplemousse
★★★★ P. F. Chang's China Bistro

econoguide 2001 Best Casino Buffets in Las Vegas

★★★★★ Carnival World Buffet. Rio Suite
★★★★★ Palatium. Caesars Palace
★★★★ Bayside Buffet. Mandalay Bay
★★★★ Bellagio Buffet. Bellagio
★★★★ Le Village. Paris–Las Vegas

econoguide 2001 Best Places to Stay in Las Vegas

★★★★★ Bellagio
★★★★★ Caesars Palace
★★★★★ Mandalay Bay
★★★★★ Paris-Las Vegas
★★★★★ Rio Suite
★★★★★ The Venetian

econoguide 2001 Best Casino Shopping in Las Vegas

★★★★ The Forum Shops. Caesars Palace
★★★★ Bellagio. Via Bellagio. Bellagio
★★★★ Grand Canal Shoppes. The Venetian

econoguide 2001 Best Attractions in Las Vegas

Casino Attractions
★★★★ Masquerade Show in the Sky. Rio Suite
★★★★ Volcano. Mirage
★★★★ Fountains at Bellagio. Bellagio
★★★★ Fremont Street Experience
★★★★ Caesars Magical Empire. Caesars Palace
★★★★ Imperial Palace Auto Museum. Imperial Palace

Thrill Rides and Theme Parks
★★★★ Adventuredome. Circus Circus
★★★★ Manhattan Express. New York–New York
★★★★ Race for Atlantis IMAX 3D Ride. Caesars Forum Shops
★★★★ MGM Grand Adventures. MGM Grand
★★★★ Speedworld. Sahara
★★★★ Speed: The Ride. Sahara
★★★★ Star Trek: The Experience. Las Vegas Hilton
★★★★ Stratosphere Tower and Rides. Stratosphere Tower
★★★★ Wet 'n Wild

Natural and Man-Made Wonders
★★★★ Hoover Dam
★★★★ Red Rock Canyon

econoguide 2001 Special Mentions

★★★★ Best cocktail waitress outfits. Rio Suites
★★★★ Best Centurion uniforms. Caesars Palace
★★★★ Gaudiest outdoor show on The Strip. Mirage
★★★★ Classiest outdoor show on The Strip. Bellagio
★★★★ Gaudiest exterior on The Strip. Excalibur
★★★★ Imitation is the sincerest flattery. (Tie). Paris–Las Vegas Casino
★★★★ Imitiation is the sincerest flattery. (Tie) The Venetian

econoguide 2001 Best Production Shows in Las Vegas

★★★★★ Cirque du Soleil's Mystère. Treasure Island
★★★★★ Cirque du Soleil presents "O." Bellagio
★★★★★ EFX. MGM Grand
★★★★★ Siegfried & Roy. Mirage
★★★★ Blue Man Group. Luxor
★★★★ Danny Gans. Stardust
★★★★ Jubilee! Bally's
★★★★ Lance Burton. Monte Carlo

Part I
Nevada Bound

Chapter 1
A Short and Irreverent History of Nevada

When they spoke of the "Wild West," it was often Nevada they had in mind.

Wild, as in a nearly virgin land when the first white explorers set foot there about the time of the American Revolution.

Wild, as in the extremes of weather from the arid deserts of the eastern part of the state to the high, snowy mountains of Sierra Nevada in the west.

Wild, as in the heady days in the 1850s and 1860s when gold and then silver were discovered south of Reno, and when for a short period of time Virginia City was the richest place on earth.

Wild, as in the early days of Las Vegas at the start of the twentieth century when the "anything goes" atmosphere of the railroad town laid the foundation for what would become Glitter Gulch and then the Strip.

Wild, as in the state of Nevada of today, a place that is just slightly ahead of, or behind, or off to one side of, anywhere else we know.

Throughout all of its history, Nevada has been looked upon as a colony for outside interests to exploit. First came the Spanish, then the British and their Canadian surrogates. When the land came under control of the young United States, Nevada was considered little more than a rest stop on the highway to California. When gold and silver were discovered in great quantities in and around Virginia City, much of the wealth was exported out of the state to California and even as far away as England.

The interests that developed much of the early commercial properties of Nevada were the railroads, and they, too, sent their money west and east. And finally, there was gambling, Nevada's one major homegrown industry. The casinos took off in the 1940s only after organized crime capitalists from New York, Chicago, Miami, Los Angeles, and elsewhere came in and exerted control. Today, the gangsters are mostly gone, but control of nearly all the major casinos and hotels rests in the hands of huge stateless corporations.

The River to the Pacific

The region that would one day be Nevada was originally part of the Spanish Empire in the New World. Father Francisco Garcés is believed to have entered the Las Vegas Valley in 1776. Garcés and other priest-explorers were expanding the Old Spanish Trail, which led from the commercial centers of Santa Fe (now in New Mexico) to the Spanish missions in southern California. Along the way, they sought to make converts if they could; more than a few Native Americans were killed in skirmishes and by disease.

There was, of course, a significant problem faced by the Spanish: getting through deserts and high mountain passes that stood between New Mexico and California. Sierra Nevada is a Spanish phrase meaning "snowy mountains." Garcés and others of his time followed the Colorado River into Nevada and did not fully explore the region geologists now call the Great Basin. And in the process, they made some significant errors on their maps and created the myth of what they called the San Buenaventura River, a great waterway that was supposed to cross the Great Basin and empty into the Pacific Ocean. In other words, they claimed there was an easy route from east to west that did not require crossing the high mountains. For much of the next half-century, trappers and explorers searched in vain for the San Buenaventura.

In 1825, Peter Skene Ogden explored parts of Nevada from the other direction, south from Canada. Working for the Hudson's Bay Company, he discovered the Humboldt River in northwest Nevada in that year. A year later, Jedediah Strong Smith, an explorer and fur trader, followed the Colorado River into southern Nevada—the same entry Garcés took fifty years earlier—and soon thereafter the 1,200-mile-long Spanish Trail became firmly established.

Smith, born in 1798 in Bainbridge, New York, went to the West as a young fur trapper and became one of the great pathfinders of our country. His group of seventeen set out from the Great Salt Lake in 1826 looking for fur trade routes to California and the Northwest. He crossed the Mojave Desert to Mission San Gabriel, California, near what is today San Diego, and may have been the first non-native to enter California from the East. Returning eastward the next year, he crossed the Great Salt Lake Desert on an epic journey through the inhospitable, waterless sands.

Another group of explorers was seeking a way to link the Mormon settlements of Salt Lake City and California, and the trailblazers sought a way to avoid the highest of the Sierra Nevada mountain passes by going south.

In 1829, Rafael Rivera, a young scout for Spanish traders, entered a valley that had a patch of tall grass about two miles long and half a mile wide—a desert oasis that offered a small amount of drinkable water. That valley, called *las vegas* (Spanish for "the meadows") became a regular stopping-off point for travelers on the westward trail.

John C. Frémont, a U.S. Army officer, conducted extensive explorations in 1843 and 1845. In 1848, at the end of the Mexican War, the territory that included what would become Nevada was acquired by the United States from Mexico for $15 million in the Treaty of Guadalupe Hidalgo.

But it took the discovery of gold at Sutter's Mill near Sacramento, California, in 1847 to begin mass migration to the West Coast, and much of the traffic passed through Nevada; during the next seven years, the population of California grew from about 15,000 to 300,000.

In 1849, Mormon settlers established a trading post at Mormon Station (now known as Genoa) in the Carson River Valley, at the base of the Sierra Nevadas. In 1855, a colony of Mormon evangelists arrived in the Las Vegas Valley and established the Las Vegas Mission in an attempt to bring their religion and knowledge to the Paiute Indians. They built a fort—importing some of the wood from mountains as far as twenty miles away—and planted crops. Although they apparently had some success in their assignments, in 1857, the settlers were recalled to Salt Lake City by Brigham Young after the church government had a dispute with the U.S. government, and the mission was abandoned.

In the late 1850s, the area around Virginia City, Carson City, and Genoa served as a staging area for settlers about to head over the Sierras to California. The Mormon Station had become a thriving commercial operation after a simple log cabin store was erected in 1851. Genoa was also the first home of the *Territorial Enterprise* newspaper, which was to become an important element of the developing Western culture.

The relatively quiet status of Nevada as a rest stop on the highway west changed mightily about this time. There had been some minor gold finds in Gold Canyon in about 1850, but the quantity was so relatively small as to be lost in the excitement over the California discoveries.

But in January of 1859, gold and then silver—the Great Comstock Lode— were found on the slopes of Mount Davidson between Reno and Carson City. By the spring of 1860, a full boom was underway at Virginia City. (One of the miners, James "Old Virginny" Finney, bestowed his name on the rough settlement of tents and cave dwellings of the first miners.)

In 1862, the U.S. Congress granted a charter to the Union Pacific Railroad to build the first transcontinental railroad, stretching from near Sacramento, California, to Missouri, where it would connect to eastern systems.

The mines in and around Virginia City had a lasting impact on the nation, bringing Nevada Territory into the Union as a source of wealth at the start of the Civil War in 1861. Many local mine owners were opposed to statehood, fearing their riches would be taxed to support the war; President Lincoln, who sought Nevada's support in Congress, pushed its statehood, which took place in 1864. Along the way, the riches of the Comstock Lode provided much of the capital for the development of San Francisco.

After the Mormons abandoned their fort in Las Vegas in 1857, a local farmer, Octavius Decatur Gass, acquired the water rights in the valley and moved into the old Mormon fort. Gass, who went on to become a major political force in the area, had come from Ohio in search of gold.

The 640-acre site, now referred to as the Las Vegas Ranch, occupied what is now the entire downtown area. A section of the old fort still stands in a city museum.

The next driving force in Nevada was the coming of the railroads. Though the Civil War held most of the attention of a war-weary America, citizens also watched as the Central Pacific and Union Pacific Railroads raced east and west toward each other in the construction of the first transcontinental railroad. The CP began on January 1, 1863, in Sacramento, California; the UP broke

> **Dear landlord.** Nevada, which entered the Union on October 31, 1864, as the 36th state, covers 110,561 square miles, the seventh largest state in the country. As big as Nevada is, consider the fact that 86 percent of the land area is owned by the federal government.

ground on December 2 of the same year in Omaha, Nebraska. The Central Pacific tracks passed through northern Nevada (Reno, Winnemucca, and Elko) to the meeting point at Promontory Point, Utah, where the Golden Spike was driven on May 10, 1869.

The main line became the lure to additional railroad construction in the state. The Virginia & Truckee Railroad, which serviced the silver and gold mines of Virginia City, was extended from Carson City to the east-west tracks at Reno.

At the start of 1905, the final spike connecting a southern railroad route between Los Angeles and Salt Lake City was driven into the desert floor about twenty miles south of what would become Las Vegas. The Tonopah & Las Vegas Railroad sprang up to link mining and ranching operations to the southern tracks.

The former Mormon ranch, which covered much of what is now downtown Las Vegas, came into the ownership of the Stewart family in 1882. Twenty years later, they sold the property for $55,000 to copper and railroad magnate William Clark, who was also U.S. Senator from Montana. He decided to make Las Vegas a division point for his San Pedro, Los Angeles, and Salt Lake Railroad and not incidentally drive up the value of his land holdings.

And so, on the morning of May 15, 1905, Clark's railroad and the closely linked Las Vegas Land and Water Company banged the opening gavel for an auction of the Las Vegas Ranch and surrounding lands. The sale was conducted from a temporary structure near the railroad station; the site today is roughly the location of the Union Plaza Hotel at the head of Fremont Street in downtown Las Vegas.

A crowd of more than one thousand bid feverishly on some twelve hundred lots; the auction continued into a second day. Spots considered prime property brought as much as $1,750, and the total net was about $265,000.

The Las Vegas Rest Stop

The first train from Salt Lake City to Los Angeles passed through the growing town of Las Vegas in 1906, and a year later a second railroad line was installed from Las Vegas northwest to Tonopah.

For most of the next quarter-century, the town thrived as a rest stop for travelers on the railroads and also as a commercial center for outlying mining operations.

The wants and needs of the miners were by most sensibilities a bit on the rough side. Many visited what passed for a town to buy basic supplies, obtain a hot bath, visit a saloon for some drinking and gambling, and find a woman for sex; the priorities were not necessarily in that order, either.

As a frontier town, Las Vegas included its share of illegal gaming parlors and a red-light district almost from the start. When the planners for the San Pedro, Los Angeles, and Salt Lake Railroad divvied up the Las Vegas Ranch, they named the area that is now between First and Second and Ogden and Stewart streets (one block in from the main drag of Fremont Street) Block 16. It was here that the first saloons—many with "cribs" out back—were located.

The Arizona Club was one of the first brick buildings in town and was generally considered the class of Las Vegas. An old photograph shows the tiny saloon along a very rough dirt road with a 50-foot-long boardwalk. The sign outside read, "Arizona Club. Headquarters for Fully Matured Reimported Straight Whiskey."

Town officials and the police turned a blind eye to the drinking, entertainment, prostitution, and gambling that took place in Block 16, which soon became known more simply as "The Block." These vices were not exactly legal, existing in a political netherworld for decades. In fact, the operators of the whorehouses were required to purchase an annual license for their operations, and the employees were subject to weekly medical examinations.

Gambling had been legal in Nevada from the time of its statehood until 1911, when reacting to a developing conservatism in the country, the legislature outlawed betting. Eight years later, the U.S. Congress instituted Prohibition, outlawing consumption of alcoholic beverages.

But that seemed to matter very little in the Wild West of Las Vegas, particularly in Block 16. Bootleggers supplied alcohol, prostitution flourished, and unregulated games of chance continued for the next twenty years.

A Dam Site

The next important event in local history came courtesy of the Federal Bureau of Reclamation when it authorized the construction of the Boulder Dam on the Colorado River about thirty miles southeast of Las Vegas. The dam was deemed necessary to control the Colorado, which regularly flooded the Imperial Valley in California and the Yuma Valley in Arizona when mountain snows melted each spring and dried to a near trickle in the summer.

Bureau of Reclamation engineers investigated more than seventy sites along the Colorado River before choosing the site of Black Canyon.

The dam was to create the 110-mile-long Lake Mead reservoir upstream and allow the controlled release of water down the Colorado River. (During the construction period, the Colorado River was diverted around the site by four huge tunnels, each fifty feet in diameter.)

Construction began in 1930 and took five years to complete. More than 5,000 workers, many of them with families, moved to the area, and Las Vegas once more was the attractive rest stop in the desert.

Not at all coincidentally, the Nevada legislature reestablished legalized casino gambling in 1931, and small casinos began catering to the construction workers. Included in the same session was a liberalization of divorce laws, requiring a short six-week residency for out-of-staters seeking to cast asunder their marriage vows.

And also not incidentally, the huge generators at the dam—renamed Hoover Dam—produced plentiful, cheap electricity that was essential to the neon signs of Glitter Gulch and the Strip and the air-conditioning within the huge hotels.

The first Las Vegas gaming license was issued in 1931 to the Northern Club at 15 East Fremont Street. Two years later, Prohibition was officially ended throughout the nation, and the consumption of alcohol became legal again.

Block 16, which continued to thrive even when most of its vices became legal, was finally killed off by a different sort of national urgency—World War II. The commander of the Las Vegas Aerial and Gunnery Range, where many thousands of soldiers were training, feared outbreaks of disease and lack of discipline among his troops. Las Vegas officials were informed that unless they cracked down on The Block, the Army would declare the whole city off-limits to servicemen. Almost immediately, the liquor and slot machine licenses of The Block were revoked. Prostitution, which operated as an adjunct to the other forms of entertainment, died off as an organized operation soon afterward.

Prostitution receded into the underworld again for the next few decades, reemerging as a legal industry in 1973 when the Nevada Supreme Court upheld the right of the state's counties to permit the activity. Brothels are legal in several Nevada counties today, and several major brothels operate outside of Las Vegas, Reno, and Carson City.

The first major casinos were established in downtown Las Vegas along Fremont Street, which eventually became known as Glitter Gulch. Joining the Northern Club in 1932 was the Hotel Apache, with a hundred rooms and the first elevator in town. With the exception of the dam workers—most of whom departed by 1936—the attraction of the casinos was almost entirely regional.

The war contributed to the growth of the area, with the establishment of the Aerial Gunnery School and a huge magnesium processing plant, Basic Magnesium, that brought ten thousand workers to Pittman (now Henderson) between Las Vegas and Boulder City. Magnesium is a component of incendiary bombs.

It was in the 1940s, however, that Las Vegas gained national notoriety, and much of the impetus came from organized crime, led by Benjamin "Bugsy" Siegel, Charles "Lucky" Luciano, Meyer Lansky, and others.

Clever businessmen, the gangsters forged links right from the start with Hollywood. This is not to say that the movie stars of the era were directly involved with the gangsters, but there was a definite synergy between the needs of the stars and the operators of the casinos.

Clara Bow (the "It girl") and Rex Bell, film stars of the 1920s and '30s, were early adopters of Las Vegas glitz. They built a ranch and were hosts of the town; they brought many later stars, including Clark Gable, Errol Flynn, the Barrymores, and others to town for visits.

Gamblers Get Out of Town

The El Rancho Vegas was founded miles from downtown in 1941, on U.S. 91, then called the Los Angeles Highway. The hotel included sixty-three bunga-

A Short and Irreverent History of Nevada

low-like rooms, and riding stables, a showroom and, of course, a casino.

The famous Flamingo hotel opened five years later on the highway (renamed as Las Vegas Boulevard and soon to become known as the Strip) and the seeds of modern Las Vegas were sown.

If there is a true civic father to Las Vegas, it would be Benjamin Siegel; you didn't call him "Bugsy" to his face. Born in Brooklyn, Siegel was a major operator in East Coast organized crime. He was sent out West in the 1930s to run a bookmaking wire service and to look after other interests there; among other things, he also owned and operated a fleet of offshore gambling ships that served Californians.

The Flamingo was Siegel's lavish dream; at the time of its opening on December 26, 1946 (with Jimmy Durante and Abbot & Costello as opening acts), it was the southernmost hotel on the Strip. Siegel saw that building an expensive pleasure palace would draw rich—and unprofessional—gamblers.

Siegel was martyred for his cause, too. He was executed by business associates in 1947, allegedly because of claims he siphoned money from the building fund for the Flamingo.

The second big resort out of town was the Last Frontier, which featured an Old West theme; guests who flew into town were picked up at the airport in a stagecoach.

One after another, hotels and casinos were built on the Strip, moving farther southward.

The Desert Inn opened in 1950 and made its mark with its showrooms featuring some of the biggest stars of the time. The Stardust brought another sta-

Caesars Palace offers gaming lessons to all guests.

ple of Las Vegas in 1958, the fancified girlie show: the Lido de Paris was a spectacular stage show that (almost) incidentally included a stageful of topless dancers.

In 1966, Caesars Palace opened and launched the era of the opulent gambling palace, and Las Vegas as we know it was born. The idea of Las Vegas as a "family" resort accelerated in 1993 and 1994 with the opening of the MGM Grand Adventures theme park and hotel (with a casino, of course), as well as the spectacular Luxor and Treasure Island.

Today the race is on to create the most luxurious, most phantasmagorical pleasure palaces. At the front of this very expensive pack are Mandalay Bay, The Venetian, and Paris–Las Vegas.

The Biggest Little Second City of Nevada

Across the state, Reno began as a toll booth over the Truckee River, a private bridge known as Lake's Crossing. And, of course, as a rest stop for travelers heading somewhere else: to California over the Sierra Nevadas and to the wild mining towns of Virginia City and the rest of the Comstock.

Today, though Reno depends upon casinos and tourism for much of its income, it has a more diversified economy than Las Vegas.

And by the way, not all the gold mined in Nevada comes from the pockets of unlucky gamblers. Today, the state produces two-thirds of the gold mined in the United States, more than $2 billion per year; other minerals, including silver, copper, gypsum, and a bit of oil, bring in another billion or so.

Chapter 2
How to Buy the Lowest-Cost Airline Tickets and Protect Yourself from the Uncertainties of Modern Travel

Let's get real: do you prefer one airline over another because it offers a better quality sandwich-in-a-bag, plumper pillows, or three whole inches of extra legroom?

The way I figure it, one major airline is pretty much like any other. Sure, one company may offer a larger plastic bag of peanuts while the other promises its flight attendants have more accommodating smiles. Me, I'm much more interested in other things:

1. safety,
2. the most convenient schedule, and
3. the lowest price.

Sometimes I'm willing to trade price for convenience; I'll never risk my neck for a few dollars.

But that doesn't mean I don't try my hardest to get the very best price on airline tickets. I watch the newspapers for seasonal sales and price wars, clip coupons from the usual and not-so-usual sources, consult the burgeoning world of Internet travel agencies, and happily play one airline against the other.

Alice in Airlineland

There are three golden rules to saving hundreds of dollars on travel: be flexible, be flexible, and be flexible.

- Be flexible about when you choose to travel. Go to Las Vegas or Reno during the off-season or low-season when airfares, hotel rooms, and attractions offer substantial discounts.
- Be flexible about the day of the week you travel. You can often save hundreds of dollars by changing your departure date one or two days. Ask your travel agent or airline reservationist for current fare rules and restrictions.

The lightest air travel days are generally midweek, Saturday afternoons, and

> **The best policy.** If any significant portion of your trip is nonrefundable, consider buying cancellation insurance from a travel agency, tour operator, or directly from an insurance company (ask your insurance agent for advice). The policies are intended to reimburse you for any lost deposits or prepayments if you must cancel a trip because you or certain members of your family become ill. Take care not to purchase more coverage than you need; if your tour package costs $5,000 but you would lose only $1,000 in the event of a cancellation, then the amount of insurance required is just $1,000. Some policies will cover you for health and accident benefits while on vacation, but your existing health policy will probably handle such an emergency as well. In any case, travel insurance usually excludes any preexisting conditions.

Sunday mornings. The busiest days are Sunday evenings, Monday mornings, and Friday.

In general, you will receive the lowest possible fare if you include a Saturday in your trip, buying what is called an excursion fare. Airlines use this as a way to exclude business travelers from the cheapest fares, assuming they will want to be home by Friday night.

- Be flexible on the hour of your departure. There is generally lower demand—and therefore lower prices—for flights that leave in the middle of the day or very late at night.
- Be flexible on the route you will take, or your willingness to put up with a change of plane or stopover. Once again, you are putting the law of supply and demand in your favor. A direct flight from Boston to Las Vegas for a family of four may cost hundreds of dollars more than a flight from Boston that includes a change of planes in Dallas (an American Airlines hub) or Minneapolis (a Northwest hub).
- Don't overlook flying out of a different airport, either. For example, metropolitan New Yorkers can find domestic flights from La Guardia, Newark, or White Plains. Suburbanites of Boston might want to consider flights from Worcester or Providence as possibly cheaper alternatives to Logan Airport. In the Los Angeles area, there are planes going in and out of LAX, Orange County, Burbank, and Palm Springs to name a few airports. Look for airports where there is competition: try Birmingham instead of Atlanta, or Louisville instead of Cincinnati, for example.

Look for airports that are served by low-cost carriers. For example, in mid-2000 I was quoted a fare of $440 to fly from Syracuse to Las Vegas on United or American Airlines. I then checked flights from Albany, a few hours away by car but served by discounter Southwest Airlines. There I found a Southwest fare of $218, and a near-matching fare of $227 from US Airways. For a family of four, a few hours on the New York State Thruway by car or bus can save about $800.

- Plan way ahead of time and purchase the most deeply discounted advance tickets, which are usually noncancelable. Most carriers limit the number of discount tickets on any particular flight; although there may be plenty of seats left on the day you want to travel, they may be offered at higher rates.

In a significant change in recent years, most airlines have changed "nonrefundable" fares to "noncancelable." What this means is that if you are forced

to cancel or change your trip, your tickets retain their value and can be applied against another trip, usually for a fee of about $75 per ticket.
- Conversely, you can take a big chance and wait for the last possible moment, keeping in contact with charter tour operators and accepting a bargain price on a "leftover" seat and hotel reservation. You *may* find that some airlines will reduce the prices on leftover seats within a few weeks of departure date; don't be afraid to check regularly with the airline, or ask your travel agent to do it for you. In fact, some travel agencies have automated computer programs that keep a constant electronic eagle eye on available seats and fares.
- Take advantage of special discount programs such as senior citizens' clubs, military discounts, or offerings from organizations to which you may belong. If you are in the over-sixty category, you may not even have to belong to a group such as AARP; simply ask the airline reservationist if there is a discount available. You may have to prove your age when you pick up your ticket.
- The day of the week you buy your tickets may also make a price difference. Airlines often test out higher fares over the relatively quiet weekends. They're looking to see if their competitors will match their higher rates; if the other carriers don't bite, the fares often float back down by Monday morning. Shop during the week.

Low-season in most of Nevada is generally the late fall to early spring, with the quietest time of the year the weeks around Christmas and New Year's, but not including those holidays themselves.

Watch out for the huge conventions that descend on Las Vegas and grab the premium rooms and drive up the prices of all the rest.

In Reno, the winter is the offest of off-seasons, with the exception of occasional massive bowling tournament crowds. The ski-oriented resorts around Lake Tahoe are busy in the winter and sometimes sold out on weekends and holidays, but rooms are usually available during the week, except in holiday periods.

Other Money-Saving Strategies

Airlines are forever weeping and gnashing their teeth about huge losses due to cutthroat competition. And then they regularly turn around and drop their prices radically with major sales. I don't waste time worrying about the bottom line of the airlines; it's my own wallet I want to keep full. Therefore, the savvy traveler keeps an eye out for airline fare wars all the time. Read the ads in newspapers and keep an ear open to news broadcasts that often cover the outbreak of price drops. If you have a good relationship with a travel agent, you can ask to be notified of any fare sales.

The most common times for airfare wars are in the weeks leading up to the quietest seasons for carriers, including the period from mid-May to mid-June (except the Memorial Day weekend), between Labor Day and Thanksgiving, and again in the winter with the exception of Christmas, New Year's, and President's Day holiday periods.

Study the fine print on discount coupons distributed directly by the airlines or through third parties such as supermarkets, catalog companies, and direct

Funny hat fares. If you are traveling to a convention, you may be able to get in on an airline discount negotiated by the group. In fact, you may not need any affiliation at all with a convention group to take advantage of special rates, if offered. All the airline will ask is the name or number of the discount plan for the convention; that information is often published on convention materials or available through sponsoring organizations. The reservationist is almost certainly not going to ask to see your union card or funny hat.

Check with convention bureaus to see if any large groups are traveling when you plan to fly. Is this sneaky and underhanded? Perhaps. But I think it is sneaky and underhanded for an airline to charge hundreds of dollars more for the seats to the left and right of the one I am sitting in.

marketers. In my experience, these coupons are often less valuable than they seem. Read the fine print carefully, and be sure to ask the reservationist if the price quoted with the coupon is higher than another fare for which you qualify.

Consider doing business with discounters, known in the industry as consolidators or, less flatteringly, as "bucket shops." Look for ads in the classified sections of many Sunday newspaper travel sections. These companies buy the airlines' slow-to-sell tickets in volume and resell them to consumers at rock-bottom prices.

Look for ads for ticket brokers and bucket shops online and in the classifieds in *USA Today*, the "Mart" section of the *Wall Street Journal* or in specialty magazines such as *Frequent Flyer*.

Some travel agencies can also offer you consolidator tickets. Just be sure to weigh the savings on the ticket price against any restrictions attached to the tickets: they may not be changeable, and they usually do not accrue frequent flyer mileage, for example.

Don't be afraid to ask for a refund on previously purchased tickets if fares go down for the period of your travel. The airline may refund the difference, or you may be able to reticket your itinerary at the new fare, paying a $75 penalty for cashing in the old tickets. Be persistent: if the difference in fare is significant, it may be worth making a visit to the airport to meet with a supervisor at the ticket counter.

Beating the Airlines at Their Own Game

In my opinion, the airlines deserve all the headaches we travelers can give them because of the illogical and costly pricing schemes they throw at us—deals such as a fare of $350 to fly ninety miles between two cities where they hold a monopoly, and $198 bargain fares to travel 3,000 miles across the nation. Or round-trip fares of $300 if you leave on a Thursday and return on a Monday, and $1,200 if you leave on a Monday and return on the next Thursday.

But a creative traveler can find ways to work around most of these roadblocks. Nothing I'm going to suggest here is against the law; some of the tips, though, are against the rules of some airlines. Here are a couple of strategies:

Nested Tickets. This scheme generally works in either of two situations—where regular fares are more than twice as high as excursion fares that include a Saturday night stay over, or in situations where you plan to fly between two locations twice in less than a year.

Let's say you want to fly from Boston to Las Vegas. Buy two sets of tickets in your name. The first is from Boston to Las Vegas and back. This set has the return date for when you want to come back from your *second* trip. The other set of tickets is from Las Vegas to Boston and back to Las Vegas; this time making the first leg of the ticket for the date you want to come back from the first trip, and the second leg of the trip the date you want to depart for the second trip.

If this sounds complicated, that's because it is. It will be up to you to keep your tickets straight when you travel. Some airlines have threatened to crack down on such practices by searching their computer databases for multiple reservations. Check with a travel agent for advice.

One solution: buy one set of tickets on one airline and the other set on another carrier.

Split Tickets. Fare wars sometimes result in super-cheap fares through a connecting city. For example, an airline seeking to boost traffic through a hub in Dallas might set up a situation in which it is less expensive to get from Chicago to Las Vegas by buying a round-trip ticket from Chicago to Dallas, and then a separate round-trip ticket from Dallas to Las Vegas.

Be sure to book a schedule that allows enough time between flights; if you miss your connection you could end up losing time and money.

Standing Up for Standing By

One of the little-known secrets of air travel on most airlines and most types of tickets is the fact that travelers who have valid tickets are allowed to stand by for flights other than the ones for which they have reservations; if there are empty seats on the flight, standby ticketholders are permitted to board.

Here's what I do know: if I cannot get the exact flight I want for a trip, I make the closest acceptable reservations available and then show up early at the airport and head for the check-in counter for the flight I really want to take. Unless you are seeking to travel during an impossibly overbooked holiday period or arrive on a bad weather day when flights have been canceled, your chances of successfully standing by for a flight are usually pretty good.

About Travel Agencies

Here's my advice about travel agents: get a good one, or go it alone. Good agents are those who remember who they work for: you. Of course, there is a built-in conflict of interest here, because the agent is in most cases paid by someone else.

Agents receive a commission on airline tickets, hotel reservations, car rentals, and many other services they sell you. The more they sell (or the higher the price), the more they earn.

I would recommend you start the planning for any trip by calling the airlines and a few hotels and finding the best package you can put together for yourself. Then call your travel agent and ask them to do better.

If your agent contributes knowledge or experience, comes up with dollar-saving alternatives to your own package, or offers some other kind of convenience, then go ahead and book through the agency. If, as I often find, you know a lot more about your destination and are willing to spend a lot more time to save money than will the agent, do it yourself.

A number of large agencies offer rebates of part of their commissions to travelers. Some of these companies cater only to frequent flyers who will bring in a lot of business; other rebate agencies offer only limited services to clients.

You can find discount travel agencies through many major credit card companies (Citibank and American Express among them) or through associations and clubs. Some warehouse shopping clubs have rebate travel agencies.

And if you establish a regular relationship with your travel agency and bring them enough business to make them glad to hear from you, don't be afraid to ask them for a discount equal to a few percentage points.

One other important new tool for travelers is the Internet. Here you'll find computerized travel agencies that offer airline, hotel, car, cruise, and package reservations. You won't receive personalized assistance, but you will be able to make as many price checks and itinerary routings as you'd like without apology. Several of the services feature special deals, including companion fares and rebates you won't find offered elsewhere.

Overbooking

Overbooking is a polite industry term that refers to the legal practice of selling more than an airline can deliver. It all stems, alas, from the unfortunate habit of many travelers who neglect to cancel flight reservations that will not be used. Airlines study the patterns on various flights and city pairs and apply a formula that allows them to sell more tickets than there are seats, in the expectation that a certain percentage will not show up at the airport.

But what happens if all passengers holding reservations show up? Obviously, there will be more passengers than seats, and some will be left behind.

The involuntary bump list will begin with the names of passengers who are late to check in. Airlines must ask for volunteers before bumping any passengers who have followed the rules on check-in.

If no one is willing to give up their seat just for the fun of it, the airline will offer some sort of compensation—either a free ticket or cash, or both. It is up to the passenger and the airline to make a deal. The U.S. Department of Transportation's consumer protection regulations set minimum levels of compensation for passengers bumped from a flight as a result of overbooking.

You are also not eligible for compensation if the airline substitutes a smaller aircraft for operational or safety reasons, or if the flight involves an aircraft with sixty seats or less.

How to Get Bumped

Why in the world would you want to be bumped? Well, perhaps you'd like to look at missing your plane as an opportunity to earn a little money for your time instead of as an annoyance. Is a two-hour delay worth $100 an hour? How about

$800 for a family of four to wait a few hours on the way home—that should pay for a week's hotel on your next trip.

If you're not in a rush to get to Nevada—or to get home—you might want to volunteer to be bumped. I wouldn't recommend this on the busiest travel days of the year, or if you are booked on the last flight of the day, unless you are also looking forward to a free night in an airport motel.

My very best haul: on a flight home from London, my family of four received a free night's stay in a luxury hotel, $1,000 each in tickets, and an upgrade on our flight home the next day.

Bad Weather, Bad Planes, Strikes, and Other Headaches

You don't want pilots to fly into weather they consider unsafe, of course. You also wouldn't want them to take up a plane with a mechanical problem. No matter how you feel about unions, you probably don't want to cross a picket line to board a plane piloted by strikebreakers. And so, you should accept an airline's cancellation of a flight for any of these legitimate reasons.

Here's the bad news, though: if a flight is canceled for an "act of God" or a labor dispute, the airline is not required to do anything for you except refund your money. In practice, carriers will usually make a good effort to find another way to get you to your destination more or less on time. This could mean rebooking on another flight on the same airline, or on a different carrier. It could mean a delay of a day or more in the worst situations, such as a major snowstorm.

Here is a summary of your rather limited rights as an air passenger:

- An airline is required to compensate you above the cost of your ticket only if you are bumped from an oversold flight against your will.
- If you volunteer to be bumped, you can negotiate for the best deal with the ticket agent or a supervisor; generally you can expect to be offered a free round-trip ticket on the airline for your inconvenience.
- If your scheduled flight is unable to deliver you directly to the destination on your ticket, and alternate transportation such as a bus or limousine is provided, the airline is required to pay you twice the amount of your one-way fare if your arrival will be more than two hours later than the original ticket promised.
- If you purchased your ticket with a credit card, the airline must credit your account within seven days of receiving an application for a refund.

All that said, you may be able to convince an agent or a supervisor to go beyond the letter of the law. I've found the best strategy is to politely but firmly stand your ground. Ask the ticket clerk for another flight, for a free night in a hotel and a flight in the morning, or for any other reasonable accommodation. Don't take no for an answer, but remain polite and ask for a supervisor if necessary. Sooner or later, they'll do something to get you out of the way.

And then there are labor problems such as those that faced American Airlines and US Airways in recent years. Your best defense against a strike is to antici-

> **Lug-it-yourself.** If you are connecting between a charter flight and a scheduled airline, your bags will likely not be "interline" transferred—it will be up to you to pick them up and deliver them between counters.
>
> And you run the risk of losing nonrefundable tickets if you miss a flight because of a problem with an unrelated carrier.
>
> Try to avoid such combinations, or leave extra hours or even days between connections.
>
> Some tour operators offer travel delay insurance that pays for accommodations or alternate travel costs made necessary by certain types of delays.

pate it before it happens; keep your ears open for labor problems before you make a reservation. Then keep in touch with your travel agent or the airline in the days leading up to strike deadlines. It is often easier to make alternate plans or seek a refund in the days immediately before a strike; wait until the last minute and you're going to be joining a very long and upset line.

If a strike occures, an airline will attempt to rebook you on another airline if possible; if you buy your own ticket on another carrier you are unlikely to be reimbursed. If your flight is canceled, you will certainly be able to claim a full refund of your fare or obtain a voucher in its value without any penalties.

Airline Safety

There are no guarantees in life, but in general flying on an airplane is considerably safer than driving to the airport. All of the major air carriers have very good safety records; some are better than others. I pay attention to news reports about FAA inspections and rulings and make adjustments. And though I love to squeeze George Washington until he yelps, I avoid start-up and super cut-rate airlines because I have my doubts about how much money they can afford to devote to maintenance.

Among major airlines, the fatal accident rate during the last twenty-five years stands somewhere between .3 and .7 incidents per million flights. Not included are small commuter airlines, except those affiliated with major carriers.

The very low numbers, experts say, make them poor predictors of future incidents. Instead, you should pay more attention to reports of FAA or NTSB rulings on maintenance and training problems.

Tour Packages and Charter Flights

Tour packages and flights sold by tour operators or travel agents may look similar, but the tickets may come with significantly different rights.

It all depends whether the flight is a scheduled or nonscheduled flight. A scheduled flight is one that is listed in the Official Airline Guide and available to the general public through a travel agent or from the airline. This doesn't mean that a scheduled flight will necessarily be on a major carrier or that you will be flying on a 747 jumbo jet; it could just as easily be the propeller-driven pride of Hayseed Airlines. In any case, though, a scheduled flight does have to meet stringent federal government certification requirements.

A nonscheduled flight is also known as a charter flight. The term is sometimes also applied to a complete package that includes a nonscheduled flight, hotel accommodations, ground transportation, and other elements. Charter flights are generally a creation of a tour operator who will purchase all of the seats on a specific flight to a specific destination or who will rent an airplane and crew from an air carrier.

Charter flights and charter tours are regulated by the federal government, but your rights as a consumer are much more limited than those afforded to scheduled flight customers.

You wouldn't buy a hamburger without knowing the price and specifications (two all-beef patties on a sesame seed bun, etc.). Why, then, would you spend hundreds or even thousands of dollars on a tour and not understand the contract that underlies the transaction?

Before you pay for a charter flight or a tour package, review the contract that spells out your rights. This contract is sometimes referred to as the "Operator Participant Contract" or the "Terms and Conditions." Look for this contract in the booklet or brochure that describes the packages; ask for it if one is not offered. Remember that the contract is designed mostly to benefit the tour operator, and each contract may be different from others you may have agreed to in the past. The basic rule here is: if you don't understand it, don't sign it.

How to Book a Package or Charter Flight

If possible, use a travel agent—preferably one you know and trust from prior experience. In general, the tour operator pays the travel agent's commission. Some tour packages, however, are available only from the operator who organized the tour; in certain cases, you may be able to negotiate a better price by dealing directly with the operator, although you are giving up one layer of protection for your rights.

Pay for your ticket with a credit card; this is a cardinal rule for almost any situation in which you are prepaying for a service or product.

Realize that charter airlines don't have large fleets of planes available to substitute in the event of a mechanical problem or an extensive weather delay. They may not be able to arrange for a substitute plane from another carrier.

If you are still willing to try a charter after all of these warnings, make one more check of the bottom line before you sign the contract. First of all, is the air travel significantly less expensive than the lowest nonrefundable fare from a scheduled carrier? (Remember that you are, in effect, buying a nonrefundable fare with most charter flight contracts.)

Have you included taxes, service charges, baggage transfer fees, or other charges the tour operator may put into the contract? Are the savings significantly more than the 10 percent the charter operator may (typically) boost the price without your permission? Do savings cost you time? What is that worth?

Finally, don't purchase a complete package until you have compared it to the a la carte cost of such a trip. Call the hotels offered by the tour operator, or similar ones in the same area, and ask them a simple question: "What is your best price for a room?" Be sure to mention any discount programs that are applicable, including AAA or other organizations. Do the same for car rental agencies, and place a call to any attractions you plan to visit to get current prices.

McCarran International Airport

Las Vegas's airport is within a chip's throw of the Strip, about a mile from the top end of the casino district, and five miles from downtown. (702) 261-5743.

McCarran is already the ninth busiest airport in the United States and the fourteenth busiest in the world, and planners worry it will reach capacity by about the year 2008. In early 2000, Congress began work on a bill that lays the groundwork for the transfer of about 6,500 acres of federal land in Ivanpah Valley, about thirty miles south of Las Vegas near Jean, Nevada, near the southern California-Nevada border.

In other airport news, Virgin Atlantic began non-stop service from London to Las Vegas. Other new carriers include AeroMexico and the discount carrier National Airlines, which began with flights from California, Chicago, and Newark to Las Vegas; there are also hopes to expand to Washington, D.C.

McCARRAN INTERNATIONAL AIRPORT

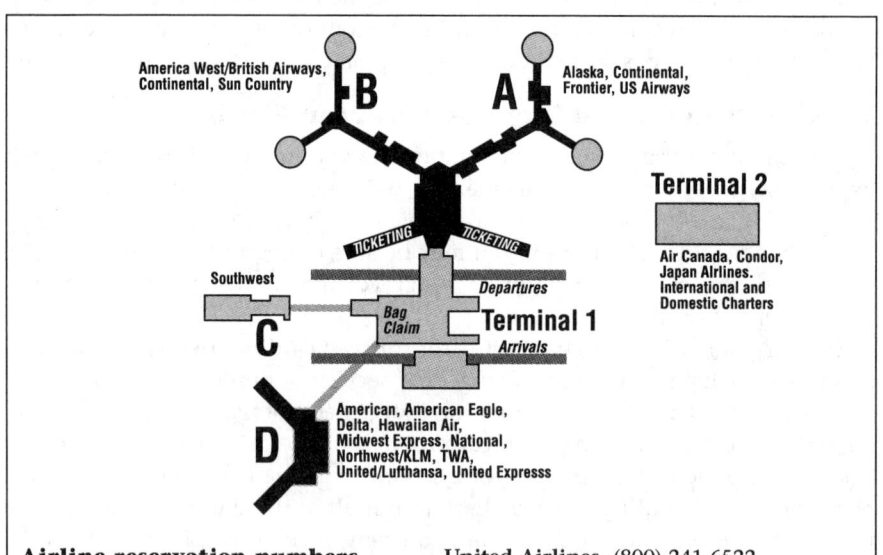

Terminal 1

- B: America West/British Airways, Continental, Sun Country
- A: Alaska, Continental, Frontier, US Airways
- C: Southwest
- D: American, American Eagle, Delta, Hawaiian Air, Midwest Express, National, Northwest/KLM, TWA, United/Lufthansa, United Expresss

Terminal 2

Air Canada, Condor, Japan Airlines. International and Domestic Charters

Airline reservation numbers

Alaska Airlines. (800) 426-0333
America West Airlines. (800) 235-9292
American Airlines. (800) 433-7300
Continental Airlines. (800) 525-0280
Delta Air Lines. (800) 221-1212
Northwest Airlines. (800) 225-2525
Southwest Airlines. (800) 435-9792
TWA. (800) 221-2000
United Airlines. (800) 241-6522
US Airways. (800) 428-4322

Airport phone directory

Main number. (702) 261-5211
Parking information. (702) 261-5121
Flight information. (702) 261-4636
Paging and information. (702) 261-5733
Lost and found. (702) 261-5134

Chapter 3
How to Sleep for Less

Negotiating for a Room

Notice the title of this section: I didn't call it "buying" a room. The fact of the matter is that hotel rooms, like almost everything else, are subject to negotiation and change.

Here is how to pay the highest possible price for a hotel room: walk up to the front desk without a reservation and say, "I'd like a room." Unless the "No Vacancy" sign is lit, you may have to pay the "rack rate," which is the published maximum nightly charge.

Here are a few ways to pay the lowest possible price:

1. Before you head for your vacation, spend an hour on the phone and call directly to a half dozen hotels that seem to be in the price range you'd like to spend. (I recommend membership in AAA and use of their annual tour books as *starting points* for your research. If you are of a certain age, join AARP.)

Start by asking for the room rate. Then ask them for their *best* rate. Does that sound like an unnecessary second request?

[True story: I once called the reservation desk of a major hotel chain and asked for the rates for a night at a Chicago location. "That will be $149 per night," I was told. "Ouch," I said. "Oh, would you like to spend less?" the reservationist said. I admitted that I would, and she punched a few keys on her keyboard. "They have a special promotion going on. How about $109 per night?" she asked.

Not bad for a city hotel, I reasoned, but still I hadn't asked the big question. "What is your best rate?" I asked. "Oh, our best rate? That would be $79," said the agent.

But, wait: "I'm a member of AAA, by the way." Another pause. "That's fine, Mr. Sandler. The nightly room rate will be $71.10. Have a nice day."]

When you feel you've negotiated the best deal you can obtain over the phone, make a reservation at the hotel of your choice. Be sure to go over the dates and prices one more time, and obtain the name of the person you spoke with and a confirmation number if available.

2. When you show up at your hotel on the first night, stop and look at the marquee outside; see if the hotel is advertising a discount rate. Here's where you

> **Showing your card.** Membership in AAA brings some important benefits for the traveler, although you may not always be able to apply the club's usual 10 percent discount on top of whatever hotel rate you negotiate. (It doesn't hurt to ask, though.) Be sure to request a tour book and Nevada maps from AAA even if you plan to fly there; they are much better than the rental car agency maps.

need to be bold. Walk up to the desk as if you *did not* have a reservation, and ask the clerk: "What is your best room rate for tonight?" If the rate they quote you is less than the rate in your reservation, you are now properly armed to ask for a reduction in your room rate.

Similarly, if the room rate advertised out front on the marquee drops during your stay, don't be shy about asking that your charges be reduced. Just be sure to ask for the reduction *before* you spend another night at the old rate, and obtain the name of the clerk who promises a change. If the hotel tries a lame excuse like, "That's only for new check-ins," you can offer to check out and then check back in again. That will usually work; you can always check out and go to the hotel across the road.

3. Are you planning to stay for a full week? Ask for a weekly rate. If the room clerk says there is no such rate, ask for the manager: the manager may be willing to shave a few dollars per day off the rate for a long-term stay.

Booking on the Internet

In many ways, the wild west still lives on the Internet. Someday the laws of economics will apply—the day when Internet companies and e-commerce outposts of traditional businesses will actually have to show a profit. Until then, though, the focus of most Web sites is to generate traffic and market share, even as they lose millions of dollars.

There are some tremendous deals available to the careful shopper. At the least, you'll be able to easily compare rates from several chains or major casino-hotels; you'll also find some special deals offered only on the Internet.

Check the web page listings for casinos listed at the end of each writeup in this book. Here are some other hotel booking web sites worth checking:

1-800-USA-HOTELS.COM	www.1800usahotels.com
Hotel Reservations Network	www.hoteldiscount.com
Choice Hotels	www.choice.com
Expedia	www.expedia.com
Travelocity	www.travelocity.com

Welcome, Conventioneers

Not all of the visitors to Las Vegas come to recreate. Each year, millions are drawn to the spectacular facilities of the Las Vegas Convention Center or the Sands Expo & Convention Center or smaller facilities at many major hotels.

The conventioneers come to town because of the lure of the casinos and entertainment, but even more importantly, they come because Las Vegas is one of the few places in the country with a huge capacity for shows as well as an available bank of hotel rooms for attendees.

The biggest Las Vegas conventions include the annual visits of CONEXPO (the Construction Industry Manufacturers Association) in March; the Consumer Electronics Show usually in January; the National Association of Broadcasters in April; Comdex (the computer industry show) in November; and the International Council of Shopping Centers in May.

Of course, we mustn't overlook the National Pizza and Pasta Association, the American Concrete Pumping Association, the Coca-Cola Collectors Club International, the International Carwash Association, and, obviously, the American Ostrich Association, which draws 2,000 people (and, we presume, a few big birds).

The leading convention facility is the Las Vegas Convention Center, at 3150 Paradise Road, about three blocks east of the Strip and adjacent to the huge Las Vegas Hilton Hotel. The convention center underwent several rounds of expansions in recent years, bringing the total capacity of the building to a staggering 1.6 million square feet. Another million square feet will open by the end of 2001, at Desert Inn and Paradise Road.

Some of the larger conventions need even more space and spill over into several large halls of the Hilton next door and from there to convention spaces around town.

The Sands Expo & Convention Center, at 201 Sands Avenue, is used primarily as the second hall for the annual Comdex computer convention, the nation's largest annual trade show.

New convention spaces at the Venetian Resort and at other hotels in Las Vegas will also be used for major gatherings.

Another facility that is used for smaller conventions and for occasional special events from the mega-gatherings is the Cashman Field Center, at 850 Las Vegas Boulevard North, just outside downtown Las Vegas.

Cashman Field Center has a 1,954-seat auditorium/theater and two exhibit halls that total 100,000 square feet of space. Outside is a stadium that is home to the AAA Las Vegas Stars baseball team April through September.

Phone bills. Be sure you understand the telephone billing policy at the hotel. Some establishments allow free local calls, while others charge as much as a dollar for such calls. (I'm especially unhappy with service charges for 800 numbers.) Be sure to examine your bill carefully at checkout and make sure it is correct.

I strongly suggest you obtain a telephone credit card and use it when you travel; nearly all hotels tack high service charges on long-distance calls, and there is no reason to pay it.

Room safety. The small safes available in some hotels can be valuable to the traveler; be sure to inquire whether there is a service charge for their use. We've been in hotels that apply the charge regardless of whether we used the safe or not; look over your bill at checkout and object to any charges that are not proper. In any case, we'd suggest that any objects that are so valuable you feel they should be locked up should probably be left home.

How to Get a Room During a Convention

For most of the year, finding a place to stay in Las Vegas is not difficult. However, the very largest of the conventions will soak up most of the rooms at the major hotels.

If you are coming to Las Vegas as part of a convention, check with the organizers for hotels that have promised space. Or, the convention may use the services of the Las Vegas Visitors' Bureau to book rooms.

The advantage of using a group's services include these: There *may* be less expensive rooms available through the convention group. And, the "official" hotel may be the location of the convention itself or on the bus route for shuttle service to the convention hall.

However, there are times when you can obtain a less expensive or more convenient place to stay by booking directly. Most major conventions, for example, only reserve blocks of rooms at the largest hotels, and there may be some rooms available directly; smaller hotels right near the convention halls are sometimes overlooked.

When the town is completely packed because of a convention, you may be able to sweet-talk your way into a room by contacting the lodging bureau handling the group. You don't have to be so bold as to lie, but you may be able to allow them to assume you are with the convention and in dire need of a room.

On the other hand, don't always assume that convention groups will be offered the lowest prices at hotels. On more than one occasion, I have obtained a cheaper price by calling a hotel directly to book a room rather than going through the lodging bureaus.

In addition, though the official hotels for a convention may be packed—and may be charging peak or even above-peak rates—nonconvention hotels may have rooms at low-season bargain rates. For example, during one of the research trips for this book, all of the major official hotels were sold out for the CONEXPO show, and the few that had rooms were asking $150 to $200 per night. Yet the huge Circus Circus hotel, which was not affiliated with the convention, had plenty of rooms at $39; ten minutes out of town hotels on Boulder Highway offered ordinary but acceptable rooms for about the same price.

One safe bet in Las Vegas is that downtown hotels will often have available rooms, even during major conventions. Of course, all bets are off during peak Christmas and other holiday times.

The Luxor

Chapter 4
Cars, Trains, and Buses

Mileage to Las Vegas

Atlanta	1,964	Grand Canyon	288	Palm Springs	280
Barstow	153	Henderson	13	Philadelphia	2,468
Boston	2,725	Hoover Dam	25	Phoenix	298
Boulder City	24	Jackpot	488	Reno	440
Carson City	430	Kingman	103	Salt Lake City	433
Chicago	1,772	Lake Havasu City	145	San Diego	337
Dallas	1,221	Lake Tahoe	470	San Francisco	564
Death Valley	160	Laughlin	93	Sparks	207
Denver	777	Los Angeles	282	Washington, D.C.	2,393
Flagstaff	275	New York City	2,548	Zion National Park	156

From the Airport to the Strip and Downtown

You'll know you're in Las Vegas the moment you get off your plane. Yep, those are slot machines in the lounge waiting to suck up your first (or last) quarters.

McCarran International Airport is just over a mile from the top of the Strip and about five miles from downtown Las Vegas.

Taxis cost about $7 to $10 to the Strip or $10 to $15 to downtown, plus tip. Cabs are usually plentiful outside the baggage area of the airport.

An alternative is to take one of the shuttle services. For about $3 to $4 to the Strip or $4 to $5 to downtown per person, you'll share the minibus with as many as a dozen or so others, and the driver will choose the order of the stops. The shuttle service may be appropriate if you are traveling alone and are not in a hurry; otherwise a taxi makes more sense.

You can also hop a ride on one of the CAT (Citizens Area Transport) buses, although between airport pickups and traffic on the Strip, they are painfully slow. The private shuttles or taxis are much better alternatives.

Renting a Car

Las Vegas, like most other major cities, is not a particularly friendly place for cars. You'll probably find it a lot easier to use taxis or walk between hotels on the strip. However, I'd recommend you consider renting a car for excursions out of the city to Red Rock Canyon, Hoover Dam, Laughlin, and other places.

McCarran Airport has a good selection of national car rental agencies, at very competitive rates. At times when there are more cars than renters (primarily non-holiday winter periods) expect to pay as little as $25 to $30 per day for a small car; in peak periods, rates reach about $40 per day for a small vehicle. Be sure to seek discounts from auto clubs, airline frequent flyer clubs, and other sources.

Be aware that the least expensive car rental agencies usually do not have their stations at the airport itself. You will have to wait for a shuttle bus to take you from the terminal to their lot, and you must return the car to the outlying area at the end of your trip. This may add about twenty to thirty minutes to your arrival and departure schedule.

Another last-minute note: as you fly into Las Vegas, read the airline's frequent flyer magazine in the seatback pocket. There are often special car rental rates advertised for destinations served by the airline. It may be worthwhile to take the ad with you to the rental counter and ask for a better rate.

Pay attention, too, when the rental agent explains the gas tank policy. The most common plan says that you must return the car with a full tank; if the agency must refill the tank, you will be billed a service charge plus what is usually a very high per-gallon rate. Other optional plans include one where the rental agency sells you a full tank when you first drive away and takes no note of how much gas remains when you return the car. Unless you somehow manage to return the car with the engine running on fumes, you are in effect making a gift to the agency with every gallon you bring back. I prefer the first option, making a point to refill the tank on the way to the airport on getaway day.

Car rental companies will try—with varying levels of pressure—to convince you to purchase special insurance coverage. They'll tell you it's "only" $7 or $9 per day. What a deal! That works out to about $2,500 or $3,000 per year for a set of rental wheels. The coverage is intended primarily to protect the rental company, not you.

Check with your insurance agent before you travel to determine how well your personal automobile policy will cover a rental car and its contents. I strongly recommend you use a credit card that offers rental car insurance; such insurance usually covers the deductible below your personal policy. The extra auto insurance by itself is usually worth an upgrade to a "gold card" or other extra-share credit card.

The only sticky area comes for those visitors who have a driver's license but no car, and therefore no insurance. Again, consult your credit card company.

Although it is theoretically possible to rent a car without a credit card, you will find it to be a rather inconvenient process. If they cannot hold your credit card account hostage, most agencies will require a large cash deposit—perhaps as much as several thousand dollars—before they will give you the keys.

And finally, check with the rental company about its policies on taking the car out of the state. Some companies will charge you extra if you are planning to take the car across a state line. In Las Vegas, this can become an issue if you travel south to Hoover Dam; the far side of the dam is in Arizona. Similarly, in Laughlin, the bridge across the Colorado River begins in Nevada and ends in

Arizona. In Reno, the California state line is nearby on the west side of the Sierra Nevadas and the popular destination of Lake Tahoe is on the line; restrictions on interstate travel are less common there.

The following are among companies serving McCarran Airport, the Strip, and downtown; check with them for the office nearest where you want to pick up a car.

Alamo Rent a Car. (702) 263-8411, (800) 327-9633.
Allstate Car Rental. (702) 736-6147, (800) 634-6186.
Avis Rent-a-Car. (702) 261-5595, (800) 367-2847.
Brooks Rent-a-Car. (702) 735-3344, (800) 634-6721.
Budget Car & Truck Rental. (702) 736-1212, (800) 922-2899.
Enterprise Rent-a-Car. (702) 870-4144, (800) 736-8222.
Fairway Rent-a-Car. (702) 369-8533.
Hertz Rent a Car. (702) 736-4900, (800) 654-3131.
Lloyd's International Rent-a-Car. (702) 736-2663, (800) 654-7037.
National Car Rental. (702) 261-5391. (800) 227-7368.
Pay Less Rent-a-Car. (702) 736-6147.
Practical Rent-a-Car. (702) 798-5253, (877) 401-7368.
Rent-a-Vette. (702) 736-2592, (800) 372-1981.
Rent-a-Wreck. (702) 474-0037, (800) 227-0292.
Sav-More Rent-a-Car. (702) 736-1234, (800) 634-6779.
Thrifty Car Rental. (702) 896-7600, (800) 367-2277.
U.S. Rent-a-Car. (702) 798-6100, (800) 777-9377.

Getting Around in Las Vegas

Navigating in Las Vegas is pretty simple. Almost every major hotel and casino is found along Las Vegas Boulevard (better known as the Strip), along Fremont Street in downtown Las Vegas, or on a cross-street to one of those two roads.

Except when there is a large convention in town, taxis are plentiful at the airport and along the Strip, and bus service is adequate. And, although it is not as common as it should be, it is quite possible to walk between and among the clusters of casino/hotels on the Upper Strip and Center Strip.

Personally, we find it mind-boggling that a visitor to Las Vegas who will ogle The Mirage or The Luxor or Excalibur can come and go without seeing even more amazing sights such as Hoover Dam or Red Rock Canyon. (And, as you will find later in this book, I cannot imagine a trip to Reno that does not include a visit to Lake Tahoe and Virginia City.)

Taxi Services

Cabs, cabs everywhere—except when there is a big convention in town, anytime you are in a hurry, or during one of Las Vegas's rare rainstorms. There are two major taxi companies that all but control the market: Yellow Cab and Whittlesea Blue Cab.

Taxi rates are about $2.40 plus $1.50 per mile.

Taxis line up at McCarran Airport to meet most flights. During conventions, taxis also arrive regularly at the front entrance to the Las Vegas

Taxi dancing. Here's a tip for visitors unable to get a cab from the convention center: walk up Convention Center Drive to the Strip and wait for a car at one of the hotels there—with luck you will be able to share a ride in a taxi that has brought a rider the few blocks you walked from the LVCC.

Nevada Commission on Tourism. Capitol Complex, Carson City, NV 89710; (775) 687-3636 or (800) 638-2328.
Lake Mead National Recreation Area. 601 Nevada Hwy., Boulder City, NV 89005; (702) 293-8907. www.nps.gov.
Nevada Division of State Parks. 1300 S. Curry St., Carson City, NV 89703-5202; (775) 687-4384. www.state.nv.us\parks\.

Convention Center. They're usually found at the main entrances of the major hotels as well.

Busing to the Tables

Las Vegas Transit operates bus routes serving much of the metropolitan area. Call (702) 228-7433 for information. The Downtown Transportation Center, at Stewart Avenue and Casino Center Boulevard, is the transfer point for many routes, open from 6:15 A.M. to 10 P.M. daily. Riders must request and pay for a transfer at the time of paying the first fare.

Route 301 connects downtown to the Strip, and **Route 303** goes from downtown to north Las Vegas. Route 301 runs twenty-four hours a day at ten-minute intervals until about midnight and fifteen minutes apart from midnight until 5:30 A.M. from the Downtown Transportation Center on Stewart Avenue to Vacation Village at the top of the Strip.

The Mall Hopper (Route 14) connects the west entrance of the Fashion Show Mall on the Strip to the Meadows and Boulevard Shopping Malls. The bus runs in an S-curve from the Boulevard Mall on Maryland Parkway across Twain and Sands to the Strip and the west entrance of the Fashion Show Mall, continuing north on the I-15 freeway to the Meadows Mall west of downtown.

For information on CAT bus schedules and routes, call (702) 228-7433.

Train Service

Amtrak. Daily high-speed Amtrak rail service between Los Angeles and Las Vegas aboard Spanish-made tilt trains and improved tracks may be on the tracks. Several Las Vegas casinos were reported to be considering purchasing blocks of seats to guarantee the success of the resumed service.

Stops were planned from Primm, the Las Vegas Strip, and downtown Las Vegas, with the trip taking about five-and-a-half hours.

And Las Vegas is hoping to be chosen for a billion-dollar federal project to build a high-speed magnetic-levitation train. Under the plan, the first link would be a forty-two-mile connection from Las Vegas to Primm; eventually the line would continue on to Anaheim, California. In mid-2000, seven localities around the nation were competing for the grant.

Part II
Las Vegas

Chapter 5
Welcome, Pilgrim

As far as I am concerned, there are two types of visitors to Las Vegas:
1. Those who have never been there before and are anxious to see if all of the strange and wonderful things they have heard are true.
2. Those who are returning to Las Vegas to see if things are really as strange and wonderful as they remember.

Either way, Las Vegas is unlike any other place on earth, with the possible exception of those other fantasy zones, Walt Disney World and Disneyland.

Coming in to Las Vegas

The best way to approach Las Vegas is to fly in on a moonlit, clear night. As your plane descends from points east, you cross hundreds of miles of barren desert that seem as lifeless as the moon. Suddenly, you'll come upon a huge oddly shaped lake in the desert held back by a tremendous dam, a pale white saucer set on end in a canyon. That's the Hoover Dam and Lake Mead.

Just minutes later you will see on the horizon an island of light, an electric oasis in the desert. About the time the pilot brings down the landing gear, you should be able to pick out some of the elements of a skyline like nowhere else on earth: a huge Egyptian pyramid, a Roman garden and amphitheater, a pirate ship, and a gaudy castle constructed of gigantic toy blocks. That's Las Vegas.

Coming in from California and points west, your jet will cross the last wall of mountains and then drop into the Las Vegas Valley. The pilot will usually hang a right turn over the spectacularly improbable Stratosphere Tower and proceed up the length of the Strip to the airport.

Welcome to Las Vegas, pilgrim.

A Place to Lay Your Head

Las Vegas claims the mantle as the first destination in America to pass the 100,000-room mark.

In mid-2000, Las Vegas offered 120,294 rooms—that's more than in New York, Paris, or Los Angeles. This includes massive new hotels such as Paris–New York (2,700 rooms), Venetian (3,000 rooms), Mandalay Bay (3,700 rooms), and Bellagio (3,000 rooms). Several thousand more, including those of the new Aladdin, are being built.

The number of rooms in Las Vegas has doubled in about ten years.

According to the Las Vegas Convention and Visitors Association, even with the huge growth in available rooms, the average occupancy level for all hotel and motel rooms in the Las Vegas metropolitan area is about 88 percent, twenty points above the national average.

Las Vegas Climate

Las Vegas has two basic weather patterns: sunny and mild, and sunny and hot.

Las Vegas averages 320 days of sunshine per year and only 4.19 inches of rain. In the summer months from June to September daytime temperatures may top 100 degrees. In the short spring and fall seasons, they usually reach the seventies during the day. In the winter, high temperatures may drop all the way down to the fifties.

Average high temperature in January	56 degrees
Average low temperature in January	33 degrees
Average high temperature in July	104 degrees
Average low temperature in July	75 degrees
Annual average rainfall	4.19 inches
Annual average snowfall	1.5 inches
Annual days with precipitation	26 days

A gondolier serenades a wedding couple indoors at The Venetian

Photo by Corey Sandler

Chapter 6
The Best of the Strip

Econoguide 2001 Best Casinos-Hotels in Las Vegas

★★★★ **Aladdin.** *Poof! Arabian nights reborn.*
★★★★★ **Bellagio.** *Prodigioso!*
★★★★★ **Caesars Palace.** *Render unto Caesar . . . in high style.*
★★★ **Circus Circus.** *Clowns, slots, jugglers, blackjack, and an indoor coaster.*
★★★ **Excalibur.** *A gaudy shrine.*
★★★★ **Hard Rock Hotel.** *Heavy metal and a casino, too.*
★★★★ **Las Vegas Hilton.** *Elvis slept here. Now the Vulcans visit.*
★★★ **Luxor.** *Pyramid power, in all of its strangeness.*
★★★★ **MGM Grand.** *You're not in Kansas anymore.*
★★★★★ **Mandalay Bay.** *Shangri-la on the Strip.*
★★★★ **Mirage.** *A volcano out front and white tigers within.*
★★★★ **Monte Carlo.** *Only in Vegas would this place seem real.*
★★★★ **New York–New York.** *Bustling, confusing. You got a problem with that?*
★★★★★ **Paris–Las Vegas.** *Disneyland Paris . . . in Las Vegas.*
★★★★★ **Rio Suite.** *Carnival! Show us your . . . chips.*
★★★ **Stratosphere Tower.** *P. T. Barnum would feel at home.*
★★★ **Treasure Island.** *Ahoy, suckers. Beware the volcano.*
★★★★★ **The Venetian.** *Prettier than the real thing.*

⬛ MUST-SEE ★★★★ Aladdin Hotel & Casino

The tales of *1,001 Arabian Nights* arrived on the Las Vegas Strip in late 2000 with the opening of the Aladdin Hotel & Casino, the only place in town with a genie-sized lamp, giant winged horses, and the nest of a giant Roc bird.

The storied Aladdin, among the oldest hotels and casinos on the Strip (first opened in 1959 as the Tally Ho; Elvis Presley married Priscilla Beaulieu there in 1967) vanished in a gala demolition in 1998.

The $1.3 billion project includes more than 130 shops and twenty-one restaurants at the Desert Passage, claimed to be the largest retail, dining, and entertainment center on the Strip. And, unusual for Las Vegas, the hotel lobby, casino, and convention center are each located on separate floors, allowing guests to pretend there aren't a few thousand slot machines and gaming tables awaiting their arrival. Guests can also visit an outdoor pool six stories above Las Vegas Boulevard, offering spectacular views of the Strip.

And in an interesting new trend, the hotel promotes the fact that some of its guests have great views of the entertainment and architecture of its nearby spectacular neighbors: some rooms and restaurants overlook Bellagio's outdoor water show across the Strip, and about one-fourth of the rooms have views of the Eiffel Tower next door at Paris–Las Vegas.

The Aladdin includes The London Club, a luxurious European-style casino-within-a-casino. There's also Scheherazade's Palace, a higher stakes gaming area located within a two-story structure inside the casino. It will feature live entertainment visible from various locations throughout the property.

The 7,000-seat Theater for the Performing Arts, the only remaining structure from the original Aladdin Hotel & Casino complex, will be renovated and restored.

Planned restaurants include Commander's Palace, an outpost of a New Orleans favorite; the elaborate P. F. Chang's China Bistro; Anasazi of Santa Fe; The Blue Note Jazz Club of New York; Bice, a world-renowned Italian restaurant; Buddha Bar; the Macanudo Steakhouse & Club, a fine American steakhouse; and Lombardi's, a gourmet eatery.

The Aladdin Music Project, a 1,000-room hotel and 50,000 square-foot casino, will be built during Phase II of the Aladdin complex.

Aladdin Hotel & Casino. 3667 Las Vegas Boulevard South. 2,600 rooms. (877) 333-9474. www.aladdincasino.com.

MUST-SEE ★★★★★ Bellagio

We already had an Egyptian pyramid, an Arthurian castle, a Roman palace and a British man-of-war. And then there was Paris, Venice, and New York. But it was so obvious: what Las Vegas *really* needed was an Italian beach resort on an artificial lake in the desert.

Bellagio spreads its massive pair of wings opposite Bally's. The hotel draws its inspiration from the Italian city of the same name, overlooking breathtaking Lake Como. The property on the Strip didn't have a lake—this is the desert, after all, and the former home of the very dry Dunes Hotel no less—and so a nine-acre pond had to be created.

It's sometimes very difficult to justify the massive amounts of money spent on some of the hotels and casinos in Las Vegas; in the case of Bellagio, though, at least the excess is evident.

You can start with the $30 million "choreographed water ballet on the lake" outside the hotel. The show, inspired by the fabulous light and fountain productions once popular in Europe, includes 1,175 water jet heads that can shoot water 160 feet into the air, 6,200 light fixtures and a high-tech audio system. It is presented every fifteen minutes for most of the day.

Another $70 million went into O, from Cirque du Soleil, the second by that group in Las Vegas (Mystère continues at the nearby Treasure Island Resort.) The troupe performs in and above a large body of water within the 1,800-seat theater, with an exterior design similar to the Paris Opera House. I haven't the slightest idea how Paris got into this mix, although Cirque du Soleil is from French Canada, which is nowhere near Lake Como. The show is presented twice nightly, except Wednesday and Thursday. Tickets for the show are available three months in advance for hotel guests and two months ahead for day visitors.

The 3,000 guest rooms and suites are decorated with antiques and art characteristic of southern Europe, and there's an extensive use of imported marble throughout. An enormous, tiled swimming pool provides relief from the Las Vegas summer heat.

The walls of the restaurants and public areas include original art by Claude Monet, Édouard Manet, Pablo Picasso, Pierre-Auguste Renoir, Paul Cézanne, Henri Matisse, and other Impressionist masters. The ultra-luxe Via Bellagio shopping street, set in an elegant Crystal Palace-like glass arcade, features stores that include Giorgio Armani, Chanel, Gucci, Hermès, Fred Leighton, Moschino, Prada, and Tiffany & Co.

The bellmen out front are adorned with top hats; the concierge staff is outfitted in waist coats. The registration desk is set within a living fantasy garden that changes with the seasons, home to real and robotic butterflies, birds, plants, and smells.

The public areas are an elegant wash of white and gold, with flowers—real and fanciful—at every turn, including a fabulous ceiling of 1,600 blown glass flowers by artist Dale Chihuly. The Conservatory is a spectacular private botanical garden; plantings are changed four to five times each year to celebrate seasons and holidays.

In mid-2000, soon after the acquisition of the Mirage by MGM Grand, Inc., eleven of the treasures of the Bellagio Gallery of Fine Art were sold off for a total of $124 million. Three of the pieces went to former owner Stephen Wynn. The gallery was closed, but is expected to reopen to display exhibits from major museums and art institutions.

The casino held on to the collection on display at two of its finest restaurants, Picasso and Renoi, where diners are seated among works by the artists named on the front door.

There is, of course, a huge casino with about 100 table games and 2,500 slot machines. Included is an elaborate sports and race book with a huge video screen on the wall; most tables also have private televisions.

Bellagio features ten specialty restaurants, including a Las Vegas version of the famed New York French restaurant **Le Cirque**, and **Osteria del Circo**, a Northern Italian eatery; both were created by the Maccioni family.

The Bellagio general restaurant reservation number is (888) 987-7111.

Le Cirque, overlooking the lake at the hotel, is among the more formal eateries with jacket and tie required for men. Specialties include *pauprette de loup-de-mer* (black sea bass in crispy potatoes) for $34 and *dégustation d'agneau* (Colorado lamb filet with baked cranberry beans) for $38. There are just eighty seats, and preference goes to high rollers. Your best bet is to seek an early reservation, at (702) 693-8100.

Osteria del Circo features homestyle Tuscan food, complemented by a wine cellar that offers more than 500 selections from around the world. Entrees are priced from about $16 to $26; many can also be ordered as smaller-portion appetizers if you want to create your own sampler. Specialty dishes include

Bellagio
Photo courtesy of Bellagio

costaletta di vitello (veal cutlet), *maltagliati alla Bolognese* (a specialty pasta), and *tartara di Branzino* (tartare of wild striped bass in a lemon dressing).

Picasso, decorated with drawings and pottery by the artist of the same name, celebrates Mediterranean cuisine. There's also an extraordinary Spanish pottery ceiling. Entrees are priced from about $20 to $30, and there's a nightly prix-fixe menu, priced between about $65 and $75. Examples from the menu included roasted langoustines, sauteed medallion of fallow deer, and roasted pigeon. The dress code is "casual elegance." Open for dinner daily, 6 P.M. to 10 P.M.; Friday and Saturday 6 P.M. to 11 P.M.; closed Wednesday.

Aqua, located alongside the Bellagio Gallery of Fine Art and the Conservatory, is a high-tone seafood food fest. The wall decorations include a work commissioned from Robert Rauschenberg. On the plates you'll find works of art priced from about $29 to $70. Appetizers include roasted whole foie gras for $80, and caviar varieties reaching to near $100. A recent menu included Hawaiian swordfish au poivre for $31 and seared scallops with caviar for $32. A five-course tasting menu was priced at $70 per person for the whole table, offering samples for everyone. Open daily, 5:30 P.M. to 11 P.M. Reservations can be made at (702) 693-7223.

Olives is a Las Vegas extension of the well-known Mediterranean restaurant of the same name in Boston. It is located within the Via Bellagio shopping arcade. Open Sunday to Thursday, 11 A.M. to midnight; Friday to Saturday, 11 A.M. to 1 A.M.

Prime is a luxury steakhouse, styled like a 1930s chophouse and speakeasy. Entrees on our visit included veal chops, spiced rack of lamb, and tuna steak with lemon confit. Entrees are priced from about $18 to $54. Jackets are preferred. Open daily, 5:30 P.M. to 11 P.M.

Jasmine is a gourmet Chinese restaurant with European influences, decorated with authentic and replicated Chinese art. The interior design is almost French in style. Menu offerings include Imperial Peking duck, Chinoise scallops, and more ordinary dishes such as Moo Shu Pork. Entrees range in price from about $16 to $48. Open daily, 5:30 P.M. to 11 P.M.

Jasmine also offers a tasting menu priced at about $70 per person, with a minimum of two at a table. On a recent visit, the menu included Imperial minced squab, honey-glazed barbecued baby back ribs, Fa Dew clam soup, Maine lobster in ginger and scallion, wok-seared beef tenderloin in black pepper sauce, and an exotic crème brulee dessert.

Shintaro, a most elegant (and expensive) Japanese restaurant, specializes in fresh seafood, sushi, and teppanyaki. The unusual sushi bar appears to be floating on dazzling blocks of ice. The Kaiseki seven-course meal was priced at $95; kaiseki means "stone in pocket," referring to an old Japanese folk tale roughly equivalent to the English "stone soup" fable. A teppanyaki dinner is priced at $55.

Noodles features regional noodle dishes from Thailand, Japan, China, and Vietnam. Chinese dim sum is available every day. Open daily, 11 A.M. to 3 A.M.

Sam's American has an open kitchen, befitting this casual eatery serving the best of regional American fare. Styled like a stone-age Flintstones set, entrees for lunch and dinner are priced from about $12 to $30. Examples include Indian-style crab cake for $16, chicken Paillard for $13, and grilled salmon Nicoise for $15. Open daily, noon to 3 P.M.; for dinner, Sunday to Thursday, 5:30 P.M. to 11 P.M. and Friday and Saturday, 5:30 P.M. to midnight.

And if you're in the mood for fine caviar, champagne, or smoked salmon, there's **The Petrossian Bar**, which specializes in all of the above.

Finally, the **Bellagio Buffet** is almost as elegant as the formal dining places in the hotel, one of the Econoguide bests with Asian and seafood specialties.

Bellagio is located along the Strip at the former site of the Dunes Hotel. There were no (real) sand dunes in sight, but there was a heck of a golf course out back of this Strip veteran. The hotel and particularly the casino had a checkered past right from the moment of its opening in 1955, with numerous failures and near failures. The Dunes was also revered among some aficionados of Vegas for its pioneering contribution to local culture: the topless show.

In 1993, the Dunes finally sank beneath the oncoming wave of development by Mirage Resorts. Actually, the hotel collapsed in a spectacular implosion that was part of the grand opening ceremonies for Mirage's Treasure Island hotel and casino; the demolition itself became the dramatic conclusion to a perfectly dreadful made-for-TV movie to promote the Treasure Island.

Bellagio, along with the Mirage and Treasure Island, were taken over in early 2000 by MGM Grand, Inc.

Room rates at Bellagio range from about $159 to $499 for basic accommodations; rooms are considerably larger than the norm in Las Vegas. Expect lower prices during slow periods and premium rates during holidays and conventions. There are also nine 6,000-square-foot villas for invited guests and a floor of luxurious penthouse suites.

Bellagio. 3400 Las Vegas Boulevard South, 3,000 rooms. (702) 693-7111. www.bellagiolasvegas.com.

MUST-SEE ★★★★★ Caesars Palace

Old Caesar—and his palace on the Strip—has been around a long time and has had to face all sorts of challenges to his glory over the years. Rest assured, though: Caesars Palace retains its position as one of the great, unnatural wonders of the world. Caesars Palace is a must-see among must-sees.

Think of Caesars Palace as a realization of Hollywood's vision of ancient Rome as seen through the jaded eye of a Las Vegas decorator.

Everything about this place is grand. The Roman Forum casino is a riot of red and gold. The sports book is among the most spectacular theater-like settings at any casino. The various restaurants include some of the most opulent settings on the Strip. And the casino employees offer equal-opportunity gawking for both sexes: there are gods and goddesses in short, short togas at most every turn.

And the spectacular **Forum Shops at Caesars** feature more than seventy specialty retailers and restaurants set in a re-creation of the skies of ancient Rome. Even more splendid excess is due with another expansion of the mall underway. *See Chapter 11 for full details on this must-see shopping mall.*

A dining and entertainment highlight is **Caesars Magical Empire.** *For details about magical Caesars Magical Empire, see Chapter 10.*

A $600 million Caesars Palace expansion was completed in late 1997 with the unveiling of the twenty-nine-story Palace Tower, which includes 1,134 guest rooms, with the top two floors made up entirely of suites serviced by a central concierge lobby. The tower is decorated with exterior fluted columns with Corinthian capitals and capped with three dramatic pediments creating a classic Greco-Roman facade. The center pediment bears a gold-leafed profile of Caesar, framed by a laurel wreath.

One of the toniest health club and spas in town occupies the second floor of the new tower, including Tectrix virtual reality bikes. The Garden of the Gods pool area was enlarged to more than four acres, including four large and two outdoor whirlpool spas, and faux stone lifeguard stands.

The Story of Caesars

When Caesars Palace was built in 1966, it was set far back from the Strip, partly for zoning reasons in the second wave of construction and partly because at the time it was believed that the new hotels would be destinations in and of themselves and that visitors would drive up the grand driveway to a parking space. The front yard of the hotel is filled with a mind-boggling collection of strange stuff, including a 20-foot-tall statue of Augustus, almost two dozen spouting fountains, and a lucky Brahma.

There are also several lengthy people-mover sidewalks intended to suck pedestrians from the curbside of the Strip all the way back to the entrance of the hotel; in 1989 an additional people mover was installed at the far northern corner of the Caesars Palace property. Coincidentally, of course, that put the Caesars moving walkway right next to the moving sidewalk for the new Mirage hotel next door. By the way, the sidewalks move only one direction—into the casino. When you are ready to leave, you'll have to walk to the Strip, or you can call a cab if you have any money left in your pockets.

Caesars World, which includes Caesars Palace in Las Vegas, Caesars Atlantic City, Caesars Tahoe, and other properties, was purchased in mid-1999 by Park Place Entertainment for a cool $3 billion. Park Place was created at the end of 1998 out of the gaming division of Hilton Hotels and a subsequent merger with Grand Casinos. Park Place also owns Bally's and Paris–Las Vegas.

Basic room rates start as low as $95 for a single and $110 for a double room at ordinary periods of the year. Deluxe rooms start at $135 for a single and $150 for a double; superior at $160 and $175. One-bedroom suites begin at $475; two bedrooms start at $610. However, during the quietest times of the year, prices drop into double digits for basic and deluxe rooms. At peak times, prices can double.

Like most other Las Vegas hotels, the quietest time of the year is usually around Christmas, excluding the holiday itself and New Year's Eve. Available rooms at that time are often offered at significantly less than the rack rate. However, Caesars Palace has been working hard to fill up its rooms during slack periods with guests from Asian locations, including Hong Kong.

Olympic Tower. The main tower includes dozens of room types. A typical deluxe room is the Olympic Square King, which includes marble and mirrors and a Jacuzzi in each room. Round

---

Armless in Vegas. The grounds around Caesars Palace include replicas of some of the most famous statues of antiquity. In front of the fountains at the main entrance of the hotel is a re-creation of the famous *Victory at Samothrace* statue, sculpted about 300 B.C. by an unknown artist; the original is in the Louvre Museum in Paris.

In front of the elliptical pool at the entrance is a copy of the *Rape of the Sabines*; the original was done by Giovanni da Bologna in 1583.

Elsewhere, you'll find reproductions of Michelangelo's *David* and *Bacchus*. On a more contemporary note, at the entrance to the Olympic Casino stands a statue of the boxer Joe Louis, who worked for the casino as a greeter after he retired from the ring.

Michelangelo's casino. At the top tier of the portico entrance to the World of Caesar is a marble statue of Apollo, the Greek and Roman god of sunlight, prophecy, music, and poetry. According to its makers, it is carved from stone taken from the same quarries that Michelangelo is believed to have used.

> **A real fake.** The Brahma Shrine on the north lawn of Caesars Palace is a replica of one of the most popular Buddhist shrines in Thailand. The original was installed more than thirty years ago at the Erawan Hotel in Bangkok to ward off bad luck after the hotel suffered various mishaps during construction. The statue is credited with fixing the problem.
>
> The Las Vegas version was a gift to the hotel from a Thai newspaper and Hong Kong high roller in 1983. Cast in bronze and plated in gold, the statue is housed in concrete covered with tiny pieces of beveled glass.
>
> Thai-Buddhist tradition associates Brahma with creation. The four faces of the shrine represent the Four Divine States of Mind: loving kindness, compassion, sympathy, and equanimity.
>
> Since its formal dedication, many visitors have made various offerings—from flowers to money—in search of a divine state of mind, or at least good luck at the tables.
>
> Although Caesars Palace rakes in coins regularly, this is one area where it does not hold a house advantage. The money tossed into the shrine is returned to charities in Thailand.

Kings—featuring round beds—are also available. Standard rooms in the Roman Tower have a rack rate of about $145 per night.

Regular suites rent in the range from about $850 to $1,000 per night, depending on the number of bedrooms. The largest suites can link together eight bedrooms, perfect for the large family or the high roller traveling with a nanny, bodyguard, chef, or other staff members.

Fantasy Suites. It's not that they are free; Caesars prefers to call them "priceless." Suffice it to say they would cost a small fortune if you were in fact able to rent them; they are offered without charge to invited guests including celebrities, members of royal families, and (of course) the highest of the high rollers visiting Caesars Palace.

I visited a few of the two-story extravaganzas, including the 4,000-square-foot Jupiter Suite, which featured glass curtain walls, two bedrooms, five TVs, a karaoke music system, and a pair of servants. The slightly skewed wall sconces were designed by the studio of the extremely skewed Salvador Dalí.

There are a total of ten Fantasy Suites: two in Roman decor, three with Egyptian themes, and five as Las Vegas re-creations of ancient Pompeii. As guests arrive on their interior balconies, they are greeted by a fiber-optics sky depicting the night sky as it is believed to have looked on the evening of the birth of Caesar Augustus.

An entire wall of each room is given over to an entertainment system that includes five video screens, two compact disc players, and a karaoke machine. A master control panel can send different music to different rooms. In fact, there's more than two miles of wiring in each suite for entertainment, motorized bedroom and living room draperies, color wheel effects on the ceiling, and other lighting.

In the rotunda at the entrance to the central people mover, **The World of Caesar** includes a miniature city of Rome as it might have looked two thousand years ago. The hotel spent $2.5 million on just this little bit of decoration. The effect is enhanced with technology, including video projection.

Eating Your Way Through Caesars Palace

The hotel offers a world of fine dining, from one of the most opulent buffets to one of the most sybaritic and expensive feasts in town.

Palatium. One of the best buffets in Vegas. A lovely setting with open-air boundaries just off the spectacular Race and Sports Book. Buffet offerings change from day to day. One indicator of class: the buffet shrimp comes prepeeled.

The buffet is open for breakfast, lunch, and dinner Monday through Friday; special brunches are served Saturday and Sunday. A seafood buffet, including a whole lobster, is offered Friday from 4 P.M. to 10 P.M., and Saturday from 4:30 P.M. to 10 P.M.

The Palatium now offers an Emperor's Feast Dinner and a Champagne Dinner as an option to the usual dinner buffet. The Emperor's Feast, served Monday to Saturday, includes the dinner buffet, one whole Maine lobster and unlimited Caesars champagne, at a cost of $30 per person. The Champagne Dinner, served Sunday to Thursday, includes the dinner buffet plus unlimited Caesars champagne, at a cost of $20 per person. The Caesars Palatium Champagne Brunch is offered on Saturday and Sunday, from 8:30 A.M. to 3:30 P.M. at a cost of $14.99, excluding holidays; children ages 4 to 12 are half price and children ages 4 and younger eat free of charge when accompanied by a paying adult.

In the spring of 2000, two of Caesars' best-known restaurants were shuttered to make way for a new group of ultra-luxury suites that front on the hotel's pool.

Palace Court served classical French cuisine in a museum-like setting beneath a domed stained glass ceiling. **Bacchanal** was, well, a bacchanal, about as close to Roman orgy as most of us could hope for. Food and wine and Centurions and lovely serving wenches were plentiful.

Empress Court. Named in *USA Today* as one of the top gourmet Chinese restaurants in the country, the kitchen focuses on Hong Kong–style Cantonese cooking, although there are touches of Malay, Thai, and Indonesian cuisine. This is not your neighborhood chow mein palace; the service is white glove elegant.

Entrance is via a dramatic staircase that encircles a koi pond and leads to a coral reef aquarium at the restaurant's door. Within the kitchen is a more pur-

---

Burger palace. Feature films made at Caesars Palace include *Oh God! You Devil*, with George Burns; *The Electric Horseman*, starring Robert Redford, Jane Fonda, Willie Nelson, and Valerie Perrine; and Mel Brooks' *History of the World—Part 1*.

Parts of the 1988 Academy Award-winning *Rain Man* starring Dustin Hoffman and Tom Cruise were filmed in a suite at Caesars Palace. Hotel legend includes the story that every night star Hoffman would order 200 or so hamburgers from the tiny **Post Time Deli** off the Race and Sports Book for the crew. He apparently knows his chopped meat; the burgers are made from the trimmings of the filets from the hotel's butcher shop and are among the best values at Caesars Palace. Burgers are priced at $5.25, with deli sandwiches including Reubens and Philly Cheese Steak going for $6.25.

The snack bar was moved near the Palatium when Caesars Magical Empire was added.

> **Unlike father.** On December 31, 1967, daredevil Evel Knievel attempted to jump over the Caesars Palace fountains on a motorcycle; twelve years later, his son Robbie Knievel avenged his father's unsuccessful attempt.
>
> In 1981, an entire racetrack was created for the first of four Grand Prix auto races on site.
>
> In 1991, Wayne Gretzky led the Los Angeles Kings to victory over the New York Rangers in the Palace's first ice hockey event, the NHL's first outdoor game since 1925.

> **Check your horse, sir?** The Circus Maximus Showroom at Caesars Palace was used for the scene in the film *The Electric Horseman* when Robert Redford rode his horse down off the stage and into the casino.

poseful giant aquarium, stocked with live rock cod, Dungeness crab, lobster, and other seafood used in meals. The galley itself includes some extraordinarily hot grills used in preparation of specialties.

The Empress Court menu includes prix-fixe dinners at about $55 per person, as well as a la carte offerings. One offering included crispy crab claws, minced squab in crystal wrap, seafood wonton soup, sauteed prawns, stir-fried prime sirloin and chicken with oyster sauce, and mango pudding delight.

Individual entrees range from about $20 to $55. On a recent visit, items include braised abalone with fish maw in oyster sauce, pan-fried scallops with double eggs, and bird's nest with bamboo fungus. Open for dinner only from 6 P.M. to 10:30 P.M., Thursday to Monday. Reservations: (702) 731-7731.

Terrazza. An elegant garden spot alongside the Garden of the Gods pool area, the menu changes from casual fare for breakfast and lunch to formal Italian dining for dinner.

The 284-seat restaurant features an exhibition kitchen with a wood-burning brick pizza oven. A la carte offerings include pasta, meat, pizza, and more. Specialties include penne with baby shrimp in a light Brodetto sauce, and grilled herb-infused mahi mahi. Dinner entrees are priced from about $17 to $36.

Terrazza is open for lunch Wednesday through Saturday from 11:30 A.M. to 3 P.M. On Sunday, the brunch menu is served from 10:30 A.M. to 3 P.M. Dinner is served every night from 5:30 to 11 P.M. Reservations: (702) 731-7731.

Hyakumi. The name means "100 tastes," and you'll find at least that many at this handsome room. The elaborate and authentic interior and exterior designs were inspired by traditional upscale Japanese residences, including both traditional and contemporary elements. The interior includes a teahouse, garden, and an azalea-lined dry riverbed. Interior landscaping includes authentic Japanese flora and accents.

Hyakumi features prix-fixe teppanyaki feasts priced at an impressive $56. Of course, if you want to substitute Kobe beef for the prime tenderloin, the price rises to $199 per person.

You can also order a la carte Japanese offerings such as yosenabe, seafood and vegetables in fish broth served in a paper pot with ponzu sauce, sea bass teriyaki, or unaju, barbecued fresh water eel on rice.

The bar offers ten varieties of sake, rated on a dry-to-sweet chart, sold in small glasses or small bottles with prices reaching $180.

Dinner is served nightly from 6 P.M. to 11 P.M. Reservations: (702) 731-7731.

Café Roma. Your basic twenty-four-hour restaurant . . . with a global view and Caesars Palace class. It draws its menu from all around the world.

A breakfast buffet is offered Monday to Friday, 7 A.M. to 11 A.M., at a cost of $11.95 per person. A lunch buffet is offered Monday to Friday, noon to 2:30 P.M., at a cost of $13.95 per person. And a dinner buffet is offered Sunday to Thursday, and Friday and Saturday, 6 P.M. to 11 P.M., at a cost of $17.95 per person. On weekends, a brunch buffet is served from 7 A.M. to 2:30 P.M. at $13.95 per person.

Sport lights. The spectacular Race and Sports Book at Caesars Palace uses sixty panels made up of 1.5 million yellow, red, and green light-emitting diode (LED) panels that display computer-produced data including track conditions, horse and jockey names, and other information.

The largest of the video screens is thirty-two feet wide by twenty-six feet high.

A new Café Roma was expected to open September 2000, and the present room will be remodeled into a high-limit gaming area

Nero's. They don't fiddle around in this elegant seafood and steak house, an elegant mix of modern and classical themes. Open for dinner nightly, with entrees priced from about $25 to $50 and including dishes such as grilled swordfish with pan-fried risotto cakes, roasted Sonoma squab with parsnip puree, and grilled sirloin with sautéed oyster mushrooms.

On a recent visit, specialties included pan-roasted veal loin chop with leak and goat cheese tart and carmelized beets for $38, and grilled swordfish with sweet potato puree for $28.

La Piazza Food Court. A high-tone food court with offerings from Japanese ramen soups and bento boxes to Chinese stir-fry, Italian pasta and pizza, Mexican specialties, and an all-American deli.

Cleopatra's Barge. A re-created boat set in a small pond; it'll never set sail, but when things really get rocking at this cocktail lounge, the place starts rolling.

And don't overlook the dining possibilities at The Forum Shops at Caesars, including Chinois, The Palm, La Salsa, Bertollini's, Planet Hollywood, Spago, and the Stage Deli. *You'll discover more about these restaurants in Chapter 11.*

And just off the casino floor is **Caesars Magical Empire**, offering fine dining and upclose magic. *See the description in Chapter 10.*

Caesars Entertainment

Omnimax Theatre. Go into space, under the sea, deep into the Grand Canyon, or into an atom in one of the highest-tech movie theaters anywhere. The 386 seats of the Omnimax recline to permit full view of the huge fifty-seven-foot-tall screen. The films are shot on 70-mm film with a frame size ten times larger than standard 35-mm media. A nine-channel "sensaround" system engulfs the audience in sound.

Ticket prices are about $7 for adults. Seniors (over 55), juniors (4–12), military personnel, and hotel guests pay $5. Show times vary, but shows typically run hourly from 2 P.M. through 10 P.M. during the week, and from 1 P.M. to 11 P.M. on Friday and Saturday. Information: (702) 731-7900.

Circus Maximus Showroom. The main showroom at Caesars Palace is used for headliner acts and an occasional Broadway production or television show. It is typically set up with more than one thousand seats; booths are designed in the shape of Roman chariots.

Caesars Palace. 3570 Las Vegas Boulevard South; 2,471 rooms; (702) 731-7110, (800) 634-6661. www.caesars.com.

MUST-SEE ★★★ Circus Circus

From the sublime to the ridiculous: another must-see attraction.

For many of us, our expectations of Circus Circus were molded by the lurid account of Hunter S. Thompson in his gonzo classic, *Fear and Loathing in Las Vegas*. Just about everything Thompson wrote about in that book, including the acrobats tumbling overhead, the motorcyclists roaring around within a ball, and the general atmosphere of a Roman Circus, is true—although, alas, things are not quite as wild as his mind's eye saw them.

In any case, Circus Circus is one of the great grind joint successes of Las Vegas. It has cheap rooms (including an RV park), cheap meals, and lots and lots of low rollers at the tables. The hotel obviously makes its money on the quantity of action, not the size of the bankrolls at play. (Some wags have called Circus Circus the K-mart of gambling establishments.)

Upstairs over the casino floor is an indoor carnival, midway, and video arcade that will entertain (and draw allowance money) from the kids while their parents drop the rent money downstairs. And then there is the famed circus, up over the main casino; the acrobats, rope walkers, jugglers, and other acts perform about once an hour and then disappear so they don't distract too much from the gambling. Shows are presented daily from 11 A.M. to midnight.

The thirty-five-story West Tower added 1,000 more rooms; a walkway from the tower includes ten retail outlets, entrance to the Circus Circus Theme Park, and two new restaurants. Stivali is an elegant Italian eatery; the chefs hand-selected olive trees for the olive oil used there and supervise the harvest. Really.

Other rooms are found in two separate towers, connected by a shuttle tram to the main building. Circus Circus often has the least expensive major hotel rooms in town; the rooms, especially in the main tower, are quite acceptable. Midweek rates generally start at about $39.

At the back of the hotel is **The Adventuredome**, a five-acre entertainment park that presents a Las Vegas–eye view of the Grand Canyon, including 140-foot man-made peaks, a ninety-foot re-creation of Havasupai Falls, and a river. The entire park is covered by a pink dome called The Adventuredome. The Fun House Express is an IMAX thrill ride simulator. *See the description of The Adventuredome in Chapter 10 of this book.*

A "hurricane zone" of slot machines produces a multimedia storm with thunder and lightning every fifteen minutes; during a storm, the jackpot is increased.

The **Circus Buffet** is served beneath a red-and-white circus tent ceiling, an assault on the eyes, even by Las Vegas standards.

The Steak House, open for dinner only from 5 P.M. to midnight, has entrees in the range of $14 to $33 and is one of the better cuts-of-meat palaces in town. And even nicer, it's a dark, quiet, and private sanctuary from the circus. Entrees are priced from about $17 to $30. On Sundays, there's a champagne brunch served from 10 A.M. to 2 P.M., featuring steak, filet mignon, and seafood on ice, and priced at $25. Reservations are suggested.

Stivali Italian Ristorante is a traditional Italian eatery offering classic sauces and pastas, fresh-baked breads and pizzas. Complimentary appetizers are offered during weekday cocktail hours; Stivali is open daily for dinner.

The **Skyrise Snack Bar** offers coffee shop specialties. The **Pizzeria** features freshly baked pizzas, calzones, and salads and is open from 11 A.M. to midnight daily. The **Blue Iguana Las Vegas** offers Mexican fare 24 hours a day.

Circus Circus Hotel/Casino. 2880 Las Vegas Boulevard South; 3,744 rooms; (702) 734-0410, (800) 634-3450. www.circuscircus-lasvegas.com.

MUST-SEE ★★★ Excalibur

To truly enjoy this place, you've got to buy into the concept: King Arthur's Castle on the Strip. Part of the Mandalay Resort Group empire (formerly Circus Circus), Excalibur looks as if it were constructed out of a child's toy blocks. It's a place where the staff is drilled to finish conversations with, "Have a royal day."

The best approach to the Excalibur is by night. The colors of the 265-foot-tall bell towers and the castle's fairy tale shape are amazing enough, but even weirder when looked at between the Egyptian pyramid of the Luxor and the tropical gardens of the Tropicana. What a city!

As only befitting a place like this, each evening a fifty-one-foot-long fire-breathing Dragon battles a robotic Merlin every hour on the hour from 6 P.M. until midnight in the moat at the front entrance. The Glockenspiel Fairy Tale is played out over the giant clock at the rear entrance, with shows at the top and the bottom of each hour from 10 A.M. until 10 P.M.

If anything, Excalibur is even more overwhelming inside. The designers seem to have collected all of the missing high ceilings from the older casinos on the Strip and taken them to Nevada extremes. More so than at most other places in Vegas, the establishment's theme is carried through in almost every detail—the decorations, costumes, restaurants.

In keeping with its orientation toward family visitors, the Excalibur is one of the few casinos in Las Vegas that welcomes cameras: still, movie, and video. (In keeping with state law, though, you must keep children younger than twenty-one away from slot machines and gambling tables.)

Like many other casinos, there are no windows within the cavernous interior; one of the only ways to tell the time of day is to listen to the cocktail waitresses. As dawn breaks, they add orange juice and coffee to their cocktail offers.

The parapets of Excalibur
Photo by Corey Sandler

The Excalibur was holder of the title as the world's largest resort hotel for several years, with 4,008 rooms in four twenty-eight-floor towers. Today, it is certainly the world's largest resort hotel set inside a castle with a moat, a drawbridge, a jousting tournament, and a western dance hall.

There are four levels to the hotel; you will enter from the main parking lot or front entrance to Level I, which is, of course, the casino floor and registration desk. An escalator descends to the lower level **Fantasy Faire**, home of **King Arthur's Arena**, the **Magic Motion Machines**, and **Fantasy Faire** games. Or, you can take an escalator up to Level II, the Medieval Village, home of the **Round Table Buffet, WCW Nitro Grill**, the **Sherwood Forest Café**. One more level up takes you to Level III, which includes the **Canterbury Wedding Chapel**, banquet rooms, and more dining.

There is, of course, a casino, and it's a whopper with nearly three thousand slot machines and a hundred blackjack and craps tables, roulette wheels, and more, spread out over three acres. The casino includes a central pavilion for high-rolling slot players. The poker room features eighteen regular tables and two pai gow poker tables.

The Sports Book at Excalibur is obviously not a priority at this K-mart of a casino; bettors are seated on ordinary metal banquet chairs, with only a dozen or so medium-sized monitors scattered about.

The Excalibur's 900-seat showroom is unlike any other in Las Vegas. To begin with, the floor of the stage is dirt rather than polished wood, and many of the stars have four legs.

The evening program is "Tournament of Kings," an original musical pro-

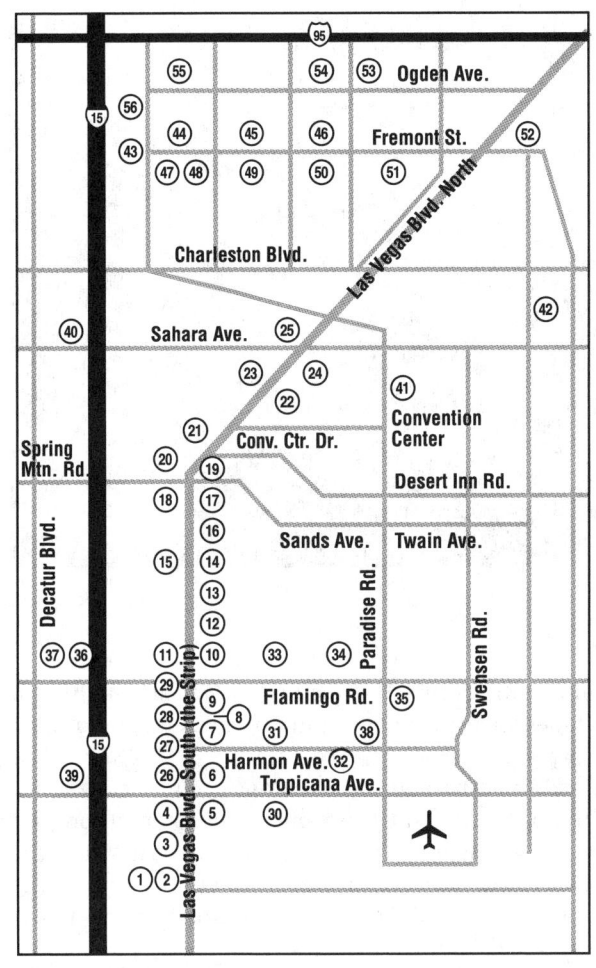

Las Vegas Strip

1. Four Seasons
2. Mandalay Bay
3. Luxor
4. Excalibur
5. Tropicana
6. MGM Grand
7. Aladdin
8. Paris–New York
9. Bally's
10. Barbary Coast
11. Caesars Palace
12. Flamingo Hilton
13. O'Shea's
14. Imperial Palace
15. Mirage
16. Harrah's
17. Venetian
18. Treasure Island
19. Desert Inn
20. Frontier
21. Stardust
22. Riviera
23. Circus Circus
24. Sahara
25. Stratosphere Tower
26. New York–New York
27. Monte Carlo
28. Holiday Inn–Boardwalk
29. Bellagio

Near the Strip

30. San Remo
31. Alexis Park
32. St. Tropez
33. Bourbon Street
34. Maxim's
35. Continental (closed)
36. Rio Suites
37. Gold Coast
38. Hard Rock
39. Orleans
40. Palace Station
41. Las Vegas Hilton
42. Showboat

Downtown

43. Plaza
44. Las Vegas Club
45. Binion's Horseshoe
46. Fremont
47. Golden Gate
48. Pioneer
49. Golden Nugget
50. Four Queens
51. Fitzgeralds
52. El Cortez
53. Gold Spike
54. Lady Luck
55. California
56. Main Street

The Strip
Courtesy of Las Vegas News Bureau

duction based on the legend of King Arthur. Presented twice each night at 6 and 8:30 P.M., the show includes jousting, dragons, fire-wizards . . . and dinner. Tickets are about $34.95 per person.

The story begins when Arthur gathers his fellow kings of Europe for a no-holds-barred competition to honor his son Christopher. The competitions, on horseback and on foot, grow increasingly intense. And then just when the party seems over, the evil fire wizard Mordred attacks, theatening to throw the land of Avalon into an age of fire and shadows. I don't want to spoil it for you, but I think you can guess who wins and who loses.

When you buy your ticket, you will be assigned to a reserved place. According to insiders, the best seats are up high in the center; in football terms, at the fifty-yard line. Avoid the end zones and stay up high to avoid the dust from the horses.

The **Fantasy Faire** level offers carnival games as well as a pair of "dynamic motion simulators" dubbed **Merlin's Magic Motion Machines**, which can take riders on a wild ride, without ever leaving the room. There are six different "rides," changing during the course of a day, shown in a pair of identical forty-eight-seat theaters. Rides include "Space Race," an outer-space demolition derby directed by George Lucas and "Devil's Mine Ride," a wild and crazy journey through underground caves and caverns. Other experiences include "Desert Duel," a bone-jarring desert race over dirt trails; "The Revolution," a simulation of one of the wildest roller coasters at the Magic Mountain amusement park, and "Runaway Train," a breakneck plunge through tunnels and steep mountain passes on a train with no brakes. Ticket prices are about $3 per ride. Note: You must be at least forty-two inches tall and in good health to ride the simulator.

The **Medieval Village** re-creates one vision of an ancient village, with shops, restaurants, strolling magicians, jugglers, and singers. Free ten-minute shows are presented every half hour on the Court Jester's Stage from 10 A.M. to 10 P.M. Many are a bit on the corny side but fun for the youngsters.

The **Fantasy Faire** itself is an unusual mix of modern video arcade and pinball machines with medieval theme carnival games. If you're into shooting galleries, be sure to check out the Electronic Crossbow with animated, moving figures in the line of fire.

Excalibur Beds and Breakfasts

Room rates start at about $49 for weekdays and $65 to $75 on weekends. The basic rooms are comfortable but a bit garish and inexpensive in appointments.

Each of the restaurants at Excalibur is a spectacular exercise in decoration and theme. Some of the food is decent, too. It's a not-very distinguished food factory; if you've got the time, cross the road to the Luxor or move on up a full step to the MGM Grand for nearby buffet fare.

The **Steakhouse at Camelot** offers gourmet dining in an intimate setting reminiscent of a royal chamber in a castle. There's a show kitchen, an impressive wine cellar, and a cigar room. With just 144 seats, reservations are necessary at busy times. Open for dinner from 6 to 10 P.M. Sunday through Thursday, and from 5 to 11 P.M. on Friday, Saturday, and holidays. Entrees range in price from about $12 to $65.

Among recent additions is the wholly incongruous **WCW Nitro Grill**. The restaurant/wrestling ring is the first in what is hoped to be a new chain celebrating the world of WCW wrestling.

About WCW and Nitro: if you've got to ask, you're obviously not a fan of the bizarre wrestling "competitions" on television and pay-per-view.

The restaurant is centered around a ring. Don't expect your waiters to duke it out for you, though; the area is used for autograph sessions with WCW stars and other notables. And you can relax through a big screen showing of regular WCW shows several nights of the week.

Menu items include things like Nelson's Famous Ribs, available in full Nelson and half Nelson portions. There's Jimmy Hart's Pasta and a Hogan burger. You can begin your meal with appetizers like broken chicken fingers or wrestling rings, and wash it all down with a selection from the "whine list."

There is also, of course, a gift shop. The establishment replaced Wild Bill's Saloon and Steakhouse.

Regale Italian Eatery is open for lunch and light dinner from 11 A.M. to 2:30 P.M. daily, and from 5 P.M. nightly. The fare is basic Italian, including antipasto, spaghetti, lasagna, and pizza in your basic trattoria setting. Entrees such as lasagna or ravioli and small pizzas are priced from about $10 to $18.

Sir Galahad's Prime Rib House. Open every night for dinner at 5 P.M., the specialties include prime rib from the Traditional English cut to the whopping

King Arthur cut, priced from about $17 to $39. Seafood and poultry dishes are also available. Reservations are recommended for the 234-seat eatery.

The **Sherwood Forest Café is a** twenty-four-hour coffee shop, with offerings that include Chinese dishes. Entrees range from about $12 to $22.

Excalibur Hotel & Casino. 3850 Las Vegas Boulevard South; 4,008 rooms; (702) 597-7777, (800) 937-7777. www.excalibur-casino.com.

MUST-SEE ★★★★ Hard Rock Hotel and Casino

In Las Vegas, where the unusual is merely ordinary, the Hard Rock Hotel is heavy metal in a hard place. Welcome to the only Las Vegas casino with the world's largest guitar on the roof and a chandelier made from thirty-two gold saxophones.

Every guest is issued a "backstage pass" room key. And rather than limousines, hotel guests are chauffeured in rock 'n' roll purple Suburbans with bodacious sound systems.

Located three blocks in from the Strip on Paradise Road, the relatively small hotel opened with a loud splash in 1995. The Hard Rock unveiled its eleven-story, 330-room expansion in 2000, doubling the size of the hotel and casino and including thirty-five luxury suites.

New restaurants include **Pink Taco**, a high-tone Mexican diner. The room features thoroughly new but decidedly old-looking corrugated metal, aged and distressed wood, and bare-bulb lighting fixtures. Visitors can sip ice-cold margaritas and cervezas to accompany hot enchiladas prepared in an open-air taqueria.

Nobu is an exotic Japanese restaurant, based around the cooking of Chef Nobu Matsuhisa, who operates eateries bearing his name in London and New York. Trees line a pathway leading to the entry, while the sushi bar glows from within a curved plane of river rock.

AJ's Steakhouse is an homage to Arnie Morton, the legendary Chicago restauranteur and father of Hard Rock's Peter Morton. Just past a '50s-style marquee advertising "Cocktails" is a small restaurant decorated in dark woods, tufted oxblood leather, and an elevated bar that has bronze rails and a black granite countertop. Oil paintings of legenedary boxers line the walls.

The Counter is a small but elegant lunch counter, a place where waffle irons, blenders, and sizzling grills make a modern return.

Hard Rock was founded by Peter Morton in 1971 with a cafe in London. Today the company owns and operates cafes in places including Los Angeles, San Francisco, Newport Beach, Chicago, Houston, New Orleans, Honolulu, Maui, San Diego, Las Vegas, Phoenix, Washington, Universal Studios Florida, Sydney, Australia, and Tel Aviv, Israel.

There is, of course, a casino, with 800 slot and video poker machines and thirty-seven table games. Some 250 of the slot machines have handles shaped like Fender guitars, and roulette tables are shaped like pianos. And then there are the gambling chips: $5 Red Hot Chili Pepper "Give It Away" chips, the $25 Purple Jimi Hendrix "Purple Haze" chip, and the $100 Tom Petty "You Got

Lucky" chip. The casino cashier's counter sits beneath a large sign that reads: "Bank of Hard Rock. In Rock We Trust."

Memorabilia on display includes one of Elvis's gold lamé jackets, Harley Davidson motorcycles from Guns 'n Roses and Motley Crue, and guitars from Nirvana, Pearl Jam, ZZ Top, Aerosmith, Bruce Springsteen, Van Halen, Chris Isaak, Lenny Kravitz, and many others. An Elvis suit and guitar are on display outside the HR store. And a San Francisco Giants uniform worn by Willie Mays adorns a mannequin outside the Sports Book. "The Joint" is Hard Rock's live music theater; it seats an intimate 1,400, a relatively small room in these days of stadium concerts for 25,000 of your closest friends.

In addition to the Hard Rock Cafe next door, restaurants in the hotel and casino include the **Mr. Lucky's 24/7** coffee shop, and **Mortoni's**, an Italian gourmet restaurant serving dinner only.

Although the enterprise is certainly intended to make a profit, there is an undercurrent of social consciousness beneath the glitz. Some of the machines are designated to pay their profits to the National Resources Defense Council and Conservation International. There are recycling bins and water-saving measures. And leftover restaurant food is donated to local charities.

Hotel amenities include the **Hard Rock Beach Club**. Music plays underwater in the lagoon-like pool, which has a sand bottom and rock outcroppings. French doors open the rooms to the outside air, an unusual feature in Las Vegas. The walls are decorated with pictures by famous rock photographers.

Basic room rates were $75 to $250 from Sunday through Thursday and $135 to $300 on weekends; suites started at $250 per night.

Hard Rock Hotel and Casino. 4475 Paradise Road; 340 rooms; (702) 693-5000, (800) 473-7625. www.hardrock.com.

MUST-SEE ★★★★ Las Vegas Hilton

Elvis slept here! In fact, this place is so large that he may still be roaming the halls somewhere, looking for the elevator.

Actually, in a perfect Las Vegas remake, Elvis has been replaced by a passel of Ferengis, Romulans, and the crew of the USS *Enterprise* at Star Trek: The Experience at the Hilton. The Experience is part theme park and part futuristic casino. *For details about the theme park, see Chapter 10.* To learn more about the casino, read on, voyager.

The Hilton is directly next to the Las Vegas Convention Center and its own 220,000-square-foot convention facilities and meeting rooms are often used for spillover from shows such as the Comdex computer exposition. Its rooms are among the first to sell out for major conventions, too.

The hotel's showroom was the site of the late-model Elvis Presley's glitter-era performances from 1969 until his reputed death in 1977. One of Elvis's costumes, an understated red, white, and blue number with a large American eagle, has been installed in a case near the entrance of the hotel near the registration desk; it was worn in a January 1972 engagement.

In recent years, the showroom was home to a production of Andrew Lloyd

> **Elvis sighting number one.** Elvis Presley made 837 sold-out appearances in 15 engagements at the Hilton from 1969–1977. From time to time, the hotel has exhibited various pieces of Elvis memorabilia.

> **Elvis sighting number two.** Elvis had his own intimate 5,000-square foot hideaway on the 30th floor of the Hilton, used during his appearances there. After Elvis' death, the maintenance staff at the Hilton filled in two bullet holes in the walls and actually redecorated the place! Obviously, they had no sense of history.
>
> In 1994 the entire place was gutted and incorporated into one of three spectacular suites, each 10,000 to 15,000 square feet in size and costing a cool $45 million to build.

Webber's *Starlight Express*; in early 1998, the theater reverted to its previous incarnation as a headliner showroom.

A Hotel and Casino, Too

The three thirty-story towers include 3,174 rooms and suites. The 1,500-seat showroom, used for major shows and boxing matches, has one of the largest stages in Las Vegas. Recreational facilities include a large pool (it actually sits above the ceiling of the main casino), tennis courts, a health club, and a nine-hole putting green.

There is, of course, a casino, and it provides a large and attractive field in which to dream. Recent renovations have upgraded the chandeliers throughout. There are sixty-five game tables and more than a thousand slot machines. A Sports and Race Book with more than fifty television monitors and projection screens is one of the most spectacular in town.

And there is also the SpaceQuest Casino, part of the Star Trek Experience expansion of the hotel. Here, visitors can travel to the twenty-fourth century to . . . gamble. (This is Las Vegas, remember.)

The SpaceQuest Casino, though, is quite a trip, with a setting that places you aboard a futuristic space station orbiting 1,500 miles above the earth. Glance up to catch the view through three large space windows that reveal the earth below as well as space limousines picking up and delivering the highest of the high rollers.

There are more than 400 slot machines at SpaceQuest; this is the future, so instead of pulling a slot handle, you can spin the wheels by passing your hand through a light beam.

There is, of course, a gift shop and a spacey bar.

Standard room rates start at about $85 but can climb sharply—if available at all—during conventions. The best rates can be obtained at Christmastime, with the exception of New Year's Eve. **Classic Suites** on the upper floors are for high rollers only.

Three fabulous "sky villas" at the top of the Hilton include the 12,600-square-foot **Villa Conrad**, a two-story home away from home decorated in French style; the larger **Villa Tuscany**, which has a private garden; and the 15,400-square-foot **Villa Verona**, modestly modeled after the Palace of Versailles.

The Villa Tuscany includes a bathroom that has gold-plated bathtub faucets and a fireplace. The lush draperies sweep aside to reveal a spectacular view of the Spring Mountains and the man-made marvel of the Strip. If the interior feels too confining, the guest can step out to a private putting green and pool.

And, of course, a butler and private chef are on call at all times.

As with other super-suites at Caesars Palace, The Mirage, the MGM Grand, and elsewhere, the suites are priceless—mere visitors to Las Vegas cannot rent them at any price. All of the fuss is aimed at enticing an estimated 200 of the world's richest gamblers, almost all of them foreigners. They get the rooms for free, and the casinos hope they will reciprocate by losing thousands at the table.

The fanciest restaurant in the building is **Bistro Le Montrachet**, which is very French. A wine cellar offers more than 400 varieties. And, check out the beautifully sculpted pear in a sugar cage at the entrance. Among the specialties, priced from about $32 to $36, is *le filet de Saint Pierre* (poached filet of John Dory with leek pasta in a creamy saffron, wild mushroom, and tomato sauce). Open for dinner only from 6 to 10:30 P.M.; it is closed Tuesday and Wednesday.

The Reef is a seafood restaurant that offers an upscale setting and menu. Specialties on a recent visit included sautéed scallops with mushroom shallot cream, Dijon herb crusted halibut, and broiled twin Australian lobster tails. Entrees are priced from about $20 to $54. The Reef is open nightly from 5:30 to 10:30 P.M.

Andiamo is the home of Northern Italian specialties and homemade pasta, offered daily for dinner from 5:30 to 10:30 P.M. Closed Sunday and Monday. There's an impressive espresso and cappuccino counter at the entrance, and diners can see the chefs at work behind a glass wall. Specialties include *medaglioni di vitello andiamo* (two veal medallions sautéed and served with creamy rosemary sauce and asparagus), and *costoletta di vitello con spugnole* (Provini veal chop sautéed with morel mushrooms and pine nuts in marsala sauce). Entrees are priced from about $15 to $30.

Benihana Village features two traditional Japanese restaurants, **Hibachi** and **Robata**. At Hibachi, chefs chop, slice, and grill your food at your table. Offerings range from about $15 to $40. Robata offers seafood specialties, prepared in Japanese fashion. Dinner is complemented by the animated musical show "Jambirdee" and a fireworks display over the Benihana Musical Waters.

The **Garden of the Dragon** features gourmet Chinese dishes from 5:30 to 10:30 P.M. In addition to basic Chinese fare, you'll also find some unusual offerings such as sizzling lamb (tender lamb loin sliced with Chinese fresh vegetables, served sizzling at the table) and steamed whole flounder (whole flounder steamed in the Cantonese style and garnished with scallions, ginger, and soy sauce). Prefixe dinners are about $22 to $27; individual entrees are also sold.

The **Hilton Steakhouse** offers charbroiled steak, ribs, fish, and chicken priced from about $18 to $52. Open 5:30 to 10:30 P.M. Offerings include several cuts of steak, such as a 36-ounce double New York strip sirloin for two, priced at nearly $60; center-cut pork chops; and large-cut filet mignon. Other entrees include fresh swordfish steak, skewer of tiger shrimp, and lemon oregano chicken.

Also available is **MargaritaGrille**, a casual Mexican restaurant. Offerings include *albondigas* (Mexican vegetable soup with meatballs), *chili con queso,* fajitas, chimichangas, *flautas,* and burritos.

Paradise Café is a twenty-four-hour coffee shop.

The **Buffet of Champions** is open for breakfast during the week from 7 to 11 A.M.; lunch is served from 11 A.M. to 2:30 P.M.; dinner is from 5 to 10 P.M. A champagne brunch is offered Saturday, Sunday, and holidays.

Las Vegas Hilton. 3000 Paradise Road; 3,174 rooms; (702) 732-5111, (800) 732-7117. www.lv-hilton.com.

MUST-SEE ★★★ Luxor

The real and imagined treasures of another desert empire come to near life in the fabulous Luxor, a 2,521-room, thirty-story, pyramid-shaped complex. The interior of the hotel—a vast hollow pyramid—is about as spectacular a sight as you'll see on the Strip. The designers of the Luxor conceived of it as a simulation of a vast archeological dig where the mysteries of ancient Egypt are revealed as though the interior was a vast excavation site. Replicas of Egyptian artifacts, including a full-sized reproduction of King Tut's tomb, are on display.

As you approach, the hotel appears to be a huge sand-colored pyramid; the rooms of the hotel occupy the exterior steps of the structure. Out front is a huge replica of the Sphinx, the mythical Egyptian creature with a human head and the body of a lion. The figure was often meant to symbolize the pharaoh as an incarnation of the sun god, Ra. Blazing out of the top of the pyramid is a forty-billion-candlepower light—claimed to be the most powerful beam of light in the world; orbiting Space Shuttle crewmembers fulfilled a PR person's dream when they reported seeing it from space. The light is actually forty-seven separate xenon units mounted in the top of the pyramid.

The pyramid, a symbol of eternal life believed by the Pharaohs to be a "stairway to the stars," offers three levels of entertainment. The Hanging Gardens of Babylon occupy the front entrance, while lagoon-like pools and a beach are at the rear entrance.

The Luxor has gone upscale a bit, eliminating some of the touristy gimmicks such as the river cruise and some of the less-than-extraordinary multimedia shows. The lobby and public areas have received handsome new appointments, and a semi-private baccarat and high-limit gaming area has taken center stage in the casino.

It's very appropriate that the exceedingly strange Blue Man Group has taken up long-term residence on stage in this weird and disconcerting place.

A computer-controlled light system makes the understated resort visible for earthbound visitors as well; there are some 3,000 strobes in an intricate special effects display that sends streaks of light up the sides of the pyramid.

A set of three moving walkways transport you up from the casino at Luxor, across Tropicana Avenue, and down into the Excalibur, a journey from ancient Egypt to merry olde England.

Guests are transported to their floors on inclined elevators moving at a thirty-nine-degree angle up the sides of the pyramid, or on more conventional vertical lifts.

The Best of the Strip

The rooms themselves have an unusual feature that may be a bit disconcerting to some visitors; the outside window wall is slanted sharply since it is part of the exterior of the pyramid. Other visitors may find the view of the interior atrium a bit dizzying; the interior balconies extend all the way up to the twenty-seventh floor, while the top three floors—mostly suites—have interior hallways. And residents of one of the first few floors of the hotel may find a great deal of pedestrian traffic right outside their doors.

The rooms are nicely appointed, from standard guest rooms (as low as $59 in off-season and more than twice that during conventions and at peak times) to the Jacuzzi Suites (starting at $150) and the spectacular upper-level rooms including the Presidential Suite that rents for several thousand dollars per night.

> **The real thing.** Luxor, on the east bank of the Nile about 315 miles southeast of Cairo, is near the site of Thebes, the capital of ancient Egypt. The temple at Luxor was built by Amenhotep III and dedicated to Amon-Re, king of the gods, the sun god. Nearby are the Valley of the Kings, where the tomb of Tutankhamen was discovered in 1922; the Valley of the Queens; and the magnificent monuments of Karnak.

Within the 90,000-square-foot casino area—about twice the size of most of the Strip's gambling rooms—the Egyptian theme is carried through with reproductions of artifacts, columns, and tombs found in the temples of Luxor and Karnak.

The gourmet room is **Isis**, which serves continental fare as well as seasonal specialties for a pre-fixe rate of about $34. Guests enter along a colonnade walk of caryatid statues and through glass doors emblazoned with gold-embossed "wings of Isis." Within the restaurant on the Mezaanine level overlooking the casino is a vaulted ceiling decorated with gold Egyptian stars. Dinner is served nightly from 5 to 11 P.M. Reservations are suggested.

The **Sacred Sea Room**, an attractively decorated hideaway, includes entrees priced from about $16 to $40, with dishes including linguine and clams, New York steak, and veal chops. Murals and hieroglyphics of ancient fishing holes line the walls. Fresh vegetables complement each meal, with a lazy Susan salad bar at each table. Dinner is served nightly from 5 to 11 P.M.

For hearty appetites, there's the **Luxor Steak House**, an elegant eatery paneled in cherry wood. Steaks and chops are priced from about $17 to $40. Dinner is served nightly from 5 to 11 P.M. Reservations are suggested.

More adventurous dishes are offered at **Papyrus**, including Polynesian, Pacific Rim, Szechwan, and Cantonese fare. Dishes are priced from about $13 to $40. A replica of a wall in a Mayan ruin stands at the rear of the dining room, which is open to the atrium's height. One specialty is the Papyrus Hot Rock Sampler; your waiter will cook marinated meats, shrimp, and vegetables on a heated slab at tableside. Dinner is served nightly from 5 to 11 P.M.

The **Pyramid Café's** menu offers a wide range of salads, plus entrees including burgers, grilled Pacific salmon, and fried chicken, priced at about $6.

Think of the **Nile Deli** as a New York Jewish delicatessen on the banks of the Nile. Large sandwiches, Philly cheesesteaks, reubens, lox on a bagel, and other delicacies are priced from about $7 to $10. The buffet at the Luxor is the awkwardly named **Pharaoh's Pheast**, which replaced the strangely named Manhattan Buffet beneath the apex of the pyramid.

And there is, of course, an ancient shopping bazaar. The hotel features a 1,200-seat oval showroom for a nightly special effects production show; the entrance to the arena is decorated to resemble the ancient tombs of the pharaohs in the Valley of the Kings.

The third level offers the Luxor IMAX Theatre, the Luxor Museum with some artifacts and replicas of Egyptian antiquities, and a set of multimedia attractions of varying appeal. *For details, see the section on Las Vegas attractions in Chapter 10.*

Two stepped pyramid-shaped towers, located between Luxor and Excalibur, added 1,950 guest rooms in recent years. A moving walkway, located between the East and West Towers, will transport guests to and from Excalibur.

Luxor's splashy lounge is RA, which features a spectacular light and sound system and nonstop dancing music. The club includes luxury VIP booths, a 110-seat sushi and oyster bar, and valet service at the south entrance to Luxor. RA is open Wednesday through Saturday from 10 P.M. to 6 A.M. A semi-formal dress code is enforced.

Luxor's Oasis Spa features sixteen treatment rooms, circuit training and weight rooms, a full range of body treatments, hydrotherapy, and the like.

Giza Galleria in the East Tower adds shopping outlets that include the Cairo Bazaar, offering Egyptian antiquities and artifacts; Treasure Chamber, offering authentic treasures from royal tombs; and jewelry and clothing stores.

The Egyptian-themed Luxor Theater offers 1,200 theater-style seats for the exceedingly strange Blue Man Group, which is kind of like Cirque du Soleil meets Stomp. The theater is located at the southwest corner of the pyramid and connects to the main casino by a dramatic foyer. There are two shows nightly from Wednesday to Saturday, and single shows Sunday and Monday. For show information, call (702) 262-4400.

Luxor Hotel/Casino. 3900 Las Vegas Boulevard South; 4,476 rooms; (800) 288-1000, (702) 262-4000. www.luxor.com.

MUST-SEE ★★★★ MGM Grand

The MGM Grand is a decidedly strange and somewhat wonderful place, a Las Vegas version of Oz for adults and children of all ages. There's a rainforest, a robotic comedian, a spaceship that lands twice nightly, and a gigantic gilded lion facing the Strip that is as much of a symbol of the promise and threat of Las Vegas as anything else in town. Oh, and it also features a huge hotel and casino and one of the widest ranges of restaurants in town.

Rising above the gilded lion at the Strip and Tropicana Avenue is a spectacular tower of a sign, boasting an impressive video screen visible by day and night, broadcasting scenes from the hotel's EFX show and other events.

And there's also MGM Grand Adventures, a small theme park with rides, shows, restaurants, and shops. *For more details on the theme park, see Chapter 10.*

Alongside the gilded lion, the casino has linked a set of pedestrian bridges that connect the four corners of the Strip and Tropicana Avenue; you can walk from the MGM to New York–New York or the Tropicana, and connect to a bridge to the Excalibur and from there by tram to Mandalay Bay.

Speaking of lions, the hotel has opened a three-level lion habitat within the casino, home to about a dozen living, growling symbols of the MGM empire; about five will be on display at any one time. The habitat is under the supervision of animal trainer Keith Evans who cares for seventeen lions, three tigers, and two snow leopards at his Las Vegas home, known to some as "The Cat House." Admission to the area will be free; you can, though, plunk down $20 for a special "photo opportunity" with some of the creatures. The habitat is open daily from 11 A.M. to 11 P.M.

MGM has brought back the infamous Studio 54, one of the ultra-trendy landmarks of New York's 1970s disco scene. The three-story nightclub is located in the former Emerald City, just off the spectacularly improved Lion Entrance on the corner of Las Vegas Boulevard and Tropicana Avenue.

MGM Grand's Studio 54 showcases state-of-the-art sound, music, and lighting, and four dance floors and bars. There is also an exclusive invited-guest area and several semi-private lounges that can hold up to 400 people; total capacity is about 1,200. The decor of the club features artwork from New York's original dance club and techno-chic scaffolding and lighting; there is, of course, a mirrored ball over the dance floor.

The bartenders and host are part of the performance, and they enforce a dress code with the emphasis on flash. "Dress spectacular" demands the sign at the door; show up in a T-shirt reading "I'm with Stupid," baggy jeans, or a silly hat and you'll be sent to your room. If you're allowed in, you'll have to pay a $20 cover charge on Friday and Saturday, or $10 during the week. The cover charge, though, applies only to men; ladies are free. The club is closed on Monday and Sunday.

Near the Strip entrance is an outpost of the **Rainforest Café** chain. The entrance to the two-story, 500-seat restaurant and store is beneath a forty-foot cascading waterfall. There is almost always a long wait to get in; make your reservation at the elephant's head and plan to dine early or late to avoid crowds.

The **Magic Mushroom Juice and Coffee Bar** includes a playful animatronic gorilla family. There's also a robotic alligator moving back and forth in a steamy pond; he is a target for coins. Alongside the gift shop are stands for live parrots and other birds; a naturalist will answer questions from time to time. Other highlights include several huge aquariums. Take the escalator toward the sky bridge for a good view into the restaurant. Lunch and dinner entrees, which include burgers, sandwiches, salads, and pasta dishes, are generally in the range of $9 to $18. The restaurant opens at 7 A.M. daily and stays open until midnight during the week, until 1 A.M. on Friday and Saturday.

An expansion just for the high-rollers, the Mansion at the MGM Grand, is inspired by Tuscan architecture, these private suites and villas range from 3,000 to 14,000 square feet. The Mansion features exquisite villas and suites that are entirely enclosed by an atrium highlighted by formal gardens and indoor and outdoor pools.

The new lion rests atop a twenty-five-foot pedestal at the corner of the Strip and Tropicana Avenue; weighing fifty tons, it is the largest bronze sculpture in the United States. The sculpture is framed by water fountains and extensive landscaping. Video display screens at the exterior and interior of the Strip entry are among the largest ever constructed.

The spectacular EFX show—one of the Econoguide Bests of Las Vegas—occupies the 1,700-seat MGM Grand Theater. This is a ninety-minute jaw dropper of an evening. The $41 million production, which boasts a seventy-person cast and more special effects than much of the rest of the Strip combined, was recast in 1999 with the arrival of the biggest, or at least the tallest star on Broadway, singer and dancer Tommy Tune; he renewed his contract into at least the end of the year 2000. Tune takes on the roles of Merlin, the wise man and sorcerer of the Arthurian legend; P. T. Barnum, the legendary circus entrepreneur; magician Harry Houdini; and H. G. Wells, the English science fiction writer. The story is a bit, shall we say, thin . . . but the show is a lot of fun and the special effects and stagecraft is truly amazing, including a huge flying saucer that somehow arrives on stage, plus numerous fire effects and explosions.

EFX is presented nightly at 7:30 and 10:30 P.M.; the show is dark Sunday and Monday. Tickets were about $70 for preferred view seating, and $49.50 for other seats. Children's tickets were $35 for all shows.

The hotel and casino are certainly grand and worth a visit, but the overall tone is down a notch from places like Caesars Palace or the Mirage. It is also one of the few hotel complexes we know of that requires the use of a map; we suspect some of the bellhops keep copies in their back pockets, too.

The **Grand Theatre** is a handsome Vegas showroom, wider than it is deep with a stage about three city buses wide and decorated in red and black. The tables and booths seat about 1,700. The relatively cozy **Hollywood Theatre**, with 630 seats, features headliners.

The **Sports Book**, to the left of the Grand Theatre, has a gigantic screen capable of handling a single event like the Super Bowl, or being split into as many as twelve separate images for various sporting events.

We also mustn't overlook (as if we could) the **MGM Grand Garden** special events center. This arena, modeled after New York's famed Madison Square Garden, offers seating for up to 15,200 for championship boxing. There's nothing very grand about the arena itself, except for its ability to change its configuration for events from ice shows, hockey games, and basketball games to prize fights and concerts. According to the designers, it can be transformed in four hours from a major exhibition hall to an arena for sporting events or concerts. The Garden was the site of the much-publicized opening night concerts by Barbra Streisand, plus a Millennium eve show.

In the hotel, standard rooms are about 446 square feet in size; 744 suites range in size from 675 to 6,000 square feet. (A bit of perspective here: a typical three- or four-bedroom home is 2,000 square feet or less.)

Standard rooms are decorated in Wizard of Oz, Hollywood, Southern, and Casablanca styles. They are larger than average and fairly quiet. Suites include traditional, Marrakech, Oriental, Bahamian, and Las Vegas designs. The Grand Class on the twenty-ninth floor includes fifty-two two-story suites primarily reserved for VIP guests and celebrities; the three Presidential Suites include wrap-around glass windows, a full kitchen with private chef and butler, and no less than twenty-one telephones, including one in the personal suite elevator. There is even a semi-private restaurant that you have to know about and be known before you can enter.

In mid-2000, the MGM Grand opened a satellite check-in desk at McCarran Airport, the first of its kind at any U.S. airport. Guests can check in and pick up their room keys, make restaurant reservations, and purchase show tickets.

The huge casino encompasses a total of 171,500 square feet, including about 3,500 slot machines, 165 gaming tables, and a Race and Sports Book. The casino is divided into four themed areas: Emerald City, Hollywood, Monte Carlo, and Sports.

Other Eateries

At the very center of it all is **Wolfgang Puck's Café**, a Nevada outpost of the successful California chef's unusual restaurants. Puck's circular eatery is a high concept pizzeria. It is open from 11 A.M. to 11 P.M.

Most of the other restaurants are clustered in a corridor that leads from the casino to the MGM Grand Garden and the MGM Grand Adventures area.

Hot restaurants at MGM include **The Hollywood Brown Derby**, a re-creation of the California original, featuring its famed Cobb salad, steaks, and other American fare. **Tre Visi** and **La Scala** are cheek-to-jowl fancy and informal Italian eateries. La Scala is run by restauranteur Franco Nuschese, owner of the popular Café Milano in Washington, D.C.

Neyla, a Mediterranean grill on the Studio Walk, opened in late 1999. Diners can try different types of "mezza," a series of appetizers including salads, plump stuffed grape leaves, dips, kabobs, spicy sausages, and spinach pies, accompanied by wood-fired flat breads. On a recent visit, entrees included strip steak with seven spices and Bulgarian feta cheese, and pan-roasted Moroccan tuna with chickpea salad. The restaurant is open from 11 A.M. to 10 P.M. Sunday through Thursday, and until 11 P.M. on Friday and Saturday.

Gatsby's, located in a most magnificently posh room, features fine French cuisine with an eclectic California flair. Offerings at Gatsby's include a combination of pan-seared Kobe beef, guinea hen, and Louisiana ostrich with sun-dried tomatoes and green peppercorn reduction for $40, and sautéed lobster with pickled mango relish for $65. Desserts include Caesar's Chocolate Ooze Cake for $9, and The Tartanic, lemon meringue on a pool of raspberry crème Anglaise for $8. A tasting menu is about $75. The restaurant is open daily from 8:30 A.M. to 10:30 P.M.

Mark Miller's Grill Room, a transplant from Santa Fe, specializing in Cowboy Rib Steaks, with an average check of about $38 to $45 per person.

Ricardo's, a 320-seat Mexican restaurant, features both fine and casual dining, entertainment, a walk-up margarita bar, and a taco bar.

Celebrity chef/author Emeril Lagasse brings his New Orleans blend of modern Creole/Cajun cooking with **Emeril's New Orleans Fish House** restaurant featuring his signature dish, Emeril's New Orleans barbecue shrimp. Fresh fish is flown in daily.

Dragon Court is a high-tone Chinese eatery, quiet and off the busy track. The small menu includes braised shark fin and chicken in brown sauce for $30, as well as more ordinary offerings such as beef with oyster sauce for $13.50 and pork chop with black pepper sauce for $15. Other items we saw: golden fried egg yolks, pu-pu platters, and honey-glazed barbecue ribs.

The **One-Liners Fast Food Court** features a **Nathan's**, a **McDonald's**, and **Hamada Oriental Express.**

Check out the robotic version of comedian Foster Brooks doing one of his routines at the bar near the elevators to the hotel rooms. It takes a while before you realize that the guy sitting at the bar telling stories is not just your ordinary drunk. He is a professional, electronically operated drunk.

The Grand Oasis includes a swimming pool with beach. Nearby is the **Grand Health Club & Spa**, a fitness center that includes six Jacuzzis.

For parents who want to park the kids somewhere away from the casinos and showrooms for a while, the MGM Youth Center will accommodate children from ages 3 (out of diapers) to 12 at its location near the theme park. Rates from 8 A.M. to 5 P.M. are about $6 per hour for guests of the hotel and $8 per hour for others; the hourly charge rises by one dollar from 5 P.M. to midnight. There is a two-hour minimum and a five-hour maximum; beepers are available to the most nervous of parents.

Also available is the **Wizard's Midway & Arcade**, downstairs from the concourse to the theme park, and featuring an impressive collection of the latest video games. If you've got any stomach left after gambling or visiting the theme park, you may want to try the **G360** virtual reality arcade game; you'll "fly" your craft into a dogfight and then come back to a carrier landing. If you're anything like the pilots I saw, you'll spend most of the time upside down trying to figure out which way is up.

The **MGM Grand–Bally's Monorail**, privately funded by the casinos, follows a 1.6-mile route north-south along Audrie Lane on Bally's property, crossing Harmon Avenue and proceeding along an internal boulevard on MGM Grand property.

This is not a thrill ride. In fact, it's a fairly slow somewhat boring short trip between the backside of the MGM Grand Hotel (with a peek into MGM Grand Adventures) and the even-more undistinguished backside of Bally's. Two trains of six forty-passenger cars are available; the potential top speed is fifty miles per hour, but we've never seen the monorail break into a trot, much less a dash.

The companies believe the line may turn out to be the first leg of a system that will one day link downtown, the Strip, the Las Vegas Convention Center, and McCarran International Airport. As this book went to press, MGM was leading the charge for such a major project.

The monorail links what is now the top end of the Strip—MGM Grand,

The Best of the Strip   57

Tropicana, Luxor, Excalibur, and the New York–New York—to the Center Strip. Bally's is next door to the Aladdin Hotel on one side and the Imperial Palace on the other, and a few blocks away from Caesars Palace and the Mirage. The Mirage, of course, is linked by trolley to its neighbor, Treasure Island.

MGM Grand, Inc., controlled by billionaire Kirk Kerkorian, bought control of rival Mirage Resorts in early 2000. The company now owns fourteen casinos, including five of the most spectacular casinos on the Strip: the MGM Grand, New York–New York, Mirage, Bellagio, and Treasure Island.

MGM Grand. 3799 Las Vegas Boulevard South; 5,000 rooms; (702) 734-5110, (800) 929-1111. www.mgmgrand.com/lv.

MUST-SEE ★★★★★ Mandalay Bay

The Road to Mandalay runs through the south end of the Strip.

Mandalay Bay Resort and Casino is one of the most striking hotels in Las Vegas, a surprise at the top end of the Strip. Not as ostentatious as Paris or the Venetian, or with its nose stuck so high in the air as Bellagio.

In a town where almost nothing is what it seems to be, or ends up like it is promised to be, Mandalay Bay stands apart. This is an attractive, fun, and dare I say it, classy addition to Las Vegas.

Set in a mythical place vaguely inspired by Kipling's poem about Mandalay, the hotel includes some of the most best-looking and most enticing restaurants in any casino in the real world of Las Vegas.

The 3,700-room, $950 million Mandalay Bay occupies the former site of the Hacienda Hotel and Casino; it is the first of a series of developments expected to blossom on the "miracle mile" of resorts under the Mandalay Resorts flag at the top end of the Strip. An automated tram links Mandalay Bay to the Excalibur and Luxor resorts.

Mandalay Bay's attractions include an eleven-acre tropical lagoon featuring a sand-and-surf beach, a three-quarter mile lazy river ride, and a swim-up shark tank; and world-class restaurants created by top-rated chefs behind some of the most acclaimed restaurants in New York, Los Angeles, and Miami.

The forty-three-story hotel and casino has a "forbidden city" theme with waterfalls, terraced gardens, and mythical statuary. A cable car links Mandalay Bay to the Excalibur Hotel, with a loading station at the intersection of The Strip at Flamingo Road. The tram makes a stop at the Luxor Resort on its return from Mandalay Bay.

The 12,000-seat **Mandalay Bay Events Center** will be the setting for superstar concerts and major sporting events. The arena was christened with a concert given by opera singer Luciano Pavarotti.

The **Mandalay Bay Theatre**, a 1,700-seat Broadway-style theater, debuted with the hit musical *Chicago*. The theater includes a full orchestra pit.

The 2,000-seat **House of Blues** is used for concerts, and there's a 600-seat restaurant on the ground floor. The club will also manage an International House of Blues Foundation Room, located on the top floor of the hotel, for VIPs and special events.

The huge hotel includes more than a dozen formal and informal restaurants. Formal dining spots are small, expensive, and exclusive.

Among the more many unusual offerings is **Rumjungle**, located along the hotel's restaurant row, nicely isolated from the beeps and squawks of the casino. Water cascades down dramatic glass walls throughout the eatery; theatrical lighting sets the mood late at night. Live cocktail lounge entertainment starts nightly at 11 P.M. The menu spreads across Latin, Caribbean, and African fare; the restaurant is from the creators of China Grill.

A star offering is the Fire Pit dinner, served to everyone at the table. Dish after dish of salmon roasted in a banana leaf, grilled corizo, Martiniquan lamb skewer with green curry coconut glaze, hulihuli chicken, and more. Adults, about $34, children $19.

Across the row is **Wolfgang Puck's Trattoria del Lupo**, an upscale restaurant set within a small piazza in Milan with views of the pasta, charcuterie, and bakery production areas. The menu focuses on Northern and Southern Italian specialties and include Puck's well-known exotic pizzas. Entrees include roasted Alaskan halibut with lemon and pancetta, for about $24, and braised lamb shank with caramelized onion and saffron, for about $26. The 200-seat restaurant is open for lunch and dinner.

A huge statue of Lenin, in headless post Cold War form, stands outside the elegant and quirky **Red Square**, an outpost of Miami's South Beach original.

Decorated in Romanov splendor, in red and black with onion domes and high ceilings, the restaurant's showpiece is its extensive vodka collection that includes private vodka lockers; the bar offers more than a hundred varieties as well as all manner of infusions, martinis, and cocktails.

One star of the menu is kulebyaka, a fillet of salmon filled with mushroom, egg, and fresh dill wrapped in a puff pastry. Other offerings include filet Stroganoff, chicken Kiev, and Roquefort-crusted filet mignon. Entrees range from about $17 to $30. The restaurant serves dinner only.

The fanciest and liveliest lobster pound in town is **Rock Lobster**, at the point of the V-shaped restaurant row, and closer to the casino floor. Dishes, priced from about $8 to $30, range from burgers, and lobster pot pies to steak, shrimp, salmon, and lobster dinners. Specialty drinks follow the same theme, with libations including Bloody Shrimp, the Lobster Trap, and Soused Lobster.

The ultra-chic **Aureole** is a cousin to Charlie Palmer's acclaimed New York restaurant, featuring seasonal American dishes. The interior of the 383-seat room was designed by the eclectic Adam Tihany, centered around a unique four-story wine tower; wine stewards strap on harnesses and are hoisted up the tower to make selections from the "cellar in the sky." Aureole is open for dinner only.

An elegant turn to the far east, **Shanghai Lilly** is encased in polished wood, mirrors, and glass; dishes are served on fine Limoges china. Chinese entrees, ranging from about $16 to $75, include basics like Kung Pao chicken and moo shu pork to unusual and pricey offerings like abelone with sea cucumber, shark's fin with Dungeness crab or Maine lobster sashimi.

Across the row is **China Grill**, described as a China-inspired brasserie. Its broader menu reaches across Asia, with offerings from China, Korea, Japan, and elsewhere. The eatery is part of a group of restaurants in New York, Miami Beach, and Beverly Hills. Entrees, ranging from about $26 to $60, include a massive two-pound Porterhouse steak with kimchi and orange maple dressing, Japanese Panko-crusted veal, and sesame-speckled skate. Open for dinner only.

The **Border Grill**, a modern and upscale version of a southwestern taqueria, is a Los Angeles favorite owned by the "Too Hot Tamales" pair of Mary Sue Milliken and Susan Feniger. Its gourmet Mexican fare for lunch and dinner features dishes such as grilled skirt steak with garlic and cilantro, sautéed rock shrimp with toasted ancho chilies, and grilled breast of turkey. One unusual dish is mulitas de hongos, which layers grilled Portobello mushrooms with guacamole, manchego cheese, black beans, poblano chiles, and tomatoes. Entrees are priced from about $18 to $25; lunch prices are a bit less expensive.

Just off the casino floor is the 600-seat **House of Blues**, largest restaurant in the hotel, offering down-home cooking and music. A larger concert hall is nearby. Entry to the restaurant is through a version of a Mississippi backyard with candles hung from low-hanging trees and a constant symphony of crickets. Specialties, priced from about $14 to $20, include slow-cooked baby back ribs, Creole jambalaya, and crawfish and shrimp etoufee. The restaurant offers a gospel brunch on Sunday mornings.

Also in the vicinity is the **Noodle Shop**, offering Chinese and Hong Kong dishes priced from about $8 to $15.

The 504-seat **Bay Side Buffet** includes "action stations" for breakfast, lunch, and dinner. The **Verandah Café** at the Four Seasons offers indoor and outdoor seating for breakfast, lunch, and dinner including Mexican, Californian, Italian, and Oriental food.

Room rates range from about $100 to $299, with specials during slow times of the year and higher prices during holidays and convention periods.

The Four Seasons at Mandalay Bay is a hotel within the hotel, occupying 424 rooms on the thirty-fifth through thirty-ninth floors. The premium hotel, owned by Mandalay Bay but managed by Four Seasons, has its own entrance, check-in, five-star dining, pool and spa, and convention area. Room rates at Four Seasons are among the highest in Las Vegas, averaging a bit under $200 per night.

The Hacienda was imploded, on national television, on New Year's Eve at the end of 1996. When it was built in 1956 near McCarran Airport, the Hacienda was miles away from the rest of the Las Vegas action. The Hacienda was a haven for low rollers. Among its pioneering efforts were some of the first gambling junkets; at one time it maintained its own fleet of thirty airplanes to bring the sheep in to be shorn.

During the years, though, the Strip extended south to encompass the Hacienda and eventually it found itself in the reflected gaudy glow of the Excalibur, Luxor, and the nearby MGM Grand. The Hacienda and some forty-seven surrounding acres were purchased in 1995 by Circus Circus Enterprises; the company also bought seventy-three acres to the south of the Hacienda at Russell Road. In 1999, Circus Circus renamed itself Mandalay Resort Group.

The company expects to eventually cover all key segments of the Las Vegas tourism and gaming markets on its Masterplan Mile, where it will own or control as many as 20,000 rooms within the coming years, including its existing Excalibur and Luxor properties.

By the way, Kipling's poem, *On the Road to Mandalay*, is a wistful remembrance by a soldier of the native girl he left behind in Mandalay in Burma (now Myanmar). "For the wind is in the palm-trees, and the temple bells they say: `Come you back, you British soldier; come you back to Mandalay!'"

Mandalay Bay Resort & Casino. 3950 Las Vegas Boulevard South. 3,700 rooms. (702) 632-7777. www.mandalaybay.com.

MUST-SEE ★★★★ Mirage

Every desert needs a mirage, although few are quite so phantasmagorical.

The Mirage is a sight to behold inside and out, but any description of the hotel has to start with the live volcano out front that spews smoke and fire a hundred feet in the air from an artificial lagoon.

When the hotel first opened in 1989, locals were unsure which was more entertaining: the aerial show from the volcano or the continuous fender benders it caused on the Strip out front.

The Mirage was the first Strip outpost of what became the bizarre and successful empire of Stephen Wynn; that all came to an end in March of 2000 when the Mirage, along with sister resorts Treasure Island and Bellagio, were acquired in a takeover by MGM Grand.

The man-made, computer-controlled fifty-four-foot-tall volcano puts on a three-minute show every fifteen to thirty minutes from dusk to midnight, spitting steam, gas-fed flames, and "lava" created with the aid of a sophisticated lighting scheme. During the show, the pumping system moves 5,000 gallons of water per minute. As part of the construction, a thousand real palm trees were moved to the site; some of the trees nearest the flames, though, are constructed of steel and concrete.

The $630 million, 100-acre site has three thirty-story towers with 3,049 rooms, including one- and two-bedroom suites, eight villa apartments, and six lanai bungalows that have private gardens and pools. The top five floors of each tower are reserved for tower and penthouse suites.

On the Strip in front of the Mirage are huge (ego-sized) busts of Siegfried and Roy and one of their white tigers. Despite the size of the statues, they are not easy to spot from the hotel itself or from a car on the Strip. To pay proper homage, you'll need to walk on the west side of the Strip between Treasure Island and the Mirage.

The driveway delivers visitors to a white porte cochere that has full-length louvered shutters that suggest arrival at a colonial government house. Entering through the main doors, you walk into a ninety-foot-high indoor atrium that has sixty-foot-tall palm trees; a central forest includes tropical orchids and banana trees, an indoor waterfall, and lagoons.

Behind the hotel's registration desk is a huge fifty-three-foot-long, 20,000-gallon coral reef aquarium stocked with sharks, rays, and other sea life from the Caribbean, Hawaiian Islands, Tonga, Fiji, the Marshall Islands, Australia, and the Red Sea. The aquarium really is worth a look, if you can find the check-in area in the complex maze of the casino.

Public areas are decorated in high-tone marble, teak, and rattan. In the atrium, the bent palm trees are necessarily fake, but they are covered in real bark. Almost every other piece of greenery is real.

The tropical theme is carried through in most of the rooms at the Mirage, featuring lush colors, rattan, and cane. The highest of the high rollers can rent one of six lanai bungalows, each with its own private garden and pool.

For non-bungalow-dwellers, the Mirage has a pool—actually a series of wandering, interconnected lagoons linking two palm tree–lined islands—where guests can swim, relax in cabanas, lunch at the Paradise Café, or enjoy drinks at the Dolphin Bar. A full-service spa and salon is also available for guest use.

> **Color scheming.** The original color scheme for the Mirage was almost entirely drawn from a palette of muted earth tones—peach, beige, and green. The increasing influx of high rollers from Asia has brought about some redecoration to reds, blacks, and yellows—colors apparently more pleasing to Asian sensibilities. The registration desk—or the keepers of the comp rooms for the guests of the casino—will color coordinate rooms to appeal to the taste of individual guests.

Basic room rates run from about $79 to $350, with suites starting at $375 and ascending to $950 per night for a two-bedroom penthouse suite. Rates may be lower at slowest winter periods.

The Mirage is one of just a few casinos in Las Vegas with $500 slot machines; there is a small nest of them in an alcove near the **Caribe Café**. The slots have a top payoff of $40,000 for a single coin. By the way, if you sit and play the $500 machines for a while, you'll be offered a free catered meal. Of course, they'll want you to eat it at the machines, feeding those expensive tokens all the while.

Nearby is the **Salon Privé**, a private gambling room for the highest rollers, where tens or even hundreds of thousands of dollars can hang on a single card in blackjack or baccarat, a roll of the dice in craps, or a spin of the roulette wheel. If you want to play, the casino will staff every table in the room in case you change your mind on which game to play.

Speaking of excesses in entertainment, the Mirage is the long-time home of Siegfried and Roy, who put on one of the most spectacular and expensive magic and stage shows anywhere. They appear forty weeks per year—if you are determined to see their show, check with the hotel to avoid dark weeks. They sell out almost every one of their shows twice nightly at 7:30 and 11 P.M. (except

> **Tiger, tiger.** Two or three tigers are usually on display in the habitat at the Mirage at all times, with new groups moved in several times each day.

> **No dolphin served here.** Several bouncing baby calves have been born in the Mirage's dolphin habitat. Each dolphin has its own signature whistle, and it is believed that the mother is able to recognize her own baby by listening for the sound.
>
> By the way, don't feel guilty about ordering a tuna sandwich at the Mirage. The hotel has a "dolphin safe" policy for all of its restaurants. And the hotel also bars the sale of fur in any of its boutiques.

Wednesdays and Thursdays.) Tickets were priced at $89.35 each, including two drinks, in mid-2000.

The production, which premiered in February 1990, is presented in the **Theatre Mirage**, a 1,500-seat theater.

Siegfried and Roy have established their own Royal White Tiger breeding line. Their family has grown to a current total of thirty-three tigers. Not all of them appear in the show, and those that do are regularly given time off for good behavior. Unlike more common tigers that have black and gold markings, the white tiger is white with black stripes, pink paws, and ice blue eyes. And the purest of the species have no stripes at all; there are only a few dozen white tigers in the world, making them among the rarest of species.

You can visit some of these beautiful creatures through the glass wall near the walkway entrance on the south side of the hotel. The re-creation of their native Himalayan world is open to the sky. There is a path that leads up almost to the roof; if you see an especially large pussycat outside your room one morning, don't open the door.

And there is a hallway that runs from the exhibit area to their cages and the showroom, allowing the animals to be walked to work. We'd suggest you avoid opening unmarked doors in the casino. (Just kidding . . . we think.)

Another interesting animal exhibit is the **Dolphin Habitat**, a 1.5 million-gallon tank for bottlenose dolphins located out back and open to the public for a nominal fee. Four connected pools, an artificial coral reef system, and a sandy bottom replicate a natural environment. The facility houses only dolphins that were either born at or relocated from other facilities. According to the Mirage, no animals are taken from the wild for the display.

And then there is the **Secret Garden of Siegfried & Roy**, a habitat for snow white tigers, white lions, snow leopards, an Asian elephant, and other animals that appear—and disappear—with Siegfried and Roy on stage. Admission to both the Dolphin Habitat and the Secret Garden is a bit steep, at $10; on Wednesday when the garden is closed, admission to the dolphins is $5.

Some of the stars of the exhibit include the white lions of Timbavati ("the river that never dries out"); Gildah, one of less than 50,000 Asian elephants left in the world, and offspring of Siegfried & Roy's conservation program, including the first male white lion cubs in the Western Hemisphere.

The Secret Garden is open for viewing weekdays except Wednesday from 11

A.M. to 5:30 P.M., and on weekends and holidays from 10 A.M. to 5:30 P.M. The Dolphin Habitat is open every day on the same schedule.

In 2000, the hotel opened the 1,260-seat **Danny Gans Theatre** to house the Danny Gans show, which stars . . . Danny Gans. The singer and impressionist, a Las Vegas staple at Rio Suites for many years, has signed up for an eight-year run, performing forty-four weeks a year, five nights a week.

The Mirage also features a collection of some of the best and most attractive restaurants in Las Vegas.

The unusual **Samba Grill** is a riot of Brazilian colors, sounds, and food set in a small faux-rainforest just off the casino floor. The highlight here is the All You Can Eat Rodizio Experience, and quite a happening it is: the Brazilian barbecue, priced at about $29 per person, includes sausage, turkey, churrasco beef, and salmon. Items are also available a la carte.

Onda, a classy Mediterranean eatery, offers entrees by chef Todd English priced from about $20 to $35. Specialties include veal scallopine over Parmesan risotto, traditional Italian neighborhood lasagna, and pan-roasted Chilean sea bass over shrimp and Swiss chard.

Also recently added was **Renoir**, one of the fancier and priciest establishments in town; the star chef behind the eatery is Alessandro Stratta. Examples from the menu include roasted squab with foie gras for $35, wild turbot with hearts of palm for $42, and braised veal cheeks with Swiss chard for $30. A tasting menu with samples of many of the dishes goes for $95 plus $55 if you order the suggested wines.

An appetizer portion of Beluga caviar sold for $105 for a an ounce-and-a-half. Oh, and then there were the desserts, priced at $9.50: they included honey-roasted Anjou pear with lemon pound cake and brown butter Armagnac sauce, and a warm chocolate truffle and raspberries in phyllo dough with ice cream. Open Thursday to Tuesday, 6 P.M. to 10:30 P.M.; closed on Wednesday. Reservations are recommended. (702) 791-7223.

Among our favorites is **Moongate**, a gourmet Chinese restaurant that serves spicy Szechwan and subtle Cantonese cuisine in a lovely setting that includes a starfield ceiling, a live cherry tree, and tasteful jade objects and statuary; the hotel reportedly spent $2.5 million on decorations alone. Open for dinner only, from 5:30 to 11 P.M., Moongate offers entrees that range from about $10 to $70. On a recent visit, fancier entrees included braised shark's fin with crabmeat for $47, fresh abalone and sea cucumber with lettuce in clay pot for $68, as well as moo shu pork for $16.50.

Next door, and sharing the starfield ceiling, is **Mikado**, set in a very elegant Japanese garden. Your chef can prepare teppanyaki dishes of chicken, steak, lobster, or vegetables at your table from about $32 to $46. Individual sushi pieces are priced from $4 to $8. Other offerings include a Japanese vegetarian delight for $16, a yakitori combo for $24.50, and chirashi (thinly sliced assorted raw fish and sushi) for $30. The restaurant is open for dinner only, 6 P.M. to 11 P.M.

An informal option is the **Noodle Kitchen**, offering simple Asian dishes that include congees (rice porridge) with toppings including beef, sea bass, abalone, and priced from about $9 to $25. Other entrees include Soya Chicken for $10 and roast duck for $10.

Kokomo's specializes in steaks and seafood in an "outdoor" setting within the atrium's tropical rain forest. Breakfast is served Thursday through Sunday; lunch Monday to Friday, 11 A.M. to 2:30 P.M.; brunch Saturday and Sunday, 8 A.M. to 2:30 P.M., and dinner nightly, 5 P.M. to 10:30 P.M.

An interesting alternative for lunch, or for dinner, is the **California Pizza Kitchen** located near the sports bar. They use wood-fired ovens to create some of the strangest—and tastiest—pizzas in town. Pies go for $10 for individual size; also available are salads and pasta dishes. No reservations are accepted, and lines can build during busy times. Open Sunday to Thursday, 11 A.M. to midnight; Friday and Saturday, 11 A.M. to 2 A.M.

The Mirage's **Buffet** is located in an attractive, bright room just off the casino floor. It is officially described as being set in an English garden at Bermuda, although we didn't quite see the connection. The food is good, but it is obvious that the Mirage feels it does not need the lure of a spectacular buffet to bring in the gambling visitors.

The Mirage. 3400 Las Vegas Boulevard South; 3,049 rooms; (702) 791-7111, (800) 627-6667. www.themirage.com.

MUST-SEE ★★★★ Monte Carlo Resort & Casino

A tip of the hat to one of the classic gambling palaces of Europe—the famed Place du Casino in Monaco—the Monte Carlo Resort & Casino brings fanciful arches, chandeliered domes, marble floors, ornate fountains, and gaslit promenades to the Las Vegas desert.

The thirty-two-floor tower, with 3,002 rooms including 259 suites, is located on the west side of the Strip, between Flamingo Road and Tropicana Avenue, and is a joint project of the Mirage and Gold Strike Resorts, which has since been purchased by Circus Circus Enterprises, now Mandalay Resort Group.

Within the Monte Carlo is an outpost of **Andre's French Restaurant**, a long-time, insiders' favorite in its location near downtown Las Vegas. The two-story hotel restaurant, designed as a Renaissance chateau and outfitted with Versace china and Sambonnet silver, seats fifty-five downstairs and forty-two upstairs in three small dining rooms. Owner Andre Rochat's wine menu offers more than 700 selections. Open daily, 6 P.M. to 11 P.M.

The **Market City Café** offers Italian fare served in whopping portions at moderate prices. A huge antipasto bar features a host of delicacies such as marinated fennel, grilled eggplant, and fresh mussels. The main menu includes pastas, pizzas, and grilled entrees.

Dragon Noodle Company is an Asian-themed restaurant and tea emporium. **Blackstone's Steak House** offers hearty meals.

The **Monte Carlo Pub & Brewery** features half a dozen specialty ales brewed on the premises, to accompany fresh pizzas, sandwiches, and pasta; the setting is an old warehouse atmosphere. There's also a food court with **Nathan's, McDonalds, Sbarro,** and others.

Outside is an exotic pool area with waterfalls, a pool and spa, a wave pool, and the "Easy River" innertube ride. There's also a Surf Pond, with twelve cannons that force strong currents of air into the water, creating surf up to ten feet high.

Magician Lance Burton, a Las Vegas staple, performs twice nightly in the 1,200-seat **Lance Burton Theatre**.

And there is a 90,000-square-foot casino with 2,200 slot machines.

The $344 million resort is a joint venture between Mirage Resorts (now part of MGM Grand) and Circus Circus Enterprises, an unusual merger of high-roller and low-roller management; a similar arrangement took place in Reno between Circus Circus and the Eldorado, resulting in the Silver Legacy.

Monte Carlo Resort & Casino. 3770 Las Vegas Boulevard South; 3,002 rooms; (702) 730-7777, (800) 311-8999. www.monte-carlo.com.

MUST-SEE ★★★★ New York–New York Hotel & Casino

At the northwest corner of Tropicana and the Strip, the Statue of Liberty faces the MGM Lion and holds her lamp against the wretched excesses of the Excalibur castle.

In a town of superlatives, somehow the designers of New York–New York have managed to pull off a relative miracle: this casino and hotel is candy for the eyes and a whole lot of fun both inside and outside. The Strip has been heading in this direction for some time: New York–New York is where Universal Studios meets Las Vegas. I kept looking for King Kong.

The Monte Carlo
Courtesy of Las Vegas News Bureau

This place has added a completely new skyline to the south end of the Strip: a re-creation of Manhattan, complete with a dozen "skyscrapers," including replicas of the Empire State Building, the Chrysler Building, the AT&T Building, the 55 Water Tower, and other landmarks of Manhattan. Out front is a 150-foot-tall replica of the Statue of Liberty and a re-creation of the famed Brooklyn Bridge. The towers, which contain the hotel rooms, are built at about one-third scale with some clever touches that make them seem real. The tallest, of course, is the Empire State Building, which even in its reduced scale stands 529 feet tall.

Inside the eighteen-acre casino area are New York neighborhoods and landmarks including the Ellis Island Immigrant Receiving Station (the registration desk), a (plastic) tree-filled Central Park, Grand Central Station Terminal, and Wall Street. You can stroll the narrow lanes of a romanticized Greenwich Village. There's also the Coney Island Emporium, an amusement area with carnival games, arcade machines, bumper cars, laser tag, and a fiber-optic fireworks show. Nearby is the entrance to the Manhattan Express, a wild roller coaster that twists, loops, and dives around the perimeter and through the center of the hotel like a subway train gone berserk. *For more details, see Chapter 10.*

Restaurants include **Il Fornaio**, where each month a different chef celebrates a particular region of Italy. There's also an Il Fornaio Bakery, offering all manner of biscotti, cornettos, espresso, and cappuccino.

Gallagher's Steakhouse brings a New York beef emporium; outside its doors on the casino floor is a huge freezer with several steers' worth of aging beef. **Chin Chin**, a Los Angeles favorite, offers gourmet Chinese fare prepared in an exhibition kitchen. **America**, a twenty-four-hour restaurant, takes you on a road trip around the country that includes menu items from across the nation. **Gonzalez Y Gonzalez** is a Mexican cafe with outdoor courtyard, complete with lanterns, pinatas and a tequila bar.

The most enticing part of New York–New York is at the back of the casino floor, a high-tone food court with streetscapes of New York City. Steam rises from manhole covers, tables are set on porches of brownstones, and overhead the roller coaster zooms by like a demented A-train. Along the cobblestone streets of Greenwich Village, Little Italy, and the Fulton Fish Market areas, are some pretty appropriate selections such as bagels, pizza, and hotdogs.

Lord of the Dance, a high-energy dance show, owned the resort's 1,000-seat showroom in mid-2000.

Hotel rooms start at $89 midweek and $129 weekends.

The $460 million project began as a joint venture of MGM Grand and Primadonna Resorts, which operated three highly successful casinos and resorts on the Nevada–California state line: Buffalo Bill's Resort & Casino, the Primadonna Resort & Casino, and Whiskey Pete's Hotel & Casino. In 1998, Primadonna was purchased by MGM Grand.

New York–New York Hotel & Casino. 3790 Las Vegas Boulevard South; 2,035 rooms; (702) 740-6969, (800) 693-6763. www.nynyhotelcasino.com.

★★★★★ Paris–Las Vegas Casino Resort
MUST-SEE

Ooh, la la. Paris arrived on the Las Vegas Strip with the opening of the opulent

Paris–Las Vegas Casino Resort, on a plot south of Bally's Casino facing the Bellagio Resort.

Paris is an ambitious but cartoony Disneyland Paris. Some will appreciate the little touches like the cocktail waitresses dressed in French gendarmes caps and little else, and the supports of the Eiffel Tower that poke through the ceiling of the casino. The ironwork in the casino is just for show, though; the real imitation tower stands a bit further west, closer to the Strip.

The $760 million hotel casino was built by Park Place Entertainment, which also owns Bally's, Caesars Palace, and Hilton.

The thirty-three-story resort re-creates Parisian landmarks, including a 540-foot half-scale replica of the Eiffel Tower that has a French restaurant and an observation level. Other recreated sites include the Arc de Triomphe, Champs Elysées, the Paris Opera House, the River Seine, and the Rue de la Paix.

Designers consulted Gustav Eiffel's original 1889 drawings to help them build their replica; unlike the original, this tower's pieces are welded together, although designers added cosmetic rivets everywhere as they appear on the real thing. Three of the recreated Eiffel Tower's legs spring from the resort's casino floor, jutting through the roof of the gaming area. Guests can dine on gourmet French cuisine in the restaurant on the seventeenth level of the tower, or ride an elevator to the observation deck. The main restaurant district lies along the rue de la Paix, under a fake blue sky and movie-set false fronts.

La Rotisserie des Artistes is an unusual two-story dining room that has an open kitchen on the first level. A pair of ornate spiral staircases ascend to the balcony where there are more seats. The wait staff, attired in traditional long white aprons, black vests, white shirts, and bow ties will offer entrees such as Scottish pheasant with tarragon mustard sauce and desserts that include classics such as tart tatin, raspberry clafoutis, and creme brulée.

Trés Jazz is a New World/Caribbean/French bistro in wood, polished aluminum, and leather, with entrees from about $24 to $40, such as filet mignon au poivre, duck à l'orange, mango-glazed lamb shank.

A stylish Parisian-style street café housed within the Louvre facade, **Mon Ami Gabi** offers the only street-level seating on the Las Vegas Strip. The eatery serves breakfast, lunch, and dinner, with fresh-baked breads and pastries, along with specialties such as gratinee of white French onion soup and a variety of quiches. By night, candlelit dinners include traditional cassoulet and shallot steak.

Le Provençal is an informal version of a European village restaurant. Waiters and waitresses serve the French-Italian cuisine native to the Provence region; when the spirit moves, they'll break into song. Guests can also order provincial wines decanted from large barrels located in the dining area, or order from an extensive list of wines that are local to Provence.

La Chine melds French and Chinese fare in a room of dynastic pottery with gold and blue accents. Intriguing entrees, prices from about $15 to $30, include an enoki mushroom sirloin roll.

And then there is **Le Village Buffet**, the latest entrant in the "can you top this?" competition in Las Vegas. The buffet celebrates the five provinces of France with action stations. Chefs prepare meals that include duck braised with Reisling wine from Alsace, rock crab salad from Brittany, sautéed sea bass with artichoke crust from Provence, coq au vin from Burgundy, and fricasee of scallops with roasted forest mushrooms from Normandy. The buffet is set within a village-like setting, with tables in the indoor town square and in a casual dining room by a fireplace. The small room fills quickly; you can make an approximate reservation for a seat as mealtime approaches.

Other casual dining areas include **JJ's Boulangerie**, a French bakery where guests will sit nearby the bakers kneading dough, creating pastries, and removing racks of baguettes from the display oven. The fresh bread is delivered to other restaurants at the resort by bicycle.

Paris–Las Vegas brings 2,916 guest rooms, including 295 suites, a two-acre pool area, an 85,000-square-foot casino, 160,000 square feet of meeting and convention space, six specialty restaurants, and a 1,500-seat showroom.

The x-shaped hotel with four wings and a central core connects to the short monorail line between Bally's and the MGM Grand.

Rooms are priced between $129 and $239.

Paris–Las Vegas. 3045 Las Vegas Boulevard South. (702) 946-7000 or (888) 266-5687. www.paris-lv.com.

MUST-SEE ★★★★★ Rio Suite Hotel & Casino

Hot, hot, hot! This is one fun place, a bit of Rio de Janeiro about a mile west of the Strip. It's a bright and cheery place of flowers, flowered shirts, and the hottest cocktail waitress uniforms in town, more of a swimsuit than an outfit, actually. Dancers in pink thong bikinis and dancers with trained birds parade through the casino from time to time.

And the hotel rooms at the Rio are among the nicest in town, spacious and attractive and offering views of the mountains or the distant Strip.

The Rio is only about a mile from the Strip, although it's not an easy walk because of the highways in the area; you'll need to use a car, cab, or the hotel's shuttle bus to get there.

Even by Las Vegas standards, the Rio story has been a jackpot success. The original building opened in 1990 and was from the start a wild and crazy place; it was almost immediately too small. Construction of a new tower was completed in 1994, and that same year work was begun on a third suite tower and a new parking garage. In 1997, the Rio completed construction of a forty-one-story tower with 1,037 more rooms, bringing the total to 2,563.

In late 1998, the Rio was purchased by Harrah's Entertainment, parent company of the Harrah's casinos and resorts.

Recent additions include a sprawling convention center and a new 1,500-seat showroom. As if all this wasn't enough, there are rumors of a new 3,000-room hotel on forty-three acres northeast of the existing property; the new hotel may have its own, different theme. The first phase of the project includes a new access road to the Las Vegas Strip, an extension of Twain Avenue. Also in the works is a pedestrian walkway on the Flamingo Road overpass.

There were also reports that the Rio was hoping to encourage the reestablishment of Amtrak train service to Los Angeles, and had offered to construct a station on its property along existing railroad tracks.

(And the area around the burgeoning Rio may become a hub of its own; the owners of the Fiesta Casino Hotel have purchased thirty-five acres across Flamingo Road from the Rio and Gold Coast, presumably to develop the land as another resort.) No plans have yet been disclosed.

The Rio also owns the Rio Secco Golf Club in Henderson, featuring a 7,250-yard championship course.

The headline-grabber in the new area is the Masquerade Show in the Sky in the Masquerade Village casino. The show, presented on the hour every other hour from midday until late night, includes a cast of thirty-six dancers, musicians, aerialists, and costumed stiltwalkers. The show is dark Wednesday.

And guests can even purchase tickets to dress in Mardi Gras finery and ride aboard one of the floats; the privilege went for about $15, with tickets for sale at the Play Rio ticket sales counter. Most of the performers pass by above the casino floor on floats that travel a 950-foot track. There are three different parades, each about twelve minutes long, presented on a rotating schedule through the day. Some of the acts include indoor bungee flying and singers within representations of butterflies, crabs, lobsters, and dolphins. The floats include:

- Brazil, adorned with flowers and maracas, with five petals that move up and down to carry six performers and several guests;
- the Venetian Gondola, which allows four performers and several guests to fly above the crowd carried by swans that have telescoping necks and flapping wings; and
- the two-sided Faces of Masquerade, with Giacomo the court jester on one side and Gypsy the fortune teller on the other. A performer hiding within controls movement, sound, and interactive conversations with guests.

There are plenty of good places to view the Masquerade Show, including the center of the upper balcony or on the casino floor in front of the main stage. Be aware, though, that security may shoo away any children who stop on casino level; families are better off on the upper level.

The Rio's signature restaurant is **Napa**, an attractive, airy room with windows looking out on the valley. Offerings include roasted diver daikon with Maine scallops, venison osso buco, and chorizo-crusted turbot. Entrees range in price from about $8 to $26.

Fortune's is a classy Chinese restaurant near Fiore with entrees ranging in price from about $26 to $48. Samples from the menu included steamed chicken with cloud ear fungus, sauteed clams with vermicelli noodles, and steamed minced pork with salty fish. The restaurant is decorated with ancient Chinese artifacts worth more than $100,000, including a mirror that has gilt dragons from the Tang Dynasty (A.D. 618–907) and an eighteenth-century jade bowl carved into the shape of a chrysanthemum and made for the Qing Court. Fortune's is above the Fiore Rottiserie and is open for dinner only from 5 to 11 P.M.

Bamboleo is an attractive Mexican cantina above Masquerade Village. Open from 1 A.M. to 11 P.M.; entrees are in the range of about $10 to $28.

Set amidst a live re-creation of a rain forest, **Mask** specializes in a wide variety of Asian foods from Japanese to Thai, as well as live teppan grill cooking and a full-service sushi bar. The stylish restaurant is open for dinner nightly from 5 to 11 P.M.

And then there is the **Voo Doo Café**, high above Las Vegas on the fiftieth and fifty-first floors, offering a breathtaking view of the skyline of the Strip. Visitors can take the elevator to the terrace just for the view.

The Voo Doo menu features New Orleans and Cajun fare, with entrees priced from about $12 to $48. Specialties include Tuna Napoleon, on garlic mashed potatoes and spinach Rockefeller, and Softshell Crab LaFayette, which is crab stuffed with corn bread dressing.

And the floorshow after 7 P.M. includes the lounge's fire-breathing, bottle-juggling bartenders. Voo Doo is open nightly.

Among specialty drinks is "What the Witch Doctor Ordered," including four rums, peach schnapps, banana liqueur, fruit juices, and dry ice, for two close friends and priced at $21. And there's "Sexual Trance" in a twisted stem glass, mixing Absolut citron, Midori, Chambord, and fruit juices, at a mere $7.

(By the way, there are only some forty-one actual floors in the tower. In keeping with Japanese and American superstitions, the unlucky numbers of four and thirteen are skipped, along with a few others for marketing purposes.)

Antonio's Ristorante serves northern Italian fare, nightly from 5 to 11 P.M.

The two levels of the Masquerade Village include a selection of upscale stores.

The **Wine Cellar Tasting Room and Retail Shoppe** bills itself as the "world's largest and most extensive public collection of fine and rare wines" and features wine appreciation instruction, weekly tasting seminars that include dinner, and a complete line of tasting accessories and gifts. The collection, valued at some $6 million, includes as its centerpiece the Chateau d'Yequem, with bottles from every vintage between 1855 and 1990. The cellars are open daily for tours.

The shops include a large Nicole Miller outlet, Guess Footwear, Speedo Authentic Fitness, and Napa Valley Gourmet. Reel Outfitters is the first Orvis outlet, selling fly-fishing gear, outdoor fashions, luggage, and other items including shotguns . . . in a casino. They also organize and run fishing and hunting tours into Utah.

All rooms at the hotel are considered suites, capacious 600-square-foot rooms. Standard rates start at about $80 on slow weekdays to $340 and more during busy weekends; the oversized rooms include a sofa and dressing area.

And then there are the Rio's smorgasbord offerings. Quite simply, the Rio is home to not just one great buffet, but the two best buffet rooms in town: the **Carnival World Buffet** and the upscale **Village Seafood Buffet**.

The Carnival World Buffet is a pretty, bright room right off the casino floor, offering a whole range of unusual—and unusually good—selections, from cooked-to-order Brazilian stir-fry to sushi to steaks and chops.

Breakfast features made-to-order omelettes, waffles, pancakes, sausage, bacon, fresh salsa, fruit, and a variety of fritters. Just when we were ready to waddle on out, we discovered the dessert section, which is the fulfillment of many a sweet tooth's wildest dream: a bakery where you can sample any food simply by pointing to it.

The expanded buffet added a sushi and teppanyaki bar, a fish and chips station, and a burger and fries joint—all included in the basic price. A "butcher shop" occupies center stage of the buffet; here you can select a steak, chop, or piece of fish for just a few extra dollars and have it grilled to your specifications while you wait.

I especially enjoy the Brazilian stir-fry counter where you get to choose from vegetables including mushrooms, asparagus, onions, broccoli, bean sprouts, carrots, and tomatoes, plus herbs and spices including cilantro, garlic, and ginger; then you choose from pork, lamb, chicken, or beef and watch as a chef cooks it all with a special sauce. Other sections of the buffet include international offerings: American, Mexican, Japanese, Chinese, and Italian. My son, a sushi aficionado, spent his time shuttling back and forth to the Japanese counter.

The Rio's buffet is (rightfully) very popular, and long lines can build; arrive early or late to get in without waiting. On an average day, the buffet serves 7,000 people; the record crowd arrived on a Fourth of July weekend, with 11,000 diners chowing down 7,000 pounds of crab legs and shrimp, 6,000 pounds of meat, 3,000 pounds of pasta, and 8,000 cakes and pastries.

The **Village Seafood Buffet** is, somehow, one step above its cousin at the other end of the casino. Tucked into a room at the end of the Masquerade Village, the buffet includes all-you-can-eat crab legs, shrimp, and other shellfish, as well as a Japanese stir-fry counter where you can add shrimp, fish, mussels, or calamari to vegetables of your choice. And the dessert section includes some of the richest and finest cakes and sweets around.

The Village buffet is the highest-priced casino smorgasbord in town, but still a great deal if you enjoy fresh seafood. Another hot place at the Rio is **Buzios Seafood Restaurant**, an oyster and seafood bar with an open show-kitchen.

The Rio's elegant **Fiore**, near the hotel's Beach Club, is a quiet sanctuary down a glass-walled hallway; you can eat in the lovely dining room or move out onto the open-air porch. Entrees, priced from about $26 to $48, include pasta, veal, chicken, and beef dishes.

Another interesting restaurant is the **All-American Bar & Grille**. Luncheon fare includes burgers for $5 to $7 and salads for $6 to $11. Dinner selections are priced from about $15 to $50. The setting is a small, dark sports bar with pennants on the wall; the walls are open to the casino.

You're really going to like this place. Did I remember to mention the buffet and the cocktail waitress outfits?

Rio Suite Hotel & Casino. 3700 West Flamingo Road; 2,563 rooms; (702) 252-7777, (800) 888-1808. www.playrio.com.

MUST-SEE ★★★ Stratosphere Tower

In modern-day Las Vegas, every hotel and casino needs a "hook" to draw the crowds. The **Stratosphere Tower**, which opened in the spring of 1996, offers the highest hook of them all: the nation's tallest free-standing observation tower at 1,149 feet. Just to make things even more wild, there are two thrill rides bolted to the tower (we trust) more than a hundred stories in the air: the **Big Shot** zero gravity simulator, and the **Let It Ride High Roller**, the world's highest roller coaster, starting at 909 feet above ground and zooming around the Tower's pod. *For details on the Stratosphere Tower's thrill rides, see Chapter 10.*

In Las Vegas, where so much is simulated and re-created, the Stratosphere Tower is the real thing. Four high-speed, double-deck elevators travel at 1,400 feet per minute, zooming visitors to the top of the tower—three times taller than any other building in Las Vegas—in forty seconds.

The tower is equipped with a special lighting system that provides a nightly light show, visible throughout the Las Vegas Valley.

There is a rotating restaurant at the 832-foot level, the "Top of the World" with a spectacular view of the Strip and the Las Vegas Valley, an outdoor and a glassed-in observation platform, and three wedding chapels more than 700 feet in the air.

Oh, and there is a sprawling, colorful casino with a World's Fair theme at the base of the tower . . . and 1,500 suites and guest rooms.

Inside is Las Vegas' first Eiffel Tower, or at least a plywood cutout version of the lower legs. (The second set of legs is within the Paris–Las Vegas casino, and the third, a scale replica of the whole thing, stands outside Paris on the Strip.)

The place is huge, stratospheric you might say; at times it seems completely hollow inside. Many of the rooms are booked to package tours or conventioneers.

The tower began life as the creation of the wild and woolly Bob Stupak, the creator of the Vegas World Casino that previously stood on the site.

Groundbreaking took place in 1991, with completion in April of 1996—an unusually long time in speedy Las Vegas. The delays were caused by the escalating financial and operational problems faced by the freewheeling Stupak.

The legacy of Stupak, and the casino's location in a spot midway between the Strip and downtown Las Vegas, contributed to financial difficulties for the Stratosphere, and the place entered into bankruptcy proceedings in late 1997.

The new owner is famed corporate raider Carl Icahn, who has recently moved into casinos and travel. Icahn plans to expand the resort, beginning with a 1,002-room tower due to open in August of 2001.

(Icahn also owns the downscale Arizona Charlie's in Las Vegas, and in Atlantic City the Sands Hotel & Casino and the Claridge Casino Hotel as well as a travel website, Lowestfares.com. As part of his departure package from TWA in 1993, Icahn owns the right to buy $600 million worth of deeply discounted airline tickets from the carrier. Put it all together, and it sounds as if Icahn is positioned to set up a low-price casino travel package empire.)

The 97,000-square-foot casino sports about 2,400 slot machines and sixty gaming tables.

Top of the World. You'll come for the view, at 833 feet in the air, but stay to enjoy the meal. The revolving restaurant—one complete circuit per hour—features steaks and seafood. Open for dinner from 5 to 11 P.M. nightly; until midnight on Friday and Saturday. Reservations: (702) 380-7711.

Montana's Steakhouse. International cuisine, plus prime rib and steak, just off the casino floor. Open daily, 5 p.m. to 11 p.m., and Friday and Saturday from 5 p.m. to midnight.

Fellini's Tower of Pasta. Italian food at moderate prices. Open for dinner nightly from 5 p.m. to midnight. Reservations: (702) 380-7711.

For a good old American pie, sandwich, milkshake, and the like, you can visit **Roxy's Diner**, frozen in the jumping '50s and open twenty-four hours a day.

The 1,325 rooms in the World Tower rent for about $79 to $99; the 119 rooms in the renovated Regency Tower start at about $69. Suites range from $109 to $750.

By the way, Las Vegas is subject to earthquakes, harsh desert winds, and the occasional underground nuclear test in the neighborhood. The designers assure us this has all been taken into account, including computer simulations and wind tunnel testing.

The observation deck is open from 9 a.m. to 1 a.m. Sunday through Thursday, and until 2 a.m. on Friday, Saturday, and holidays. Admission is $6 for adults, $3 for children ages 4–12 and seniors ages 55 and older. Combination tickets with the thrill rides are also available, and described in Chapter 10. For information on the rides, call (702) 380-7777.

Stratosphere Tower. 2000 Las Vegas Boulevard South. (702) 380-7777, (800) 998-6937.

MUST-SEE ★★★ Treasure Island

Let's give credit where credit is due: extravagant casino developer Steve Wynn, already responsible for installing the town's only active volcano in front of his Mirage resort, was also the first person to realize that what Las Vegas was missing was its own pirate warship.

Treasure Island opened with a bang at the end of 1993, just north of its corporate cousin the Mirage; the two hotels are connected by an automated tram. Both Treasure Island and the Mirage, along with Bellagio, were taken over by MGM Grand, Inc. in early 2000.

The adventure begins with a boardwalk along the Strip and across a lagoon to the front entrance. The front of the resort has been designed as an outdoor theater modeled after Buccaneer Bay, the village in Robert Louis Stevenson's *Treasure Island* classic.

Several times each afternoon and evening, depending on the season and weather conditions, the British frigate HMS *Sir Francis Drake* sails around Skull Point to confront an eighty-foot-long replica of the pirate ship *Hispaniola*. "In the name of His Royal Britannic Majesty, King of England and all that he surveys, I order you brigands to lay down your arms and receive a Marine boarding party," the British captain warns. "The only thing we'll receive from you is your stores, valuables, and whatever rum ye might have onboard, you son of a footman's goat," is the pirate's response.

I'm not exactly sure what that means, but those are, of course, fighting words. The two ships engage in a cannon battle across the lagoon, complete with explosions, fire, and a spectacular sinking ship. Many of the thirty stunt players jump or fall from the rigging into the water below.

This is Las Vegas, after all: the pirates win. (The British captain goes down with his ship—or does he?) The schedule for the show is posted near the entrance to the casino.

The $430 million Treasure Island resort includes 2,900 guest rooms with 212 suites in three thirty-six-floor towers. All rooms and suites have floor-to-ceiling windows. Standard room rates range from about $45 to $99 and suites are from about $150 to $300.

Other facilities include **Pirates Walk**, a glittering main street village lined with retail shops, two wedding chapels, and a lavish tropical pool with slide, two cocktail bars, and a snack bar. The shopping area includes our nominee for the worst pun in Las Vegas, a clothing store called "Damsels in Dis' Dress."

The hotel also has its own slightly more imaginative version of the photographic fantasy booth that is very common in Las Vegas. You can be pictured with Siegfried and Roy and some of the tiger cubs, in the middle of the set of Cirque du Soleil, collecting gold coins coming out in a waterfall from a slot machine, or pulling up in front of the Treasure Island in a stretch limousine.

The **Buccaneer Bay Club** is a quiet, private room on the second floor off the casino that has a view of the pirate battle out front. Offerings, priced from about $25 to $40, on a recent visit included Seared Ahi tuna au poivre, horseradish crusted salmon, and mesquite grilled filet mignon. Open daily, 5 P.M. to 10:30 P.M. Children younger than 5 years old are not allowed.

The Plank is a very elegant and quiet hideaway, with a setting of an educated pirate's booty-filled library. Entrees range from about $14 to $40, including cioppino, mesquite-grilled salmon, and steak with crabmeat and béarnaise sauce. Open daily, 5:30 P.M. to 11 P.M.

Madame Ching's. Classic Szechwan and Cantonese cuisines in an elegant and refined setting. On a recent visit, specialties included walnut shrimp for $19, black mushrooms with sea cucumber for $21.50, and macadamia beef for $15. Open for dinner Wednesday through Sunday, 5 P.M. to 11 P.M. Children younger than 5 are not allowed.

Francesco's Cucina Italiana. Fine cooking like your momma probably never made, with entrees priced from about $18 to $30. Samples from the menu include fusili pasta with duck prosciutto, tagliolini pasta with porcino mushrooms and black truffles, and beef tenderloin with scamorza cheese. Open daily, 5:30 P.M. to 11 P.M. Children younger than 5 are not allowed.

Black Spot Grille. A bit away from the casino, it offers pasta, calzone, burgers, and other such fare, with prices from about $6 to $10. Open Sunday to Thursday, 11 A.M. to 11 P.M. and Friday and Saturday, 11 A.M. to 12:30 A.M.

The **Lookout Cafe** is a high-toned 24-hour coffee shop that offers dishes such as salmon, halibut, pot pie, and burgers. Prices range from about $5 to $13.

There are three themed buffets, in Italian, American, and Chinese flavors, presented in adjoining, attractive rooms. The food is a bit ordinary, though.

For the non-gamblers, there is **Mutiny Bay**, a 15,000-square-foot arcade entertainment center set in an ancient Moorish castle. It includes Disney-like animated robots, including propositioning pirates, wisecracking wenches, and various automated animals. In addition to a state-of-the-art collection of video arcade machines (including the most unusual, Ridge Racer, a racing simulator that puts the controls within a *real* red sports car), there is a collection of carnival games, complete with barkers. One favorite entertainment is Castle Climb, which pits three participants in a race to scurry up one of three twisting rope ladders.

There is, of course, a casino: a sprawling 90,000-square-foot affair.

Entertainment at Treasure Island is built around a permanent 1,500-seat home for the **Cirque du Soleil**, the decidedly strange French-Canadian circus troupe. Cirque du Soleil (French for "circus of the sun") is one of the youngest of the great circuses of the world, begun in 1984 in Montreal, Quebec. Its genesis stemmed from a group of street performers gathered by Guy Laliberte.

What we've got here is a one-ring human circus, without animals, air cannons, motorcycles, or the other high-tech trappings of other shows. The emphasis is on strange and wonderful human performances. Mystère is the current production. In mid-2000, tickets were priced at $75 for adults. Shows were presented nightly except Monday and Tuesday, at 7:30 and 10:30 P.M.

Treasure Island. 3300 Las Vegas Boulevard South; 2,900 rooms; (702) 894-7111, (800) 944-7444. www.treasureisland.com.

MUST-SEE ★★★★★ Venetian

The canals of Venice, complete with gondolas and gondoliers, on a spit of sand in the Las Vegas desert. Seems logical to me.

Venetian Casino Resort opened in the spring of 1999 on the former site of the Sands opposite the Mirage, with replicas of some of Venice's best-loved landmarks, including the Bridge of Sighs, the Doge's Palace, the Rialto Bridge, and the Campanile Tower. Oh, yes: there's also a canal running along the Strip and the shopping district within, with singing gondoliers plying their trade for visitors.

And to give you a sense of the size of this place: most of the buildings were recreated more or less in their actual size. This is no half-scale model.

The first phase of the $2 billion project delivered 3,306 suites; another 3,000 or so suites are due in the **Lido Resort**, the second phase already underway. Standard rooms are an expansive 700 square feet with private bedrooms, sunken living rooms, and over-sized bathrooms constructed of Italian marble. Each includes a private fax machine with a personal number; the machine also doubles as a computer printer and copier.

The resort includes the **Grand Canal Shoppes** with 140 retail shops, about twice the size of the huge Forum Shops at Caesars Palace (although Forum Shops plans its own expansion in 2000).

The mall area features a quarter-mile Venetian streetscape with intimate "piazza"-style settings and a 630-foot "grand canal." Running its length will be a fleet of functional gondolas, singing gondoliers, and waterside cafes crossed by Venetian bridges. They even release doves into the perpetual painted blue skies overhead.

The attention to detail in the construction of this resort is amazing. Stones have been hand-weathered to make them look old. Stop to spend the time to

The Venetian's front plaza; Treasure Island lies across the Strip

Photo by Corey Sandler

gawk at the amazing sixty-five-foot-high dome at the entrance to the casino; the trompe l'oeil art on the dome is worthy of a real palace. The walls and alcoves of the hotel are filled with hand-painted frescoes and pieces of art. The Campanile includes a working set of bells; the Archangel Gabriel at its top is eleven feet tall and six feet wide.

The indoor gondolas are beautiful replicas of antique boats from Venice, with one minor improvement: they include a tiny electric motor and propellor, controlled by a foot pedal.

In this town of superlatives, the spectacular Grand Canal Shoppes is among the most amazing shopping districts you will find, a more modern version of The Forum Shops at Caesars Palace. *For a listing of the stores along the canal, see Chapter 11.*

The Great Hall is a wonder of spectacular ceiling paintings, wall frescoes, ironwork, a fabulous stone floor . . . plus a Brookstone store and a Warner Bros. Restaurant. They almost fit in.

And the Venetian includes more than a million square feet of meeting space that will be used to book conventions and meetings that should keep the massive complex busy every day.

The Best of the Strip 77

The resort includes an outpost of the famed Canyon Ranch Spa Club of California. Adjoining a five-acre pool deck modeled after a Venetian-style garden, the spa includes massage, skin care, and body treatment rooms, a forty-foot rock climbing wall, a movement therapy and Pilates studio, a spinning gym, therapeutic Watsu pools, and a medical center.

Out front on the second and third floors of the St. Mark's Library building, for reasons that make sense only in Las Vegas, is a branch of the Madame Tussaud's wax museum, a British company by way of Paris. Madame Tussaud's Celebrity Encounter is unusual in that it encourages visitors to touch and pose with its lifelike statues. More than a hundred celebrities are in the decidedly eclectic collection. A few random selections: Muhammad Ali, Jodie Foster, Madonna, and Ivanna Trump.

> **Some are more equal than others.** Pay attention to the payoff rates promised on slots and video poker machines. Some machines in the same casino will have different payouts. One way to check this is to look at the payout for a full house in poker; one bank of machines offered a standard 40:1, while another set of machines promised 50:1.

Tickets for the museum are about $12.50 for adults, and $10 for children ages 4–12. A discounted family pass for two adults and two children is also available.

A free entertainment, the Birds of Venice, features a flock of trained white doves released several times each afternoon for a circle around the front of the hotel.

There is, of course, a huge casino at the Venetian, within the Doges Palace.

There are more than 3,000 restaurant seats at The Venetian. Within the recreated Ca'D'Oro Palace is a version of Manhattan's famed **Lutéce**, behind a very subtly marked doorway off the casino floor near the race and sports book. The menu and prices are not posted out front, either; if you've got to ask, you may not want to know.

But since you asked me, you'll find lobster, steak, and salmon dishes priced from about $30 to $60.

Lutéce draws its name from the ancient Celtic name for Paris, the birthplace of French gastronomy. The restaurant at the Venetian is an outpost of the famed haute cuisine eatery in New York. The menu includes modern French delicacies and classic influences. Among the highlights is a nightly prix fixe menu degustation.

Examples from the menu include a salad of tender lobster and mango and uncooked slices of Atlantic salmon with a tomato-coriander coulis. Entrees include beef short ribs slow-braised in dark beer, Maine sea scallops in a warm black-truffle vinaigrette, and roasted lobster bathed in cognac butter.

Lutéce, located on the Casino level, has ninety-five inside seats and sixty-five out on the terrace and is open for lunch and dinner.

Most of the other eateries are located on Restaurant Row off the casino floor.

Piero Selvaggio, who also owns and operates L.A.'s Primi and Posto, brings a version of his **Valentino's Italian Grill** to the Venetian. The cuisine is contemporary and traditional Italian, with entrees produced from about $15 to $30. Many of the ingredients in the kitchen are imports from Italy, including white truffles, fresh porcino mushrooms, burrata cheese from Puglia, and Mediterranean and Adriatic Sea fish. On a recent visit, the menu included spicy chicken Paillard and a New York steak with Tuscan barbecue sauce.

Chef and owner Stephan Pyles, a renowned Texan chef and host of a PBS cooking series, operates **Star Canyon**. The cuisine comes in highly seasoned ranch house portions based on multicultural history of the Lone Star State, executed with classic French culinary techniques. The kitchen features a wood-burning oven and large rotisserie and grill.

No real cowboy ever dined at a fancy chuckwagon like Star Canyon, but urban types can pretend and eat well on hearty fare, such as a bone-in Cowboy Ribeye or grilled lamb chops; entrees range from about $20 to $35. Some of the more interesting fare is on the appetizer menu, with offerings that include a tamale tart, chilled shrimp and jicama soup, and molasses grilled quail.

Signature recipes include bone-in ribeye with pinto bean-wild mushroom ragout and red chile onion rings. Side dishes include grilled sirloin-sweet potato enchiladas with queso freco and black bean relish, and chile relleno with smoked chicken and wild mushroom enchiladas.

Star Canyon's 300-seat dining room can be best described as "high concept cowboy," mixing contemporary and historical elements of the West.

Los Angeles celebrity chef and author Joachim Splichal's **Pinot** offers steak, poultry, pastas, seafood, and wild game, complete with a large rotisserie and an oyster bar that sports waiters in rubber boots. Entrees (priced from about $20 to $30) include butternut squash gnocchi and pan-seared venison loin.

Most of the decor was imported from France, including the wooden French door facade from a hotel in Lyon, the copper pots, kitchen utensils, as well as the Coq d'Or, the large weathered cast-iron rooster that stands guard at the entry.

Restaurateur Kevin Wu and master Hong Kong chefs Lai Lam and Chiu Kee Yung established the highly regarded Royal Star Seafood Restaurant in California. In combination with Chinese cuisine expert, Theresa Lin, they created the **Royal Star** at The Venetian.

Appetizers include a variety of specialties that have their origins in various regions of China, ranging from the familiar (lettuce cups) to the exotic (giant scallops). Seafood entrees include crab, lobster, fish, prawns, shrimp, and geoduck, all taken from a live tank. There is also a large offering of classic and creative meat, poultry, and vegetarian dishes. There's also a separate dim sum kitchen, served tableside in traditional carts. The 200-seat restaurant is on Restaurant Row; meals are served from 9 A.M. to midnight.

The décor blends shimmering slate floors and wood accents, within cool celadon walls. A silver-leafed ceiling and elegant chenille upholstery surround authentic Chinese artifacts that complete the fusion of contemporary design with traditional Chinese art.

The ultra-high end Asian eatery is almost hermetically sealed off from the casino floor and passers-by. I watched as a Chinese family watched a pair of waiters artfully carving a huge Royal Peking Duck at tableside. Entrees range from about $18 to $60.

The **Delmonico Steakhouse** is a combination of a venerable New Orleans steakhouse with one of today's best-known and flashiest chefs, Emeril Lagasse. The 320-seat restaurant, open for lunch and dinner, has an earthy but modern Tuscan look. Dishes include traditional steak, seafood, and poultry dishes, as well as Lagasse's Creole specialties.

Gian Paulo "Zeffirino" Belloni, a fourth-generation chef in his family, brings authentic Italian technique to **Zeffirino** at The Venetian, located canalside at The Grand Canal Shoppes.

The 450-seat restaurant, open for lunch and dinner, focuses on seafood; specialties include filet of sole piccola, lobster tail, fresh fish, grilled fish, zuppa, and pizzarettes and pastas. Specialty oils, pastas, spices, tomatoes and other ingredients are imported from Italy; breads and pastas are baked on the premises.

According to insiders, Pope John Paul II has a secret passion for the Zeffirino family's pesto, and receives an annual parcel of pesto and sausages.

Within the Grand Canal Shoppes overlooking the canal, chef Wolfgang Puck and his designer wife Barbara Lazaroff have created **Postrio**, an informal bistro café on the Piazza San Marco and an elegant San Franciscan–European formal dining room, serving American cuisine with Asian and Mediterranean influences. Offerings range from gourmet pizzas to a four-course experience, complete with fine wine.

The menu includes grilled quail with spinach and soft egg ravioli; foie gras terrine with fennel, haricot verts and walnut toast; grilled lamb chops with tamarind glaze, shoestring potatoes and peanut sauce; Chinese-style duck with mango sauce and crispy fried scallions; along with fresh-daily baked breads, pastries, and pastas.

Created by the founders of Il Fornaio, **Canaletto** features the food and wine of the Veneto region of Northern Italy. Chef Maurizio Mazzon, a native of Venice, offers fresh seafood, beef, game and poultry cooked in wood-fired rotisseries and grills, as well as northern Italian staples such as risotto, gnocchi, and polenta. The restaurant's unusual wine list spotlights the lesser-known wines of northeast Italy.

Canaletto's two-story architecture incorporates many facets of Venetian-inspired design. "Outside" tables surrounding a forty-foot-tall statue sit in the heart of St. Mark's square, much like the cafes lining the original Piazza San Marco. Past Canaletto's elegant double-arched bar, luxurious navy blue-striped booths under sixteen-foot-tall ceilings offer a more refined dining experience. Polished hardwood floors blend into terrazzo tile leading to the exhibition kitchen. Spectacular Venetian lights and chandeliers crafted by the artisans of Murano cast a flattering glow.

Casual diners can head for the **Grand Lux Café**, from the creators of The Cheesecake Factory. Or, they can sample a marketplace menu of authentic Mexican dishes with an American ambiance from the father of southwestern cuisine at **Taqueria Canonita**.

The Taqueria's menu includes authentic Mexican dishes such as tacos, tamales, tostados, gorditas, and rellenos made with grilled and roasted meats, vegetable, and seafood. Tacos al carbon features beef, chicken and pork varieties served on fresh, hand-made corn tortillas, accompanied by spicy, creamy slaw. Other entrees include quesidillas with shrimp and mango and carbrito barbacoa with black beans, featuring spit-roasted barbecued young goat with clay pot black beans.

The décor features a high-ceiling and central exhibition kitchen. It is located canalside at The Grand Canal Shoppes.

At the **WB Stage 16**, guests dine on the "set" of four of Hollywood's memorable Warner Brothers productions: Gold Diggers, Casablanca, Ocean's Eleven, and Batman. The menu offers a blend of international cuisine.

There is also a 500,000-square-foot meeting center that complements the existing Sands Expo Center's 1.6 million square feet of convention space. The combination of the hotel, meeting center, and Sands Expo Center makes The Venetian the world's largest hotel and convention complex under one roof.

The Venetian Resort Hotel Casino. 3355 Las Vegas Boulevard South. (702) 414-1000, (800) 494-3556. www.venetian.com.

Chapter 7
The Rest of the Strip

Econoguide 2001 Casinos-Hotels in Las Vegas

★★★	**Alexis Park**. *Mama don't allow no gambling round here.*
★★	**Bally's**. *Bally-who? Attractive but generic.*
★	**Barbary Coast**. *Shaky old San Francisco.*
★★	**Desert Inn**. *The Rat Pack wouldn't know the place today.*
★★	**Flamingo Hilton**. *Bugsy sleeps with the fishes; the casino's tired, too.*
★	**New Frontier**. *Survived a near-death experience; waiting for a rebirth.*
★	**Gold Coast**. *Coasting along.*
★★	**Harrah's Las Vegas**. *Old school, with some modern flash.*
★	**Imperial Palace**. *The parking garage is its best feature.*
★	**Maxim's**. *Minimal.*
★★	**Orleans**. *High-end for the low-rollers.*
★	**Palace Station**. *Lively.*
★	**Riviera**. *Old money.*
★★★	**Sahara**. *A casbah with a coaster.*
★★	**San Rémo**. *Off the frenzied Strip.*
★	**Stardust**. *Past its prime.*
★★	**Tropicana**. *Squeezed out.*
	Algiers. *Its future lies in the distant past.*
	Holiday Inn/Boardwalk. *Ferris Wheel for dummies.*
	O'Shea's. *Low-roller mecca on the Strip.*
★	**Sam's Town**. *Boomtown.*

★★★ Alexis Park

This is one of the favorite hotels for visitors to Las Vegas who either don't want to visit the casinos, or who want to be able to find a better-than-decent hotel room without having to navigate through a quarter-mile of flashing neon and jangling slot machines. The Alexis Park is half a mile east of the Strip, and any time you need to visit an Egyptian pyramid, a pirate galleon, or an Arthurian castle you can get there from here.

The hotel includes 500 better-than-average rooms, including many multi-room suites. Several small, pricey restaurants offer gourmet fare. Guests can use a fully equipped health spa. Because the hotel does not have the casino to bring in profits, room rates are a bit on the high side for Las Vegas, ranging from about $125 to $1,000 per night.

Alexis Park Resort. 375 East Harmon Avenue; 500 rooms; (702) 796-3300, (800) 582-2228.

★★ Bally's

A quality joint, well kept up but without much of an identity, Bally's includes a large convention facility often used for overflow exhibits from some of the larger trade conferences, so the place really jumps when a big show is in town.

Attractive but generic, it now stands as a suburb of Paris, to which it is connected. The walk from Bally's to Paris is worth the effort just to see the spectacular stained glass cupola at the place where the two hotels come together.

Some of the function rooms and decorations still bear reminders of the former incarnation as the original MGM Grand, with names such as the Garland and Gable ballrooms. The original 2,100-room hotel opened in 1973 with all the hoopla of a Hollywood premiere; Cary Grant was master of ceremonies for the event, and the ribbon was cut by Fred MacMurray and Raquel Welch. An additional 732-room tower was added in 1981.

A few years back, the hotel underwent another major transformation with the construction of a $14 million dramatic moving walkway structure from the Strip to its front door and the installation of a mirrored-glass facade to the main building. Dramatically illuminated arches in changing colors beckon passersby into the hotel; of course, there aren't that many pedestrians on this part of the Strip, but it's the principle of the thing, we guess.

There is definitely an attempt to go upscale a bit; Bally's will almost certainly benefit from the presence next door of its sister resort, Paris–Las Vegas.

A monorail links Bally's to the MGM Grand at the top of the Strip.

The nearly 3,000 rooms at the hotel range from standard kings and doubles to Hollywood Suites and the extravagant Royal Penthouse Suites, which rent for about $2,500 per night.

The **Big Kitchen Buffet** is one of Las Vegas's more attractive buffet rooms. Well isolated from the casino, the only reminder of where you are lies in the keno boards and runners. If one of your measures of class is whether the shrimp in the shrimp cocktail is peeled or not and whether the orange juice served at breakfast is fresh or not, Bally's Big Kitchen passes on both counts. By no means as impressive or large as the Rio, it is nevertheless one of the better buffets in town.

Bally's Steakhouse is a simple, elegant, large room, originally called Barrymore's, decorated in blacks and whites. Entrees range in price from about $25 to $50. Specialties include herb-marinated chicken breast, plus steaks and filet mignon. A special **Sterling Brunch Sunday** is served in Bally's Steakhouse.

Chang's is an Asian eatery featuring Hong Kong dishes with Taiwanese and Mandarin influences. They serve dim sum from 11:30 A.M. to 2:30 P.M. and dinner from 6 to 11 P.M. The phone number is (702) 739-3388.

The **al Dente** restaurant offers light Italian specialties. Pizzas and pastas range from $11 to $14. We also saw grilled chicken with garlic, mushroom, sausage, potatoes, and lemon for $17, and *pescespada salmorrigglio*, fresh swordfish lightly grilled with garlic, lemon, olive, and Italian parsley for $22.50.

Open Saturday to Monday, 6 P.M. to 11 P.M.; Tuesday and Wednesday, 5:30 P.M. to 10:30 P.M.; closed Thursday and Friday.

A particularly interesting restaurant at Bally's is **Seasons**, with a wide range of American offerings. The menu on one visit included offerings from about $30 to $50 such as ballotine of rabbit in roasted pine nuts and sage, Pacific mahimahi in lobster sauce, roast rack of lamb in rosemary and garlic, or a grilled veal chop in chantarelle sauce. The phone number is (702) 739-4651.

The **Sidewalk Café** is open twenty-four hours and includes a wide range of sandwiches, appetizers, and finger foods. Offerings, priced from about $5 to $15, include chicken wings, Cobb salad, veal cutlet Parmesan, and the self-declared Bally's Famous Reuben.

Jubilee! at the **Jubilee Theater**, one of the most expensive and elaborate stage shows ever produced, has been running for sixteen years. You'll see such events as the sinking of the *Titanic* and the destruction of the temple by Samson. The 190-foot-wide stage is fifteen stories high from the bottom of the pit to the roof; it includes five separate areas to accommodate the massive set pieces. There are three main elevators and eight smaller ones to move scenery. Special effects include dry ice fog, real flames, and a tank that drops 5,000 gallons of water for the last moments of the *Titanic*.

> **Smoky memory.** Most of the guests at the huge high-tone Bally's Las Vegas have forgotten the images that filled network news shows on November 21, 1980, when the main wing of what was then called the MGM Grand burned for several awful hours, killing eighty-four guests and employees and injuring hundreds of others.
>
> After renovations—including extensive fire detection and fireproofing efforts—the hotel was sold to the Bally Corporation in 1985. Today, Bally's may well be one of the safer hotels in Las Vegas with fire detection, control systems, and alarm systems at every turn. There's even a safety lecture broadcast on the in-house video system.

Bally's Las Vegas. 3645 Las Vegas Boulevard South; 2,814 rooms; (702) 739-4111, (800) 634-3434. www.ballyslv.com.

★ Barbary Coast

A small place, almost possible to overlook in the glare of its neighbors, but actually worth a look-see. The Barbary Coast is decorated in a turn-of-the-century San Francisco motif with lots of wood, stained glass, and chandeliers. Dealers wear garters on their arms; cocktail waitresses wear the adornments where they were meant to reside, for all the world to admire.

Except for the McDonald's in the basement, you could almost believe you had been transported back in time. Actually, even the McDonald's sign is constructed from stained glass.

The few rooms at the Barbary Coast are elegantly appointed; they are mostly kept for regular clientele. There is no pool, no showroom, and few other amenities except a pleasant ambiance—which is not a bad thing for a hotel/casino.

Drai's Supper Club is a Hollywood and Beverly Hills favorite, served by its own elevator off the casino floor. On a recent visit, entrees priced from about $25 to $30, included crispy duck confit, braised osso bucco, pepper steak filet mignon, and blackened ahi tuna.

The menu at **Michael's** highlights Continental cooking and fine wines, and the **Victorian Room** offers round-the-clock dining and a wide variety of low-cost offerings, including Chinese food.

Barbary Coast. 3595 Las Vegas Boulevard South; 400 rooms; (702) 737-7111, (800) 634-6755. www.coastcasinos.com/barbary/.

★★ Desert Inn

Named after the considerably greener and officially gambling-free hotel in Palm Springs, California, the Desert Inn debuted in 1950. In typical Las Vegas fashion, the grand opening was a blast: ceremonies were made to coincide with the test of an atomic bomb outside of town. Today, it is a relatively small upscale enclave in the heart of things on the Strip.

Its most famous owner was the reclusive Howard Hughes, who moved into a penthouse suite on Nov. 23, 1966; when he was asked to leave six months later to make room for casino high rollers, he bought the place instead. Its various owners after that have included Kirk Kerkorian, ITT Sheraton, Caesars World, and Starwood. In early 2000, Las Vegas legend Stephen Wynn purchased the Desert Inn after he was squeezed out of Mirage Resorts when that mega-group was purchased by MGM Grand. Wynn said he planned to start all over, with the Desert Inn as his point of re-entry on the Las Vegas Strip.

In recent years the Desert Inn completed a $200 million expansion and renovation . . . and reduction. The hotel capacity was brought down to 715 upgraded rooms. The main casino is dark and elegant with a high ceiling and chandeliers; a small balcony overlooks the pit. Rooms are nicely appointed; some near the pool have cabana entrances to the water.

The Desert Inn Golf Club, a 7,193-yard, par-72 course, is among the top rated courses in the country and the home of many championship events. The par-3 seventh hole, which includes a long carry over water to a heavily bunkered green, is considered one of the most difficult on the PGA Tour.

The nice variety of restaurants includes **Ho Wan**, a Szechwan eatery that offers prix-fixe meals at about $26 per person for appetizer, pot stickers, sweet and sour soup, and *kung pao*. Dishes ordered from the menu range from $16 to $65. On a recent visit, unusual specialties included abalone with vegetables for $65, pan-fried salty squids with pepper, and baked salt spare ribs. Shark's fin soup is offered for about $22.

The Chairman's first office. Frank Sinatra made his Las Vegas debut in 1951 at the Desert Inn; it was the Sands, though, that served as his performing home for many years.

The two finest restaurants at the Desert Inn are **Portofino** and **Monte Carlo**, sharing the same grand glass elevator and marble foyer at the back of the hotel.

Portofino is an elegant Italian restaurant, with entrees from about $16 to $45. An example: *paglia e fieno* (green and white pasta with pancetta, peas, and mushrooms in a rosa cream sauce).

Monte Carlo offers French cooking in a very elegant peaches and cream setting. Entrees range in price from about $25 to $42, and include *le Vieux favori* (steak Diane flamed in wine sauce with fresh mushrooms) for about $26.

Terrace Pointe, the resort's twenty-four-hour restaurant creates the illusion of dining al fresco as guests overlook swaying palms and a tropical lagoon.

Desert Inn Hotel & Country Club. 3145 Las Vegas Boulevard South; 715 rooms; (702) 733-4444, (800) 634-6906. www.thedesertinn.com.

★★ Flamingo Hilton

Las Vegas is one of the only places in the world where present owners proudly promote the gangster roots of the founder of the enterprise.

Today the Flamingo Hilton has just come out from under a massive transformation that includes a sixth new tower, a new entrance, and a water playground out back.

The original Flamingo was the invention in 1946 of Benjamin "Bugsy" Siegel, among the first of many underworld figures to recognize they could make money from legal gambling at least as easily as they could from illegal activities.

Siegel built his 100-room pleasure palace in a spot that was at the time in the middle of nowhere, six miles south into the desert. He spent an astronomical $6 million and in the process began the world of Las Vegas glitz, a style that has not yet stopped escalating.

Less well known, though, is the fact that Bugsy's Flamingo had a very short life: it closed in January 1947 after just fourteen days in business. Bugsy may have been a terrific gangster and certainly was possessed of a showman's vision, but he apparently was not the best businessman.

The hotel reopened later that year under new management, including front man for a different leading light of the underworld, Meyer Lansky. Lansky held onto a hidden interest in the hotel until late in the 1960s.

Still standing well into the 1990s was the Oregon Building, a rather unassuming low structure that included the fourth-floor penthouse once occupied by Bugsy Siegel. Features of the apartment reportedly included a trap door exit to a basement tunnel that led to a neighboring building.

The Hilton Corporation became the first major hotel chain to "legitimize" the Las Vegas casino market when it purchased the Flamingo in 1971. Since then, the company has been adding to the hotel complex almost continuously, building a series of huge towers with a total of nearly 4,000 rooms.

The sixth tower at the site opened in late 1996 along with a flashy new facade. In back, where Bugsy's suite once stood, there are now fifteen acres of tropical gardens and swimming pools. Live entertainment in the area includes a dozen flamboyant flamingos plus a dozen tiny African penguins. Koi and goldfish fill the surrounding ponds, along with colorful ducks and graceful swans. Future residents at the hotels may include cranes and perhaps some exotic marsupials, such as wallabies.

Among the restaurants is **Alta Villa**, a family coffee shop with a few offerings slightly more ambitious than ordinary, such as applewood smoked salmon with

> **Like mother.** Liza Minelli's first contractual appearance in Las Vegas occurred in 1965 at the Sahara; eight years earlier, her mother Judy Garland had brought her onstage during an appearance at the Flamingo.

> **Dino and the kid.** Dean Martin and Jerry Lewis made their Las Vegas debut at the Flamingo in October of 1948; by 1952, their movies made them the top box-office draw in the country.

asparagus. Set in an Italian village, dinner is served nightly with entrees from about $12 to $20.

At **Conrad's**, a world of wood, brass, and mirrors encircles a show kitchen where specialties, priced from about $30 to $40, include poached veal tenderloin, garlic crusted medallions of monkfish, ostrich Rossini, and baby suckling pig.

The **Peking Market** looks like a transported Oriental marketplace. Open nightly except for Monday and Tuesday, entrees range from about $10 to $32.

The **Paradise Garden Buffet** basks in a tropical theme. And there is **Bugsy's Deli**, named after the gangster benefactor of the place.

In recent years, the Flamingo Showroom has been home to a touring company of the Radio City Rockettes.

Flamingo Hilton. 3555 Las Vegas Boulevard South; 3,642 rooms; (702) 733-3111, (800) 732-2111. www.hilton.com.

★ The New Frontier

The New Frontier, which emerged in 1998 from six years of near-suspended animation—a six-year, four-month labor strike called by five unions against the former owners—may be about to head farther west. Plans call for the demolition of the hotel by 2001 and the construction of a new mega-resort: The City by the Bay.

The new hotel and casino will salute San Francisco with Fisherman's Wharf, a reproduction of the fishing quays; Chinatown; Lombard Street, a replica of the crookedest street in the world; and Coit Tower, a 300-foot concrete shaft with views of the Strip. Planned restaurants include Alcatraz, where guests will be served in the cell block, and Napa Valley, a fully operational winery.

The 2,512-room hotel is expected to open in September of 2002.

Until the wrecker's ball arrives, the signature joint of the New Frontier is **Gilley's Saloon, Dancehall and Bar-B-Que** where you can eat, drink, dance, and ride the mechanical bull if you so choose. Specialties include "Gilley's Kick-Ass Texas BBQ." The dance hall is open Tuesday through Friday from 4 P.M. until very late, and on Saturdays and Sundays from 11 A.M. There is no cover charge; tables surround the dance floor.

Restaurants include **Margarita's Mexican Cantina** on the floor of the casino, serving fajita, burritos, and other south-of-the-border fare priced from about $6 to $17. The upscale **Phil's Angus Steakhouse** offers steak, poultry, and seafood entrees priced from about $12 to $40.

Frontier Hotel and Gambling Hall. 3120 Las Vegas Boulevard South; 986 rooms; (702) 794-8404, (800) 634-6966. www.frontierlv.com.

★ Gold Coast

A K-mart of a casino aimed at the low rollers, hidden behind a tremendous, blank stucco front wall, the Gold Coast features a sea of slot machines, including what seems to be an unusually large number of video poker machines. The Gold Coast sits next door to the Rio, a mile west of the Strip.

The main point of distinction for this hotel is the second-floor, seventy-two-lane bowling alley (can you envision the noise level when all the lanes are in use?). There are also two movie theaters and a bingo hall. At the back of the casino is a large dance hall featuring country and western high-kicking, with free classes offered. A liquor store sits directly off the casino.

There has been some attempt at creating an old California theme with pressed-tin ceilings and chandeliers, though not anywhere nearly as successfully as at the Barbary Coast on the Strip.

The **Buffet** is an unusually ordinary setting in one of the corners of the casino. **Mediterranean Room** offers pasta, veal, and chicken with entrees ranging in price from $7 to $25 in an ordinary room with a keno display. The **Cortez Room** offers chicken, steak, seafood, and a prime rib special in the range of $8 to $25. The **Monterey Room** is a twenty-four-hour coffee shop that includes Chinese dishes among its fare.

Gold Coast Hotel & Casino. 4000 West Flamingo Road; 750 rooms; (702) 367-7111, (800) 331-5334. www.coastcasinos/goldcoast/.

★★ Harrah's Las Vegas

This place has been through changes, from what was once the largest Holiday Inn in the world to one of the largest Mississippi riverboats on dry land to a new incarnation as a celebration of carnival around the world.

Harrah's underwent a $200 million renovation and expansion in 1997, including completion of a thirty-five-story tower with 986 rooms and seventy-four suites, and an all-new facade that sinks the former riverboat from sight.

Among the highlights of the reworked casino is a ceiling mural with fiber-optic fireworks. At Carnaval Court, outside on the plaza, the phantasmagorical Carnaval Fantastique show is presented a few times each night.

Entertainment includes the 525-seat **Commander's Theatre**, where in 2000, country and western star Clint Holmes presented "Takin' It Uptown." The hotel also offers an improvisational comedy show.

The **Fresh Market Square** buffet is new and improved. The new twenty-four-hour **Club Cappuccino** features all sorts of coffee, naturally, and is supervised by the hotel's very own Certified Roast Master. **Asia** brings a mix of Chinese and Asian cuisine in an intimate setting. **Café Andreotti's** offers Italian specialties in a setting of the Tuscan Hills.

The Range Steakhouse offers a dramatic view of the Las Vegas Strip along with its upscale menu. They love chops here—veal, pork, lamb, and beef—prices from about $30 to $40 with toppings like pistachio salsa butter.

Harrah's Las Vegas Casino Hotel. 3475 Las Vegas Boulevard South; 2,699 rooms; (702) 369-5000, (800) 634-6765. www.harrahs.lv.com.

★ Imperial Palace

An eclectic place with a vaguely Oriental theme, this deceptively large hotel (2,700 rooms) sprawls up, down, left, and right from its location at the heart of the Strip, across from the Mirage and Caesars Palace.

The Imperial Palace claims the title of the largest privately owned hotel casino in the world, a one-man band begun in 1972 at the old Flamingo Capri Motel by owner Ralph Engelstad. Construction of the various towers of the complex began in 1974 with a melange of Oriental themes. Recent renovations include adding an Oriental pagoda-like ceiling over the casino in golds and reds; the old crystal chandeliers still hang incongruously. The back half of the casino is pretty much untouched.

By Las Vegas standards, the IP is a bit on the ordinary side, although it has one distinction that is a secret to many visitors. Hidden away on an upper floor of a parking garage in back is an amazing collection of antique and unusual cars. Even if you are not the sort to gush over a classic 1928 Cadillac Dual Cowl Phaeton or an antique 1906 Ford Model K Touring Car restored to mint condition, there are other reasons to visit the museum. Concentrate instead on the history of vehicles used by world leaders, or come close to the transportation of some of the greatest stars of the twentieth century. *Look for more details on the car collection in Chapter 10.*

There's a nominal admission charge for the museum that almost no one pays; look for free passes at the entrance or ask a floor manager in the casino. The official rate is $6.95 for adults and $3 for children 12 and younger; the museum is open every day, late into the night. Work your way all the way to the back and up an escalator and an elevator to the car museum.

Treasures of the eclectic collection include Marilyn Monroe's pink Lincoln, a 1926 McFarlan owned by heavyweight champion Jack Dempsey, a roomful of Deusenbergs, Johnny Carson's 1939 Chrysler, and cars ridden in or owned by luminaries from Hitler to Mussolini to Kennedy and Nixon.

The large casino is a busy place and you may need to drop bread crumbs to find your way back to your room. The best rooms can be found in the newer tower; the hotel features an Olympic-sized swimming pool and a health and fitness center. The long-running show at the Imperial Theatre Showroom is "Legends in Concert," which features re-creations of musical greats, including Elvis (surprise!), the Beatles, Buddy Holly, Liberace, Roy Orbison, Nat King Cole, Marilyn Monroe, and Judy Garland. "Legends" is presented twice nightly, except Sunday.

The Imperial Palace features a double-handful of restaurants, including the **Teahouse**, a twenty-four-hour coffee shop, and the **Emperor's Buffet**. Just to make things confusing, there is also a slightly more upscale buffet, for dinner only, the **Imperial Buffet**, which is served in the Teahouse after 5 P.M.

From April to October, adventurous sorts can visit the Imperial-style **Hot Hawaiian Luau**, described as an authentic poolside luau complete with a lavish buffet, unlimited mai tais and piña coladas, as well as a full-scale Polynesian show.

Embers, tucked away on the fifth floor, offers steak, seafood, and Continental dishes in an intimate setting; it is open from 5 P.M. Wednesday through Sunday with reservations suggested. Menu offerings, priced from about $12 to $25, may include items such as orange roughy sautéed with macadamia nuts and Alaskan king crab legs with lemon drawn butter.

Seahouse. A seminautical setting with offerings including stuffed mushrooms with crabmeat and shrimp fettuccine. Entrees range from about $15 to $25. Open from 5 P.M. Friday through Tuesday with reservations suggested.

Other self-describing eateries include **Rib House** (from 5 P.M. Tuesday through Saturday), **Pizza Palace** (daily from 11 A.M. to midnight), and **Burger Palace**. Betty's Diner features ice cream, sandwiches, hot dogs, and snacks.

The **Ming Terrace** restaurant features Mandarin and Cantonese cuisine and is open daily from 5 P.M. Among out-of-the-ordinary offerings are egg flower soup, black mushroom and sea cucumber stew, and sour cabbage with beef. Entrees range from about $9 to $29.

The bars in the casino area bear Japanese names: Geisha, Ginza, Kanpai, Mai Tai, Nomiya, and Sake. Probably the most unusual watering hole in the hotel is the **Duesenberg Lounge** in the Duesenberg Room of the Auto Collection; aside from the decidedly unusual setting, you will also want to check out the antique western bar itself, which is straight out of the "Gunsmoke" era.

Imperial Palace Hotel & Casino. 3535 Las Vegas Boulevard South; 2,700 rooms; (702) 731-3311, (800) 634-6441. www.imperialpalace.com/vegas/.

★ Maxim's

Only in Las Vegas would a place like this be overshadowed. Maxim's is on Flamingo Road, a half-block in from Caesars Palace and the Mirage, and down the street from Bally's.

The hotel was sold to timeshare developer Premier Interval Resorts in 1999, and its future is uncertain.

Maxim's Hotel/Casino. 160 East Flamingo Road; 800 rooms; (702) 731-4300, (800) 634-6987.

★★ Orleans Hotel & Casino

One of America's liveliest cities is represented in this resort several blocks west of the Strip on Tropicana Avenue. It's Mardi Gras all the time here, although it's impossible to visit here without comparing it to the nearby Rio Casino, which celebrates the Carnival atmosphere of Brazil with exuberance, extravagance, and eensy-weensy cocktail waitress uniforms.

Well, the Orleans is attractive and fun in its own way, including an above-average buffet and skimpy cocktail waitress uniforms, but the voltage level is much lower.

The hotel's facade combines French, Spanish, and Plantation Colonial influences in an interesting jumble. Guest rooms include 810 "Petite Suites" and thirty one- and two-bedroom suites in a twenty-two-story tower. The main casino sits beneath an attractive high ceiling, flanked by French Quarter–like verandahs and ironwork.

Eateries include the **Canal Street Grille**, an elegant steak and seafood restaurant. Entrees include Pacific salmon in lime ginger sauce and blackened gulf shrimp with pecan rice, classical slow-roasted prime rib, and steaks or chops served with a choice of seven sauces.

Don Miguel's is a Mexican restaurant decorated in brass and mirrors. Specialty entrees include chicken baldastano, filet Colorado, and snapper cascabel, with tequila flan for the final touch.

Vito's offers an Italian menu on the second floor overlooking the casino. Specialties include five-cheese lasagna, calamari oscar, veal marsala, and *gamberoni con prosciutto* with pasta dishes priced from $6.95 and entrees from about $11 to $25.

The **Courtyard Café** is a twenty-four-hour coffee shop that serves New Orleans specialties, including barbecue shrimp or a muffuletta, and Chinese dishes such as Singapore noodles, moo-shu pork, Peking duck, and Szechwan salmon. A very ordinary fast food restaurant, **Terrible Mike's**, is located adjacent to the Race and Sports Book, with offerings that include beer-steamed Vienna hot dogs, chili, burgers, and deli sandwiches.

The **French Market Buffet** is set in a wrought iron and red brick re-creation of New Orleans, and features some unusual offerings, including gumbo, jambalaya, crawfish, blackened turkey, and other Creole fare. Come here for a buffet with a difference.

The 827-seat **Orleans Showroom** is used for headliner performances. The **Bourbon Street Cabaret** features classic jazz, blues, and zydeco.

The hotel also includes a seventy-lane bowling alley, a 500-seat food court; a New Orleans–themed restaurant/nightclub/lounge with live entertainment; an assortment of bars and cafes; retail shopping areas; a 3,420-seat, twelve-screen stadium seating movie theater; a child care center; and an arcade.

The Orleans is owned by Coast Hotels, which also owns the Gold Coast and the Barbary Coast in Las Vegas.

Orleans Hotel & Casino. 4500 West Tropicana Avenue; 804 rooms; (702) 365-7111, (800) 675-3267. wwwcoastcasinos.com/orleans/.

★★ Palace Station Hotel & Casino

The Palace is off the beaten track for most visitors, but it's a favorite of Las Vegas locals primarily because of its restaurants.

It's no small place, with more than 1,000 rooms and a large and lively casino with 2,200 slots and a 600-seat bingo parlor. Out-of-towners can use the hotel's shuttle bus for free transport to the Strip, about a mile east.

The hotel suffered a catastrophic flood and roof collapse over the casino pit in mid-1998 after a record rainfall; no one was hurt, but think of all the gambling that was lost! The casino rebuilt the pit with an updated Victorian theme that includes polished wood columns and moldings, stained glass accents, and vintage cast iron chandeliers with the aura of an Old West dance hall.

The **Broiler** is a local favorite for seafood. Typical offerings include mesquite broiled mahimahi, halibut, catfish, red snapper, and other fish for $11 to $15.

Landlubbers can also order steak and chicken dishes. Entrees are priced from about $17 to $35. Open daily from 11 A.M. to 11 P.M.

The Feast is called an "action buffet" by the management, because many of the dishes are prepared for guests as they wait. The Feast often wins "best" ratings from the locals, although on my visits it ranked in the second tier below spectacular offerings such as those of the Rio, Caesars Palace, and Bellagio.

The **Guadalajara Bar & Grille** offers authentic Mexican food along with Tex-Mex cuisine and Southwestern fare. Specialties are priced from as low as $10 all the way up to $40. The Guadalajara Bar & Grille is also known for its inexpensive margaritas. Open daily from 11 A.M. to 11 P.M.

The **Iron Horse Cafe** offers coffee shop food twenty-four hours a day. Iron Horse also serves Chinese food from 11 A.M. to 5 A.M., with graveyard specials nightly from 11 P.M. to 5 A.M. For lighter fare, there's the **Pasta Palace**, featuring pasta, scampi, veal, and pizza cooked in a woodburning oven, with entrees priced from about $9 to $20. It's open daily for dinner from 4:30 to 11 P.M. Nightly specials include steak or lobster dinners.

Palace Station Hotel & Casino. 2411 West Sahara Avenue; 1,028 rooms; (702) 367-2411, (800) 634-3101. www.stationcasinos.com.

★ Riviera

A grand creation intended to bring a touch of the Côte d'Azur to the desert floor, the Riviera collapsed into bankruptcy almost immediately after its opening in 1955. (The opening act was Liberace, earning a then-spectacular $50,000 per week. In 1956, film and radio star Orson Welles appeared on stage with a magic act.) A series of subsequent owners, including the Chicago mob, took over with a tremendous spurt of new construction that culminated in another bankruptcy in 1983.

The Riviera includes one of the largest casinos in town, at 125,000 square feet. Although there is not much pedestrian traffic on the Strip, the casino does have an open front like some of the downtown joints. Inside is a riot of reds and golds.

Odd Couple number one. Marlene Dietrich and Louis Armstrong appeared together at the Riviera in 1962.

The Riviera added an 85,000-square-foot convention and visitors center in 1999. The new facility, designed for conventions and entertainment events and located behind the hotel, will accommodate up to 3,500.

The hotel is the long-time home of *Splash*, a water-theme production show, and *Crazy Girls*, an adults-only topless revue which has been in place for more than a decade; a bronze statue of the cast's backsides stands at the hotel's entrance. More than a few rolls of film have also been exposed there.

Elvis sighting number four/Odd Couple number two. Elvis Presley posed on stage in 1956 in a gold lamé jacket at the Riviera piano while Liberace, wearing Elvis' rocker duds, whipped at a guitar.

The **Rik'Shaw** is an ordinary name for a lovely place to eat. A variety of entrees range in price from about $9 to $26.

An overly simple name for another nice place is **Ristorante Italiano**, a classy Italian eatery decorated with brass, brick, and statuary with a fake skyline of Rome outside the painted "windows." It also has one of the more elaborate espresso machines in town. Specialties are priced from about $12 to $30.

Kady's Coffee Shop is an all-day coffee shop. Sandwiches, burgers, and entrees range from about $6 to $15. At the time of our visit, an overnight special offered one pound of snow crab legs for $10, or steak and lobster for $8.88.

Kristofer's offers chicken, steak, filet mignon, and lobster tail, from about $22 to $37.

The Riviera buffet is called the **World's Fare Buffet**. Special themes are Mexican on Monday, Italian on Tuesday, Oriental on Wednesday, Hawaiian on Thursday, international on Friday and Saturday, and Western barbecue on Sunday.

Riviera Hotel & Casino. 2901 Las Vegas Boulevard South; 2,071 rooms; (702) 734-5110, (800) 634-6753, (800) 634-3420. www.TheRiviera.com.

★★★ Sahara Hotel & Casino

In one of the more successful remakes of a Strip golden oldie, the Sahara completed in late 1997 a $100 million reconstruction program that included a spectacular tent-like porte cochere leading to the main entry, a new pool area with gazebo, spa, cabanas, and outdoor snack bar, and, of course, an expanded casino. The facade facing the Strip was redone with fountains and palm trees.

The dowdy old plaster camels and bedouins that used to grace the front of the hotel have been touched up and moved to a small oasis along the road.

And apropos of nothing else, there is also a sub-theme within the casino of auto racing, with a high-tech simulator, a racing restaurant, and scattered road machines in the casino.

And then there is **Speed: The Ride**, a wild roller coaster that blasts through a hole in the front wall of the NASCAR racing simulator at the back of the hotel and through the sign out front on the Strip. The track ends in front with a track that runs straight up to the sky; the cars then fall back to earth and backwards to the starting gate. Go figure. *For more details, see Chapter 10.*

> **I wanna hold your cash.** The Beatles put on a pair of concerts in 1964 under the sponsorship of the Sahara, but held at the large Las Vegas Convention Center. Tickets for the show averaged $4, and the Beatles were paid $25,000 for the appearance.

The Sahara opened in 1952 and was an immediate sensation for the size and gaudiness of its outdoor sign. Actually, it can draw its lineage back to the Club Bingo, which opened in 1947 and featured a 300-seat bingo parlor. It was sold, remodeled, and opened as the Sahara five years later. At the time, it was the first casino visitors would come to as they left downtown. The hotel was sold in 1995 to William Bennett, the former chairman of Circus Circus, and he has turned on the money spigot to renew the place.

The Rest of the Strip

Speedworld, a $15 million virtual reality attraction, uses twenty-four interactive three-quarter-scale Indy car simulators to give riders the look and feel of racing on a mile and a half oval at the Las Vegas Motor Speedway or in a phatasmagorical zoom up the Strip at 200 miles per hour. The virtual experience is provided by a 133-degree wrap-around screen, realistic sound, and a moving car body. *See Chapter 10 for full details.*

In 2000, the Sahara added an outpost of the NASCAR Café themed restaurant.

Future plans may include a new 1,000-room tower. Bennett is staying coy about plans for the thirty-nine-acre plot across the road from the Sahara.

The showplace restaurant is the **Sahara Steakhouse**, a private and quiet room decorated in reds and blacks. All the usual suspects—prime rib, steak, shrimp, and lobster—are priced from about $25 to $60. The **Caravan Coffee Shop** offers nightly specials such as New York strip steak for $7.95. The **New Sahara Buffet**, which seats 1,120 close friends, is upstairs and away from the bustle. It includes three "action stations" for Oriental, Italian, and traditional carving. On the third floor is **Paco's Hideaway**, a Mexican eatery that offers entrees beginning at $4.95.

Sahara Hotel & Casino. 2535 Las Vegas Boulevard South; 2,000 rooms; (702) 737-2111, (800) 634-6411. www.saharahotel.com.

★★ San Rémo Casino & Resort

The San Rémo began as a lure to the business traveler, and as such delivers pleasant rooms and service. There is, of course, a casino, too. Recent expansions have added a bit more glitz and a lot more rooms.

The San Rémo is located about a block east of the Strip, next door to its flashy corporate neighbor, the Tropicana.

Saizen at San Rémo, a Japanese dining and sushi bar, offers a wide range of dishes from tempura to tonkatsu to teriyaki, as well as sushi. The **Paparazzi Grille** offers steak and seafood. **Pasta Rémo** offers fine Italian dining from 5 P.M. to midnight. Lighter fare, including Italian subs and salads, is available at **Luigi's Deli**. The **Ristorante dei Fiori** coffee shop and buffet is open twenty-four hours. The **Buffet** is available for breakfast, lunch, and dinner.

The stage show at the hotel in 2000 was "Les Trix," a revue with all of the Las Vegas staples: showgirls, music, and magic. The show was presented nightly except Monday.

San Rémo Casino & Resort. 115 East Tropicana Avenue; 711 rooms; (702) 739-9000, (800) 522-7366.

★ Stardust

A venerable establishment, if you are somehow able to overlook an extremely checkered history of involvement by various factions of organized crime. For many years, the hotel was a semi-legit operation of the Chicago mob, a connection that ended with the discovery of a massive "skimming" scandal—the raking off of profits from gaming operations before they were taxed.

The Stardust was famous for its reproduction of the "Lido de Paris" floorshow, which saved millions on costume expenses for its showgirls, many of whom were dressed only in, err, stardust. The Lido finally departed a few years back, after more than thirty years on stage. In late 1999, the Stardust announced a ten-year deal with the "king of Las Vegas." Singer Wayne Newton will perform in the Wayne Newton Theater forty weeks a year.

Some parts of the Stardust have more sparkle than others: the newer West Tower building is quite nice, the old strips of low motel buildings at the back of the hotel are generally not the sort of place you'd want to write home about, and the East Tower is somewhere in between.

The classy **William B's Steakhouse** is decorated like a Chicago steakhouse in mahogany, brass, blacks and whites. Entrees range from $16 to $40. Specialties include petite filet mignon, king porterhouse, and boneless double center cut pork chop. Veal or chicken dishes are prepared in your choice of style—Oskar, marsala, angelo, francaise, parmigiana, piccata, and William B (coated with flour and served with avocado and crab).

The **Tres Lobos Mexican Restaurant and Cantina** is open for dinner only, Tuesday through Saturday, with entrees priced from $7.95 to $13.95. Food is attractively presented in this lively room, decorated like the open courtyard of a Mexican mansion.

There's a branch of the **Tony Roma's** chain, offering a full slab of baby back ribs, barbecue chicken and ribs combo, or a half barbecue chicken, priced from about $9 to $16. **Toucan Harry's** is an attractive coffee shop. The Stardust's buffet is **Coco Palms**.

Stardust Resort & Casino. 3000 Las Vegas Boulevard South; 2,100 rooms; (702) 732-6111, (800) 634-6757. www.stardustlv.com.

★★ Tropicana

An interesting mix of colorful Miami schmaltz and flashy Las Vegas glitz, the Trop is among the favorite "old" hotels on the Strip. First built in 1957, it has had its share of mob intrigue and corruption through the years. It was recently restored under the ownership of the Ramada Corporation.

Once alone at the top of the Strip, now it is almost possible to miss in the flow of the flashy Excalibur, Luxor, and MGM Grand across the road. Recently, though, they added to the overdose at the corner with a tropical village facade, complete with huge Easter Island-like statues and a new main entrance; in case you still miss it, a nightly laser light show is presented. Overhead walkways connect the Tropicana and the MGM, Excalibur, and New York–New York casinos.

> **Is that a deed in your pocket?** Mae West was not only a successful entertainer, but she had a way with real estate, buying half a mile of undeveloped land on the Strip between the eventual site of the Dunes and Tropicana.

The leaded, stained-glass ceiling above the tables in the casino is worth a peek, and lovers of Miami staples such as dancing water fountains and chandeliers will not be disappointed. Machines sit under a blue sky in a forest of bamboo trees. Overall, it's a lively place, well kept up.

With a tropical theme, there is emphasis on watery decorations, including a five-acre water park that has lagoons, spas, waterfalls, and what is claimed as the world's largest indoor/outdoor swimming pool. There are dozens of exotic birds and fish in surrounding cages and pools. There is even a swim-up blackjack table. The entire area is carefully lit at night, including a laser light show.

Standard rooms are somewhat ordinary, jutting off long boring hallways.

The long-playing show at the Trop is the "Folies Bergere," which features $5 million in sets and costumes. The show is still based on the Paris original, including cancan dancing and splits, and spectacular costumes . . . and some dancers who seem to have left parts of their outfits in the dressing room.

The Tropicana opened on the Las Vegas Strip April 4, 1957, and the Folies opened some two years later in December of 1959. The current edition of the longest running production show in Las Vegas history includes some of the best production numbers from past Folies, as well as new sequences. Folies Bergere plays at 8 P.M. for a dinner or cocktails show, with prices starting at $28.95, and a cocktail show at 10:30 P.M. for $22.95. Information: (702) 739-2411.

The Trop offers the rather ordinary **Island Buffet** for breakfast and dinner. **The Golden Dynasty** offers Chinese cuisine nightly except Wednesday and Thursday from 5 to 10:45 P.M.

Mizuno's Japanese Steakhouse offers teppanyaki dining nightly from 5 to 10:45 P.M.

Pietro's Gourmet Dining is a Las Vegas favorite, extended into a casino. Entrees range from about $20 to $35; on a recent visit the menu included breast of chicken Kiev, Veal Sorrentino, and Steak Diane. Open for dinner Thursday to Monday from 5 to 11 P.M.

The Savanna offers the "Wild Side of Dining" starting with steaks and moving on from there. Well off the casino floor, entrees range in price from about $14 to $30. On a visit, the menu included basil pesto crusted roasted rack of lamb. The eatery is open nightly, except Sunday and Monday, from 5 to 11 P.M.

Tropicana Resort and Casino. 3801 Las Vegas Boulevard South; 1,910 rooms; (702) 739-2222, (800) 634-4000. www.tropicana.lv.com.

Algiers Hotel

An old-style motor court that has rooms centered around a pool, located across the Strip from Circus Circus. Nothing fancy but it's a decent place to stay and a good value; the inner courtyard is surprisingly peaceful.

If you're a guest, be sure to check out the black-and-white photos of the hotel in its heyday; they're located near the registration desk.

Algiers Hotel. 2845 Las Vegas Boulevard South; 105 rooms; (702) 735-3311.

Holiday Inn/Boardwalk

While most eyes were fixed on the fabulous new mega-resorts up and down the Strip, the Holiday Inn snuck in with a small hotel and casino, which opened at the end of 1995. The Boardwalk has actually been around for awhile, although hardly anyone noticed.

In 1998, the hotel was purchased by Mirage Resorts, and in mid-1999, that company disclosed its intention to build yet another meagresort on the property; in early 2000, Mirage was itself purchased by MGM Grand, Inc. and the Boardwalk's future once again became uncertain.

The Boardwalk, with 654 rooms, is the largest Holiday Inn in America. The designers of this place did a very sneaky thing, putting what looks like a wild roller coaster on the exterior of the building; it was enough to make us look for the ticket booth the first time we drove by. The coaster is just for show, alas. So, too, is a Ferris Wheel out front that carries a full load of lifelike tourist dummies. Inside is a lively K-mart of a casino that caters to the low rollers.

Restaurants include the **Cyclone Coffee Shop**, open daily from 7 A.M. to 11:30 P.M. **The Deli**, which offers foot-long Coney Island hot dogs and other such gourmet fare, is open twenty-four hours a day. **The Surf Buffet** offers American, Italian, Mexican, and Oriental selections daily. **Caffe Boardwalk** serves Italian fare priced from about $10, daily from 5 P.M. to 11 P.M.

Holiday Inn/Boardwalk. 203 rooms. 3740 Las Vegas Boulevard South. (702) 735-2400, (800) 635-4582. www.hiboardwalk.com.

O'Shea's Casino

O'Shea's is a mecca for the low roller on the Strip, albeit at a pretty toney location. Now part of the Hilton family, it is located next to the Flamingo Hilton and across the road from Caesars Palace. The casino features nickel slots, offers cheap beer, and promises to cash out-of-state checks.

Interesting for a glimpse of the old-style wood and mirror ceiling over the pit; if you look left and right, though, you're likely to spy a Burger King, Subway, or Baskin Robbins.

O'Shea's Casino. 3555 Las Vegas Boulevard South; (702) 697-2711.

★ Sam's Town Hotel & Gambling Hall

Catering mostly to locals, Sam's Town is your basic Old Western boomtown on the outside, with a clanging and flashing casino within. But if you work your way deep inside to the hotel registration desk you'll find a spectacular glass-roofed atrium known as Mystic Falls Park that has trees and birds, sitting areas, bars, and restaurants. The Sunset Stampede, a laser light and water show, is offered several times daily within the park.

Sam's Town is located on the Boulder Highway south of Flamingo Road. One unusual feature is a Western dance hall on the second floor. Restaurants include the **Diamond Lil's** steakhouse and **Mary's Diner**, a re-creation of an old diner. **The Great Buffet** is a pleasant room with reasonable offerings.

Sam's Town Hotel & Gambling Hall. 650 rooms. 5111 Boulder Highway. (702) 456-7777, (800) 634-6371.

Chapter 8
Downtown Las Vegas

Econoguide 2001: Best Casinos in Downtown

★★★	**Golden Nugget.**	*A gilded lady of a certain age.*
★★★	**Main Street Station.**	*Uptown in a downtown kind of way.*
★	**Binion's Horseshoe.**	*Has character and characters.*
★	**Fitzgerald's.**	*McCasino.*
★	**Four Queens.**	*An unimpressive hand.*
★	**Golden Gate.**	*Recoup your losses at the shrimp cocktail bar.*
★	**Jackie Gaughan's Plaza.**	*Flashy, by downtown standards.*
★	**Lady Luck.**	*A woman of a certain age.*
★	**Las Vegas Club.**	*People come here to gamble.*
★	**Sam Boyd's Fremont.**	*Less than memorable.*

Downtown Las Vegas was where it all started, and though the flashiest and largest of the casinos have moved south to the Strip, the ingredients just may be in place for an exciting rebirth of Fremont Street.

The "Fremont Street Experience"—a space-age space frame with lights, sound . . . and casinos . . . covered the top of the famous Glitter Gulch at the end of 1995, and many of the casinos downtown put millions into impressive additions and renovations. Thus began the redevelopment of the downtown area. Once you park your car in one of several parking garages, there are at least ten major casinos within walking distance—and under cover.

And the city has joined in a plan to construct Neonopolis@Fremont Experience, a $99 million retail and entertainment complex at Fourth and Fremont Streets. The project is supposed to include several dozen retail shops, eleven movie screens, and entertainment, with an opening planned by mid-2001.

For years, the neon splash of Glitter Gulch was used as the picture to represent all of Las Vegas. The lights of the various signs were so bright in the narrow man-made canyon that pedestrians enjoyed electric noon at midnight. The stretch was used as the setting for many movies, including *Honey, I Blew Up the Baby*, *The Stand*, and *Diamonds Are Forever*.

While the Strip has gone in for flume rides, white tigers, and Oz and has catered—a bit schizophrenically—to families as well as to the highest of the high rollers, downtown Las Vegas has been the home of the serious gambler. The payoffs on the slot machines near Fremont Street are just a bit better than up on the Strip, and the house rules for many table games are just a tad more liberal.

Downtown is also the home for some of the lower forms of entertainment and commerce, including strip clubs and pawn shops; you can just pass them by if that's not what you're looking for.

The latest conception of the future of downtown, then, is as the "adult Las Vegas." Think of it as the Glitter Gulch Theme Park and Indoor Gambling Mall and you'll get the idea.

The canopy does not completely enclose the street—it's more of a high-tech tinkertoy than a solid roof—but the result is still an interesting mix of inside and out.

The $70 million "Fremont Street Experience" put a five-block-long, 100-foot-high cover over the main drag. Beneath the canopy is a 1.4 million-light "sky parade" and light show. Several times a night, the space frame comes to life with a ten-minute music and light show about cowboys, stampeding buffaloes, and dollar signs in the sky. The show is controlled by thirty-one computers, including thirty within the space frame and a single master computer.

The library of shows changes from season to season; in 2000 shows were offered every hour on the hour from dusk to midnight. For information on shows and special events, call (800) 259-3559.

At the head of Fremont Street is a parking garage that has 1,500 parking spaces, plus the Plaza Shops with 50,000 square feet of store space, and the Promenade Shops at Fremont Street, a blend of patio cafes and marketplace shopping in kiosks, street carts, and pavilions.

Although some of the side streets of downtown are a bit scary, even to the locals, a visitor who parks in one of the casino parking garages is unlikely to be exposed to the seedier side of town. Most casinos offer free parking for several hours if you get your parking ticket validated inside; there is no requirement that you spend a dime at the tables or machines.

And you can easily stay on the Strip and commute to Fremont Street, or the other way around; it's a fifteen-minute drive by highway and a bit slower (but more interesting) to drive the length of Las Vegas Boulevard.

The Fremont Street Experience also features special events, including a Holiday Festival that displays a fifty-foot Christmas tree, an ice rink for public skating and special entertainment, and a New Year's Eve party.

Casino developer and champion promoter Bob Stupak's plans for a fifteen-story boat-shaped *Titanic*-themed hotel at the north end of the Las Vegas Strip hit a political iceberg in mid-1999, and another scheme to bring back to life the long-closed Moulin Rouge, also seems to have returned to the vapors.

MUST-SEE ★★★ Golden Nugget Hotel & Casino

Part of the Mirage dynasty, the Golden Nugget is the class of downtown. The lively casino is decorated with a San Francisco theme, painted in white and gold with ornate chandeliers and ceiling fans. The new tower at the hotel is a local landmark with its brilliant gold reflective glass; there are a total of 1,907 rooms, including one- and two-bedroom suites, twenty-seven luxury apartments in the Spa Suite Tower, and six penthouse suites in the North Tower.

Amenities include an outdoor pool and whirlpool, full-service spa and beauty salon, fitness center, and the Golden Nugget specialty shops. Entertainment in the Theatre Ballroom features the "Country Fever" musical revue, bringing a touch of "Strip" entertainment downtown.

Be sure to walk deep into the casino to a display case near the registration desk to check out a few real golden nuggets. The most impressive is the Hand of Faith Nugget, which is claimed to be the world's largest piece of unrefined gold. Weighing in at 875 troy ounces (almost sixty-two pounds), it was discovered with a metal detector in 1980 by a young man prospecting behind his trailer home near Wedderburn, in Victoria, Australia.

As aficionados of the brewing art, we were most impressed with the central **38 Different Kinds of Beer Bar**, which delivers guess-how-many-kinds of guess-what. Actually, there may be more than thirty-eight types at the time you visit; some beers are available in standard and light versions.

Each of the Golden Nugget restaurants is a small gem, too. They include:

Stefano's. A truly lovely small room, well insulated from the casino. Decorated like a real Venetian hideaway, only cleaner and newer. You'll be served by flocks of waiters in long aprons.

Lillie Langtry's. Nearby is another quiet, lovely room, decorated in gold and mirrors and serving Cantonese fare by way of San Francisco. (Miss Lillie, also known as the Jersey Lily, was a famous English actress who made her name in the United States with a tour in the 1880s that included the Wild West; she was the Madonna of her day.)

California Pizza Kitchen. An outpost of the California-based wood-fired pizza chain (another location is within the Mirage on the Strip) it features more than twenty-five varieties of pizza ranging from the traditional to the unusual in personal sizes priced from about $7 to $10 on regular or honey-wheat dough.

Golden Nugget, Las Vegas

We were also intrigued by the possibility of a *moo-shu* chicken calzone. The Pizza Kitchen is hidden away in a side room near the registration desk.

Golden Nugget Buffet. The best of the downtown buffets, and one of the most popular in town, especially for the Sunday champagne brunch when the wait can extend to hours. Come early, make an advance reservation, or try to curry some favor with a pit boss for the Sunday special.

Carson Street Café, modeled after a European sidewalk cafe, serves breakfast, lunch, and dinner twenty-four hours.

Golden Nugget Hotel & Casino. 129 East Fremont Street; 1,907 rooms; (702) 791-7111, (800) 634-3454. www.goldennugget.com.

MUST-SEE ★★★ Main Street Station

An exciting addition to downtown, the Main Street Station brings a touch of Victorian elegance, including historical treasures, opulent chandeliers, stained glass windows, and four antique railroad sleeping cars.

A walkway from the Fremont Street Experience to the Main Street Station includes World War I–era street lamps from Brussels, Belgium. Overhead in the

Under the Fremont Street Experience space frame
Photo by Corey Sandler

casino is a chandelier from the Figaro Opera House in Paris. The casino cashiers' cage windows feature the bronze grillwork of the teller windows from the Barclay Bank of London.

One of the railroad cars, now used as the Main Street Cigar Bar, was the personal coach of author Louisa May Alcott. Another of the cars was used by Buffalo Bill Cody and hosted Annie Oakley and Teddy Roosevelt.

The signature eatery is the **Pullman Grille**, open for dinner nightly except Tuesday and Wednesday and featuring steak and seafood. The **Triple 7 Brewpub** offers five microbrews produced on site, wings, burgers, and sushi. The **Garden Court Buffet** follows the Las Vegas "action buffet" trend, including designer pizza and pasta, antipasto, and a barbecue.

Sky high. North Las Vegas, a few miles beyond downtown, is the home of Nellis Air Force Range. The North Las Vegas Air Show takes place each fall, usually near the end of October, drawing tens of thousands of visitors. Events include all sorts of aircraft, hot air balloons, vintage autos, and various celebrations of Indian heritage.

The casino is connected by an enclosed pedestrian bridge to the California Hotel and Casino which, like Main Street Station, is also owned by Boyd Gaming Corporation; other properties owned by Boyd include The Fremont and the Stardust Resort & Casino.

Room rates start at $35 weekdays and $40 on weekends.

Main Street Station. 200 North Main Street; 406 rooms; (702) 387-1896, (800) 713-8933. www.mainstreetcasino.com.

★ Binion's Horseshoe Hotel & Casino

One of the eclectic oddities of Nevada, and worth a visit for that reason alone, Binion's is a rambling, dim place semidecorated in dark browns, blacks, and reds. Benny Binion was one of Las Vegas's old-time gambling men who ran a casino, which is quite a different thing from today's business people who own gambling casinos. However, it is worth noting that Steve Wynn, the flamboyant developer of Belladio, the Mirage and Treasure Island, was a protégé of Binion in his younger days; Wynn now owns the Desert Inn.

Binion created his Horseshoe in the late 1940s out of two old downtown properties, the Apache Hotel and the Eldorado Casino. Today the casino has absorbed an entire city block, including the old Mint Hotel next door.

The casino is considered a haven for the "serious" gambler, with some of the highest limits in Las Vegas.

Alas, one of the place's quirky charms was sold off in early 2000: the framed million dollars in rare $10,000 bills went to a local collector for a reported $6 million. Something like five million visitors went home with souvenir photos taken in front of the cash.

You'll also find the Poker Hall of Fame on the right wall of the casino, with pictures of the famous and infamous players of all time.

Before you leave, go for a ride on the glass-walled elevator for a great view of downtown. And on the twenty-fourth floor is one of Las Vegas's grandest

> **No day of rest.** Sundays are surprisingly busy days at many casinos, bringing out the locals for brunches. It's also a common arrival day for big tour groups.

> **Pawn shop plaza.** How bad can things get? There is a group of pawn shops between the Golden Nugget and the Pioneer Club on both sides of Fremont Street. There is no *Econoguide* to hock shops; I can't recommend these shops as places to buy or sell.

> **Truth in advertising.** On the Strip heading into downtown, keep an eye out for the tiny Normandie Hotel on the left, a rather jarring pink stucco motor court. On one visit, the sign outside said, "Elvis Slept Here."
> We suspect it was on an off night.
> (By the way, the other side of the sign read "Highly Recommended by Owner.")

monuments to beef, **Binion's Ranch Steak House**. It's a spectacular room and one of the best beeferies around.

Gee Joon offers Chinese cuisine. The overnight special on one visit to the **Coffee Shop** was a ten-ounce New York strip steak with salad, potato, rolls, and butter for $4.50. The **Horseshoe Buffet** features nightly themes including Tex-Mex, Bayou, Italian, and BBQ. On Friday nights, it offers its Seafood Buffet, a downtown favorite that includes giant shrimp, crab legs, salmon, oysters, mussels, a carving station for prime rib, and seven hot entrees.

Binion's Horseshoe Hotel & Casino. 128 East Fremont Street; 354 rooms; (702) 382-1600, (800) 937-6537.

★ Fitzgeralds Casino and Holiday Inn

If you have any question about whether this place intends to cater to the low rollers or the high rollers, a quick glance at the ubiquitous advertisements for the hotel should tell you: a regular come-on at Fitzgeralds is a free burger at the McDonald's within the casino.

In the core of the casino is a world of Irish green, including what is claimed to be a piece of the Blarney stone, a collection of four-leaf clovers, and a gaggle of leprechauns. In other words, lots of luck. The thirty-four-story tower is downtown's tallest casino/hotel.

The signature eatery is **Limerick's Steakhouse**, open for dinner except Tuesday and Wednesday. The background is an Irish castle.

Vincenzo's Italian Café serves northern Italian cuisine for lunch and dinner in a patio setting around a show kitchen; specials start at $5.95.

Fitzgeralds. 301 East Fremont Street; 638 rooms; (702) 388-2400, (800) 274-5825. www.fitzgeralds.com.

★ Four Queens

By Las Vegas standards, the Four Queens is a relatively understated hotel decorated in blue and beige with mirrored ceilings with a small but lively casino.

The hotel was first built in 1964 and supposedly drew its name from the fact that former owner Ben Goffstein had four daughters. During the years, the hotel has expanded to 720 rooms with twin nineteen-story towers, and it occupies the entire block at Fremont and Third Streets.

Hugo's is one of the better eateries in Las Vegas. The meal begins with a make-your-own salad from a tableside cart laden with offerings from bay shrimp to roasted pine nuts to hearts of palm. Entrees are priced from about $24 to $49.

At the more casual **Magnolia's Veranda**, you can try the Four Queens' Dip, a pair of French rolls filled with sliced beef and Swiss cheese, served au jus. Entrees are priced from about $5 to $15.

The casino has gone through rocky financial straits in recent years.

> **Where do they get the coins?** The Four Queens claims the title for the world's largest slot machine, duly noted in the *Guinness Book of World Records*. The Queens Machine is 9 feet, 8 inches tall and 18 feet long. Six people can play the slot, for $1 to $5 per pull, at the same time.

Four Queens Hotel & Casino. 202 East Fremont Street; 720 rooms; (702) 385-4011, (800) 634-6045. www.fourqueens.com.

★ Golden Gate Hotel & Casino

Built in 1906 as the Hotel Nevada, the Golden Gate is the oldest hotel in Las Vegas. A restaurant, the **Bay City Diner**, is set in 1930s San Francisco.

The best thing here is the nondescript **San Francisco Shrimp Bar and Deli** way at the back: the 99-cent shrimp cocktails that aren't half bad. Take two, they're small. The fake-crab cocktails are the same price, and are even better.

In recent years, Golden Gate has worked to return the hotel's exterior to a 1930s San Francisco look, with window awnings and planter boxes, and a hedge on the roof.

Golden Gate Hotel & Casino. 1 Fremont Street; 106 rooms. (702) 382-6300.

★ Jackie Gaughan's Plaza Hotel and Casino

An attractive and well-kept hotel at the head of Fremont, it was for many years known as the Union Plaza, as a reminder of the former railroad interests that once controlled Las Vegas and of the railroad station that formerly occupied the spot. The hotel today is still connected to the Amtrak station at one end and the Greyhound terminal at the other.

The hotel was opened in 1971 on the spot where the land auction of 1905 took place. At the time, it had the largest casino in Las Vegas, a distinction that has since been passed up the Strip many times.

The Plaza offers a wide range of gambling opportunities, beginning with rarely seen penny slots and nickel progressive jackpot machines and moving upward from there.

The casino also occasionally features one of our least favorite come-ons: an instant tax refund stand. Why don't we like that? Even assuming you come to the desk with a professionally prepared tax return, what you are essentially doing is taking out a short-term loan at a very high interest rate; by some calculations, the cost of the loan can be the equivalent of as much as 100 percent in interest. If you are that hard up for an instant return of your tax refund, you

> **Las Vegas Chamber of Commerce.** 711 East Desert Inn Road, Las Vegas, NV 89109; (702) 735-1616.
> **Las Vegas Convention and Visitors Authority.** 3150 Paradise Road, Las Vegas, NV 89109; (702) 892-0711. www.lasvegas24hours.com.

might want to consider whether you really should be spending the money in a casino once you obtain it.

The signature restaurant at the Plaza is the **Center Stage**, on the second floor of the tower with a spectacular view up Glitter Gulch. The eatery is open from 4:30 P.M. to midnight, with dinners priced from about $10. The **Plaza Diner** on the first floor serves breakfast, lunch, and dinner twenty-four hours a day.

John "Jackie" Gaughan's group also owns the **El Cortez Hotel** in downtown, the **Las Vegas Club, Western Hotel & Bingo Parlor**, and the **Gold Spike**.

Gaughan's Plaza. 1 Main Street; 1,037 rooms; (702) 386-2110, (800) 634-6575. www.jackiegaughan.com.

★ Lady Luck

One block in from Fremont on Ogden and Third Streets, this is one of the livelier places in downtown.

The **Burgundy Room** offers entrees such as tournedos *rossini* and fresh halibut.

The **Winner's Café** coffee shop offers specials that include a broiled chopped sirloin with soup or salad for about $4, a prime rib dinner for about $5, and a New York steak dinner for about $10.

The **Banquet Buffet** offers breakfast, lunch, and dinner.

Room rates range from about $40 to $80. Lady Luck Casino Hotel. 206 North Third Street; 792 rooms; (702) 477-3000, (800) 523-9582. www.ladyluck.com/lasvegas/.

★★ Las Vegas Club

A lively, informal small club with a high mirrored ceiling, the Las Vegas Club holds a special attraction for baseball and blackjack fans.

The casino claims the most liberal blackjack rules in the world; the somewhat complex rules do seem to reduce the house advantage, at least for experienced and knowledgeable players. Among the special rules are these: you can double down on any of the first two or three cards; you can surrender your original two cards for half your bet; you can split and resplit aces up to two times; you can split and resplit any pair any time you choose, and any hand of six cards totaling twenty-one or less is an automatic winner. The Las Vegas Club somewhat compensates for its loose rules by dealing cards from a multideck shoe, reducing the edge for card counters.

But back to the atmosphere: you'll notice things are a bit different when you see the uniforms worn by the dealers; instead of white shirts and string ties, they are each decked out in baseball jerseys. The cocktail waitresses wear cheerleader outfits.

Take the hint and head toward the back of the casino to examine the great collection of old sports photos and memorabilia—mostly baseball and boxing—near the Dugout Restaurant. Photos on the wall date back as far as the 1920s.

Among the favorite sports stars is former speedster Maury Wills; you'll find his original 1950 minor league contract to the Hornell Baseball Association in upstate New York. He was paid a whopping $150 a month with a $500 signing bonus. Also on display are Wills' shoes from 1962, the year he set a major league record with 104 stolen bases. (Wills, by the way, had a short career on stage in Vegas; among his appearances was in a show at the Sahara in 1969 where he played saxophone.)

Great Moments Room. Specialties, priced about $13 to $20, include *scaloné,* a combination of abalone and shrimp sautéed and finished with light white wine and garlic sauce, for about $14.

Las Vegas Club Hotel & Casino. 18 East Fremont Street; 410 rooms; (702) 385-1664.

> **Camp Las Vegas.** Fremont Street is named after John Charles Frémont, a nineteenth-century American explorer who established a camp near Las Vegas Springs in 1844.

> **Elvis sighting number five.** The King's first Las Vegas appearance took place at the New Frontier in downtown in April of 1956, and it wasn't a smashing success. At the time, it seemed that the King of Rock 'n' Roll's appeal was to younger crowds than those coming to Las Vegas. In 1969, he returned and made the first of a long series of appearances at the International Hotel (now the Las Vegas Hilton).

★ Sam Boyd's Fremont Hotel & Casino

One of the first "carpet joints" in downtown, it also featured one of the first block-long neon signs in the neighborhood. The joint is always jumping.

Paradise Buffet. The weekend Champagne Brunch, served Sunday from 7 A.M. to 3 P.M., is one of the better deals in downtown. It includes breakfast omelettes and eggs cooked to order, herring, sour cream, smoked salmon, New York strip loin, ham, turkey, and salads for $8.95.

The buffet's Seafood Fantasy is served Tuesday, Friday, and Sunday from 4 P.M. for $14.95. (The "regular" dinner is offered other nights for $9.95.) *See the section on buffets for hours and prices.*

The hotel includes a branch of the **Tony Roma's** chain, open for dinner from 5 to 11 P.M. Specialties include prime rib, steak, and chicken, with prices ranging from about $15 to $25.

The **Second Street Grill** has for several years been a gourmet eatery in search of a good menu; it was previously billed as a California–Pacific Rim mix, but more recently it has moved more toward steak house fare with entrees from about $25 to $35.

The **Paradise Cafe** offers American and Chinese cuisine for $15 or less. Open Monday to Thursday, 7 A.M. to 2 A.M. and Friday to Sunday, all day.

Sam Boyd's Fremont Hotel & Casino. 200 East Fremont Street; 452 rooms; (702) 385-3232, (800) 634-6182. www.vegas.com/hotels/fremont/.

Street Casinos

Not all of the casinos in Las Vegas are billion-dollar enterprises with thousands of slot machines and spectacular settings. Some are small, full of character, and populated with characters. Some are so tacky you'll want to take a shower immediately after you make a break for the exit.

The best of the little places can be found in downtown along Fremont Street, which on a busy night becomes an outdoor block party with visitors strolling from one casino to the next.

Here are our four favorite street-level joints in downtown; you can stop in at all of them in a single visit.

Mermaid's

A lively storefront sawdust casino, all slots, bouncy music, and special promotions. In an earlier incarnation, this was Sassy Sally's Casino.

Mermaid's. 32 Fremont Street; (702) 382-5777.

Pioneer Club

The Pioneer Club, home of the huge animated neon cowboy sign on Fremont Street that locals know as "Vegas Vic," went dark in 1995, leaving a gap in the bridgework of the "Fremont Street Experience." There are hopes that Vic and his joint will be resurrected, perhaps by the Golden Nugget next door or another company.

La Bayou Casino

A vaguely New Orleans-themed storefront, formerly the Coin Castle.

La Bayou Casino. 15 East Fremont Street; (702) 385-7474.

El Cortez Hotel

A corner of this now-sprawling downtown casino and hotel, at the corner of Fremont and Sixth Streets, constitutes the oldest continuously operating casino in Las Vegas. The El Cortez opened in 1941 as a Western-themed casino and hotel with about eighty rooms. A fourteen-story, 200-room tower opened in 1983.

El Cortez. 600 East Fremont Street; 308 rooms; (702) 385-5200, (800) 634-6703.

The Clubs

You cannot come to Las Vegas without being assaulted by ads for "topless entertainment." We're not trying to influence you, but if that's what you want, two examples can be found on Fremont Street, under the skeletal protection of the space frame: the **Golden Goose** ("World Class Topless Girls") and **Glitter Gulch** ("Topless Girls of Glitter Gulch").

Chapter 9
Las Vegas Showrooms and Nightlife

Econoguide 2001: Best Production Shows
- ★★★★★ **Cirque du Soleil's Mystère.** Treasure Island
- ★★★★★ **Cirque du Soleil Presents O.** Bellagio
- ★★★★★ **EFX.** MGM Grand
- ★★★★★ **Siegfried & Roy.** Mirage
- ★★★★ **Blue Man Group.** Luxor
- ★★★★ **Danny Gans.** Mirage
- ★★★★ **Jubilee!** Bally's
- ★★★★ **Lance Burton.** Monte Carlo
- ★★★ **Les Folies Bergere.** Tropicana
- ★★★ **The Great Radio City Spectacular.** Flamingo Hilton
- ★★★ **Wayne Newton.** Stardust

With a few notable exceptions, some of the best entertainment buys in America can be found in Las Vegas, with lavish stage shows, superstars, and fabulous music. Why are the prices generally reasonable? In a word, gambling. Las Vegas, Inc., uses the shows and the buffets and anything else they can to try to lure you into the casino. You'll walk past every slot machine and gaming table they can possibly put in your way between the front door and the showroom; then you'll have to walk back past them on your way out.

Before you buy your ticket, be sure you understand what's included. A common deal includes two drinks, usually from a selection of house brands; both drinks are usually served before the show begins. Additional drinks and snacks are billed at lounge prices. Some shows offer dinner, again usually from a limited menu (and rarely worth writing home about). The final question is: does the ticket include gratuities for your servers?

Another important thing to know about Vegas shows: in the past, most of the shows did not offer assigned seating and you were at the mercy of the maître d'. High rollers, and those who slipped the guy at the door $10 or $20 or more, got the best tables. Recently, though, many of the showrooms have gone over to assigned seats, on a first-come, first-served basis; high rollers still get the very best places. In any case, there are very few really bad seats in the showrooms, which are most often designed to be wider than they are deep with a lot of front row tables across the very wide stage.

The worst seats will put you at a long table perpendicular to the stage. You will share your evening with ten or twelve strangers at the table. The best seats, although usually not the closest, are the first tier of couch-like booths.

Production Shows

The major shows tend to settle in for long runs, but nothing is forever. Be sure to call beforehand; you'll need a reservation for most shows in any case.

Many of the Las Vegas revues include scantily clad or topless dancers, and many comedy acts are R-rated; some showrooms have PG-rated early shows for families and those easily offended (what are you doing in Las Vegas in the first place?).

Bally's. Jubilee! ★★★★ Singing, dancing (some topless), and fantastic production numbers. Tuesday and Sunday 7:30 P.M., Saturday, Monday, Wednesday and Thursday 7:30 and 10:30 P.M. Dark Tuesday. $49.50 to $66 including tax. Must be 18. (702) 739-4111.

Bellagio. Cirque du Soleil presents O. ★★★★★ Friday through Tuesday 7:30 and 10:30 P.M. Dark Wednesday and Thursday. $100 main floor, $90 balcony. (702) 693-7722.

Boardwalk. The Dream King. ★★ Daily 8:30 P.M. except Sunday and Monday. $27.95. (702) 730-3194.

Excalibur. Tournament of Kings. ★★ Production show with live jousting, sword fighting and pyrotechnics. Dinner shows nightly at 6 and 8:30 P.M. $36.95 with meal. (702) 597-7600.

Flamingo Hilton. Flamingo Showroom. The Great Radio City Spectacular with the Rockettes. ★★★ Dinner show 7:45 P.M., cocktail show at 10:30 P.M. Dinner from $52.50; cocktail show $42.50 with two drinks. Dark Friday. (702) 733-3111.

Flamingo Hilton. Bugsy's Celebrity Theatre. Forever Plaid. ★★★ Nightly 7:30 and 10 P.M. $24.95. Dark Monday. (702) 733-3333.

Harrah's Las Vegas. Takin' It Uptown, starring Clint Holmes. ★★ Nightly 7:30 P.M., plus 10 P.M. on Thursday and Saturday. $49.45. Dark Wednesday. (702) 369-5222.

Imperial Palace Hotel. Imperial Theatre. Legends in Concert. ★★ 7:30 and 10:30 P.M. nightly. Dark Sunday. $34.50, including two drinks. (800) 351-7400, (702) 794-3261.

Jackie Gaughan's Plaza. Boylesque with Kenny Kerr. ★★ Shows at 8 and 10 P.M. except Sunday and Monday. $31.85. (702) 386-2444.

Luxor. Luxor Theater. Blue Man Group. ★★★★ Sunday and Monday at 7 P.M., Wednesday to Saturday, 7 P.M. and 10 P.M. Dark Tuesday. $60.50 and $71.50. (702) 262-4400 or (800) 557-7428.

Luxor. Luxor Live Theatre. Lasting Impressions with Bill Acosta. ★★★ Sunday at 7:30 P.M. and 10 P.M., Tuesday at 7:30 P.M. and 9:30 P.M., Wednesday to Saturday 7:30 P.M. Dark Monday. $29.95. (702) 262-4400.

Mandalay. Mandalay Theatre. Call for shows. (702) 632-7580.

MGM Grand. Grand Theatre. EFX. ★★★★★ A dancing, singing, and special effects spectacle with a cast of 70. Nightly 7:30 and 10:30 P.M. Tuesday through Saturday. Dark Sunday and Monday. $51.50 for upper level seating, $72 preferred seating, and $37 for children 5–12. (702) 891-7777, (800) 929-1111.

The Mirage. Siegfried & Roy Theatre. ★★★★★ Siegfried and Roy magic spectacle. Twice nightly at 7:30 and 11 P.M. Dark Wednesday and Thursday. $95. Appearances forty weeks of the year. (702) 792-7777.

The Mirage. Danny Gans Theatre. **Danny Gans.** ★★★★ Tuesday through Thursday and Saturday and Sunday at 8 p.m. $67.50 and $90. (702) 796-9999.

Monte Carlo. Lance Burton Theatre. ★★★★ Lance Burton, Master Magician. Tuesday through Saturday 7 and 10 P.M. Dark Sunday and Monday. $34.95 for main floor and mezzanine seats; $44.95 for balcony. (702) 730-7160 or (800) 311-8999.

New York–New York. Michael Flatley's Lord of the Dance. ★★★ Tuesday, Wednesday, and Saturday at 7:30 and 10:30 P.M. Thursday and Friday 9 P.M. Dark Sunday and Monday. $50 during week, $60 Friday and Saturday. (702) 740-6815.

Rio. Copacabana Showroom. David Cassidy with Sheena Easton. ★★★ Nightly Wednesday to Friday and Sunday at 8 P.M., Tuesday and Saturday at 7 P.M. and 9:30 P.M. $58, includes 1 drink. (702) 252-7776.

Riviera Hotel. Splash Theatre. Splash. ★★★ Musical variety nightly at 7:30 and 10:30 P.M. Adults only. $40.50 or $50.50 for VIP seating. (702) 794-9433.

Riviera Hotel. La Cage Theater. An Evening at La Cage, starring Frank Marino. ★★★ Nightly at 7:30 and 9:30 P.M., plus 11:15 P.M. show on Wednesday. Dark Tuesday. $22.95, including two drinks. (702) 794-9433.

Riviera Hotel. Crazy Girls adult entertainment. ★★ Nightly 8:30 and 10:30 P.M., midnight show on Saturday. $20.95, including two drinks. Dark Monday. (702) 794-9433.

Riviera Hotel. The Riviera Comedy Club. Nightly at 8 and 10 P.M., plus 11:45 P.M. on Friday and Saturday. $15.95, including two drinks. (702) 794-9433.

San Remo. Les Trix. ★★ Nightly at 8 and 10:30 P.M.. $25.99, including two drinks. Dark Monday. (702) 597-6028.

Showboat. Call for show information. (702) 385-9164.

Stardust Hotel. Wayne Newton Theatre. Wayne Newton. ★★★ Monday to Friday at 9 P.M., Saturday at 8 P.M. and 11 P.M. Dark Sunday. $49.95, including one drink. (702) 732-6325.

Stratosphere Tower. American Superstars. ★★ Sunday to Tuesday at 7 P.M., Wednesday, Friday and Saturday at 7 P.M. and 10 P.M. Dark Thursday. $29.65. (702) 380-7711.

Treasure Island. Cirque du Soleil's Mystère. ★★★★★ Wednesday through Sunday 7:30 and 10:30 P.M. Dark Monday and Tuesday. $75. (702) 894-7722, (800) 392-1999.

Tropicana Hotel. Tiffany Theatre. The Best of Folies Bergere. ★★★ Music and dance show. Dinner show 7:30 P.M. (covered show; children 5 and older are permitted), admission starts at $46.95. Topless show at 10 P.M.; children must be

16 years and older. Admission starts at $41.95. Dark Thursday. (702) 739-2411.

The Venetian. C2K Showroom. André-Philippe Gagnon. ★★★ Wednesday through Sunday at 7 p.m. $45, $75, and $92.

Celebrity Shows

Boulder Station. Railhead Saloon. (702) 432-7575.

Caesars Palace. Circus Maximus Showroom. (702) 731-7333, (800) 445-4544.

Desert Inn. Crystal Room. (702) 733-4566.

Gold Coast. Gold Coast Showroom. (702) 367-7111.

Hard Rock Hotel. The Joint. (702) 226-4650.

Las Vegas Hilton. Showroom. (702) 732-5755.

Mandalay. Mandalay Bay Events Center. (702) 632-7580. House of Blues. (702) 632-7580.

MGM Grand. Hollywood Theatre. (702) 891-7777. MGM Grand Garden. Ice shows, sporting events, celebrity shows.

New Frontier. Gilley's Saloon. (702) 794-8200.

The Orleans. Orleans Showroom. (702) 365-7075.

Palace Station. Trax. (702) 367-2411.

Rio. Club Rio. (702) 252-7776.

Riviera. Mardi Gras Plaza. (702) 794-9433.

Sahara. Congo Room. (702) 737-2515.

> **On the rocks.** The drinking age in Nevada is twenty-one, and in most of the state there are no closing hours for liquor sales or consumption. Visitors from states that have more restrictive laws will be surprised to see other laxities, including free drinks at casinos. You don't suppose the casinos (and their partner the state) are happy to see customers a bit loosened, do you?

A Selection of Nightclubs Outside of the Casinos

The Beach. Sports bar and club. 356 Convention Center Drive. (702) 731-1925.

Club Utopia. It takes all sorts: techno, hip hop, acid jazz, and reggae on various nights and in various rooms. 3765 Las Vegas Boulevard South. (702) 736-3105.

The Drink. A celebration of booze. 200 East Harmon Avenue. (702) 796-5519.

The Hop. 1650 E. Tropicana Avenue. (702) 310-5060.

Play It Again Sam. Eat, drink, and be moody in a re-creation of Rick's Café Americain from Casablanca. 4120 Spring Mountain Road. (702) 876-1550.

Tommy Rocker's Cantina & Grill. A misplaced beach bar, home of the Las Vegas Parrot Head Club. 4275 South Industrial Road. (702) 261-6688.

Chapter 10
Mama Don't Allow No Gambling 'Round Here: Area Attractions

Econoguide 2001: The Best Attractions in and Around Las Vegas
Casino Attractions
- ★★★★ **Masquerade Show in the Sky.** Rio Suite
- ★★★★ **Volcano.** Mirage
- ★★★★ **Fountains at Bellagio.** Bellagio
- ★★★★ **Fremont Street Experience**
- ★★★★ **Caesars Magical Empire.** Caesars Palace
- ★★★★ **Imperial Palace Auto Museum.** Imperial Palace

Thrill Rides and Theme Parks
- ★★★★ **Adventuredome.** Circus Circus
- ★★★★ **Manhattan Express.** New York–New York
- ★★★★ **Race for Atlantis IMAX 3D Ride.** Caesars Forum Shops
- ★★★★ **MGM Grand Adventures.** MGM Grand
- ★★★★ **Speedworld.** Sahara
- ★★★★ **Speed: The Ride.** Sahara
- ★★★★ **Star Trek: The Experience.** Las Vegas Hilton
- ★★★★ **Stratosphere Tower Rides.** Stratosphere Tower
- ★★★★ **Wet 'n Wild**

Although you sometimes have to squint through a forest of slot machines and neon lights to see it, there is life outside of the casinos. Hidden to most visitors to Las Vegas is a wide variety of cultural and outdoor activities.

Hardly qualifying as cultural highlights, but still fun are diversions such as **Caesars Magical Empire, MGM Grand Adventures, Grand Slam Canyon, Wet 'n Wild,** and **Star Trek: The Experience** at the Las Vegas Hilton.

★★★★Star Trek: The Experience at the Las Vegas Hilton

For decades, visitors to Las Vegas have been boldly going where no one has gone before. But all that is prologue to an extraterrestrial thrill at the Las Vegas Hilton, a one-of-a-kind $70 million collaboration with Paramount Parks.

After a visit to the Museum of the Future—a collection of "real" artifacts, uniforms, and weapons from the Star Trek universe—you'll be escorted into a shuttlecraft. Everything seems to go well until your travel is interrupted by a transport beam. When the beam stops, you'll find yourself on the bridge of the Federation Starship *Enterprise*; what's more, you have passed through a temporal rift in the space–time continuum and have arrived in the year 2371.

According to Commander Will Riker, bad things are afoot: Captain Picard has been kidnapped, and the Klingons have hatched a plan to eliminate one of Picard's ancestors so that Picard will never be born. Apparently, someone in your group is that ancestor. So you'd better high-tail your way out of here.

And so you're off to take a Turbolift (you might call it a futuristic elevator) to the transport vehicle. That sounds like a good idea, until the Klingons somehow manage to latch on to your cab and send it into a free fall. (Your helpful elevator operator may inquire whether any of his passengers suffered "protein spills" on the way down.)

Finally, you're at the portal to the Shuttlecraft Goddard. Try to sit in one of the first three rows for the best view of your return voyage. The screens in front of you and overhead show a spectacular view of a battle in deep space that extends all the way down to a high-speed run through the Strip from the Excalibur Hotel to the Las Vegas Hilton.

The attraction is a few steps beyond the groundbreaking *Back to the Future* attractions at Universal Studios in Orlando and Hollywood, adding actors and several special effects to a whiz-bang multimedia motion platform. The simulator uses a six-axis platform, similar to those used to train military jet pilots and NASA astronauts. The cast of a few dozen actors does a good job of staying in character throughout the experience, which takes about twenty-two minutes.

There are two queues—the first leads from the entrance of a shopping promenade at the Hilton to the ticket windows, and a second more lengthy line winds its way past an exhibit of Star Trek artifacts known as the History of the Future to the entrance of the attraction itself. If the second queue is full when you arrive, you can expect about a forty-five-minute wait until you reach the attraction itself. Tickets are assigned to a specific boarding time and are available at the Hilton as early as three days in advance.

To experience the shuttlecraft ride/motion simulator, you must be at least forty-two inches tall. Pregnant women and people with heart or back conditions are advised not to visit. Photography is not allowed during the "Voyage Through Space." Alas, visitors cannot sit in the captain's chair on the bridge.

The casino and the promenade are open to visitors, without charge. Tickets for the Experience were priced at $15.95 in 2000; you could also visit just the museum for $10.05. Open daily from 11 A.M. to 11 P.M.

For information, call (888) 462-6535, (702) 697-8717, or visit the web page at www.startrekexp.com.

At **Quark's Bar and Restaurant**, you can be the first from your corner of the galaxy to sample Romulan Ale, a specially brewed blue beer. Other unusual concoctions include a Ferengi Freeze, Vulcan Volcano, and the Harry Mudd Martini. The Warp Core Breach for Two blends several rums, vodka, blue Cucaçao, cranberry, pineapple, grapefruit, guava, orange juice, grenadine, and more, served on a platform of dry ice. Specialty drinks range from about $5 to $14, higher when served in souvenir glasses.

At the 180-seat restaurant, specialties include the Talaxian Turkey Wrap, Dr. Bashir's Roasted Veggie Pizza, and Romulan Warbird, which looks very much like a charbroiled chicken breast in lemon, lime, and orange zest vinaigrette. There are also a few contemporary dishes from Sisko's Restaurant in New Orleans, including Bayou Linguini. Entrees range in price from about $8 to $18.

At the exit is the SpaceQuest Casino, a 20,000-square-foot area that has more than 430 slots and videogames. The slots have no handles; players pass their hand through a beam of light to spin the reels. Note that kids are not permitted to loiter at the casino, which is located at the show's exit.

You enter into a casino traveling through space. Overhead, a set of three huge "windows" display changing scenes of the galaxies, views that are rendered in high-resolution on computer. The earth appears out the windows, about 1,500 miles away: dawn over North America, noon over the Mediterranean Sea, sunset over Asia, and night over the South Pacific. If you watch carefully, you'll see intergalactic trucks delivering Pepsi (one of the more unusual commercials you're likely to see anywhere) as well as space limousines and taxis depositing visitors.

There are, of course, slot machines and blackjack tables . . . but these are tewnty-fourth-century money grabbers with fiber-optic lighting and multimedia effects. The spectacular roulette tables include fiber-optic elements, and computers read the drop of the ball and display winning combos; table games use hologram-like chips with an exploding SpaceQuest logo.

By the way, the SpaceQuest Casino is not the first Hilton in space; a Hilton hotel was featured on Space Station One in the film, *2001: A Space Odyssey* in 1968, and on Mars in *Total Recall* in 1990.

Star Trek: The Experience at the Las Vegas Hilton
Courtesy of Las Vegas News Bureau

★★★★ Speedworld at the Sahara

Here's your chance to experience most of the thrills and none of the risk of driving at 220 miles per hour around a Grand Prix racetrack: Speedworld at the Sahara is a high-tech hoot. Or, you can strap yourself into a slingshot roller coaster and cruise along the Las Vegas Strip at speeding ticket velocity.

Speed: The Ride burst through the front wall of the NASCAR Café and through the sign at the front of the Sahara in May of 2000. The unusual roller coaster sends riders up the starting hill with linear induction motors that propel the cars without old-fashioned chains; a second set of motors is out front of the casino along the Strip.

The coaster reaches a top speed of seventy miles per hour as it moves through the Sahara's huge marquee sign. After an inverted loop the cars climb up a nearly vertical incline and then fall backwards through the entire track, returning to the NASCAR Café after its two-minute trip.

Tickets for the coaster in 2000 were $6 for those fifty-four inches and taller.

The other fast attraction at the Sahara is **Speedworld**, created by a company that has manufactured flight and tank simulators for the military. This $15 million installation at the back of the Sahara casino, puts you within the cockpit of an Indy-class race car on a six-axis motion base with a 133-degree wraparound projection screen.

You can't flip the car, and crashes into the wall or another car register as a shudder; other than that, though, the feel of the simulator is said to be very close to the real thing. After my uncertain and somewhat dizzying trip around the track, I'm willing to take that on faith.

Strapped into place in a three-quarter scale Indy car, you'll feel the wind in your face and the tilt of the track. You can choose an automatic transmission, or shift for yourself with a semi-automatic clutchless system with six forward speeds. (The semi-automatic yields about a 10 percent boost in speed, but new drivers will have more than enough to worry about just staying on the track and probably should opt for the auto transmission.)

There are twenty-four cars, split into groups of eight. The groups can race separately or all cars can be on the track. There are two eight-minute courses, one a simulation of the Las Vegas Motor Speedway, and the other a somewhat unusual road course up the Las Vegas Strip (most of the major hotels and landmarks are recognizable along the way, but they don't quite match their locations on the map.) The course on the Strip is more interesting, but the Speedway is more challenging and realistic.

The attraction is open daily from 10 A.M. until 11 P.M. on Friday and Saturday and until 10 P.M. other nights. Tickets for a single race were $8 in 2000; drivers must be at least forty-eight inches tall and there is a weight restriction of 300 pounds for entry into the very tight confines of the simulator cockpit.

Even if you don't take a drive, it's worth the time to stand along the rail and watch the contestants; in Las Vegas, where almost anything goes, you might want to place a bet among friends about the results of any particular race. Car fans can also gawk at some real NASCAR, CART, and Indy cars parked in the aisles near the simulators.

The 3-D theater shows include an Iron Man Stewart off-road truck race (perhaps the best film), a stock car adventure with Richard Petty that ventures on and off the track, and an Indy Car Challenge. Tickets for the 3-D theater were $3 in 2000; visitors must be at least forty-two inches tall. (702) 737-2111.

★★★★ Caesars Magical Empire

Enter into a magical 2,000-year-old world of Caesar, with the help of some late twentieth-century technology. The theme of the Magical Empire is *Credus Quod Habes et Habes*, or "What you believe to be true is true." I took my family for an evening in the Empire, and here is what I believe: this is one of the most entertaining dinner shows in Las Vegas or anywhere else.

Visitors descend into catacombs that lie beneath Caesars Palace, with an entrance adjacent to the Caesars Palace Palatium Buffet and the Race Book.

The adventure begins in the **Chamber of Destiny**. On arrival, guests are escorted through the fog-filled **Catacomb Maze**, along an aqueduct of cascading waters, and down a hallway filled with artifacts and lined with imposing doorways. The journey ends at the ten dining chambers of the gods, each the site of a three-course meal for twenty-four guests.

You'll have your own personal stand-up comic/sorcerer as your host; he'll spill forth a combination of old Roman jokes and modern references, involving the small audience into his routine.

A typical menu includes a fine salad and nicely prepared chicken, salmon, veal, or vegetarian dishes. Unlimited wine and soft drinks are included.

By the way, we don't often comment on personal facilities, but in the case of the Magical Empire, be sure to check out the rest rooms in the catacombs. Whose face is that in the mirror?

Your dinner ends with your host disappearing before your eyes and reappearing at the back of the room.

After dinner, guests are free to wander through the other attractions of the Empire. The centerpiece is the **Sanctum Secorum**, filled with illusions and the Lumineria show, a combination of sound, light, a thirty-foot spiraling flame effect from the central pit, and a visit by the great Caesar himself. Flanking the large chamber are two elegant lounges, the **Grotto Bar** and the **Spirit Bar**, each home to its own small illusions and surprises, including Invisibella, the phantom piano player. Special cocktails are as much as $15 in a souvenir goblet.

There are, surprisingly, no blackjack tables in the sanctum and only a few poker machines at the bars. Near the Grotto Bar a "haunted" piano answers your questions with songs.

Finally, there are two theaters in the Empire. The **Secret Pagoda** presents masters of "close-up" magic in an intimate seventy-two-seat room. The **Sultan's Palace**, which seats 144, features top magicians for larger illusions.

The strong point of the Magical Empire is close-up magic, so you won't have to view a set of tigers on a video screen half a block away. Cards, balls, even magicians disappear in a small room.

Prices in 2000 were about $75.50 for dinner, with admission limited to ages 12 and older. Half-price tickets for children ages 3 through 10 are also available. Expect to devote about three hours to the experience. For reservations call (702) 731-7333 or (800) 445-4544.

Visitors at Caesars can also view the Fire and Fantasy Lumineria show for free from 11 A.M. to 4:30 P.M. And the central people mover from the Strip offers a peek into the Sanctum Secorum through the eyes of the dragon on the wall.

★★★★ MGM Grand Adventures

If Las Vegas is Disneyland for adults, then perhaps MGM Grand Adventures is Las Vegas for kids . . . of all ages. The theme park is small and somewhat limited but nevertheless offers some worthy diversions for an afternoon or evening away from the slot machines.*

The park has shrunk in recent years. Lightning Bolt, an indoor roller coaster that was too tame and too short was moved; the hokey Backlot River Tour and the Deep Earth Exploration simulator were closed. The hotel's swimming pool and a new convention center take up much of the former space.

The **Lightning Bolt** ride was moved to the back corner of the park and expanded. Out of the dark now, it is somewhat longer and faster, with 2,400 feet of track, two drops and a three-minute ride.

The **SkyScreamer** is claimed to be the world's tallest skycoaster. This is a very strange ride: participants are strapped into a harness and pulled backward to the top of a large arch and then set free to zoom forward toward the earth and then back up again. It's like a combination of a bungee jump and a roller coaster. Adult rides are about $35 for one person, $30 each for two, and $25 each for three riders; all prices include admission to the park.

There are eight "areas" in the tightly packed park: **Casablanca Plaza**, **New York Street**, **Asian Village**, **French Street**, **Salem Waterfront**, **Tumbleweed Gulch**, **New Orleans Street**, and **Olde England Street**. Scattered around the park you'll find a collection of fast food restaurants.

There are a number of strolling entertainers and mini-attractions, including my personal favorite: a sumo wrestling arena. The park came to a standstill with laughter one day as my two children, suited up in gigantic padded costumes and helmets, fulfilled their dream of whacking each other with mallets.

As you descend the escalator into the park from the MGM Grand, you'll arrive in Casablanca. Given a choice, most people go to the right, and that is the general flow around this park—a counterclockwise tour. Therefore, if the park is very busy you might want to go against the flow and head to the left.

Parisian Taxis is a bumper car ride with a few French street signs.

Are you ready to go **Over the Edge**? It's a pleasant little journey through a nostalgic old saw mill that has quaint scenery and rustic charm. This log flume ride takes you down into two wet dropoffs.

---

* If you're a fan of theme parks, you might want to pick up a copy of *Econoguide 2001—Walt Disney World, Universal Orlando* or *Econoguide 2001—Disneyland, Universal Studios Hollywood*, both by Corey Sandler and published by Contemporary Books.

The **Gold Rush Theatre** at the back of the park between Over the Edge and the relocated Lightning Bolt roller coaster has been used in the past for You're in the Movies, a high-tech entertainment that combines live action with video magic. The large **Magic Screen Theatre** is used for live stage performances. Various specialty acts rotate through the theater over the course of the year.

Grand Canyon Rapids is your basic raft ride (four to six per boat) through rapids and down a "blasting tunnel" drop; this is definitely a wet ride.

The **Dueling Pirates** show is a stunt performance that will entertain the kids pretty well. It does, though, suffer a bit by comparison to the (free) battle fought in the lagoon outside Treasure Island down on the Strip.

The park is outdoors, and nights and winter days can be a bit chilly. Check with the park for operating hours. In the off-season, the park is open from 11 A.M. to 7 P.M.; in the summer, the park can be open until as late as 10 P.M.

Admission rates can vary according to the season; in the dead of winter, the park has been closed or open only on a limited schedule. If you are traveling to Las Vegas in the winter and are promising the kids (or yourself) a day at the theme park, be sure to check with the park ahead of time for its schedule. Admission to the park was $12.95 in early 2000. For more information, call the park at (702) 891-7979.

Luxor

The hollow interior of the Luxor pyramid was originally conceived as an ancient Egyptian playground, featuring attractions created by special effects designer Douglass Trumbull (also responsible for the spectacular *Back to the Future* ride at Universal Studios in Orlando, Florida). The attractions, alas, proved to be somewhat of an ancient dud.

In Search of the Obelisk is a fifteen-minute simulation that includes a runaway elevator into the tomb and then a frenzied chase sequence within a pyramid with some interesting special effects. Tickets were $7 in 2000. **King Tut's Museum** includes an audio guided tour. Tickets were $5 in 2000. The **IMAX 3D Theatre** offers films projected on a 68-by-84-foot screen; 3-D films employ the IMAX Personal Sound Environment, a headset that incorporates liquid crystal shutters synchronized to the film. Tickets were $8.95 in 2000.

Luxor sold a "Master Pass" in 2000 priced at $23.95; it included admission to the Obelisk show, the Museum, and three IMAX films. (702) 262-4000.

★★★★ The Adventuredome

Only in Las Vegas could they come up with something like this: **The Adventuredome**, a five-acre indoor entertainment park that presents a Las Vegas–eye view of the Grand Canyon, including 140-foot man-made peaks, a ninety-foot re-creation of Havasupai Falls, and a river. The entire park, attached to the **Circus Circus Hotel and Casino** is covered by a pink space-frame dome known as an Adventuredome. It was originally dubbed **Grand Slam Canyon.**

The **Fun House Express** multimedia experience is a computer simulation of a roller coaster ride that uses 3-D IMAX images projected onto a 180-degree video screen and three pitching and bucking fifteen-seat theaters. Guests must be forty-two inches or taller for the four-minute ride. There's a story, too: it seems that Jimmy the clown is mad at his boss; so he sends visitors to his rickety old fun house ride on a drop into . . . Clown Chaos.

The park includes the world's only indoor double-looping roller coaster. If you're not already dizzy from the gambling, the neon, the buffets . . . then you are ready for the **Canyon Blaster** at Grand Slam Canyon. I'm not sure I was ready, but I went for a ride anyway; I survived, but I'm having a hard time reading the notes I took while on the ride.

You'll know this is a serious ride as you walk around The Adventuredome; the floor shakes beneath your feet as the cars rumble by. The Canyon Blaster emphasizes speed and twists and turns over height; its track circles in and around much of the sphere. There are two loops, two corkscrews, and some interesting views of the hotel and the Strip if you keep your eyes open.

The **Rim Runner** is a three-and-a-half-minute indoor water flume ride, with much of the raft ride in the dark. "This is a wet ride. You will get soaked," warn the signs. In case you are not fully prepared, the gift shop sells disposable ponchos for a dollar or two.

Grand Slam Canyon is open every day and into the night; call for current hours. Admission is free and in 2000, individual tickets cost $3 to $6, depending on the ride. An unlimited-rides pass sold for $16.95 for those forty-eight inches and over, $12.95 for those thirty-three to forty-eight inches, and free to

The Canyon Blaster speeds by a dino in The Adventuredome
Photo by Corey Sandler

the littlest visitors. Circus Circus has changed its admission policy numerous times in recent years.

The busiest times at the park come weekends and holidays, with nighttime crowds larger than in the morning and afternoon. (702) 794-3939.

★★★★ Wet 'n Wild

For a cooling antidote to a hot day on the Strip, try Wet 'n Wild, located south of the Sahara Hotel/Casino on Las Vegas Boulevard South.

The park, which operates from about May 1 to October 1 of each year, includes **Royal Flush**, which sends riders down one of a pair of chutes at speeds of up to forty-five miles per hour and into a fog bank.

Bomb Bay is about as close as you are likely to get to a free-fall; think of it as a bungee jump without the bungee. One person at a time slips into a capsule at the top of a seventy-six-foot-high water slide, which is then moved into a vertical position with the lucky occupant standing almost straight up inside. Then the bottom drops out and the rider drops nearly straight down the watery chute.

The **Banzai Banzai** is a double-slide water coaster, allowing a pair of riders to race each other down to a 120-foot-long runway pool at the bottom.

There are, of course, a few slightly less wild but just as wet rides, too. Ticket prices in 2000 were $25.95 for adults, $13 for seniors, children forty-eight inches and shorter are $19.95, children younger than 3 years old are free. *You will find a discount in the coupon section of this book.*

Wet 'n Wild. 2600 Las Vegas Boulevard South; open in season; call (702) 737-7873 for information. www.wetnwild.com.

★★ Flyaway Indoor Skydiving

Only in Las Vegas would this sound only slightly out of the ordinary: a vertical wind tunnel powered by an airplane propeller.

Lucky participants fly in a column of air twelve feet across and twenty-two feet high, moving at airspeeds of up to 115 miles per hour. They wear flight suits and helmets, but no parachutes are necessary. And yes, there is a heavy-duty screen between divers and the engines' propeller.

Training classes are scheduled every half hour and the whole experience takes about an hour, including a fifteen-minute flight session shared by five flyers.

In 2000, prices for a first flight were $35. Check with Flyaway for height, weight, and age restrictions. Hours of operation are generally 10 A.M. to 7 P.M. daily, and until 5 P.M. on Sunday.

Flyaway. 200 Convention Center; (702) 731-4768.

★★★★ Manhattan Express at New York–New York

People actually pay for this: the Manhattan Express is the world's first roller coaster to feature a "heartline" twist-and-dive maneuver. A heartline roll is similar to the sensation felt by a pilot during a barrel roll, when the center of rotation is the same as the passenger's center of gravity. In the twist-and-dive

The Manhattan Express loops around the New York skyline
Photo by Corey Sandler

portion of the ride, the train rolls 180 degrees, suspending riders eighty-six feet above the casino roof before diving directly under itself.

The portion of the ride visible from the Strip is only a small piece of the fun; most of the track runs out back over the parking lot. A good view of the track is from the sidewalk on Tropicana, or from across the road at Excalibur.

Riders board sixteen-passenger trains from within the New York–New York casino and then ascend a 203-foot lift. The first drop of seventy-five feet is just a warm-up for the fifty-five-degree, 144-foot second drop that passes within a few feet of the hotel's valet entrance at sixty-seven miles per hour. The ride is also unusually long, lasting just short of four minutes; it will probably seem a lot longer to you.

Tickets for the coaster are $10. The ride is open Sunday through Thursday from 10 A.M. to 11 P.M., and until midnight on Friday and Saturday.

There are lockers near the entrance for personal possessions—you don't want to carry anything droppable from the coaster.

New York–New York also includes one of the largest arcades and carnival game rooms in town. For information, call (702) 740-6969.

★★★★ Race for Atlantis IMAX 3D Ride at Caesars Forum Shops

The metropolis of Atlantis comes to life within the Forum Shops of Caesars Palace, the first permanent giant-screen IMAX 3D motion simulator ride.

According to tradition, the winner of a chariot race between the gods held every thousand years becomes ruler of Atlantis for the next millennium.

Mama Don't Allow No Gambling 'Round Here 121

Humans are chosen to race their chariots against a field of fierce competitors, including Neptune, the reigning monarch, and Ghastlius, champion of evil.

The ride was created by the team that produced Back to the Future—The Ride at Universal Studios in Hollywood and Orlando, an attraction that is considered one of the benchmarks of amusement parks.

This is the first permanent giant-screen IMAX 3D motion simulator thrill ride. The screen is eighty-two feet in diameter, and four twenty-seven passenger motion simulator bases can move in any of six directions. Also, the ride is home to the world's largest indoor water-based fog system.

Riders are outfitted with an E3D electronic headset, which includes the IMAX Personal Sound Environment system and the liquid crystal shutters that, when synchronized via infrared signal with the IMAX 3D projector, produce the ride's immersive environment.

Adults $9.50, children younger than 12 $6.75, seniors over 55 $8.50.

Race for Atlantis. Forum Shops, Caesars Palace; (888) 910-7223.

★★★★ The Stratosphere Tower

The **Stratosphere Tower**, the nation's tallest free-standing observation tower at 1,149 feet, is topped off by a pair of the highest thrill rides in the world: the **Big Shot** zero gravity simulator, and the **Let It Ride High Roller**, the world's highest roller coaster, starting at 909 feet above the ground and zooming around the Tower's pod.

The **Let It Ride High Roller** travels around on the top of the tower on 1,865 feet of track; the nine four-passenger cars make three clockwise rotations around the tower, banking at thirty-two-degree angles.

The **Big Shot** ride was designed by a major bungee jumping company and offers the same sort of a straight up-and-down terror ride, thrusting sixteen passengers 160 feet in the air along a 228-foot mast extending like a needle from the top of the tower. Traveling at speeds of up to forty-five miles per hour, the ride shoots passengers from the 921-foot level of the tower to the 1,081-foot level and then lets them freefall back to the launching pad. Riders experience up to four Gs as they near the top, and negative Gs on the way down.

In 2000, tickets for the elevator to the top of the tower were $6 for adults ($10 including a buffet meal), and $3 for seniors and children ages 4-12 ($7 with the buffet.) Tickets for the elevator and the High Roller were $9; for the Big Shot $10, and for both rides and the elevator, $14. You could add a buffet to the price for $4 more during the week or $7 on weekends. For information, call (702) 380-7777.

Museums

Barrick Museum of Natural History. University of Nevada at Las Vegas's collection includes a selection of lizards, snakes, and spiders guaranteed to make your skin crawl; there's also an impressive display of arrowheads. On the campus of UNLV at 4505 South Maryland Parkway; open Monday through Friday, 8 A.M. to 4:45 P.M., and Saturday 10 A.M. to 2 P.M.

Boulder City Hoover Dam Museum. Historic artifacts of the construction of Hoover Dam. Open daily 10 A.M. to 5 P.M. and Sunday noon to 5 P.M. Admission is adults $2, children $1 and seniors $1. 1305 Arizona Street in Boulder City; (702) 294-1988.

Clark County Heritage Museum. A collection of area history, including railroad rolling stock and memorabilia; Heritage Street, a collection of historic homes in a park setting; and a time line from prehistoric to current times. Open daily except holidays, 9 A.M. to 4:30 P.M. Adults $1.50, children $1. 1830 South Boulder Highway; Henderson; (702) 455-7955.

Guinness World of Records Museum. Part of an expanding chain of exhibits under license from the famous recorder of world records and strange accomplishments, the museum includes models and replicas that inform about such things as the largest number of hard-boiled eggs eaten at one sitting, the smallest ridable bicycle, the largest human being, the world's oldest man.

The museum in winter is open every day from 9 A.M. to 5:30 P.M. and in summer until 7:30 P.M., at 2780 Las Vegas Boulevard South, on the Strip north of Circus Circus and across from Wet 'n Wild and the Sahara Hotel/Casino; call (702) 792-3766 for hours and information. Adults $4.95, $3.95 for students and seniors, and $2.95 for children ages 5 to 12. *You will find a discount in the coupon section of this book.*

Imperial Palace Antique Auto Collection. With more than 200 antique and classic cars, one of the most impressive collections anywhere. One corner of the museum is a room full of twenty-five or so Duesies worth more than $50 million; classic Duesenberg cars, including Jimmy Cagney's 1937 Model J. More contemporary and a bit more flashy is Liberace's pale cream 1981 Zimmer Golden Spirit, complete with candelabra. There is, of course, an Elvis car: a pale blue 1976 Eldorado. Also on display is a 1938 Cadillac V-16 touring sedan (with backseat bar) owned by W. C. Fields.

Presidents Row includes John F. Kennedy's 1962 Lincoln Continental "Bubbletop," Lyndon Johnson's 1964 Cadillac, Dwight Eisenhower's 1952 Chrysler Imperial, Harry S. Truman's 1950 Lincoln Cosmopolitan, Franklin D. Roosevelt's 1936 V-16 Cadillac, and Herbert Hoover's 1929 Cadillac.

From the darker side of history are vehicles including Al Capone's 1930 V-16 Cadillac, Adolf Hitler's 1936 Mercedes-Benz 770K, Benito Mussolini's 1939 Alfa Romeo, and Emperor Hirohito's 1935 Packard.

And in keeping with the generally offbeat atmosphere of Las Vegas, also on display is Howard Hughes's 1954 Chrysler, which comes equipped with an elaborate air purification system in the trunk intended to protect Hughes from the germs that afflict us mortals.

The oldest cars on display include an 1897 Haynes-Apperson, a two-cylinder, four-seat surrey that ran on naptha; and an 1898 LaNef, a three-wheeler with tiller steering. Rare cars include a few Tuckers, a 1903 Lenawee, and a 1913 Stanley Steamer bus.

The museum is open every day from 9:30 A.M. to 11:30 P.M. Listed prices are $6.95 for adults and $3.95 for children 5 to 12. Free tickets are usually available in the casino. Open daily; 3535 Las Vegas Boulevard South; (702) 731-3311.

Las Vegas Art Museum. Three galleries that offer displays of local and national artists changing monthly. The main building was constructed in the

1930s from wooden railroad ties. Open Tuesday through Saturday, 10 A.M. to 5 P.M., and Sunday 1 to 5 P.M. Within Lorenzi Park, 3333 Washington Avenue. Admission $3 adults, $2 children, students $1; (702) 360-8000.

Las Vegas Natural History Museum. Wildlife, an educational gift shop, and a nice collection of dinosaurs, including the skull of a T-rex. Open daily from 9 A.M. to 4 P.M.; 900 Las Vegas Boulevard North; adults $5.50, students and seniors $4.50, children (4 to 12) $3; (702) 384-3466. *You will find a discount in the coupon section of this book.*

Las Vegas Southern Nevada Zoological Society. Nevada's only public zoo, the small collection includes a Bengal tiger, a lion, a few monkeys, and indigenous wildlife; there's also a petting zoo. 1775 North Rancho; (702) 648-5955.

Liberace Museum. "Mr. Showmanship" is gone, but the glitter remains. Much of his collection of costumes, pianos, candelabras, and cars stands vigil in this museum, operated by The Liberace Foundation for the Performing and Creative Arts, which provides educational grants to schools and colleges.

Some of his outfits were wilder than those worn by showgirls on the Strip, including a suit made of ostrich feathers. There are some eighteen Liberace-special pianos, five Liberacemobiles, including a Rolls Royce covered with mirror tiles; and jewelry including a piano-shaped ring containing 260 diamonds in a gold setting with ivory and black jade keys.

The main museum includes the Piano, Car, and Celebrity Galleries; the annex includes the Costume and Jewelry Galleries and a re-creation of Liberace's office and bedroom from his Palm Springs home. The library includes personal mementos including a lifetime's press clippings and photographs.

The museum is five minutes east of the Strip on Tropicana in a strip mall. The collection is spread amongst three sites: a collection of pianos and cars is found in a freestanding building near Tropicana; and two storefronts in the plaza display some of Liberace's fabulous outfits, furniture, and personal effects, including photos. There is, of course, a gift shop; it's one of the only places I know where you can buy fake rhinestone vests and all manner of piano-themed neckties, scarves, and costume jewelry.

Treasures of the museum's collection include:
- an empress chinchilla and blue silk brocade outfit valued at $600,000;
- a $1 million Rolls Royce Phantom V Landau Limousine, one of only seven made, covered with rhinestones and mirror tiles and formerly used to drive Liberace on stage for grand entrances;
- red, white, and blue jeweled hot pants worn at a Radio City Music Hall celebration of the hundredth birthday of the Statue of Liberty; and
- a fabulous antique desk reputed to be among the possessions of Czar Nicholas II, taken from the Imperial Palace in St. Petersburg and sold after the Russian Revolution. Almost Alice in Wonderland–like with loopy curves and filigrees, Liberace used it in the office of his Tivoli Gardens Restaurant.

The museum is located at 1775 East Tropicana Avenue; (702) 798-5595. The minimum tax-deductible donation is $6.95 for adults, $4.95 for seniors and students. Children younger than 12 are admitted free. Open Monday to Saturday 10 A.M. to 5 P.M.; Sunday 1 to 5 P.M.

Lied Discovery Children's Museum. A hands-on place for kids, including Toddler Towers, a model of the Space Shuttle, a radio station, a collection of computer toys, and more. Tuesday to Sunday 10 A.M. to 5 P.M. Closed Monday except most school holidays. Across from Cashman Field, 833 Las Vegas Boulevard North; adults $5, juniors (2 to 17) and seniors $4; (702) 382-3445. *You will find a discount in the coupon section of this book.*

Lost City Museum of Archeology. Artifacts and interpretations of Pueblo Grande de Nevada, the so-called Lost City of the Anasazi Indians, who occupied the area for about 1,200 years until the year 1150. Located in Overton, sixty miles northeast of Las Vegas via I-15, at 721 South Highway 169; adults $2. Open daily from 8:30 A.M. to 4:30 P.M.; (702) 397-2193.

Nevada State Museum & Historical Society. The history of southern Nevada from the dawn of native culture some 13,000 years ago to the present, including the Hoover Dam, Nevada's role as a nuclear test site, and its mining industry. Take I-95 to Valley View. 700 Twin Lakes Drive in Lorenzi Park. Admission $2; children younger than 18 free. 9 A.M. to 5 P.M.; (702) 486-5205.

Searchlight Museum. A small outpost of the Clark County Heritage Museum, it chronicles the history of the former mining town of Searchlight and the story of famed Hollywood fashion designer Edith Head and screen stars Clara Bow and Rex Bell, all of whom lived there. Open daily 9 A.M. to 4:30 P.M. Admission $1.50 adults, children 3 to 15 and seniors $1, younger than 3 free. Searchlight Community Center, sixty miles south of Las Vegas; (702) 297-1682.

Commercial Attractions

Bonnie Springs Ranch/Old Nevada. *See the section on Red Rock Canyon in Chapter 15.* Highway 159, 23 miles west of Las Vegas. Open seven days a week from 10:30 A.M. to 5:30 P.M., with tickets priced at about $6.50 for adults, seniors $5.50, and $4 for children; (702) 875-4191.

Secret Gardens. Mirage Hotel, 3400 Las Vegas Boulevard South; open 11 A.M. to 3:30 P.M. weekdays, 10 A.M. to 3:30 P.M. weekends. Closed Wednesday. Admission $10, children under 3 free; (702) 791-7188.

Holy Cow Brewery Tour. Self-guided tours are offered weekdays at 11 A.M., 1 and 3 P.M. 2423 Las Vegas Boulevard South; (702) 732-2697.

Omnimax Theatre. A giant dome theater, just off the gambling floor and a better bet for families and adults than most other entertainment on the Strip. Caesars Palace, 3570 Las Vegas Boulevard South; (702) 731-7900.

White Tiger Habitat. Mirage Hotel. 3400 Las Vegas Boulevard South; open 24 hours; free admission; (702) 791-7111.

Dance

Academy of Nevada Ballet Theatre. (702) 898-6306.
　Department of Dance Arts, UNLV. (702) 895-3827.
　Las Vegas Civic Ballet Association. (702) 229-6211.
　Theatre Ballet of Las Vegas. (702) 458-7575.

Chapter 11
Local Protocol: Sex, Marriage, Shopping, Comps, and Tipping

Sex, Sex, Sex

There, I got your attention, didn't I? That is the philosophy of Nevada, too, and especially Las Vegas. The casinos and hotels and just about everything else in town are tied to sex, from the costumes on the cocktail waitresses, the togas on the greeters at Caesars Palace, and the production shows to the more-directly-to-the-point topless bars.

Getting past the idea of sex as tease, there is also a small but apparently thriving industry in prostitution in much of the state.

Prostitution is perhaps no more common in Nevada than it is in most other parts of the country, and certainly on a par with most convention and entertainment centers. It is, though, legal in several parts of the state, and there are about 36 legalized houses or "ranches" in the state. The industry is centered just outside of Reno and up or down the road from Las Vegas. For the record, the Nevada Supreme Court upheld the rights of the counties to legalize and regulate brothels; Clark County, which includes Las Vegas, and Washoe County, home of Reno, are among the few that do *not* permit brothels.

In Las Vegas, though, the streets are littered with brochures from "escort" services that offer what they describe as "in-room entertainment" and other such euphemisms. And Reno is ringed by special service companies.

Many of the companies masquerade as massage services ("Cathy's College Girls of Reno Hotel Guest Massage Service"), entertainment bureaus ("Plato's Retreat"), or escort services.

Among the brothels are the Cherry Patch Ranch an hour out of Las Vegas, the Mustang Ranch 1, six miles east of Reno in Lockwood, and the Sagebrush Ranch just outside of the state capitol in Carson City.

In this day and age it would be remiss of us not to warn that using the services of a prostitute is a highly dangerous activity. There is the chance of exposure to disease, including AIDS; and there is the possibility of being robbed on the street or in your hotel room. For what it is worth, the safest place to pay for sex is at one of the regulated brothels. In any case, a much safer diversion

> **This explains a lot, doesn't it?** As if Las Vegas wasn't already one weird place, consider the fact that fifty or so miles north and west of town is the neighborhood nuclear test site.
>
> From its start in the depths of the Cold War in 1951 through today, there have been nearly 700 tests of nuclear bombs. At first, the explosions were conducted in the atmosphere and it was not an unusual sight to see a mushroom cloud cresting over downtown Las Vegas. Since the 1960s, the explosions have taken place underground.
>
> The Nevada Test Site at Yucca Flat is part of the huge Nellis Air Force Range. The test site is 1,350 square miles, about the size of the entire state of Rhode Island. In case you had your heart aglow in anticipation of a tour, though, we're sorry to disappoint you: the entire area is off-limits.

is to read the entertainment section of the *Yellow Pages* in your hotel room for a few dirty laughs.

Getting Hitched

Speaking of more socially acceptable forms of expression, the idea of Las Vegas as a wedding—and divorce—mecca dates back to the same "anything goes" mentality that gave birth to the gambling industry and other adventures. Today, Las Vegas and Reno continue to have a thriving wedding industry, offering the added lure of the grand hotels and casinos. More than 100,000 couples tie the knot in Las Vegas each year.

If you are impressed by celebrity name-dropping, check out some of the ads or billboards for the wedding chapels. According to the proprietors, those who have done the deed at their establishments include Joan Collins, Mia Farrow, Eddie Fisher, Michael Jordan, Jon Bon Jovi, Demi Moore, Dudley Moore, Mickey Rooney, Frank Sinatra, Elizabeth Taylor, and Bruce Willis.

Most of the major hotels offer elegant chapels for ceremonies ranging from the ridiculous to the sublime. You can get married dressed as King Arthur and Guinevere at the Excalibur, in a toga at Caesars Palace, or as just about anything else at any of a number of chapels. And there are dozens of small establishments that do nothing else but service the needs of the betrothed.

The busier chapels will require advance reservations, but many of the chapels in Las Vegas can also deal with walk-in customers. For those in a hurry, there is a drive-up window at the Little White Chapel, where for about $30 and a few minutes you can kiss the bride before you get back into traffic. At the other end of the spectrum—but by no means the limit to what you can spend—the MGM Grand Hotel & Casino has a $1,000 package with a room and a rented maid of honor and best man.

If you are planning to get married in Las Vegas, check with the County Clerk's office for the current legalities. For recorded information on marriages in Clark County, call (702) 455-4415. You can also obtain information about the process on a web page at www.co.clark.nv.us/recorder/recindex.htm.

Civil Ceremonies

If you want to have a quick civil ceremony in Las Vegas you can hop over to the office of the Commissioner of Civil Marriages at 136 South Fourth Street, one block from the Marriage License Bureau. You can walk in single and stroll out married during the same hours that the County Clerk is open. The fee for a ceremony is $25 Monday through Friday from 8 A.M. to 5 P.M., and $30 for late nights, weekends, and holidays.

You must have at least one witness besides the person performing the ceremony. Don't count on finding an extra clerk in the office; people have been known to hire strangers from the street for a quick stand-in.

Chapel Ceremonies

For many visitors, though, a civil ceremony at the commissioner's office is not what it is all about. Instead, they want to do it up in grand (by Las Vegas standards) style at one of the dozens of wedding chapels. You can get just about anything you want, from a choir of Elvis impersonators to a chapel on wheels to a ceremony in King Arthur's Court. Rates vary and reservations are necessary at some—but not all—of the chapels.

> **Wedding cam.** You can take a peek inside the Little White Chapel and see weddings in progress on the internet, at www.discovery.com/cams/wedding/wedding.html.

Here is a listing of some:

A Chapel by the Courthouse. 201 Bridger Avenue; (702) 384-9099, (800) 545-8111.
Candlelight Wedding Chapel. 2855 Las Vegas Boulevard South; (702) 735-4179.
Chapel of the Bells. 2233 Las Vegas Boulevard South; (702) 735-6803.
Chapel of Love. 1431 Las Vegas Boulevard South; (702) 387-0155.
Cupid's Wedding Chapel. 827 Las Vegas Boulevard South; (702) 598-4444.
Graceland Wedding Chapel. 619 Las Vegas Boulevard South; (702) 474-6655.
Las Vegas Wedding Gardens. 200 West Sahara Avenue; (702) 387-0123.
Little Chapel of the Flowers. 1717 Las Vegas Boulevard South; (702) 735-4331.
Little Church of the West. 4617 Las Vegas Boulevard South; (702) 739-7971.
Little White Chapel. 1301 Las Vegas Boulevard South; (702) 382-5943, (800) 545-8111.
San Francisco Sally's Victorian Chapel. 1304 Las Vegas Boulevard South; (702) 385-7777.
Silver Bell Wedding Chapel. 607 Las Vegas Boulevard South; (702) 382-3726.
Wee Kirk o' the Heather. 231 Las Vegas Boulevard South; (702) 382-9830.

Here are some of the hotel chapels in Las Vegas:

Bally's Wedding Chapel. Bally's Casino Resort; (702) 892-2222.
Canterbury Wedding Chapel. Excalibur Hotel & Casino; (702) 597-7260.
Circus Circus Chapel of the Fountains. Circus Circus Hotel/Casino; (702) 794-3777.
Plaza Chapel. Union Plaza Hotel; (702) 386-2110.
Riviera Royale Wedding Chapel. Riviera Hotel; (702) 794-9494.
Shalimar Wedding Chapel. Shalimar Hotel; (702) 382-7372.
We've Only Just Begun Wedding Chapel. Imperial Palace; (702) 733-0011.

Money, Money, Money

Arriving with foreign currency? No problem. Every major casino will be glad to exchange your marks, yen, bucks, or pounds, or whatever, into cash—or gambling chips. They'll extract a fee in the form of a discount from the actual exchange rate; you will probably get the best deal at a commercial bank.

Travelers checks are no problem at hotels, casinos, restaurants, or stores in Las Vegas; some places may require a photo ID card.

Need to cash a check? No problem for guests at a major hotel, although some establishments may enforce a limit on the amount they will release each day. At the casinos, the cashier will often cash checks for clients known to the casino, or in some way guaranteed by a credit card.

Need a loan? Most casinos will extend "markers" (credit vouchers) to gamblers who apply for such a loan in advance of their visit. Unsecured loans on the spot are more difficult to obtain.

Need a cash advance? Most major casinos have installed automated teller machines that permit withdrawal of cash from bank accounts or as cash advances against credit cards. Bank machines generally work with one of the national syndicates such as Plus, Cirrus, or Instant-Teller. If you choose to take a cash advance, be sure to read the disclaimer on the machine carefully; some systems apply a hefty service charge to the amount of money you are withdrawing, over and above any interest the holder of your credit card will charge.

A notch down on the pecking order are check-cashing businesses that specialize in out-of-state personal checks, money orders, and even savings account passbooks. You'll need personal identification, and you can expect to pay a fee that will increase with the complexity of the verification and transfer of funds.

And then there are the pawnshops of Las Vegas, filled with jewelry, cameras, furs, and other items left behind to raise cash. There are more than four pages of listings in the local phone book. If you are that desperate for cash, perhaps you should seek counseling of a different sort than is available in these pages.

Comprehending Comps

Let's get one thing out of the way: there is no such thing as a free lunch, not even in Las Vegas.

There are, however, "comp" lunches, breakfasts, dinners, drinks, hotel rooms, shows, airline tickets, and more. That's comp as in complimentary, but as we say, they're not quite free.

The distinction is this: almost all of the casinos in Nevada offer all sorts of freebies to gamblers. They do so because they know that, over the long haul, they will win and you will lose.

The system starts with free drinks for players, which is actually one of the more insidious come-ons in marketing. Not only does it encourage players to sit at the slot machine or at the gaming table, but alcohol dulls the senses, reduces inhibitions, and otherwise aids in the removal of cash from your wallet.

The next step up is the provision of free meals. At a smaller casino, the process might be as simple as this: the pit boss, perhaps alerted by the dealer to your consistent gambling, will drop by and hand you a card good for dinner. It might be a free pass to the coffee shop or the buffet, or you may be "comped" into the gourmet restaurant. Either way, it's a reward for playing at the casino, and it also keeps you on the premises before and after the meal.

At larger casinos, the process has become a bit more complicated. Ask the floor manager or the pit boss to "evaluate" your play; he or she may actually

Local Protocol: Sex, Marriage, Shopping, Comps, and Tipping 129

chart your bets or may consult with the dealer. Generally, a comp rating will be given based on several hours of play at a consistent level.

Many casinos now use electronic means to track the play of visitors at slot and video poker machines; they will issue a magnetically coded card that is placed in readers attached to the slots to record the amount of action. The cards can be cashed in for free meals or shows after a certain amount of play. You can also be monitored while you are playing by casino hosts watching the results of your play on a computer monitor.

A tip: you can increase your "action" by having both halves of a couple play on the same account.

Some casinos have a slightly less sophisticated means of tracking slot players, relying on records kept by change booths or strolling change attendants. There is, of course, more of an opportunity to cheat here; one scheme would be to change a few hundred dollars in bills into coins but only play a small portion of the silver.

It doesn't hurt to ask one of the supervisors about how you can be evaluated. If you don't like the answer, you can always take your business elsewhere.

It all comes down to the amount of "action" you will provide the casino. Action is the amount of money you will put at risk over a particular period of time. For example, if you bet $25 per hand in blackjack for four hours a day over a three-day weekend, you are giving the casino something like $7,500 in action; at most middle-of-the-road casinos that should be worth a free hotel room for the length of your stay.

There is no official rulebook to the distribution of comps. Smaller casinos more desperate to attract action may be more generous than the bigger places. However, the most spectacular casinos—places such as Caesars Palace and the Mirage—offer the most spectacular comps to the highest of rollers. The two-story, 4,000-square-foot Fantasy Suites at Caesars Palace, for example, are described by the casinos as "priceless" because they cannot be rented by guests. They are offered as comps, along with free meals, room service, shows, limousine service, and other amenities to people for whom money must truly hold no meaning.

According to insiders, the serious freebies start at about the $25 per hand level for free rooms. "RFB" players, who receive rooms, food, and beverages, generally are $75 to $125 per hand gamblers. The penthouses, limousines, and other perks are usually offered at about the $150 per hand level.

Some hotels are more up front about their comp programs than others. For example, the Flamingo Hilton in Reno issues a rate card for players in its Club Flamingo slot system, which uses a magnetic card to record action.

At the Flamingo Hilton in Reno, players can earn rewards ranging from a pair of free passes to the buffet to meals at the coffee shop or food court to admission to the Heavenly Bodies showroom and, for the highest rollers at the slots, free meals at the Top of the Hilton gourmet restaurant.

Playing time is based on six handle pulls per minute (once every ten seconds) using the maximum number of coins for each machine. In other words, if you are playing at a $1 machine, the club payoffs are based on betting the maximum number of tokens—usually five—for that machine. Fewer coins bet or fewer handle pulls per minute will require more playing time.

The quickest way to freebies is to play a $5 machine where you can obtain a dinner buffet, coffee shop, or food court pass for two for one hour of play. (At $25 per pull, six times a minute, this means you are risking $9,000 in hopes of obtaining $20 worth of food.)

More reasonable requirements apply to the 25-cent machines. The Reno Hilton will give the same meals described above to a player who puts in five hours. (That's $1.25 per pull, six times a minute—a mere $2,250 in action.) For five hours of work. For $20 worth of food.

Of course, unless you are completely luckless, you should be able to avoid losing all of your money. Slot machines generally pay back between 90 and 99 percent of money bet. Remember, though, that this percentage applies over the very long haul and includes the very rare huge jackpot payoffs.

For table players, the Flamingo Hilton Reno offers comp packages that begin with discounts on hotel rooms for visitors willing to put down $10 at a time for four hours a day; free rooms for bettors playing $35 a hand for four hours a day; free room and buffet or coffee shop meals and drinks for $75 bettors; and free rooms, gourmet meals, and drinks for a player betting $100 at a time for four hours a day. If you are willing to bet even more and establish your credentials beforehand, the hotel will offer reimbursements of your airfare.

If you want to earn comps, keep in mind a few pointers. It is against your own interests to move from casino to casino, since you are diluting your influence in this way. (And don't think that casinos don't know this. That's why they have all of those "clubs" for loyal patrons.) And, if you change from one area of the casino to another, be sure that whoever is evaluating you is aware of where you are going and can transfer supervision.

Note that we have not talked about winning versus losing here. At any particular moment, the casino doesn't really care whether a player is ahead or behind. They know which way the dollars will eventually flow; in fact, if you're ahead of the game, they very much want you to stick around at their casino until the odds start to run the other way.

A Guide to Tipping

Las Vegas, Reno, and Lake Tahoe are very much dependent on the tourist and conventioneer, and tipping is an essential element of the economy. In fact, it has its own name in the casino: toking. You will have an extraordinary opportunity to grease the palms of dozens of strangers on your visit, but it's not necessary to pay everyone you meet.

Here's a guided tour to outstretched hands.

Transportation. The standard tip for taxi drivers is in the range of 15 percent to 20 percent of the fare; you might want to give more for a driver who helps with the bags or one who puts out his or her cigarette at your request.

Valet Parking. A tip of about $1 to $2 is standard.

Bartenders and Cocktail Waitresses. Most casinos offer free drinks to players at the tables and some extend the privilege to slot players; a tip of 50 cents per drink or $1 per round is standard.

Restaurant Servers and Room Service. Again, a tip in the range of 15 percent to 20 percent is standard. A sore point among some waiters and waitresses are visitors to buffets who don't leave money for the people who clear away your dishes and bring you drinks.

If you have received a free meal, check to see if your comp includes a gratuity for the staff; if it does not, you should leave a tip equal to 15 percent to 20 percent of what the bill would have been.

Bell Captains and Bellmen. The usual rate is about $1 to $2 per bag; give $1 or $2 to a bellman who summons a cab for you.

Bingo and Keno Runners. A small tip every few cards, and a larger tip with a winning card.

Dealers. A small tip, in the form of cash or a chip a few times an hour is standard. Some dealers might prefer that you place a small bet for them every once in a while, especially if you are winning; ask them how they'd like to be toked. In theory, this will not give you any special advantage at the table, but it might earn you more friendly treatment.

Maids. About $1 per day per person is standard; more if you have created an unusual amount of work or if extra services have been provided.

Showroom Maitre d'Hotel. In the past, nearly every casino showroom had a maitre d' out front who determined where each guest was seated. Ignore him and you might end up in the back corner behind the coffee pot; make him happy and you would end up down front and center. The current trend, though, is toward reserved seats at most shows—especially the more expensive ones. Therefore, tipping the maitre d'—if there is one—is optional.

Shop Until You Drop in Las Vegas

If you've got any money left in your wallet—or if you are traveling with a spouse who prefers to gamble on clothing or accessories instead of the roll of the dice—Las Vegas offers several major shopping areas.

Fashion Show Mall

The **Fashion Show Mall**, located directly on the Las Vegas Strip at 3200 Las Vegas Boulevard South, at the head of Convention Center Drive and next to the Mirage, is a large mall with some 150 shops, including a wide range of clothing and specialty stores. It is within walking distance of most Center-Strip motels and the Las Vegas Convention Center. Valet parking is available. Hours are Monday to Friday 10 A.M. to 9 P.M., Saturday 10 A.M. to 7 P.M., and Sunday noon to 6 P.M. For information, call (702) 369-8382.

Restaurants at the mall are a cut above your basic mall food court. They include **Chin's**, a gourmet Chinese restaurant. Dive! is a Los Angeles import with involvement by movie director Steven Spielberg. It puts diners within a re-creation of a submarine with simulated underwater scenes moving past the "windows"; the menu includes a range of subs, of course, including the nuclear

Sicilian Sub Rosa, Fajita Sub, and Soft Shell Crab Sub. **Sfuzzi** is a gourmet Italian restaurant. Another import is **Morton's**, a well-known steak house.

Women's Fashions: Abercrombie & Fitch; Ann Taylor; Benetton; Cache; Casual Corner; Contempo Casuals; Judy's; Lillie Rubin; Liz Claiborne; The Limited; Marshall-Rousso; Mondi; Nicole Miller; Petite Sophisticate; Private Collections; Talbot's; Wet Seal.

Shoes: Bally of Switzerland; Bianca; Brass Boot; Footlocker; Joyce-Selby; Lady Foot Locker; Leeds; Norman Kaplan; Rococo; Scarpe.

Cards, Gifts, Toys, and Books: Carlan's Gifts; Discovery Channel; Disney Store; Expanding Wall; Papyrus; Serendipity Gallery; Waldenbooks.

Art Galleries: Centaur Sculpture; Gallery of History; Rock & Hollywood Gallery, Southwest Spirit, Walt Disney Gallery, Wyland Galleries.

Apparel, Specialty: Banana Republic; Miller Stockman Western Ware; North Beach Leather; St. Croix Shop; Victoria's Secret.

Men's and Family Apparel: Abercrombie & Fitch; Benetton; Brats; Custom Shop Shirtmakers; Camouflage; The Gap; Harris & Frank; JW; Lauren & The Boys; Melwan's; Miller's Outpost; Oak Tree; Schwartz Big & Tall; Shirt Shoppe; Steve Gordon's; Uomo Uomo Sport; Zeidler & Zeidler.

Jewelry: Bailey Banks & Biddle; Chainery; Fashion Shop Jewelry; Gold Factory; Lundstrom Jewelers; Weisfield's; Whitehall; Zales.

Specialty: Abercrombie & Fitch; Antique Emporium; Bag & Baggage; Collegetown USA; Electronics Boutique; El Portal Luggage; Futuretronics; Gallery of Collectibles; Gloria Jean's Coffee Bean; La Perfumerie; Lenscrafters; Louis Vuitton; Omni Chemists; Sam Goody's; San Francisco Music Box; Sharper Image; Suncoast Motion Picture; Sun Shade Optique; Tennis Lady Tennis Man; Vignettes.

Department Stores: Dillard's; Macy's; May Company; Neiman-Marcus; Saks Fifth Avenue.

The Boulevard Mall

The **Boulevard Mall** is a typical group of shops decorated with plants under an atrium. There's an open, bright feeling—sort of like being outdoors. It is located at 3528 South Maryland Parkway, at the intersection with Desert Inn Road, about five minutes east of the Strip. It claims the mantle as the largest mall in Nevada. Hours are 10 A.M. to 9 P.M. weekdays, from 10 A.M. to 8 P.M. on Saturdays, and 11 A.M. to 6 P.M. on Sundays. For information, call (702) 735-8268.

Accessories: Afterthoughts; Best of Times; Carimar; Claire's Boutique; Sporting Eyes; Sunglass Designs.

Men's Apparel: Coda; Harris & Frank; J. Riggings; JW; Oak Tree; Pacific Wave; Schwartz' Big & Tall; Structure; Zeidler & Zeidler.

Men's and Women's Apparel: Colorado; County Seat; The Gap; GapKids; Going to the Game; Gymboree; Hot Cats; Howard & Phil's Western; Sports Logo; Wilson's Leather Experts.

Women's Apparel: Cacique; Casual Corner; Charlotte Russe; Contempo

Casuals; Express; Lane Bryant; Lerner; The Limited; Petite Sophisticate; Roland's of Las Vegas; Victoria's Secret; Wet Seal.

Cards, Gifts, and Specialty: African & World Imports; Amy's Hallmark; Bath & Body Works; The Body Shop; Country Hutch; Disney Store; Hot Topic; Just a Buck; The Mole Hole; The Nature Co.; San Francisco Music Box Co.; Sanrio Surprises; Sesame Street General Store; Spencer; Things Remembered; Tinderbox; Trader's West.

Services: Glamour Shots; Great Expectations Hair Salon; iNatural Cosmetics; Kiddie Kandids; Lens Crafters Optique; Prestige Travel; Stark Express Shoe Repair; Styles Hair Salon; Trade Secret Beauty Salon.

Shoes: Bostonian; Dolci's; Famous Footwear; Foot Action; Foot Locker; Kids Foot Locker; Kinney Shoes; Lady Foot Locker; Leed's; Naturalizer; Nine West; Wild Pair.

Pets, Hobbies, and Entertainment: B. Dalton Bookseller; Champs Sports; Energy Express; Frisky Pet Center; KayBee Toy & Hobby; Radio Shack; Ritz Camera; Sam Goody; Software Etc.; Suncoast Motion Picture Co.; Wherehouse Records.

Home Furnishings: The Bombay Co.

Jewelers: Bailey Banks & Biddle; The Chainery; J. Burton Jewelry; Lundstrom Jewelry; The Jewelers; Tiffin's Jewelers; Whitehall Jewelers; Zales.

Department Stores: Broadway Southwest; Dillard's; Marshall's; JC Penney; Sears; Woolworth's.

The Meadows Mall

North of Downtown near U.S. 95 at Valley View Boulevard, the 140-store two-level mall includes Dillard's, The Broadway, JC Penney, and Sears. The mall provides its own Downtown Trolley that shuttles back and forth to the Downtown Transportation Center. Open weekdays from 10 A.M. to 9 P.M., and weekends, on Saturday from 10 A.M. to 7 P.M. and on Sunday from 10 A.M. to 6 P.M. For information call (702) 878-4849.

Factory Outlets

Belz Factory Outlet World. 7400 Las Vegas Boulevard South, I-15 at the Blue Diamond exchange, south of Las Vegas. Open daily 10 A.M. to 9 P.M., and Sunday 10 A.M. to 6 P.M. Call (702) 896-5599.

Stores include Adolfo II; Amity Leather; Afterthoughts; Aileen; Bass Apparel; Blue Wave; Bon Worth; Bruce Alan Bags; Bugle Boy; Burlington Brands; Buxton; Carter's Childrensware; Chez Magnifique; County Seat; Corning/Revere; Crown Jewels; Danskin; Designer Labels for Less; Ducks Unlimited; Ellen Ashley; Hushpuppies; Kitchen Collection; Kitchen Place; Leather Loft; L'egg's/Hanes/ Bali; Levi's; Lucia; Music 4 Less; Naturalizer; Nike; Oneida; Osh Kosh b'Gosh; Perfumania; Pfaltzgraff; Prestige Fragrance; Publishers Warehouse; Ribbon Outlet; Ross Simons; Ruff Hewn; Springmaid Wamsutta; Stone Mountain Handbags; Stride Rite; Swank; Toy Liquidators; Trader Kids; Van Heusen; Village Hatter; Westport Ltd.; Whims/Sarah Coventry; and Young Generations.

Other Stores

Here are a few of our favorite stores located outside of shopping malls.

Bare Essentials. Leather, lace, and lingerie—the stuff of life. 4029 West Sahara; (702) 247-4711.

Bell, Book & Candle. 1725 East Charleston Boulevard; (702) 386-2950. Crystal balls, magic potions, and classes in witchcraft.

Bookstar. 3910 South Maryland Parkway; (702) 877-1872. One of the largest and best-stocked bookstores anywhere. And it's open late into the night; stop off on the way to the airport.

Cowtown Boots. 2989 South Paradise Road. (702) 737-8469. A factory outlet for handmade leather boots from cowhide to snakeskin to Teju Lizard.

Desert Indian Shop. 108 North Third St.; (702) 384-4977. Art and artifacts of the west.

The Magic Shop. Riviera Hotel; 2901 Las Vegas Boulevard South; (702) 696-9869.

Sunglass City. 506 Fremont St.; (702) 388-0622. The eyes have it; watches, too.

If you're determined to bring a bit of Las Vegas home with you (and if you've left a bit of money in your wallet or on your credit card) you may want to visit one of several stores that sell gambling equipment. Be sure you investigate state and local laws before you bring back machines.

Bud Jones Co. 3640 South Valley View Boulevard; (702) 876-2782. Casino supplies, offered to the public, too.

Gamblers Book Club. 630 South Eleventh; (702) 382-7555; (800) 634-6243. They take their games seriously here, offering the biggest collection of gambling arcana we know of, as well as a fine collection of local history, travel, and fiction.

Gamblers General Store. 800 South Main Street; (702) 382-9903. Open to the public for slot machines, poker machines, personalized poker chips, and craps tables.

Paul-Son Dice and Card. 2121 Industrial Road; (702) 384-2425. Gambling equipment, including used dice and cards from major casinos.

And for those with a very special predilection, you may want to visit the **Seventh Dimension** shop for your spiritual articles and metaphysical supplies. They apparently prefer ESP instead of telephone numbers; you may, or may not, find the place on Las Vegas Boulevard North at Charleston Boulevard

China in Las Vegas

There's a little bit of Asia about a mile west of the Strip, in the 4000 block of Spring Mountain Road. The **Las Vegas Chinatown Plaza** includes Chinese and Vietnamese restaurants, an Asian supermarket, and jewelry and gift shops with wares from around the world. For information, call (702) 221-8448.

Feeling Lucky?

Earlier in this chapter we mentioned the sad fact that some visitors to Las Vegas end up leaving more than merely their money behind; pawnshops are well stocked with rings, necklaces, musical instruments, cameras, and just about anything else that can be carried in for quick cash at a deep discount.

If you are a particularly adventurous shopper and you are able to tell the difference between a dud and a diamond, an Instamatic and a Nikon, and a Gibson and garbage you may want to go to a pawnshop to buy.

Be aware that most of these operations are not in the nicest parts of town, and few spend any money at all on decorations. There are more than a dozen pawnshops in Las Vegas and many more throughout the state; for some reason, they seem to be clustered wherever you find casino districts.

Hail Caesars!

And then there are the **Forum Shops at Caesars**, which has to qualify as among the most otherworldly, spectacular shopping venues anywhere in the world. In other words, perfectly appropriate for Las Vegas.

The storefront facades and common areas are designed to appear like an ancient Roman streetscape, with huge columns and arches, central piazzas, ornate fountains, and classic statuary.

Overhead, on a barrel-vaulted ceiling, a painted dome emulates the Mediterranean sky. The sky turns from daylight to sunset to dawn to full daylight over the course of two hours; the sun rises in the east and sets in the west.

And just when you thought The Forum Shops at Caesars had reached its outlandish limit, consider this: work was expected to begin by mid-2000 on yet another expansion, of another 250,000 square feet.

A re-creation of the Pantheon, one of the greatest architectural masterpieces in Roman history, will serve as the focal point of an entrance to a new, multi-level specialty retail, restaurant and entertainment complex, which will connect to the existing Roman-themed shopping plaza at Caesars Palace.

The Pantheon, flanked by a pedestrian plaza, will be a 150-foot-high replica of the majestic Roman icon and will stand at the northeast corner of the Caesars Palace property.

An earlier expansion added the Roman Great Hall, an eighty-five-foot-tall open space featuring "Atlantis," a show that merges human and animatronic figures. *See Chapter 10 for details.*

The area includes a huge FAO Schwarz store, with a giant hobby horse parked like a Trojan Horse at its entrance; a spectacular two-floor Virgin Megastore selling music, books, and software; Gap and Gap Kids; Abercrombie & Fitch; Emporio Armani; Lacoste; The Polo Store/Ralph Lauren; and Niketown.

Restaurants include The Cheesecake Factory, Chinois (a Wolfgang Puck restaurant), and Torrefazione Coffee at the Virgin Megastore Cafe. And then there is the Caviarteria, which offers specialty foods; on a recent visit the menu included a smoked wild boar sandwich for $8, Icelandic gravlax for $10, and a Caspian caviar sampler: beluga, oscetra, and sevruga from $25 to $100, depending on the size of the portion. Caviarteria is a branch of the New York and Beverly Hills originals.

A gathering place is the Atlantis statue at the back of the addition. Atlas, Gadrius, and Alia struggle to rule Atlantis while projected images on walls simulate a descent to the ocean floor and smoke, fire, fog, and fountains fill the air. The whole thing is surrounded by a 50,000-gallon saltwater aquarium.

The Forum Shops
Courtesy of Las Vegas News Bureau

Realistic animatronic statues appear at least as lifelike as some slot machine players at three in the morning. Shows are presented daily on the hour, beginning at 11 A.M.

The Forum Shops were attached onto the north side of Caesars Palace, and the main entrance connects to the main casino. There is now an entrance and exit at the far end of the Forum Shops, allowing visitors to come into the shops without having to meander through the casino, or saving the need to double back at the end of a tour; the door may not be open in the evening, though.

Amazingly, there are no casinos within the Forum Shops area itself—although there are a few banks of slot machines right by the entranceway just to ease the transition. It has to be the only place in the world where an actor dressed as Bugs Bunny (at the Warner Brothers Studios Store) poses within thirty feet of slot machines.

The Forum shops are open daily from 10 A.M. to 11 P.M., and until midnight Friday and Saturday; some restaurants and shops are also open earlier and later.

At the casino entrance to the mall is the **Quadriga** statue, four gold-leafed horses, a charioteer, and five heroic arches, an ancient symbol of great achievement. (*Quadriga* is a Latin word for a team of four, and is pronounced *kwod-reye-ja*.) As you look at the fountain, Jupiter is perched up top. Mars faces Gucci. Diana the Huntress checks out Louis Vuitton, and Venus and Plutus keep an eye on the casino.

At the far end of the U-shaped mall is the spectacular **Festival Fountain.** It may look like marble, but it is not; every hour on the hour, starting at 10 A.M., the statuary comes to life.

Local Protocol: Sex, Marriage, Shopping, Comps, and Tipping

In the animated tableau, Bacchus, god of merriment and wine, hosts a party with Apollo, Plutus, and Venus. The seven-minute show stars Bacchus, who has already had more than a few sips from his goblet. He enlists the power of Apollo (god of music), Venus (goddess of love), and Plutus (god of wealth) in preparing a party for all of the guests gathered around his fountain.

When the party is over, the statues return to marble-like silence. The statues are on a rotating platter and make a complete circle.

The best seats are probably on the floor, about ten or fifteen feet back from the statues. Young kids may become fidgety after a minute or two, and most adults will not want to see the show a second time. Like most free entertainment in Las Vegas, it's worth every penny you pay for it.

Also within is an outpost of the **Disney Store** chain, among the most unusual locations for such a wholesome outlet: inside a gambling casino next to a Victoria's Secret and across from Planet Hollywood.

Women's Fashions: Ann Taylor; Bebe; Caché; Express Compagnie Internationale; Plaza Escade; St. John.

Specialty Apparel: A/X Armani Exchange; Beyond the Beach; The French Room; Gianni Versace; Gucci; Guess; North Beach Leather; Rose of Sharon—Size 14 and Up; Versus; Victoria's Secret.

Specialty Shops: Animal Crackers; Antiquities; Brookstone; Christian Dior; Davante; Disney Store; Endangered Species; Field of Dreams; Kids Kastle; Louis Vuitton; Magic Masters; Magnet Maximus; Museum Company; Porsche Design; Sports Logo; Stuff'd; Sunglass Hut; Warner Brothers Studios Store; West of Santa Fe.

Men's Apparel: Bernini; Cuzzens; Kerkorian; The Knot Shop; Structure; Vasari.

Jewelry: Bulgari; M. J. Christensen; N. Landau Hyman; Roman Times; Zero Gravity.

Shoes: Avventura; Just for Feet; Shoooz at the Forum; Stuart Weitzman; Via Veneto.

Art Galleries: Galerie Lassen; Thomas Charles Gallery.

Food: Bertolini's; Chocolate Chariot; La Salsa; Palm Restaurant; Planet Hollywood; Spago; Stage Deli; Sweet Factory; Swensen's Ice Cream.

Warner Brothers Studios Store. Look up over the entrance for statues of Sylvester the Cat, the Tazmanian Devil, and Daffy Duck—in togas! The inscription over the door reads "Warnerius Fraternus Studius Storius," which is a rough Latin approximation for Warner Brothers Studios Store.

Inside the shop, let your eyes drift upward to spot the Gremlins hiding at ceiling level. At the back of the store is a video wall showing snippets of classic and current WB movies and cartoons. A pair of computer paint programs allows kids to colorize their own cartoons. Nearby is Marv's Matomic Service, a crawl-through space for kiddies.

And then there are the things on sale: sweatshirts, T-shirts, stuffed animals, toys, and souvenirs with a Warner's theme, for children of all ages. Also on sale is a selection of original cels from WB cartoons, with prices ranging from about $100 to $7,000 and more.

Just for Feet. An "interactive shoe store" with more than 100,000 pairs of sports shoes in a 12,000-square-foot space that includes a small basketball court and a treadmill so customers can try out their footwear in real situations. They've even got tennis shoes for babies.

Magic Masters. A wood paneled room designed to look like Houdini's library. (Check out some of the framed photographs on the wall.) There's a secret door to the left of the counter that leads to a small room where secrets are unveiled to the buyer.

Chinois. Wolfgang Puck shares the marquee with his wife Barbara Lazaroff with a wide-ranging Asian menu; small entrees are priced at about $15 to $20. Items on a recent visit included Thai basil shrimp, stir-fried Hoisin pork, and spicy Shanghai noodles.

Palm Restaurant. An elegant extension of the famed New York eatery. Among its offerings is a $12 prix-fixe lunch menu that includes petite filet mignon, prime rib, or pasta. Dinner offerings include seafood crab cakes for $26, a New York strip steak for $27, and a 36-ounce double steak for two for $57; a variety of salads is also available.

Planet Hollywood. Don't count on meeting the Hollywood film star of your dreams; they're busy counting their money earned from this successful chain of fancified burger joints decorated with cinema stuff. You can contribute, though: hamburgers are $6.50, vegetable burgers $6.75, barbecued pizza goes for $9.95, and a Mexican shrimp salad for $10. Dinner platters include St. Louis Ribs for $12.95, and grilled ranch chicken for $10.95. There is also a merchandise counter out front where you can purchase Planet Hollywood merchandise.

Spago. Not your average pizzeria. Specialties at the open-air cafe, which sits under the beautiful artificial Roman sky, include spicy chicken pizza with caramelized red onions and chili pesto for $12; Mediterranean fish soup with lobster and couscous for $24, and grilled tuna with tomato-fennel salsa and crisp smoked salmon ravioli for $23.

Bertolini's. The most spectacular setting in the Forum, this "sidewalk cafe" Italian eatery faces the Fountain of the Gods. Specialties include unusual pizzas for about $9 and pasta dishes from about $10 to $14. It's the place to see and to be seen at, although the noise of the water in the fountain can become a bit overbearing.

Porsche Design. "Design is neither form nor function alone, but the synthesis of the two." So says F. A. Porsche, grandson of the legendary automaker Ferdinand Porsche; he began as a designer at the Porsche plant in Stuttgart where he was instrumental in the design of the famed 904 and 911 series of cars. He went on to set up his own design house in the Austrian town of Zell am See, working for clients including makers of motorcycles, large-screen televisions, cameras, computers, furniture, and lamps. In 1991, F. A. Porsche was named chairman of the family auto business.

His store showcases some of his company's elegantly functional forms, including sunglasses, pipes, and shavers.

Antiquities. Not to be missed, this unusual store facing the Festival Fountain is proof of the theory that one man's garbage is another's collectible investment. Where else can you buy a beautifully restored Coke machine, a classic jukebox, or a fortune-telling machine?

The owners of the store include among their treasure mines the backyards of the deep South and the cellars of Brooklyn; recovered items are repaired, repainted, and in some cases improved. Everything works just as it did when the items were new.

On one visit we found a 1942 Wurlitzer Model 950 Gazelle jukebox, the one with colored liquid bubbles and neon. Only 3,400 were made, and the unit on display required more than 300 hours of restoration. It was a bargain at $47,000.

Nearby was a 1940s coin-operated photo booth in working order for $9,800. Other unusual offerings included a restored 1937 Dodg'em bumper car and a Gypsy Grandma Fortune Teller from the 1940s. We saw a bleacher seat from the dear-departed Comiskey Park in Chicago; there are lots of autographed pictures and movie memorabilia, some more impressive than others.

Foto-Forum. Here's your chance to put your face on the body you've always dreamed of: a biker babe, a bikini beauty, or Southern belle for the ladies, or perhaps a hockey star, beefcake stud, or Hollywood leading man.

The shop uses computer and video wizardry to merge your face with images on file; the result can be a poster, a small portrait, a personalized coffee cup, or just about anything else.

According to the operators, the most popular image for men is (what else could it be in Las Vegas?) Elvis; for women, it's the chance to sit atop a pair of 50-D cups barely contained in a string bikini.

Cinema Ride. The Cinema Ride is a four-capsule virtual reality simulator "ride" located downstairs next to the Cyber Station video arcade. As intense as these kinds of movies are, this one is made even more frightening with the addition of 3-D glasses.

Tickets for the five-minute movies are priced at about $4; look for discount coupons at the time of your visit. You must be at least forty-two inches tall to gain admission.

The Venetian's Grand Canal Shoppes

The opulent Venetian Resort brought an indoor version of the Grand Canal of Venice to The Strip, an opulent competitor to the Forum Shops at Caesars Palace.

You can stroll down stone walkways along nearly a quarter mile of canalside shops and restauarants; many of the shops are the only ones of their kind outside of Europe.

The shopping district culminates at St. Mark's Square, beneath a seventy-foot ceiling filled with the ever-changing Venetian sky.

The mall is open Sunday to Thursday from 10 A.M. to 11 P.M., and until midnight on Friday and Saturday. For information, call (702) 414-4500.

Women's Apparel: Ann Taylor, Banana Republic, BCBG Max Azria, bebe, Burberry, Caché, For Joseph, Kenneth Cole, Lido Beach Shop, Lior, Marshall Rousso, Oliver & Co., Privilege, and Wolford.

Men's Apparel: Clothing and Accessories: Banana Republic; Bertone, Burberry, Kenneth Cole, Lio, Marshall Rousso, Oliver & Co., Pal Zileri, and Tino Cosma.

Specialty Shops: Acca Kappa, Ancient Creations, Brookstone, Canyon Ranch Living Essentials, Country Rock & Roll, Davidoff, Diamond Resorts, Dolcé due, Houdini's Magic, Il Prato, In Celebration of Golf, Lior, Lladro, Ripa de Monti, Rondo', Sephora, and Tolstoy's.

Shoes: Banana Republic, Cesare Paciotti, Jimmy Choo, Kenneth Cole, New Balance, Privilege, and Rockport.

Jewelry: Agatha, Ancient Creations, Bernard K. Passman Gallery, Ca' d'Oro, Erwin Pearl, Mikimoto, Movado, and Simayof Jewelers.

Children's Apparel & Toys: Kids Karnivale and Toys International.

Gifts: Brookstone, Buon Giorno, Ciao, and Godiva.

Restaurants: Canaletto, Chulas, Postrio, Taqueria Canonita, Tsunami, WB Stage 16 Restaurant, and Zefferino.

The Showcase Mall

Showcase Mall, North of the MGM Grand, the mall features four floors of unusual offerings, including M&M's World and Ethel M Chocolates (both offshoots of the Mars candy family). Open daily from 10 A.M. to midnight, and until 1 A.M. on Friday and Saturday. (702) 597-3122.

Chapter 12
An Index of Las Vegas Casinos, Hotels, and Motels

Like most everything else in Las Vegas, room rates are subject to the laws of supply and demand. During convention and holiday periods, a very ordinary motel room can command presidential suite rates; during quiet periods in the winter, some of the best rooms in town are offered for pocket change. The rates indicated here are approximations of standard rates.

$	$49 or less	♣	Casino/Hotel
$$	$50 to $99	LVBN	Las Vegas Boulevard North (Downtown)
$$$	$100 to $149	LVBS	Las Vegas Boulevard South (The Strip)
$$$$	$150 and more		

Alexis Park Resort. 375 East Harmon Avenue. (702) 796-3300, (800) 582-2228. $$$-$$$$
Algiers. 2845 LVBS. (702) 735-3311, (800) 732-3361. $-$$$
Ambassador East Motel. 916 East Fremont Street. (702) 384-8281, (800) 634-6703. $
Apache Motel. 407 South Main Street. (702) 382-7606. $-$$
Arizona Charlie's. ♣ 740 South Decatur Blvd. (702) 258-5200, (800) 342-2695. $-$$
Bally's Las Vegas. ♣ 3645 LVBS. (702) 739-4111, (800) 634-3434. $$-$$$$
Barbary Coast Hotel & Casino. ♣ 3595 LVBS. (702) 737-7111, (800) 634-6755. $$-$$$$
Bellagio. ♣ 3400 LVBS. (702) 693-7111. $$$-$$$$
Best Western Main Street Inn. ♣ 1000 North Main Street. (702) 382-3455, (800) 851-1414. $-$$$
Best Western Mardi Gras Inn. ♣ 3500 Paradise Road. (702) 731-2020, (800) 634-6501. $-$$$
Best Western McCarran Inn. ♣ 4970 Paradise Road. (702) 798-5530, (800) 626-7575. $$$-$$$
Best Western Parkview Inn. ♣ 905 LVBN. (702) 385-1213, (800) 528-1234. $$-$$$
Binion's Horseshoe Hotel & Casino. ♣ 128 East Fremont St., (702) 382-1600, Res. (800) 622-6468. $-$$
Blair House Suites. 344 East Desert Inn Road. (702) 792-2222, (800) 553-9111. $$-$$$$
Blue Angel Motel. 2110 East Fremont Street. (702) 386-9700. $-$$
Bonanza Lodge. 1808 East Fremont Street. (702) 382-3990. $-$$
Boulder Station. ♣ 4111 Boulder Hwy. (702) 432-7777, (800) 683-7777. $$-$$$$
Bourbon Street. ♣ 120 East Flamingo Road. (702) 737-7200, (800) 634-6956. $-$$$
Budget Inn Hotel. 301 South Main Street. (702) 385-5560, (800) 959-9062. $-$$
Budget Suites of America. 4625 Boulder Hwy. (702) 454-4625. $-$$$
Budget Suites of America. 1500 Stardust Road. (702) 732-1500, (800) 752-1501. $-$$
Caesars Palace. ♣ 3570 LVBS. (702) 731-7110, (800) 634-6661. $$$-$$$$
California Hotel Casino. ♣ 12 Ogden Street. (702) 385-1222, (800) 634-6255. $-$$

Capri Motel. ♣ 3245 East Fremont Street. (702) 457-1429. $–$$
Carriage House. 105 East Harmon Avenue. (702) 798-1020, (800) 225-2301. $$$–$$$$
Casa Malaga Motel. 4615 LVBS. (702) 739-8362. $–$$$
Casino Royale & Hotel. ♣ 3411 LVBS. (702) 737-3500, (800) 854-7666. $–$$$
Circus Circus Hotel & Casino. ♣ 2880 LVBS. (702) 734-0410, (800) 634-3450. $–$$$$
City Center Motel. 700 East Fremont Street. (702) 382-4766. $–$$
Comfort Inn-Central. 211 East Flamingo Road. (702) 733-7800, (800) 221-2222. $$
Comfort Inn-North. 910 East Cheyenne. (702) 399-1500, (800) 228-5150. $–$$$
Comfort Inn-South. 5075 Koval Lane. (702) 736-3600, (800) 228-5150. $–$$$
Convention Center Lodge. 79 Convention Center Drive. (702) 735-1315. $–$$
Crest Budget Inn. 207 North Sixth Street. (702) 382-5642, (800) 777-7737. $–$$$
Crowne Plaza. 4255 South Paradise Road. (702) 369-4400, (800) 227-6963. $$–$$$$
Daisy Motel & Apartments. 415 South Main Street. (702) 382-0707. $–$$
Days Inn Airport. 5125 Swensen Street. (702) 740-4040, (800) 325-2525. $–$$$
Days Inn Downtown. 707 East Fremont Street. (702) 388-1400, (800) 325-2344. $–$$$$
Days Inn Town Hall. ♣ 4155 Koval Lane. (702) 731-2111, (800) 634-6541. $–$$$
Del Mar Resort Motel. 1411 LVBS. (702) 384-5775. $–$$$
Desert Inn. ♣ 3145 LVBS. (702) 733-4444, (800) 634-6906. $$$–$$$$
Desert Moon Motel. 1701 East Fremont Street. (702) 382-5535. $–$$
Diamond Inn Motel. 4605 LVBS. (702) 736-2565. $–$$$
Domino Motel. 1621 South Main Street. (702) 384-6000. $
Downtowner Motel. 129 North Eighth Street. (702) 384-1441, (800) 777-2566. $–$$$
Econo Lodge. 1150 LVBS. (702) 382-6001, (800) 553-2666. $–$$$$
El Cortez Hotel. 600 East Fremont Street. (702) 385-5200. $
El Mirador Motel. 2310 LVBS. (702) 384-6570. $–$$
Excalibur Hotel/Casino. ♣ 3850 LVBS. (702) 597-7777, (800) 937-7777. $$–$$$$
Fairfield Inn by Marriott. 3850 Paradise Road. (702) 791-0899, (800) 228-2800. $$
Fitzgeralds Casino Hotel. ♣ 301 Fremont Street. (702) 388-2400, (800) 274-5825. $–$$
Flamingo Hilton Las Vegas. ♣ 3555 LVBS. (702) 733-3111, (800) 732-2111. $$–$$$
Four Queens Hotel. ♣ 202 Fremont Street. (702) 385-4011, (800) 634-6045. $$–$$$$
Sam Boyd's Fremont Hotel. ♣ 200 East Fremont Street. (702) 385-3232, (800) 634-6460. $–$$
Fun City Motel. 2233 LVBS. (702) 731-3155. $–$$$
Gables Motel. 1301 East Fremont Street. (702) 384-1637. $
Gateway Motel. 928 LVBS. (702) 382-2146. $–$$
Gatewood Motel. 3075 East Fremont Street. (702) 457-3660. $–$$
Gold Coast Hotel. ♣ 4000 West Flamingo Road. (702) 367-7111, (800) 331-5334. $–$$$$
Gold Spike Hotel. ♣ 400 East Ogden 89101. (702) 384-8444, (800) 634-6703. $
Golden Gate Hotel. ♣ 1 East Fremont Street. (702) 385-1906, (800) 426-1906. $–$$
Golden Inn Motel. 120 LVBN. (702) 384-8204. $–$$$
Golden Nugget Hotel. ♣ 129 East Fremont Street. (702) 385-7111, (800) 634-3454. $$–$$$$
Happy Inn. 3939 LVBS. (702) 736-8031. $–$$$
Hard Rock Hotel. ♣ 4455 Paradise Road. (702) 693-5000, (800) 693-7625. $$–$$$
Harrah's Casino Hotel. ♣ 3475 LVBS. (702) 369-5000, (800) 634-6765. $$–$$$$
Hawthorn Suites. 4975 South Valley View. (702) 798-7736, (800) 527-1133. $$–$$$$
High Hat Regency Motel. 1300 LVBS. (702) 382-8080. $–$$
Hitchin' Post RV Park & Motel. 3640 LVBN. (702) 644-1043. $–$$
Holiday House. 2211 LVBS. (702) 732-2468. $
Holiday Inn Casino–Boardwalk. ♣ 3750 LVBS. (702) 735-2400, (800) 635-4581. $$–$$$
Holiday Motel. 2205 LVBS. (702) 735-6464. $
Holiday Royale Apartment Suites. 4505 Paradise Road. (702) 733-7676, (800) 732-7676. $$$–$$$$
Hotel Nevada. 235 South Main Street. (702) 385-7311, (800) 637-5777. $–$$
Hotel San Rémo. ♣ 115 East Tropicana Avenue. (702) 739-9000, (800) 522-7366. $–$$$$

An Index of Las Vegas Casinos, Hotels, and Motels 143

Howard Johnson's at the Airport. ♣ 5100 Paradise Road. (702) 798-2777, (800) 634-6439. $–$$
Howard Johnson's. 1401 LVBS. (702) 388-0301, (800) 446-4656. $–$$$
Howard Johnson's Hotel & Casino. ♣ 3111 West Tropicana Avenue. (702) 798-1111. $–$$$
Imperial Palace Hotel. ♣ 3535 LVBS. (702) 731-3311, Res. (800) 634-6441. $–$$$
Jackie Gaughan's Plaza Hotel. ♣ 1 Main Street. (702) 386-2110, (800) 634-6575. $–$$$
Jackpot Motel. 1600 South Casino Center Blvd. (702) 384-7211. $
King Albert Motel. 185 Albert Avenue. (702) 732-1555, (800) 553-7753. $–$$
King 8 Hotel. ♣ 3330 West Tropicana Avenue. (702) 736-8988, (800) 634-3488. $–$$
Klondike Inn. 5191 LVBS. (702) 739-9351. $–$$$$
Knotty Pine. 1900 LVBN. (702) 642-8300. $
Koala Motel. 520 South Casino Center Blvd. (702) 384-8211, (800) 223-7706. $–$$
La Concha Motel. 2955 LVBS. (702) 735-1255. $–$$
La Palm Motel. 2512 East Fremont Street. (702) 384-5874. $–$$
La Quinta Las Vegas Airport. 3970 Paradise Road. (702) 796-9000, (800) 531-5900. $$–$$$$
La Quinta Motor Inn. 3782 LVBS. (702) 739-7457, (800) 531-5900. $$
Lady Luck. ♣ 206 North Third Street. (702) 477-3000, (800) 634-6580. $–$$$$
Lamplighter Motel. 2805 East Fremont Street. (702) 382-8791. $–$$
Las Vegas Backpacker's Hostel. 1322 East Fremont Street. (702) 385-1150. (800) 550-8958. $–$$
Las Vegas Club. ♣ 18 East Fremont Street. (702) 385-1664, (800) 634-6532. $–$$$
Las Vegas Courtyard by Marriott. 3275 Paradise Road. (702) 791-3600, (800) 321-2211. $$–$$$$
Las Vegas Downtown Thrift Lodge. 629 South Main Street. (702) 385-7796, (800) 525-9055. $–$$
Las Vegas Downtown Travelodge. 2028 East Fremont Street. (702) 384-7540, (800) 578-7878. $–$$$
Las Vegas Hilton. ♣ 3000 Paradise Road. (702) 732-5155, (800) 732-7117. $$–$$$$
Las Vegas Motel. 1200 East Fremont Street. (702) 384-5670. $–$$
Laughing Jackelope. 3969 LVBS. (702) 739-1915. $
Lee Motel. 200 South Eighth Street. (702) 382-1297. $
Lucky Lady Motel. 1308 East Fremont Street. (702) 385-1093. $–$$$
Luxor Hotel Casino. ♣ 3900 LVBS. (702) 262-4000, (800) 288-1000. $$–$$$$
Main Street Station. ♣ 300 North Main Street. (702) 387-1896, (800) 465-0711. $–$$
Maxim Hotel/Casino. ♣ 160 East Flamingo Road. (702) 731-4300, (800) 634-6987. $–$$
Meadows Inn. 525 East Bonanza Road. (702) 456-5600, (800) 932-1499. $–$$
MGM Grand Hotel. ♣ 3799 LVBS. (702) 891-1111, (800) 929-1111. $$–$$$$
Miami Beach Motel. 4213 LVBS. (702) 736-6014. $–$$
Milestone Motel. 1919 East Fremont Street. (702) 387-1650.
The Mirage. ♣ 3400 LVBS. (702) 791-7111, (800) 627-6667. $$–$$$$
Monte Carlo. ♣ 3770 LVBS. (702) 730-7777, (800) 311-8999. $–$$$
Motel 8/Mr. Deli. 3961 LVBS. (702) 798-7223. $–$$$
Motel 6. 5085 Industrial Road. (702) 739-6747, (800) 466-8356. $
Motel 6 Boulder Highway. 4125 Boulder Hwy. (702) 457-8051, (800) 466-8356. $–$$
Motel 6 Tropicana. 195 East Tropicana Avenue. (702) 798-0728, (800) 466-8356. $–$$
Nevada Palace. ♣ 5255 Boulder Hwy. (702) 458-8810, (800) 634-6283. $
New York–New York. ♣ 3790 LVBS. (888) 693-6763
Normandie Motel. 708 LVBS, (702) 382-1002. $
Oasis Motel. 1731 LVBS. (702) 735-6494. $–$$
Olympian Palms. 3890 Swenson Avenue. (702) 732-8889, (800) 879-7904. $–$$$$
Orleans Hotel & Casino. 4500 West Tropicana Avenue. (702) 365-7111, (800) 675-3267. $–$$
Palace Station. ♣ 2411 West Sahara Avenue. (702) 367-2411, (800) 634-3101. $$–$$$$
Parkway Inn. 5201 South Industrial Road. (702) 739-9513. $–$$$

Ponderosa Motel. 3325 East Fremont Street. (702) 457-0422. $
Polo Towers. 3745 LVBS. (702) 261-1000, (800) 935-2233. $$–$$$$
Quality Inn. ♣ 377 East Flamingo Road. (702) 733-7777, (800) 634-6617. $–$$$$
Queen of Hearts. ♣ 19 East Lewis Avenue. (702) 382-8878. $–$$
Ramada Vacation Suites. 100 Winnick Avenue. (702) 731-6100, (800) 634-6981. $–$$$
Regency Motel. 700 North Main Street. (702) 382-2332. $
Residence Inn by Marriott. 3225 Paradise Road. (702) 796-9300, (800) 331-3131. $$–$$$$
Rio Suites Hotel. ♣ 3700 Flamingo Road. (702) 252-7777, (800) 752-9746. $$–$$$$
Riviera Hotel & Casino. ♣ 2901 LVBS. (702) 734-5110, (800) 634-6753. $$–$$$
Rodeway Inn. 167 East Tropicana Avenue. (702) 795-3311, (800) 424-6423. $$–$$$
Rodeway Inn. 4288 North Nellis Blvd. (702) 632-0229, (800) 424-6423. $$–$$$
Royal Hotel. ♣ 99 Convention Center Drive. (702) 735-6117, (800) 634-6118. $–$$$
Sahara Hotel & Casino. ♣ 2535 LVBS. (702) 737-2111, (800) 634-6666. $–$$$$
St. Tropez Suite Hotel. 455 East Harmon Avenue. (702) 369-5400, (800) 666-5400. $$–$$$$
Sam's Town. ♣ 5111 Boulder Hwy. (702) 456-7777, (800) 634-6371. $–$$$$
Santa Fe Hotel & Casino. ♣ 4949 North Rancho. (702) 658-4900, (800) 872-6823. $–$$
Showboat. ♣ 2800 Fremont Street. (702) 385-9123, (800) 826-2800. $–$$$
Somerset House. 294 Convention Center Drive. (702) 735-4411. $–$$
Star View Motel. 1217 East Fremont Street. (702) 388-1533. $
Stardust Resort & Casino. ♣ 3000 LVBS. (702) 732-6111, (800) 634-6757. $–$$$$
Steven Motel & Apartment. 2112 North Nellis Blvd. (702) 452-8199. $
Stratosphere Tower. 2000 LVBS. (702) 380-7777, (800) 998-6937. $–$$$
Sunrise Suites. 4575 Boulder Hwy. (702) 434-0848, (800) 362-4040. $–$$
Sunrise Vista Executive Suites. 3801 East Charleston Blvd. (702) 459-7908. $$$–$$$$
Super 8 Hotel & Casino. ♣ 4250 Koval Lane. (702) 794-0888, (800) 800-8000. $–$$
Super 8 Motel. 5288 Boulder Hwy. (702) 435-8888, (800) 800-8000. $–$$
Super 8 Motel. 4435 LVBN. (702) 644-5666, (800) 800-8000. $–$$$
Tam O'Shanter Motel. 3317 LVBS. (702) 735-7331, (800) 727-3423. $–$$
Thunderbird Hotel. 1213 LVBS. (702) 383-3100, (800) 634-6277. $–$$
Tod Motel. 1508 LVBS. (702) 477-0022. $–$$
Town Lodge Motel. 225 North Seventh Street. (702) 386-7988. $–$$
Town Palms Hotel. 321 South Casino Center. (702) 382-1611. $
Towne & Country Motel. 2033 East Fremont Street. (702) 366-8576. $–$$
Travel Inn Motel. 217 LVBN. (702) 384-3040. $–$$$
Traveler's Motel. 1100 East Fremont Street. (702) 384-7121. $
Travelodge—Las Vegas Inn. 1501 West Sahara Avenue. (702) 733-0001, (800) 578-7878. $–$$
Travelodge—Las Vegas Strip. 2830 LVBS. (702) 735-4222, (800) 578-7878. $–$$$
Travelodge—South Strip. 3735 LVBS. (702) 736-3443, (800) 578-7878. $$–$$$$
Treasure Island at the Mirage. ♣ 3300 LVBS. (702) 894-7111, (800) 944-7444. $$–$$$$
Tropicana Inn. 5150 Duke Ellington Way. (702) 736-8964. $–$$
Tropicana Resort & Casino. ♣ 3801 LVBS. (702) 739-2222, (800) 634-4000. $$–$$$
Vacation Village Hotel Casino. ♣ 6711 LVBS. (702) 897-1700, (800) 658-5000. $–$$
Vagabond Motel. 1919 East Fremont Street. (702) 387-1650. $
Valley Motel. 1313 East Fremont Street. (702) 384-6890. $
Victory Budget Motel. 307 South Main Street. (702) 384-0260. $
Villa Inn. 225 LVBS. (702) 382-3878. $
Villa Roma Motel. 220 Convention Center Drive. (702) 735-4151, (800) 634-6535. $–$$
Western Hotel. ♣ 899 East Fremont Street. (702) 384-4620, (800) 634-6703. $
White Sands Motel. 3889 LVBS. (702) 736-2515. $–$$
World Trade Center Ramada Inn. 901 East Desert Inn Road. (702) 369-5750, (800) 390-1777. $–$$$
Yucca Motel. 1727 LVBS. (702) 735-2787. $

Chapter 13
Eating Your Way Across Las Vegas

Econoguide Las Vegas 2001: Best Buffets
Las Vegas Strip
- ★★★★★ **Carnival World Buffet.** Rio
- ★★★★★ **Palatium.** Caesars Palace
- ★★★★ **Bayside Buffet.** Mandalay Bay
- ★★★★ **Bellagio Buffet.** Bellagio
- ★★★★ **Le Village Buffet.** Paris–Las Vegas

Downtown Las Vegas
- ★★★ **The Buffet.** Golden Nugget (Downtown)
- ★★★ **Garden Court Buffet.** Main Street Station (Downtown)

Econoguide Las Vegas 2001: Best Restaurants
Casino Restaurants
- ★★★★ **Emeril Lagasse's New Orleans Fish House.** MGM Grand
- ★★★★ **Empress Court.** Caesars Palace
- ★★★★ **Le Cirque.** Bellagio
- ★★★★ **Bistro le Montrachet.** Las Vegas Hilton
- ★★★★ **Lutéce.** Venetian
- ★★★★ **Red Square.** Mandalay Bay
- ★★★★ **Rumjungle.** Mandalay Bay
- ★★★★ **Star Canyon.** Venetian
- ★★★★ **Zefferino.** Venetian

Outside the Casinos
- ★★★★ **Andre's French Restaurant**
- ★★★★ **Pamplemousse**
- ★★★★ **P. F. Chang's China Bistro**

Eating Your Way Across Las Vegas

Like most everything else inside and outside a casino, restaurants are part of the come-on. You'll find some of the best deals, the best food, and the wildest settings in Las Vegas. You can dine inside a Roman catacomb, a submarine, or a rain forest. You can find $5 steaks, $50 chickens, and $500 wines.

Like I've said, it's all a come-on; the goal is to get you to stroll by the slot machines and the tables on your way to and from dinner. But that doesn't mean you have to gamble on anything more than the quality of the menu.

In the listing in this chapter, I've included some of the best and most interesting places to eat in Las Vegas. You won't find fast-food outlets (although they do exist in Las Vegas and even within some of the casino-hotels), and you won't find the ordinary coffee shop. And we will also deal with that special Las Vegas creature, the fabulous buffet.

All of the restaurants listed here are worth a visit, but some are better than others. Restaurants bearing four stars earn a place among the Econoguide '01 Best Restaurants in Las Vegas. Three-star establishments offer superior dining and settings.

Las Vegas's Favorite Food: Buffets

Comedian Gary Shandling offered the best reason we've ever heard for the popularity of buffets in Las Vegas. He told us of an unlucky visitor who dropped $800 at the tables and moved on to an all-you-can-eat buffet at the casino. "By God," the man said, "I am going to eat $800 worth of food if it kills me!"

The history of buffets in Las Vegas may go back to the town's origins as a provisioning center for miners and railroad workers. Bars would compete for business by offering the proverbial "free lunch" to customers who kept their glasses full.

Today's casinos, of course, view the buffet in somewhat the same way. They figure if they can lure you into their doors with the offer of an inexpensive meal, you are quite likely to stop to play the tables or the slot machines on your way in or out. The casinos try to encourage this as much as they can by placing the buffets at the back of the casinos. The casinos also try to find ways to encourage all-night gamblers to stick around for breakfast.

Whatever the reason for the buffets, it is true that some of the offerings represent the best values for food anywhere we know of. The best of the buffets offer top-quality meals in attractive settings for a mere fraction of the price of a sitdown restaurant. (The worst of the buffets are spectacularly ordinary and unattractive, but still represent better values than McDonald's or the neighborhood greasy spoon.)

In general, the best meals are the dinner buffets and the weekend brunches; a few casinos offer spectacular breakfasts. As you might expect, the more popular buffets can build lengthy lines; the best strategy is to eat a bit early—before 8 A.M. for breakfast and before 6 P.M. for dinner.

Prices are subject to change. Call to check hours. Most buffets offer lower rates for children. Soft drinks, coffee, and tea are included with most meals; alcoholic drinks are extra.

Las Vegas Buffets

Arizona Charlie's. ★★ Wild West Buffet. (702) 258-5200. Breakfast 7 to 11 A.M., $3.75; lunch 11 A.M. to 3:30 P.M., $4.75; dinner 4 to 10 P.M., $6.75.

Bally's. ★★★ Big Kitchen Buffet. (702) 739-4111. Breakfast 7 to 11 A.M., $9.99; lunch 11 A.M. to 2:30 P.M., $11.99, and dinner 4 to 10 P.M., $15.99. Sunday Sterling Brunch in Bally's Steakhouse from 9:30 A.M. to 2:30 P.M., $55.

Bellagio. ★★★★ Bellagio Buffet. (702) 693-7111. Breakfast 7 to 10:30

Eating Your Way Across Las Vegas 147

A.M., $10.95; lunch 11 A.M. to 3:30 P.M., $13.95; dinner 4 to 10 P.M., $22. Champagne brunch Saturday and Sunday 8 A.M. to 4 P.M., $18.50.

Binion's Horseshoe.★★★ Horseshoe Buffet. (702) 382-1600. Nightly from 4 to 10 P.M., $10.95. Friday night seafood buffet, $14.95.

Boomtown.★★ Blue Diamond Buffet. (702) 263-7777. Breakfast 7 to 11 A.M., $3.99; lunch noon to 3:30 P.M., $6.49; dinner 4:30 to 10 P.M., $7.99 to $13.49. Sunday Champagne Brunch, 8 A.M. to 3:30 P.M., $7.99.

Boulder Station.★★ The Feast. (702) 432-7777. Breakfast 7 to 11 A.M., $4.99; lunch 11 A.M. to 2 P.M., $6.99; and dinner 4 to 10 P.M., $8.99. Sunday Signature Brunch at the Broiler 10 A.M. to 3 P.M., $16.99.

Buffalo Bill's.★★ Miz Ashley's Boarding House Buffet. (702) 679-5160. Breakfast 8 A.M. to 11 A.M., $5.95; lunch daily 11 A.M. to 5 P.M., $6.25; dinner 5 to 8 P.M. $6.95. Breakfast Saturday and Sunday 8 to 11 A.M., $5.95.

Caesars Palace.★★★★ Palatium Buffet. (702) 731-7110. Breakfast Monday through Friday 7:30 to 11:30 A.M., $7.99; lunch Monday through Thursday 11:30 A.M. to 3:30 P.M., $9.99, and on Friday until 2:30 P.M.; dinner daily 4:30 to 10 P.M., $14.99. A seafood buffet, including one lobster, is served from 4 to 10 P.M. on Fridays and 4:30 to 10 P.M. on Saturdays for $24.99. A lavish champagne brunch is offered Saturday and Sunday from 8:30 A.M. to 3:30 P.M. for $14.99.

Circus Circus.★★ Circus Buffet. (702) 734-0410. Breakfast 7 to 11:30 A.M., $5.49; lunch noon to 4 P.M., $6.49; dinner 4:30 to 10 P.M., $7.99. The Steak House Champagne Brunch has seatings at 9:30 A.M., 11:30 A.M., and 1:30 P.M. Sunday, $21.95.

Desert Inn.★★ Terrace Pointe Buffet. (702) 733-4444. Breakfast 6 to 11:15 A.M., $12.75; lunch noon to 2:30 P.M., $16.75. Sunday brunch 10 A.M. to 2:30 P.M., $19.50.

Excalibur.★★ Round Table Buffet. (702) 597-7777. Breakfast 6:30 to 11 A.M., $6.99; lunch weekdays 11 A.M. to 4 P.M., $7.99; dinner weekdays 4 to 10 P.M., $9.99. Weekend Prime Rib and Shrimp 4 P.M. to 10 P.M., $9.99.

Fitzgeralds.★★ Molly's Coffee Shoppe & Buffet. (702) 388-2400. Breakfast 7 to 11 A.M., $5.99; lunch 11:30 A.M. to 3 P.M., $5.99; dinner 4 P.M. to midnight, $8.99. Champagne brunch Saturday and Sunday 7 A.M. to 3 P.M., $8.99.

Flamingo Hilton.★★★ Paradise Garden Buffet. (702) 733-3111. Breakfast 6 A.M. to noon, $7.75; lunch and dinner 11:30 A.M. to 11 P.M., $13.99. Nightly Seafood Spectacular $13.99.

Fremont.★★ Paradise Buffet. (702) 385-3232. Breakfast 7 to 10:30 A.M., $5.35; lunch 11 A.M. to 3 P.M., $6.96; dinner 4 to 10 P.M., $10.71. Seafood Fantasy Sunday, Tuesday, and Friday 4 to 10 P.M., $16.08. Champagne Brunch, 7 A.M. to 3 P.M. Saturday and Sunday, $9.64.

Frontier. Cattleman's Buffet. (702) 794-8200. Breakfast 7 to 11:30 A.M., $7.95; lunch noon to 3:30 P.M., $8.95; dinner 4 to 10 P.M., $9.95. Friday Seafood Buffet 4 P.M. to 10 P.M., $15.95. Sunday champagne brunch 7 A.M. to 3:30 P.M., $9.95.

Gold Coast.★ Buffet. (702) 367-7111. Breakfast 7 to 10:30 A.M., $3.95; lunch 11 A.M. to 3 P.M., $5.95; dinner 4 to 10 P.M., $8.95. Sunday Brunch 8 A.M. to 3 P.M., $7.95.

Golden Nugget.★★★ The Buffet. (702) 385-7111. Breakfast 7 to 10:30 A.M., $5.50; lunch 10:30 A.M. to 3 P.M., $7.25; dinner 4 to 10 P.M., $9.95. Sunday Champagne Brunch 8 A.M. to 10 P.M., $10.50.

Harrah's.★★★ Fresh Market Square Buffet. (702) 369-5000. Breakfast 7 to 11 A.M., $8.99; lunch 11 A.M. to 4 P.M., $9.99; dinner 4 to 11 P.M., $14.99. Sunday brunch 10 A.M. to 4 P.M., $14.99.

Holiday Inn Boardwalk Casino.★ Surf Buffet. (702) 735-2400. Open 24 hours. 11 P.M. to 10 A.M., $4.99; lunch 10 A.M. to 4:30 P.M., $6.49; and dinner 4:30 P.M. to 11 P.M., $7.99.

Imperial Palace.★★ Emperor's Buffet. (702) 731-3311. Breakfast 7 to 11:30 A.M., $6.25; lunch 11:30 A.M. to 5 P.M., $7.50; dinner 5 to 10 P.M., $8.50. Imperial Buffet in Teahouse weekdays 7 A.M. to 3 P.M., $7.45; lunch 11:30 A.M. to 2:30 P.M. $7.45; dinner 5 to 10 P.M., $9.45. Champagne brunch buffet, 8 A.M. to 3 P.M., Saturday, Sunday, holidays, $8.45.

Lady Luck.★★ (702) 477-3000. Breakfast 7 to 10:30 A.M., $5.49; lunch 11:30 A.M. to 2:30 P.M., $5.95; prime rib and seafood dinner 4 to 10 P.M., $7.95.

Las Vegas Hilton.★★★ The Buffet. (702) 732-5111. Breakfast Monday through Friday 7 to 10 A.M., $7.99; lunch 11 A.M. to 2 P.M., $8.99; dinner 5 to 10 P.M., $12.99. Champagne brunch Saturday and Sunday 8 A.M. to 2 P.M., $11.99.

Luxor.★★★ Pharaoh's Pheast. (702) 262-4000. Breakfast 6:30 to 11:30 A.M., $8.03; lunch 11:30 A.M. to 4 P.M., $8.57; dinner 4 to 11 P.M., $12.32.

Main Street Station.★★★ Garden Court Buffet. (702) 387-1896. Breakfast 7 to 10:30 A.M., $4.99; lunch 11 A.M. to 3 P.M., $6.99; and dinner 4 to 10 P.M., $10.71, and dinner on Tuesday and Thursday, $11.75. Sunday champagne brunch 7 A.M. to 3 P.M., $8.99. Fridays seafood, $15.

Mandalay Bay.★★★★ Bayside Buffet. (702) 632-7777. Breakfast 7 to 10:45 A.M., $9.50; lunch 11 A.M. to 2:45 P.M., $9.50; dinner 3 to 10 P.M., $17.95. Sunday brunch 7 A.M. to 2:45 P.M., $15.50.

MGM Grand.★★ MGM Grand Buffet. (702) 891-1111. Brunch 7 to 2:30 P.M., $9.50; dinner 4:30 to 10 P.M., $13.95.

The Mirage.★★ Mirage Buffet. (702) 791-7111. Breakfast 7 to 10:45 A.M., $7.50; lunch 11 A.M. to 2:45 P.M., $10.67; dinner 3 to 10 P.M., $16.03. Champagne Buffet Sunday 8 A.M. to 10 P.M., $16.03.

Monte Carlo.★★ Buffet. (702) 730-7777. Breakfast 7 to 11 A.M., $6.99; lunch 11 A.M. to 4 P.M., $7.25, and dinner 4 to 10 P.M., $9.99. Sunday champagne brunch 7 A.M. to 3:30 P.M., $10.99.

Nevada Palace.★★ LaBella Restaurant Buffet. (702) 458-8810. Dinner 4 to 9 P.M., $5.99. Seafood buffet Friday, $9.99.

Orleans.★★ French Market Buffet. (702) 365-7111. Breakfast 7 to 10 A.M., $4.95; lunch 11 A.M. to 3 P.M., $6.95; and dinner 4 to 10 P.M., $9.95. Monday seafood dinner $13.95, Sunday champagne brunch 8 A.M. to 3 P.M., $9.95.

Palace Station.★★ The Gourmet Feast. (702) 367-2411. Breakfast 7 to 11 A.M., $4.49; lunch 11 A.M. to 3 P.M., $6.99; dinner 4 to 10 P.M., $8.99. Sunday brunch 7 A.M. to 3:30 P.M., $8.99.

Paris–Las Vegas.★★★★ Le Village Buffet. (702) 967-4401. Breakfast 7:30

Eating Your Way Across Las Vegas 149

to 11:30 A.M., $10.95; lunch noon to 5:30 P.M., $14.95; and dinner 5:30 to 10:30 P.M., $21.95. Champagne buffet on Sunday, 7:30 A.M. to 4 P.M., $21.95.

Primm Valley.★★ The Greens. (702) 679-5160. Breakfast Saturday and Sunday 7 to 11 A.M. $5.95; lunch 11 A.M. to 5 P.M., $6.25; dinner 5 to 10 P.M., $6.95.

Rio.★★★★★ Carnival World Buffet. (702) 252-7777. Breakfast 8 to 10:30 A.M., $8.95; lunch 11 A.M. to 3:30 P.M., $11.95; dinner 3:30 to 11 P.M., $14.95. Weekend brunch 9 A.M. to 3 P.M., $14.95. ★★★★Village Seafood Buffet dinner 4 to 10 P.M., $27.

Riviera.★★ World's Fare Buffet. (702) 734-5110. Breakfast 6 to 10 A.M., $6.99; lunch 10 A.M. to 2 P.M., $7.99; dinner 4 to 10:30 P.M., $9.99. Weekend brunch 10 A.M. to 3 P.M., $7.99.

Sahara.★★ Sahara Buffet. (702) 737-2111. Brunch 7 A.M. to 3 P.M., $5.35; dinner 4 to 10 P.M., $5.99. Weekend seafood and prime rib brunch 8 A.M. to 3 P.M., $8.50.

Sam's Town.★★ Great Buffet. (702) 456-7777. Breakfast 8 to 11 A.M., $3.99; lunch 11 A.M. to 3 P.M., $6.99; dinner 4 to 9 P.M., $8.99. Friday and Saturday seafood, $15.99. Champagne brunch Sunday 8 A.M. to 3 P.M., $8.99.

San Rémo.★★ Buffet. (702) 739-9000. Breakfast 6 to 10:30 A.M., $7.95; brunch 10:30 A.M. to 2 P.M., $7.95; dinner 5 to 9 P.M., $9.95. Brunch Saturday and Sunday, 6:30 A.M. to 2 P.M., $7.95.

Santa Fe.★★ Lone Mountain Buffet. (702) 658-4900. Breakfast 7:30 to 10:30 A.M., $4.99; lunch 11:30 A.M. to 2:30 P.M., $5.99; dinner 4 to 9 P.M., $8.49; Sunday brunch 7:30 A.M. to 2:30 P.M., $9.11. Thursday seafood extravaganza night, $13.99. Ti Amo Sunday Jazz Brunch, 11 A.M. to 5 P.M., $12.95.

Showboat.★★ Captain's Buffet. (702) 385-9123. Lunch 10 A.M. to 2:30 P.M., $5.95; dinner 4:30 to 9 P.M., $11.95. Weekend champagne brunch 8 a.m. to 3:30 p.m., $6.95.

Stardust.★★ Coco Palms. (702) 732-6111. Champagne Brunch daily 7 A.M. to 3 P.M., $10.50.

Stratosphere.★★ Stratosphere Buffet. (702) 380-7700. Breakfast 7 to 11 A.M., $5.49; lunch 11 A.M. to 4 P.M., $6.49; dinner 4 to 10 P.M., $8.99. Sunday and Friday seafood fantasy, $11.25.

Texas Station.★★ Feast Around the World. (702) 631-1000. Breakfast 8 to 10:30 A.M., $4.99; lunch 11 A.M. to 3:30 P.M., $6.99; dinner 4 to 10 P.M., $9.99. Weekend champagne brunch, 8 A.M. to 3:30 P.M., $8.99. Friday and Saturday buffet $10.99.

Treasure Island.★ Buffet. (702) 894-7111. Breakfast 6:45 to 10:45 A.M., $6.99; lunch 11 A.M. to 3:45 P.M., $7.50; dinner 4 to 10:30 P.M., $11.50. Champagne Brunch Saturday and Sunday, 7:30 A.M. to 3:30 P.M., $11.50.

Tropicana.★★ Island Buffet. (702) 739-2222. Brunch weekdays 7:30 A.M. to 1:30 P.M., $7.95, dinner 4:30 to 10 P.M., $11.95. Weekend brunch 7:30 A.M. to 2:30 P.M., $9.95.

Westward Ho. Buffet. (702) 731-2900. Brunch 11:30 A.M. to 2 P.M., $6.95; dinner 4 to 10 P.M., $8.95.

Las Vegas Restaurants

You can get just about anything you want at a Las Vegas restaurant. Most are open for lunch and dinner; weekend hours may vary. Be sure to call to confirm hours and check to see if a reservation is necessary. Most casino restaurants are open weekends; some eateries outside of the hotels are closed on Sunday.

| $ | Inexpensive (Entrees to $10) | $$ | Moderate ($10 to $20) |
| $$$ | Expensive ($20 to $40) | $$$$ | Deluxe ($40 and over) |

Casino Restaurants

Many of the better restaurants in Las Vegas can be found within the casinos. You'll find details about many of them in the writeups in Chapter 6. Not included here are casino coffee shops and fast food restaurants.

Alexis Park. (702) 796-3300.
Pegasus.★★★ Continental specialties. $–$$$
Pisces Bistro.★★ A seafood café. $$–$$$

Bally's Las Vegas. (702) 967-7999.
Al Dente.★★ Pasta, pasta everywhere.
Bally's Steakhouse.★★★ Steaks, chops, and seafood served in a New York club atmosphere. $$$–$$$$
Chang's.★★ Hong Kong, Mandarin, and Taiwanese cuisine. $$–$$$
Seasons.★★★ Steak and seafood and a seasonal menu. $$$–$$$$

Barbary Coast. (702) 737-7111.
Michael's.★★★ Goumet steak and seafood in a Victorian setting. $$$–$$$$

Bellagio. (702) 693-7111.
Le Cirque.★★★★ Classic Continental. $$$-$$$$. (702) 693-8100.
Osteria del Circo.★★★★ Tuscan delicacies. $$–$$$. (702) 693-8150.
Picasso.★★★ Mediterranean works of art. $$$-$$$$. (702) 693-7223.
Aqua. ★★★ Seafood and fine art. $$$-$$$$. (702) 693-7223.
Olives.★★★ Mediterranean sidewalk cafe. $$$. (702) 693-7223.
Prime.★★★★ Chicago speakeasy and chophouse. $$-$$$. (702) 693-7223.
Jasmine.★★★ Gourmet Chinese fare. $$-$$$. (702) 693-7223.
Shintaro.★★★★ Pacific Rim haute cuisine. $$$$. (702) 693-7223.
Noodles.★★ Regional noodle dishes of Asia. $$$. (702) 693-7223.
Sams's American.★★★ Regional American fare. $$–$$$. (702) 693-7223.
Petrossian Bar.★★★ Afternoon tea, caviar, champagne, and smoked salmon. $$$-$$$$. (702) 693-7223.

Binion's Horseshoe. (702) 382-1600.
Binion's Ranch Steak House.★★★ Victorian-style decor with a panoramic view from the twenty-fourth floor, specializing in huge steaks and prime ribs. $$$–$$$$

Eating Your Way Across Las Vegas 151

Gee Joon. ★★ Asian cuisine. "Gee Joon," the highest-ranking hand in Pai Gow, means *supreme* or *excellent*. **$$–$$$**

Boulder Station. (702) 432-7777.

The Broiler. $$–$$$ Steak and seafood.
    Guadalajara Bar and Grill. $$ Mexican specialties in a lively setting.
    Pasta Palace. $$ The name says it all.

Caesars Palace. (702) 731-7731.

Café Roma. ★★ **$$–$$$**
    Empress Court. ★★★★ A most elegant Hong Kong–style Cantonese restaurant, including abalone, jellyfish, shark's fin, and bird's nest soups using rare spices from the Orient. **$$–$$$**
    Hyakumi. ★★★★ An elaborate sushi bar with expansive (and expensive) Japanese menu. **$$$$**
    Neros Steak & Seafood. ★★★ High-tone Continental fare in an elegant room just off the casino floor. **$$$–$$$$**
    Terrazza. ★★★ An elegant spot by the Garden of the Gods pool. **$–$$$**

Forum Shops at Caesars Palace

The Palm. ★★★ The Vegas branch of the venerable New York steak and seafood house; casual and fun. **$$–$$$$**. (702) 732-7256.
    Planet Hollywood. ★★ Although the glitz of Hollywood doesn't seem quite so wild set against the backdrop of Las Vegas, this is still an entertaining eatery. **$–$$**. (702) 791-7827.
    Spago. ★★★ Trendy yuppie fare for trendy yuppies; includes an "outdoor" cafe on the streets of ancient Rome. **$$–$$$**. (702) 369-6300.
    Stage Deli of Las Vegas. ★★ Pickles on the table, corned beef to die for, and a bit of New York attitude. **$–$$**. (702) 893-4045.

California Hotel. (702) 385-1222.

Pasta Pirate. Basic Italian. **$–$$**
    Redwood Bar & Grill. Chops, seafood, and poultry. **$$–$$$**

Circus Circus. (702) 734-0410.

The Steak House. ★★★ A class act in a funky joint. **$$–$$$**
    Stivali. ★★★ Upscale Italian. **$$–$$$**

Excalibur. (702) 597-7777.

Camelot. Gourmet fare. **$$**
    Regale Italian Eatery. Pasta, pizza, and more. **$–$$**
    Sir Galahad's. A prime ribbery. **$$–$$$**
    WCW Nitro Grill. Will wrestle for food. **$–$$**

Fitzgerald's Holiday Inn. (702) 388-2400.

Limerick's Steak House. Steaks, ribs, and an Irish castle. **$$–$$$$**

Flamingo Hilton. (702) 733-3111.

Alta Villa. Italian specialties. **$$**
   Conrad's.★★★ Olde English gourmet fare. **$$–$$$**
   Peking Market.★★ A handsome Chinese eatery. **$–$$**
   Sushi Bar Hamada. **$–$$**

Four Queens. (702) 385-4011.

Hugo's Cellar.★★★ A local institution; fine steaks, seafood, and fowl. **$$$–$$$$**
   Magnolia's Veranda. Casual casino fare. **$–$$**

Fremont. (702) 385-3232.

Lanai Express. Chinese and American fare. **$$**
   Second Street Grill. American and Pacific Rim specialties. **$$–$$$**
   Tony Roma's.★★ Familiar ribs, chicken. **$$–$$$**

Gold Coast. (702) 367-7111.

Cortez Room. Steak and seafood, and lots of it. **$–$$$**
   Mediterranean Room. *Italian and French specilaties.* **$–$$$**
   Monterey Room. Casino fare, American to Chinese. **$$**

Golden Nugget. (702) 385-7111.

California Pizza Kitchen.★★ Unusual pies. **$–$$**
   Lillie Langtry's.★★ Above-the-ordinary Cantonese cuisine. **$$–$$$**
   Stefano's.★★★ Seafood and pasta in the place named after the owner, so they're on their toes. **$$$**

Hard Rock. (702) 693-5000.

Mortoni's.★★★ Trendy Italian fare from owner Peter Morton. **$$**

Harrah's. (702) 369-5000.

Asia.★★★ Elegant Chinese and Asian cuisine. **$$–$$$**
   Cafe Andreotti.★★ An attractive Italian eatery. **$$–$$$**
   The Range Steakhouse.★★★ High above the Strip. **$$–$$$**

Imperial Palace. (702) 731-3311.

Embers.★★ Intimate steakhouse setting. **$$–$$$**
   Ming Terrace. *Mandarin and Cantonese specialties.* **$–$$$**
   Rib House. Western barbecue. **$$–$$$**
   Seahouse. Cape Cod on the Strip. **$$–$$$**

Lady Luck. (702) 477-3000.

Burgundy Room.★★★ Fine wines and gourmet cuisine, surrounded by a private art collection, including works by Dalí, Erte, and others. **$$$–$$$$**
   Marco Polo.★★ Fresh pasta. **$$–$$$$**

Las Vegas Club. (702) 385-1664.
Great Moments Room.★★ Steak and seafood, off the casino floor. $$

Las Vegas Hilton. (702) 732-5111.
Andiamo.★★★ $$-$$$
    Benihana Seafood Grille.★★ Hibachi grill in a Japanese village. $$-$$$
    Bistro le Montrachet.★★★★ Elegant Continental fare. $$$
    Garden of the Dragon.★ Upscale Chinese. $$-$$$
    Hilton Steakhouse.★★ One of the classiest casino steakhouses. $$-$$$$
    Margarita Grille. Mexican favorites in a classy room. $$
    Quark's Bar and Restaurant.★★★ Your basic twenty-fourth-century diner at the Star Trek Experience. $$-$$$
    The Reef.★★★ An upscale seafoodery. $$$

Luxor. (702) 262-4000.
Isis.★★★ Fresh gourmet food and very, very old furnishings. $$$
    Millenium.★★ A tony cafe. $$
    Nile Deli. A New York kosher-style deli on the banks of the Vegas Nile. $-$$
    Papyrus. Polynesian and Chinese fare in a lush settings. $$-$$$
    Sacred Sea Room.★★★ Fine seafood fare. $$-$$$$

MGM Grand. (702) 891-7777.
Brown Derby.★★★ A Vegas version of the Hollywood original, with steaks, chicken, seafood, and salads. $$
    Mark Miller's Grill Room.★★★ Hot Southwestern fare. $$$-$$$$
    Dragon Court. A quiet Chinese outpost. $$$
    Gatsby's.★★★ California cuisine. $$$$
    Emeril Lagasse's New Orleans Fish House.★★★★ Creole and Cajun specialties and a seafood bar. $$-$$$
    La Scala.★★ A formal and elegant dining room. $$$-$$$$
    Rainforest Cafe.★★★ The great outdoors, indoors. $-$$
    Wolfgang Puck Café.★★ Trendy pizzas and other dishes at a lively restaurant on the casino floor. $$

Main Street Station. (702) 387-1896.
Triple 7 Brewpub.★★ Pub food with four signature brews and a changing specialty brew. $-$$
    Pullman Grille.★★ A steak house so intimate it bears the name of the family farm in Illinois where the corn-fed Black Angus beef is raised. $-$$

Mandalay Bay. (702) 632-7777.
Aureole. ★★★ Seasonal American dishes. $$$$
    Border Grill. ★★★ Upscale Southwestern taqueria. $$
    China Grill. ★★★ Chinese brasseries. $$$
    House of Blues. ★★ Down-home creole. $$-$$$

Red Square. ★★★ Pre-Marxist menu. $$-$$$
Rock Lobster. ★★ Elegant lobster pound. $-$$$
Rumjungle. ★★★ Brazilian liveliness. $$$
Shanghai Lilly. ★★ Upscale Chinese. $$-$$$
Noodle Shop. ★★ Hong Kong fast food. $-$$
Wolfgang Puck's Trattoria del Lupo. ★★ Northern and Southern Italian specialties. $$$

The Mirage. (702) 791-7111.

California Pizza Kitchen. ★★ Unusual pies. $-$$
Kokomo's. ★★ A Continental restaurant with seafood specialties, in a rain forest within a Las Vegas casino; we're not sure what it all has to do with a city in Indiana of the same name. $$-$$$
Mikado. ★★ Japanese specialties. $$$-$$$$
Moongate. ★★★ A lovely room with elegantly presented Oriental dishes. $$-$$$$
Noodle Kitchen. Asian soups, noodle, and rice dishes. $-$$
Onda. ★★★ Classic Mediterranean fare. $$-$$$
Renoir. ★★★ High-tone Mediterraneann. $$$-$$$$
Samba. ★★★ Brazillian rodizio. $$-$$$

Monte Carlo Resort. (702) 730-7777.

Blackstone's Steak House. ★★ Casino steakhouse fare, well done. $$-$$$
Dragon Noodle Co. ★★ Noodles, roasted meats, and other Asian fare. $$
Market City Café. A Southern Italian trattoria. $$
Monte Carlo Pub & Brewery. ★★ Pizza, pasta, sandwiches, and half a dozen microbrews. $-$$$

New York–New York. (702) 740-6969.

Chin Chin. Asian and Pacific Rim specialties. $$-$$$
Gallagher's Steakhouse. ★★ A Vegas version of the original. $$$-$$$$
Gonzalez Y Gonzales. ★★ Mexican cafe. $-$$
Il Fornaio. ★★★ A little bit of Little Italy. $$
Motown Café. ★★ Ribs, fish fry, and R&B. $$

Orleans. (702) 365-7111.

Canal Street Grille. ★★★ Use your clout to reserve a fireside table and enjoy fine steaks and seafood. $$$
Don Miguel's. ★★ Watch tortillas being made while you wait. $-$$$
Vito's Italian Restaurant and Pizzeria. Basic Italian. $-$$$

Palace Station. (702) 367-2411.

Fisherman's Broiler. Seafood in an old California setting. $$-$$$
Guadalajara Bar and Grill. ★★ Tex-Mex specialties. $-$$$$
Pasta Palace. Pasta, pasta, pasta. $-$$

Paris–Las Vegas. (702) 946-7000.

La Chine. ★★★ France meets China. $$–$$$
    Le Provençal. ★★★ French-Italian cuisine of Provence. $$–$$$
    Mon Ami Gabi. ★★ Parisian street café. $$$–$$$$
    La Rotisserie des Artistes. ★★★ French show kitchen. $$$–$$$$
    Trés Jazz. ★★★ New World/Caribbean bistro. $$$–$$$$

Rio Suites. (702) 252-7777.

All American Bar & Grille. Loud and boisterous, just off the casino floor. $$–$$$$
    Antonio's. ★★★ Traditional Italian. $$
    Bamboleo. ★★ Mexican specialties. $–$$$
    Buzio's Seafood Restaurant. ★★ Pan roasts and steamed shellfish $$
    Fiore. ★★★ The elegance of the Rio, in a hideaway off the casino floor. $$$–$$$$
    Mask. ★★ Far Eastern specialties and teppanyaki grill. $$
    Napa Restaurant. ★★★ Country French, with a phonebook-sized wine list. $$$–$$$$
    Voo Doo Café & Lounge. ★★★ Best of the Bayou with an unbeatable view from the top. $$–$$$$

Riviera. (702) 734-5110.

Kristofer's. ★★ Prix-fixe gourmet fare. $$$–$$$$
    Rik' Shaw. ★★ Gourmet Chinese. $–$$$
    Ristorante Italiano. Fancy Italian. $$–$$$

Sahara. (702) 737-2111.

Paco's Hideaway. Mexican and Tex-Mex. $–$$
    Sahara Steakhouse. ★★ Gourmet steak and seafood. $$$–$$$$

Sam's Town. (702) 456-7777.

Billy Bob's Steakhouse & Saloon. Just like it sounds. $–$$
    Diamond Lil's. Beef and poultry. $$
    Mary's Diner. Straight out of the '50s. $–$$
    Papamios Italian Kitchen. $–$$
    Willy & Jose's. Mexican and Western specialties. $–$$

San Remo. (702) 739-9000.

Paparazzi Grille. Steaks and seafood. $–$$
    Pasta Remo. Casual Italian, $–$$

Sheraton Desert Inn. (702) 733-4444.

Ho Wan. $$–$$$$
    Monte Carlo Room. ★★★ High French cuisine. $$$–$$$$
    Portofino. ★★ Mediterranean food by candlelight. $$–$$$$

Stardust. (702) 732-6111.

Tony Roma's. ★★ Another outpost of the rib chain. $–$$
   Tres Lobos. ★★ Dark and intimate Mexican. $–$$
   William B's. ★★ Gourmet steak. $$–$$$

Stratosphere. (702) 380-7777.

Top of the World. ★★★ 380-7711. Steaks, seafood, and more, served on a revolving platform 833 feet above The Strip. $$$
   Big Sky Steak House. Steak, plus BBQ ribs, beef brisket, honey-fried chicken, and all that good stuff. $$
   Fellini's Restaurant. Family Italian. $$
   Roxy's Diner. American fare. $–$$

Texas Station. (702) 631-1000.

Guadalajara. Lively Tex-Mex. $
   San Lorenzo Italian Restaurant. Wide-ranging Italian menu. $–$$
   Stockyard Steakhouse. ★ Steak, seafood, and rib platters. $–$$
   Yellow Rose Café. Casino fare. $

Treasure Island at the Mirage. (702) 894-7111.

Black Spot Grille. Burgers, salads, and pasta. $–$$
   Buccaneer Bay Club. ★★ Continental fare; the window tables offer oblique views of the naval battle out front. $$–$$$$
   Madame Ching's. ★★ Gourmet Asian fare. $$–$$$
   The Plank. An informal steak and seafood place. $$–$$$$

Tropicana. (702) 739-2222.

Golden Dynasty. ★★ Szechuan and Cantonese specialties. $–$$$
   Mizuno's Japanese Steakhouse. ★★ Teppanyaki dining nightly. $$–$$$
   Pietro's Gourmet Dining. ★★★ Mediterranean specialties. $$$–$$$$
   Savanna. ★★ Exotic fare. $$–$$$$

Venetian Resort Hotel Casino. (702) 414-1000.

Canaletto. ★★★ High-tone Italian. $$–$$$
   Delmonico Steakhouse. ★★★ Old school steakhouse. $$$$
   Grand Lux Café. ★★ From the creators of the Cheesecake Factory. $–$$$
   Lutéce. ★★★★ Modern French and oh-so-toney. $$$–$$$$
   Pinot. ★★ Elegant steak, game, and seafood. $$–$$$
   Postrio. ★★★ Informal bistro-café. $$–$$$$
   Royal Star. ★ Upscale Asian. $$–$$$$
   Star Canyon. ★★★★ High-concept chuckwagon. $$–$$$
   Taqueria Canonita. ★★ High-tone Mexican. $–$$
   Valentino's Italian Grill. ★★ Grilled pizza and entrees. $$–$$$
   WB Stage 16. ★★ Dine on the "set" of Warner Bros. productions. $$–$$$
   Zeffirino. ★★★ Fancy Italian. $$$–$$$$

Theme Restaurants

The rest of the world has already discovered Planet Hollywood and the Hard Rock Café, but the local versions of those quiet establishments are Las Vegas–style.

The Hard Rock Café has its own theme casino and restaurant on Paradise Road, equipped with a giant guitar outside and a collection of the guitars of the giants within. You'll find details about the casino in Chapter 6.

The other big franchise in town is Planet Hollywood within the Forum Shops at Caesars Palace. You'll get to stroll through the streets of ancient Rome en route to the trappings of today's glitzy Hollywood. Details of the Forum Shops are in Chapter 11.

If you like subs, you'll like Dive!, at the Fashion Show Mall on the Strip. Once an hour, the submarine-themed eatery goes into a dive—klaxons sound, lights flash, water bubbles pass through glass walls, and a good time is had by all. Dive! is partly owned by filmmaker Steven Spielberg and serves an interesting mix of foods, including submarine sandwiches.

Along the streets of New York at the spectacular New York–New York casino is a geographically challenged outpost of the Motown Café, featuring cafe food and Motown music.

Other entrants include the Harley-Davidson Café at Harmon Avenue on the Strip, and the Gordon Biersch Brewery Restaurant, at 3987 Paradise Road, serving German and American food and beer.

One major departure: the Official All Star Café, at the Showcase Mall on the Strip just north of the MGM Grand, closed in early 2000 after its parent company, Planet Hollywood filed for bankruptcy.

A Selection of Theme Restaurants

Dive!★★★ 3200 Las Vegas Boulevard South; (702) 369-3483. $–$$

Holy Cow Casino Café Brewery.★★★ 2423 Las Vegas Boulevard South; (702) 732-2697. $–$$

Motown Café.★★ New York–New York Hotel and Casino; (702) 740-6969. $$

Planet Hollywood.★★ Forum Shops at Caesars Palace; (702) 791-7827. $$

Out of the Casinos

American

Big Dog's Cafe & Casino. 6390 West Sahara Avenue; (702) 876-3647. $–$$

Big Mama's.★★ 3765 Las Vegas Boulevard South; (702) 597-1616. Big Mama McWhorter's Southern, Cajun, creole, and barbecue recipes. $–$$

The Coachman's Inn. 3240 South Eastern Avenue; (702) 731-4202. Prime ribs and sandwiches. $$

Jeremiah's Steak House. 171 East Tropicana; (702) 736-3044. $$–$$$

Kiefer's.★ 105 East Harmon Avenue; (702) 739-8000. Penthouse restaurant in Carriage House with view of the Strip. Veal, steak, and seafood specialties. $$

Mount Charleston Inn Hotel.★ 2 Kyle Canyon Rd., Mount Charleston;

(702) 872-5500. Quail, rabbit, game, and other down-home specialties in a mountain chalet. Check driving conditions in wintertime. $$

Mount Charleston Lodge. Mount Charleston; (702) 872-5408. Check for hours and driving conditions. $-$$

Peppermill Lounge. 2985 Las Vegas Boulevard South; (702) 735-4177. $-$$

Sonia's Cafe & Rotisserie.★★ 3900 West Charleston Boulevard. (702) 870-5090.

TGI Friday's. 1800 East Flamingo Road; (702) 732-9905. $-$$

Asian/Middle Eastern

Cathay House.★ 5300 West Spring Mountain Road; (702) 876-3838. A great panoramic view of the Strip. Dim sum carts. $-$$

China First. 1801 East Tropicana Avenue; (702) 736-2828. $$

Chin's.★★ Fashion Mall, 3200 Las Vegas Boulevard South; (702) 733-8899. A decidedly modern and elegant Chinese restaurant. $$

Chung King. 3400 South Jones Boulevard; (702) 871-5551. A neighborhood Chinese eatery. $

Fong's Garden. 2021 East Charleston Boulevard; (702) 382-1644. An old-line, old-style family Chinese restaurant. $-$$

Hakase. 3900 Paradise Road; (702) 796-1234. Sushi, teppanyaki tableside Japanese cooking. $$

Hamada of Japan. 598 East Flamingo Road; (702) 733-3005. Sushi, teppanyaki tableside Japanese cooking, or menu items. $-$$$

India Palace.★ 505 East Twain Avenue; (702) 796-4177. $-$$

Kosher Chinese. ★ 4580 West Flamingo Road. at Decatur; (702) 871-3262. Chinese, minus the pork and shrimp. $$

P. F. Chang's China Bistro.★★★★ 4165 Paradise Road; (702) 792-2207. Asian elegance. $-$$

Saigon.★ 4251 West Sahara Avenue; (702) 362-9978. A very ordinary storefront restaurant with extraordinary Vietnamese cooking. $-$$

Seoul B-B-Q. 953 East Sahara Avenue; (702) 369-4123. Ribs along with fish and kimchi (pickled cabbage) that will clear your sinuses for days to come. $$

Shalimar.★★ 3900 Paradise Road; (702) 796-0302. Authentic Indian menu, featuring tandoori meat, curries, unusual rice, and vegetarian specialties. $$

Tanya Restaurant.★★★ 210 West Sahara Avenue; (702) 388-9923. Thai specialties; (702) 388-9923. $-$$

Thai Spice.★★★ 4433 West Flamingo Road; (702) 362-5308. $-$$

Continental

Andre's French Restaurant.★★★★ 401 South Sixth Street; (702) 385-5016. A re-created French country home, with great attention to detail in service and food. $$$-$$$$

Aristocrat Restaurant.★★★ 850 South Rancho Road; (702) 870-1977. A quality, small Continental hideaway. $$$-$$$$

Bootlegger Ristorante and Lounge. 5025 South Eastern Avenue; (702) 736-4939. An old family eatery with a lot of character. $$-$$$$

Pamplemousse.★★★ 400 East Sahara Avenue; (702) 733-2066. Closed Monday. A changing, fresh menu of French country specialties. $$-$$$
Second Story.★★ 4485 South Jones Boulevard; (702) 368-2257. French and Continental cuisine. Enclosed porch. $$$

Delicatessens

Jerusalem Kosher Restaurant & Deli. 1305 Vegas Valley Drive; (702) 696-1644. Closed Friday evenings, all day Saturday. $$
Park Deli. 3900 Paradise Road; (702) 369-3354. $-$$

German

Café Heidelberg. 604 East Sahara Avenue; (702) 731-5310. $$
Swiss Cafe. 3175 East Tropicana Avenue; (702) 454-2270. $-$$$

Italian

Battista's Hole in The Wall.★★ 4041 Audrie Street; (702) 732-1424. A classic, comfortable family Italian restaurant. $$-$$$
Carluccio's Tivoli Gardens. 1775 East Tropicana Avenue; (702) 795-3236. Liberace's sequinned ghost is everywhere. $-$$
Cipriani Restaurant. 2790 East Flamingo; (702) 369-6711. $$-$$$
La Strada Restaurant. 4640 Paradise Road; (702) 735-0150. $$
Olive Garden. 1547 East Flamingo Road; (702) 735-0082. A national seafood and Italian chain that offers a bottomless salad bowl at your table. $-$$
Olive Garden. 1361 South Decatur Boulevard; (702) 258-3453. $-$$
Parma Ristorante. 1750 South Rainbow Boulevard; (702) 258-0680. $$
Piero's.★★ 355 Convention Center Drive; (702) 369-2305. Quality Italian pasta, seafood, and meat across the street from the Convention Center. $$-$$$$

Japanese

Kabuki Japanese.★★★★ 1150 East Twain; (702) 733-0066. $$-$$$
Mikado Express.★★ 845 South Rainbow Boulevard. A local teriyaki favorite. (702) 878-3450. $$
Nippon. 101 Convention Center Drive; (702) 735-5565. Sushi, sashimi. $-$$
Osaka.★★★ 4205 West Sahara Avenue. A local favorite. (702) 876-4988. $$-$$$
Teru-Sushi. 700 East Sahara Avenue; (702) 734-6655. $$
Togoshi Ramen. 855 East Twain Avenue, #107; (702) 737-7003. $$
Tokyo Restaurant. 953 East Sahara Avenue; (702) 735-7070. $$

Mexican

Chapala Restaurant. 3335 East Tropicana Avenue; (702) 451-8141. $-$$
Macayo Vegas. 1375 East Tropicana Avenue; (702) 736-1898. $-$$
Macayo Vegas. 1741 East Charleston Boulevard; (702) 382-5605. $-$$
Macayo Vegas. 4457 West Charleston Boulevard; (702) 878-7347. $-$$
Ricardo's Mexican Restaurants. 4930 West Flamingo Road; (702) 871-7119. $-$$

Middle Eastern

Habib's Persian Cuisine.★★★ 4750 West Sahara Avenue; (702) 870-0860. $–$$

Moroccan

Marrakech.★★ 3900 Paradise Road; (702) 736-7655. Six-course French Moroccan meal, with a belly dancer, of course. $$$

Seafood

Kim Tar.★★ 4215 Spring Mountain Road; (702) 227-3588. $–$$$
   Landry's Seafood House.★★ 2610 West Sahara; (702) 251-0101. $–$$$$
   Rosewood Grille and Lobster House.★★★ 3339 Las Vegas Boulevard South; (702) 792-9099. $$–$$$$
   The Lobster House.★★ 3763 Las Vegas Boulevard South; (702) 795-8199. $$–$$$$
   The Plank.★★ 3300 Las Vegas Boulevard South; (702) 894-7111. $$–$$$$
   The Tillerman.★★ 2245 East Flamingo Road; (702) 731-4036. $$$

Steakhouses

Cattlemen's Steak House. 2645 South Maryland Parkway; (702) 732-7726. $–$$
   Cavalier Restaurant. 3850 East Desert Inn Road; (702) 451-6221. $–$$$
   Golden Steer.★★★ 308 West Sahara Avenue; (702) 384-4470. Pounds of steak and ribs; also game, fish, and poultry in a western atmosphere between the Strip and the Convention Center. $$–$$$
   Hungry Hunter.★★★ 2380 South Rainbow Boulevard. A local fave. (702) 873-0433. $$–$$$$
   Morton's of Chicago.★★★ Fashion Show Mall, 3200 Las Vegas Boulevard South; (702) 893-3955. $$–$$$$
   Philip's Supper House. 4545 West Sahara Avenue; (702) 873-5222. $$–$$$
   Play It Again, Sam. 4120 Spring Mountain Road; (702) 876-1550. $$–$$$
   Port Tack. 3190 West Sahara Avenue; (702) 873-3345. $–$$
   Rosewood Grille.★★ 3339 Las Vegas Boulevard South; (702) 792-6719. $$–$$$
   Ruth's Chris Steak House.★★★ 3900 Paradise Road; (702) 791-7011. $$–$$$
   Yolie's Brazilian Steakhouse.★★ 3900 Paradise Road; (702) 794-0700. Marinated meats, sausage, and poultry cooked over wood-fired rotisserie. $$

Chapter 14
Sports and Recreation

Spectator Sports
Las Vegas Stars Baseball

The Las Vegas Stars, the AAA farm club of the San Diego Padres in the Pacific Coast League, one step below the majors, play a 140-game season from April through September. Home games are played at Cashman Field, which has 9,334 permanent seats and 3,000 bleachers in the outfield. Fans can also have dinner at the Club Level Restaurant and watch the game from there.

For ticket information, call (702) 386-7200, or call Ticketmaster at (702) 474-4000. Seat prices range from about $5 to $8.

The Stars are one of the most successful minor league franchises. In typical minor league fashion, there are many special promotions at games, including firework nights.

Among the present-day stars who played for the Stars in the past are Roberto and Sandy Alomar, Carlos Baerga, Joey Cora, Ozzie Guillen, John Kruk, Tony Gwynn, Benito Santiago, Kevin McReynolds, and Shane Mack.

Before the start of each season, the Stars hold the annual **Las Vegas Big League Weekend**, bringing in several major league teams for exhibition games in spring training.

To get there from the airport, take I-15 to I-93/95 South/Downtown exit, and then the Cashman Field/Las Vegas Boulevard exit. At the light on Las Vegas Boulevard turn left; at the third light you will see Cashman Field.

UNLV Runnin' Rebels

The nationally ranked college basketball team plays home games at the Thomas and Mack Center in a season that runs from mid-November through the beginning of March. Tickets are scarce for some matchups. Call (702) 895-8658.

UNLV Lady Rebels

The women's basketball team, also a national power, plays at the South Gym of UNLV. For ticket information, call (702) 895-8658.

Rodeo

The National Finals Rodeo is held in December.

Recreation
Racquetball

Las Vegas Athletic Club East. Four clubs. (702) 364-5822, West Sahara location.

Las Vegas Sporting House. Ten racquetball and two squash courts. Open twenty-four hours. 3025 Industrial Road (behind Stardust Hotel); (702) 733-8999.

Bowling

Gold Coast Hotel & Casino. Seventy-two lanes. Open twenty-four hours. 4000 West Flamingo Road; (702) 367-4700.

Orleans Hotel & Casino. Seventy lanes. 4500 West Tropicana Avenue, (702) 365-7111.

Sam's Town Hotel Gambling Hall & Bowling Center. Fifty-six lanes. Open twenty-four hours. 5111 Boulder Highway; (702) 454-8022.

Santa Fe Hotel & Casino. 60 lanes. 4949 North Rancho Drive; (702) 658-4995.

Showboat Hotel, Casino & Bowling Center. 106 lanes. Open twenty-four hours. 2800 Fremont Street; (702) 385-9153.

Horseback Riding

Bonnie Springs Old Nevada. Seven days a week through Red Canyon. Highway 159 West of Las Vegas; (702) 875-4191.

Cowboy Trail Rides/Red Rock Canyon Riding Stables. (702) 387-2457.

Ice Skating

Santa Fe Resort. The only public ice skating arena in southern Nevada, with an NHL regulation–sized rink. Figure skating and hockey lessons and leagues. 4949 North Rancho Drive; (702) 658-4900.

Roller Skating

Crystal Palace. 4680 Boulder Highway; (702) 458-0177.
   Crystal Palace. 3901 North Rancho Drive; (702) 645-4892.
   Crystal Palace. 9295 West Flamingo; (702) 253-9832.

Skiing and Sledding

Las Vegas Ski and Snowboard Resort/Lee Canyon Ski Area. Route 156, Mount Charleston. Snow and road conditions: (702) 593-9500, (702) 646-0008.

Vertical	Elevation	Lifts
1,030	9,320	3

Base: 8,290 feet. Summit: 9,320 feet.

1999–2000 Rates: Adults $28 (afternoon $22); Children $21 (afternoon $15).

A secret to many winter visitors to Las Vegas is that there is a ski hill less than an hour north of the Strip, forty-seven miles away. Las Vegas Ski and

Snowboard Resort, which used to be called Lee Canyon, is not to be confused with one of the Sierra Nevada monsters in and around Lake Tahoe, but it does offer decent skiing from about December through April. Snow-making helps out where Mother Nature fails. The resort offers shuttle bus service from Las Vegas, and you can rent ski equipment and clothing.

This is predominately an intermediate hill, with about 15 percent beginners' slopes and 5 percent expert terrain. Chairs 1 and 2 are each 3,000 feet long, rising 1,000 feet to intermediate and advanced runs; chair 3 serves Rabbit Peak for novice skiers. The **Mount Charleston Hotel** is on Kyle Canyon Road. Call (702) 872-5500 for directions; you can also consult www.skilasvegas.com.

Foxtail Snow Play Area. Lee Canyon Road, Mount Charleston. Bring your own sled, inner tube, or cafeteria tray. Check with Las Vegas Ski and Snowboard Resort for local snow conditions first.

Cross-Country Skiing. The U.S. Forest Service, 2881 South Valley View Boulevard, (702) 873-8800, has maps of Mount Charleston available for sale.

Brian Head Ski Resort. Off Interstate 15 in Brian Head, Utah. Information and lodging reservations: (800) 272-7426. www.brianhead.com.

Vertical	Elevation	Lifts
1,161	11,307	7

It's a hike at 180 miles northeast (more than three hours from Las Vegas) into Utah on Interstate 15, but the reward is a serious ski area. Brian Head has Utah's highest base elevation at 9,600 feet, drawing an average of more than 450 inches of snow per year. The resort typically opens in early November.

The ski resort is spread over two mountains and includes 53 trails. Brian Head Peak reaches to 11,307 feet; across the valley is the strictly beginner and intermediate Navajo Peak. In the 1999-2000 season, adult lift tickets were $35; young adults (13-18) $33, children (6–12) and seniors (60–69), $22. Seniors 70 and older ski free. Afternoon half days, $30 for adults and young adults; $15 children. Brian Head includes lodging packages in the Brian Head Hotel or surrounding condominiums; there are also hotels and inns near the resort.

Thrills and Spills

Flyaway Indoor Skydiving. An indoor skydiving simulator using an airplane engine for lift. 200 Convention Center; (702) 731-4768. *See Chapter 10.*

Skydive Las Vegas. Boulder City. (702) 293-1860.

Miniature Golf

Scandia Miniature Golf & Family Fun Center. 2900 Sirius Road; (702) 364-0070.

Golf Courses (Public and Semi-Private)

Angel Park Golf Club. 36 holes on Cloud Nine, Mountain, and Palm courses. Rates vary by season. Lighted driving range. 100 South Rampart Boulevard; (702) 254-4653.

Badlands Golf Club. 27-hole Johnny Miller course with view of Red Rock Canyon. 9119 Alta Drive; (702) 242-4653.

Black Mountain Golf and Country Club. 18 holes. $70 (non-resident) weekday, $80 (non-resident) weekend, including cart. 500 Greenway Road, Henderson; (702) 565-7933.

Boulder City Municipal Golf Course. 18 holes. $25 (non-resident) for 9 holes, with cart; $36 (non-resident) for 18 holes, with cart. 1 Clubhouse Drive, Boulder City; (702) 293-9236.

Craig Ranch Golf Course. 18 holes. $15 for 9 holes with cart; $26 for 18 holes with cart. 628 West Craig Road; (702) 642-9700.

Desert Inn Golf Course. 18-hole championship course. Non-guests $250. Guests $165. (702) 733-4290.

Desert Rose Golf Course. 18-hole championship course. Seasonal fees. 5843 Club House Drive; (702) 431-4653.

Las Vegas Golf Club. 4300 West Washington. 18 holes. Non-resident fees: $42 weekday and $54 weekend for 9 holes; $69 weekday and $89 weekend for 18 holes. Carts additional. (702) 646-3003.

Las Vegas National Country Club. The former Las Vegas Hilton Country Club. 1911 East Desert Inn Road 18 holes. $125 with cart Monday to Thursday, $160 with cart Friday through Sunday. (702) 796-0013.

Legacy Golf Club. 18 holes. $115 weekday and $135 weekend, with cart. 130 Par Excellence Drive; (702) 897-2187.

Los Prados Golf and Country Club. 18 holes. $35 weekday, $45 weekend. 5150 Los Prados Circle; (702) 645-5696.

North Las Vegas Community Course. 9 holes. $6 weekday, $7.50 weekend. 324 East Brooks Avenue, North Las Vegas; (702) 633-1833.

The Las Vegas National Country Club

Painted Desert Country Club. 18-hole championship target golf course. $125 fee, with cart. 5555 Painted Mirage Way; (702) 645-2568.

Red Rock Country Club. A pair of Arnold Palmer–designed 18-hole courses in Summerlin, a master-planned community west of Las Vegas. The club features views of the Spring Mountain Range and the Red Rock Canyon National Conservation area. 2250 Red Springs Drive #B, Las Vegas. (702) 360-5959. Call for prices.

Tournament Players Club at the Canyon. 9851 Canyon Run Drive, Summerlin. (702) 256-2000.

Tennis

Bally's. Eight outdoor courts, five illuminated. Reservations only. $10 per hour for guests, $15 per hour for visitors. (702) 739-4111.

Desert Inn. Four lighted courts. Fee for visitors. Lessons and rentals available. (702) 733-4577.

Las Vegas Hilton. Six courts. Free to hotel guests. (702) 732-5111.

Monte Carlo Hotel. Three courts. Guests $10 per hour, nonguests $15 per hour. (702) 730-7411.

Plaza. Four outdoor courts, all lighted. Rentals available. (702) 386-2110.

Riviera. Two courts, both lighted. Guests first, others welcome. Reservations only. (702) 734-5110.

Sports Club–Las Vegas. Two illuminated outdoor courts. $15 per person. Reservations required. (702) 733-8999.

Sunset Park. Eight illuminated courts. Courts $5 (evenings) and $3 (daytime). (702) 260-9803.

Bicycle Rentals

Bikes USA. 1539 North Eastern Avenue; (702) 642-2453.

City Streets Bike Tours. 8221 East Charleston Boulevard. Bicycle rentals for Red Rock Park and Mount Charleston, maps, and equipment. (702) 596-2953.

Parks and Scenic Areas

Floyd Lamb State Park. 9200 Tule Springs Road; (702) 486-5413.

Hoover Dam. (702) 293-8367.

Lake Mead Recreation Area.
  Boulder Beach: (702) 293-8990.
  Callville Bay: (702) 565-8958.
  Cottonwood: (702) 297-1464.
  Las Vegas Bay Marina: (702) 565-9111.
  National Park Service: (702) 293-8907.

Lee Canyon. Mount Charleston in Toiyabe National Forest, northwest of Las Vegas on Highway 95 to Highway 156. (702) 646-0008.

Spring Mountain Ranch. Blue Diamond. (702) 875-4141.

Valley of Fire. Overton. (702) 397-2088 or (702) 397-8928.

Chapter 15
Journeys North of Las Vegas: Mount Charleston, Lee Canyon, Red Rock Canyon, and Valley of Fire

As I've noted, Las Vegas is a lot more than just green felt, computer-controlled volcanic eruptions, and mock Egyptian pyramids. Few things make that point more clearly than a journey a few miles north of town along I-95.

Just past downtown the trappings of Las Vegas fall away quickly, yielding to the near-barren Mojave Desert. On the plateau to the right is the huge Nellis Air Force Base, and beyond that are two of the area's less well-known attractions: the Nellis Air Force Range that runs for almost 125 miles from Las Vegas to near Tonopah, and the Nevada Test Site, a nuclear weapons testing area included within the range.

Nellis is generally off-limits to civilians, except for occasional open houses. Visitors can tour the home of the famed Thunderbirds aerial demonstration team on Tuesday and Thursday at 2 P.M. The ninety-minute tour includes a film about the flyers, a museum, and a visit to a hangar to see an F-16. Call (702) 652-4018 for information.

The top-secret status of the Nellis base and the vast size of the area have regularly spawned all sorts of interesting rumors about goings-on in the area, including reports ranging from testing of strange military aircraft (including the Stealth bomber) to detailed reports of military experiments on captured UFOs and their alien crews. We got that last tidbit, by the way, from Elvis, who has his hideaway on the range.

Going to Dreamland

And then things get really weird. About 120 miles northwest of Las Vegas is a huge government military installation that officially doesn't exist. There are several very long runways and dozens of hangars and buildings, but according to FAA pilot charts and U.S. Geological Survey topographic maps, it just ain't there.

167

The military installation, at Groom Lake, is known to some as Dreamland; old government maps call it Area 51. When officialdom is pushed, they will acknowledge the existence of something called a "remote test facility."

According to *Popular Science*, which published an investigation of the air base in 1994, every weekday ten to twelve Boeing 737 jets depart from special terminals operated by defense contractor EG&G Corp. at McCarran Airport, or in Palmdale, California. The planes, painted white with a broad red stripe down their lengths, make low-level thirty-minute flights to Groom Lake with an estimated 1,500 to 2,000 employees per day. The carrier is sometimes identified as "Janet Airways."

What goes on there? According to unofficial observers, the base has been used for projects from testing of the ultrasecret SR-71 spy plane in the 1960s to flight tests of Soviet Sukhoi Su-22 and MiG-23 fighters somehow obtained by the military to training with F-117A Stealth attack planes. And there are those who maintain that the U.S. government has captured UFOs and kept them at the base.

There is not much chance of taking a sightseeing trip to Dreamland, though. About as close as you can get is up in the hills near the tiny town of Rachel (population about 100). The Bureau of Land Management property outside the base is patrolled by sheriff's deputies and private security forces nicknamed "Cammo Dudes"; closer in is the boundary of the base itself, which is guarded with detection devices, video cameras, and signs warning, "Use of Deadly Force Authorized."

By the way, if you go to the trouble of driving to Rachel (I-15 north to Route 93 north, picking up Route 375 westbound near Ash Springs), you'll find the Little A'Le'Inn (pronounced "alien"), its walls covered with UFO memorabilia and a large photo of the base that doesn't exist. The famous "black mailbox" view spot, said to be a great place for a close encounter of some kind or another, is at mile marker LN 29.5 on Route 375.

For years, locals and interested visitors used to hike or drive to a remote area they called "Freedom Ridge" along Groom Lake Road that offered a distant view of the sprawling air base. In April of 1995, though, the government succeeded in taking the land and closing off access. In 1996, Area 51 fans devoted their attention to hikes to the top of Tikapoo Peak within the Pahranagat National Wildlife Refuge; there a difficult ninety-minute hike leads to an even more distant view of the area. According to those who seem to make this their life's work, the government agencies that run Area 51 halt any secret operations anytime they detect unauthorized eyes, and that is why you won't see any UFOs or unusual military operations if you bother to make the climb. Turn your back, though, and they're there. (Sort of like the unanswerable question of whether the refrigerator light really does go off when the door is closed.)

Natural Wonders

On the left side of I-95 and the Strip, heading out of Las Vegas, are three expeditions worth taking. Fill up the gas tank in your car before heading out on a tour; gas stations are few and far between in this area.

Red Rock Canyon

Here is an extraordinary world of rusty red cliffs, Joshua trees, yucca plants, and sagebrush; just as otherworldly and much more real than the nearby manmade canyons of Las Vegas. It's heaven for hikers, perfect for picnickers, and a delightful drive, even if you never leave your car.

Take I-15 to the West Charleston exit and drive west on Charleston Avenue toward the hills. About ten miles out of town, Las Vegas is a garish memory and Red Rock Canyon is a garish reality. The sandstone cliffs, towering 2,000 feet above the desert floor, are an artist's palette of red, orange, yellow, pink, purple, and brown.

Check at the Bureau of Land Management Visitor Center on Red Rock Road to pick up hiking, bicycling, climbing, or general nature brochures. Marked hiking trails range from about two miles to a fourteen-mile tour to the top of the escarpment. There's also a thirteen-mile one-way driving loop with pull-offs at some of the more spectacular views, with even more "oohs" per mile than on the Las Vegas Strip.

The **Sandstone Quarry** area offers a climbing trail with access to some ancient Indian petroglyphs in Brownstone Canyon.

For much of the past 600 million years, the land that is now Red Rock Canyon was the bottom of a deep ocean basin; the western coast of North America was in present-day western Utah.

A rich variety of marine life in the waters left behind deposits of shells and skeletons more than 9,000 feet thick, which were eventually compressed into limestone and other carbonate rocks.

Large bodies of salt water became cut off from the sea and eventually evaporated, leaving behind salt and gypsum. The exposure of the sediments to the atmosphere caused some of the minerals to oxidize, changing their colors to red and orange.

Beep, beep! One of the most famous residents of Red Rock Canyon is the roadrunner. And yes, this chicken-sized bird really does streak across the desert on foot. (And though there are coyotes, too, we are not aware of a local franchise for the Acme Dynamite Company.)

Another stage in the geologic history of Red Rock Canyon occurred about 180 million years ago when the area became an arid desert. A giant dune field stretched eastward to Colorado, with sand more than half a mile deep in some areas. The shifting sands left behind curved and angled lines known as "crossbeds" that were eventually cemented into sandstone in combination with calcium carbonate and iron oxide; this is the source of some of the red rock cliffs.

Over thousands of years, at least four and possibly several other Native American cultures occupied the Red Rock area. They were drawn to the relative abundance of water in the canyon, which includes more than forty springs and catchment basins. Archaeologists have found roasting pits and a historical sandstone quarry.

In more recent times, the canyon has served as the backdrop for many Hollywood westerns, television shows, and commercials. Visitors by car now must pay $5 ($2 for motorcyclists) to drive through the loop; the fee was imposed

> **Don't be a burro.** Heed the warning signs against feeding the wild burros in the area; they bite. The state puts teeth into the warning with a $25 fine for unauthorized feedings.

by the Bureau of Land Management to maintain and finance roads, buildings, trails, signs, exhibits, and historic structures. For information, call the Red Rock Canyon Visitors Center at 363-1921.

The National Park Service plans to begin charging a fee to use the Lake Mead National Recreation Area in the next few years.

Sky's the Limit. Rock climbing in Red Rock Canyon with trained guides. For information, call (800) 733-7597 or (702) 363-4533. www.skysthelimit.com.

Bonnie Springs Old Nevada. Long before there was a serious settlement at Las Vegas there were isolated ranches like this one, which originally dates back to about 1840. Today, though, the Bonnie Springs Ranch is a somewhat tired Western theme park in a very pretty setting at the southern edge of Red Rock Canyon. The park includes a petting zoo, a small railroad, a Western street with shops, demonstrations, and the occasional shootout. Guided horseback tours of the area are also available.

Located on Highway 159, south of the exit from Red Rock Canyon in Blue Diamond. Open seven days a week, with tickets priced at about $6.50 for adults, $5.50 for seniors, and $4 for children ages 5 to 11; (702) 875-4191.

Spring Mountain Ranch State Park. An isolated ranch owned (along with hundreds of other Nevada properties) by Howard Hughes and used as a business retreat, it was originally the home of Lum of the "Lum 'n Abner" radio show of the 1930s, and then the home of Vera Krupp, widow of the German weapons maker. It is now operated by the State Park system; tours of the home are available. Call (702) 875-4141 for hours. There is a $5 entrance fee per vehicle.

Mount Charleston

About twenty miles north of town, after a long jaunt along a flat desert floor, look for the Kyle Canyon exit (Nevada Route 157) branching off to the left. From here you will begin a long, steady climb. The road is one of the more dramatic ones we know of: for much of the early part of the climb you are able to look straight into the face of the mountain ahead of you.

Mount Charleston is a serious hill, reaching to 11,919 feet, the highest peak of the Spring Mountain Range and nearly two miles above the floor of the Las Vegas Valley. Much of the surrounding area is part of the Toiyabe National Forest.

The trip is an interesting exploration of the effect of elevation on climate and plant and animal life. The yucca, Joshua trees, and creosote bushes are able to survive the intense heat and lack of rain at the desert floor. Somewhere around the 5,000-foot level you'll find junipers, scrub pine, and sagebrush. Higher up the mountain the vegetation gives way to bristlecone pines that are adapted to the extremes of cold and wind on the mountain. Bristlecones are among the longest-living things on earth, with some plants believed to be nearly 5,000 years old.

About ten miles up the road is the **Mount Charleston Hotel,** an old-timey mountain lodge (OK, so it's about twenty-five years old; it still feels like an

Journeys North of Las Vegas 171

antique) with beam ceilings and a large open fireplace. Rooms include a few suites with fireplaces. The **Canyon Dining Room** is an attractive place to eat, especially on a moonlit night. Call (702) 872-5500 for information.

At the very end of Kyle Canyon Road is a stunning resort area, first developed by the Civilian Conservation Corps during the Depression and now offering vacation homes, campgrounds, and picnic areas.

At the top of the road, the mountain continues to rise; there are a number of trails including a short walk to **Mary Jane Falls** or a more strenuous fifteen-mile hike to the **Charleston Peak** where on a clear day you can see into four states: Nevada, California, Utah, and distant Arizona. Forest Service Road 22, a branch road off of Route 157, leads to near **Robbers' Roost Caves**, a gathering of limestone caverns used as hideouts in the mid–nineteenth century by Mexican bandits who preyed on settlers and travelers in the area.

Route 158 branches off to the right, just before the Mount Charleston Hotel. This is a stunning, twisty mountain road that traverses a ridge over to Lee Canyon Road (Route 156). At the T, turn left into the mountain and climb for another four miles to reach the Lee Canyon Ski Area renamed in 1995 as the **Las Vegas Ski and Snowboard Resort**.

An alternate route to Mount Charleston is to go past Route 157 and continue on I-95 for about fourteen miles to Route 156. This road goes directly to the ski area; from there you can also cross over the upper trail (Route 158) and descend on Route 157.

Valley of Fire State Park. A bit farther away than Red Rock Canyon, but a bit wilder, this park includes spectacularly colored desert sandstone that has been sculpted by the wind and rain into fantastic shapes. The geology dates as far back as the Jurassic period.

You'll also find petroglyphs (prehistoric rock drawings) on canyon walls; they are believed to date back more than 2,000 years to the time of the Anasazi.

Trails lead to isolated parts of the park including **Mouse's Tank**, a shallow natural bowl that collects the scarce rainfall in the area. It was the hiding place of Mouse, a Paiute Indian who terrorized some of the area settlers a century ago.

Stop at the Visitor Station for maps and information, or call (702) 397-2088. You can also consult www.state.nv.us/stparks.

The Valley of Fire is about fifty miles northeast of Las Vegas, off I-15 in Overton; you can make a loop that connects to the top of Lake Mead and down to Boulder and the Hoover Dam for a nice day trip.

> **Roll of the dice.** In 1942, actress Carole Lombard was killed when her DC-3 airplane slammed into Mount Potosi southwest of Las Vegas in the Spring Mountains. She was returning from a war bonds rally in the Midwest to Los Angeles and husband Clark Gable.
>
> In remembrance of the popular Miss Lombard, an orange butterfly with black spots peculiar to the local hills was named the *Carole's fritillary*.
>
> The name holds Las Vegas significance: *fritillary* comes from the Latin *fritillus*, meaning dice box.

Temperatures in the valley can become downright brutal in the summer; the best time to visit is from September through May. Bring water and supplies with you, even for a day trip.

Overton

The small town of **Overton**, on Route 169, was once the commercial center for the early Mormon settlements in the Moapa Valley in the nineteenth century. Before then, the area was populated by Anasazi tribes who developed farms, including irrigation canals branching off the Virgin and Muddy Rivers more than a thousand years ago. The largest of their buildings, the fabled Lost City at the confluence of the Virgin and Muddy Rivers, included ninety-four rooms; that area is now below the waters of Lake Mead.

The **Lost City Museum** outside of Overton includes one of the most complete collections of ancient Pueblo Indian relics dating back thousands of years. It continues through the ancient Basketmaker cultures and through the Paiutes, who arrived about the year 1000 and whose descendants still live in southern Nevada. Outside of the museum is a replica of a Pueblo home, built as a Civilian Conservation Corps project during the Depression era. Also displayed are artifacts of the Mormon settlement of the region. The museum is open daily with a $2 admission fee for visitors 18 and older. Call (702) 397-2193 for information.

South of Overton, within the Valley of Fire State Park, is **Overton Beach**, a recreational area on upper Lake Mead. Beneath the waters east of the area is the former location of St. Thomas, a Mormon farming community; when the water level is low, parts of some of the buildings can be seen offshore.

Rhyolite, a real live dead ghost town is just off I-95 to the west of the Air Force Range, about 115 miles from Las Vegas. The town is named for the most common type of rock in the area. At its peak around the turn of the century, Rhyolite was a booming gold-mining community complete with opera house, symphony, red-light district, more than fifty saloons, six barber shops, eight physicians, and two undertakers, all to serve a population of nearly 10,000.

The town's rapid decline began with the San Francisco earthquake of 1907. By the early 1920s, the population was down to one.

Today, Rhyolite's ruins include a two-story school building from 1909, a train depot, an old jail, and the stone skeleton of the Cook Bank Building.

Each March, the Rhyolite Resurrection Festival brings the ghost town back to life through vignettes and a reunion of Rhyolite descendants.

Contact the Nevada Commission on Tourism for more information at (702) 486-2424. www.travelnevada.com.

Chapter 16
Journeys South of Las Vegas: Henderson, Hoover Dam, Boulder City, Lake Mead, and Lake Mohave

Henderson

Henderson, south of Las Vegas toward Boulder City, is Nevada's third most populous city (after Las Vegas and Reno) with more than 80,000 residents.

The town sprouted during World War II because of the Basic Magnesium plant, a huge facility that processed the mineral for use in munitions. The plant closed in 1944, but unlike the dozens of other ghost towns in Nevada, the residents of Henderson managed to find other industries. Henderson also serves as a bedroom community for workers in tourism and government installations. Downtown Henderson is (like Boulder City) somewhat frozen in time.

The Boulder Highway has been supplanted by superhighways that link Las Vegas to Boulder City and on to Los Angeles, but if you're looking for a glimpse of the past, this is still the best route to Henderson.

The **Southern Nevada Museum** on Boulder Highway includes Heritage Street, a collection of buildings from old Southern Nevada; some are houses built for the magnesium workers, early Las Vegas residences, and mining villages. An Indian Village celebrates the Native American culture of the area.

With an eye north to Las Vegas, Henderson has embarked on an ambitious series of developments in recent years, including the creation of **Lake Las Vegas,** one of the largest civil engineering projects in the country. The $100 million earthen dam has created a two-mile lake that is one day expected to be circled by 3,000 homes, several golf courses, and (of course) half a dozen hotel-casinos.

The Henderson Factory Tours

Ethel M. Chocolate Factory. Free factory tour and botanical garden and cactus display. And, yes, there are samples. Ethel was the mother of candy bar magnate Forrest Mars, the family behind the Mars Bar, M&Ms, Milky Way, and much more. The kitchens and manufacturing areas can be glimpsed behind

> **Henderson Chamber of Commerce.** 590 S. Boulder Highway, Henderson, NV 89015; (702) 565-8951. www.hendersonchamber.com.
>
> **Henderson Convention Center.** 200 Water Street, Henderson, NV 89015; (702) 565-2171.

large glass windows on the tour; for most of the year, though, the lines are only open weekdays.

The first room is the kitchen where fillings are prepared; specialized equipment includes cream beaters for butter creams and a nut sorting table. The second area includes two "enrobing lines" where nut clusters, butter creams, and caramels are drenched with chocolate. In front is the molding line where solid pieces, truffles, and cream liqueur chocolates are created. The last room is the packing area where candies are wrapped and boxed.

Call ahead to check on operating hours. There's a large shop on the property, and you can expect a few fresh samples. The cactus garden showcases more than 300 varieties of prickly plants; if that's the sort of thing you're looking for, here's a fine example. 2 Cactus Garden Drive off Sunset Road from the Boulder Highway; call for hours; (702) 458-8864.

Ron Lee's World of Clowns. Sculptor Ron Lee has made a career out of clowning around, and has a devoted following of collectors to show for it. His factory, where as many as 100 employees cast and decorate his art pieces, is open to the public; there's a small carousel, a gallery . . . and a gift shop. 330 Carousel Parkway. Open Monday through Friday 8 A.M. to 5 P.M., and on Saturday from 9 A.M. to 5 P.M.; (702) 434-1700.

Hoover Dam

If they had a casino at Hoover Dam, it would be a building that would rival Luxor, Excalibur, Caesars Palace, and MGM Grand combined. They don't, of course, and though nearly 700,000 visitors a year come to visit this incredible monument to the attempts of our species to exercise control over our environment, this means that nearly 20 million other visitors to Las Vegas don't make the forty-mile trip south. There ought to be a law. . . .

The Colorado River, which flows 1,400 miles from the Rocky Mountains in Colorado to the Gulf of California is one of the great geological forces in the West, creating spectacular natural wonders, including the Grand Canyon.

In the early days of settlement, the Colorado was the source of great respect and fear. Early settlers attempted to divert water for irrigation purposes. They were defeated by the tremendous seasonal changes from steady flow to summertime trickle to wild flooding in the spring as mountain snows melted.

Steam-powered riverboats navigated the Colorado River upstream from its mouth in the late 1800s, able to reach as far north as the Mormon settlement of Callville during certain parts of the year.

One of the most difficult parts of the 600-mile trip was passage through the Black Canyon rapids. Crews had to use a system of winches and cables strung through ring bolts anchored in the canyon walls.

It took a disastrous flood in California's Imperial Valley in 1905 to begin the move to finally tame the river. In that year, early spring flash floods washed away small earthen dams that had been created to divert water from the river to the Imperial Canal. The heavy water flow changed the course of the river and caused it to flow for the next two years into the Imperial Valley and the large Salton Sea east of San Diego, increasing the size of that body of water from twenty-two to 500 square miles; to this date the Salton Sea has not fully retreated to its turn-of-the-century size, covering about 300 square miles today.

> **High way.** The two-lane highway atop the dam connects Nevada and Arizona. By the way, Nevada is in the Pacific time zone, and Arizona is one hour later in the Mountain time zone.

The first step in harnessing the Colorado was agreement among the governments of the seven states through which it flows. In 1922 a commission, headed by Herbert Hoover, then Secretary of Commerce, produced the Colorado River Compact, dividing use of the water between Upper and Lower Colorado River Basins. In 1928, Congress passed the Boulder Canyon Project Act; construction of the dam was begun in 1931.

The first task for the construction crews in April 1931 was to deal with the water already passing through the canyon. Four huge diversion tunnels, nearly sixty feet in diameter, were dug out of the canyon walls to the left and right of the dam's eventual location. A year-and-a-half later they were ready to send the Colorado River through the tunnels and leave dry the dam's base.

More than 5,000 men worked day and night in a continuous pour of concrete that took two years—a total of 4.4 million cubic yards of concrete for the dam and supporting structures. Although there is a common belief that some of the ninety-four workers who died during the dangerous construction project are entombed within the concrete, dam tour guides will tell you otherwise.

The dam itself is described as an arch-gravity structure. Still the highest concrete dam in the western hemisphere, it rises 726 feet above the bedrock of Black Canyon. It is 660 feet thick at its base and forty-five feet thick at the top, with a span of 1,244 feet across the canyon.

The dam was completed in 1935, two years ahead of schedule, which has to be a record for a government project. The diversion tunnels were closed in February of 1935, and Lake Mead began to form behind the dam. The first power generator began operation in 1936; the seventeenth and final generator went on line in 1961.

The dam cost about $175 million to build at the time, and the cost has been repaid through revenues from the generation of power and the supply of water.

The energy distribution from the dam sends about 19 percent of the power to the state of Arizona, about 25 percent to Nevada, 28 percent to the Metropolitan Water District of Southern California, and the remainder to various municipalities in California, including Los Angeles.

The Lake Mead reservoir, which built up behind the dam, extends for 110 miles and usually stores about two years of average Colorado river flow, which is released as needed for irrigation and power generation. Water stored in the lake irrigates more than one million acres of land in the United States and half a million acres in Mexico.

Power source. As important as the large hydroelectric plants of Hoover Dam and Davis Dam are, conventional thermal plants using fossil fuels produce more than 75 percent of the Nevada electrical power.

Down the drain. Nearly all the state's streams and rivers drain internally into lakes or dry lake beds known as playas, or sinks. The major exception is the Colorado River.

The Humboldt rises in the northeast and flows west to disappear into the Humboldt Sink; and the Walker, Carson, and Truckee Rivers rise in the Sierra Nevada and flow east to the Walker, Carson, and Pyramid Lakes. Many other streams are dry for most of the year, filling their banks only in the spring with snow melt or after the rare summer rainfall.

Like a rock. The U.S. Bureau of Reclamation continued to own and operate Boulder City, controlling almost every detail until 1960 when it gave up dominion and the town was incorporated. Only then was alcohol permitted to be sold; today, Boulder City continues as the only city in Nevada that bans public gambling.

The generators produce about four billion kilowatt-hours of energy per year, enough for 500,000 homes. The gravity-fed generators are non-polluting, and of course, water flow is a renewable resource.

Another effect of the dam is to clear the once-muddy waters of the Colorado for much of its downstream passage and within Lake Mead itself.

Tours of the dam are conducted by the Bureau of Reclamation daily except for Thanksgiving and Christmas. The tour passes down through the body of the dam to the generating stations and out onto the walkway near the diversion tunnels at the base of the dam.

Tours are offered from 9 A.M. to 4:15 P.M. Tickets are $8 for adults, $2 for children ages 6–16, and $7 for seniors older than 62 years. For information, call (702) 293-8321. There's also a more impressive "hard hat" tour for $25 per person.

An impressive visitors' center, cantilevered out from the rock wall of the canyon on the Nevada side, was completed in 1995; Congressional critics pointed out that the price tag for the visitors' center was higher than the cost of the dam itself.

The visitor center includes a three-compartment rotating turntable, which seats 145 people in each compartment. The audience sees a trio of historical films.

Davis Dam, downstream of Hoover Dam, was completed in 1953. That rock and earth wall controls the flow of water from Lake Mohave. Self-guided tours are available at Davis.

Boulder City

Boulder City is a planned community created by the U.S. Bureau of Reclamation as housing for some of the construction workers for the dam and for administrative offices. The construction of the town coincided with a period of architectural design and government master planning; the result was a designed town with a great deal of un-Nevada-like greenery and parks.

As a former government company town, Boulder has the distinction of being the only town in Nevada that prohibits gambling.

Journeys South of Las Vegas

The **Boulder City/Hoover Dam Museum** is worth a visit to ogle the impressive collection of construction photos. The museum is located within the historic Boulder Dam Hotel at 1305 Arizona Street, erected for the use of government VIPs during the time the dam was under construction. www.accessnv.com/bcmha/.

> **Boulder City Chamber of Commerce.** 1305 Arizona Street, Boulder City, NV 89005; (702) 293-2034.
> **Boulder City Visitor Center.** 100 Nevada Highway, Boulder City, NV 89005; (702) 294-1220.

Lake Mead

It seems odd to speak of a fabulous outdoor wonderland such as Lake Mead as a creation of man, but so it is.

Before Lake Mead was formed when the diversion tunnels of Hoover Dam were closed in 1935, this area was almost untouched by humans. Indian tribes once inhabited some of the canyons. Explorers like John Wesley Powell went deep into the Grand Canyon and other areas and passed through the region; the first foreign settlers included fur trappers, Mormon settlers, and hardy prospectors.

Anson Call established Callville, a Mormon colony, in 1864 with a trading post to service emigrants on their westward passage along the Colorado River. Callville was abandoned five years later, although the walls of part of the settlement were still in place when the entire region—including many ancient Indian sites—was flooded by the waters of the developing lake. It is a good question to ask whether Hoover Dam could have been built under today's historic preservation and environmental impact laws.

In any case, Lake Mead today is an incredible contrast of desert and water, mountain and canyon, magnificent wilderness and the triumph of man-made technology.

Lake Mead National Recreation Area includes the 110-mile-long Lake Mead, the sixty-seven-mile-long Lake Mohave, which backs up behind the smaller Davis Dam at Laughlin, the surrounding desert, and the isolated Shivwits Plateau in Arizona, which connects into the Grand Canyon National Park.

Together, the two huge (274 square-mile) lakes sparkle in one of the driest, hottest places known to man.

In summer, daytime temperatures rise above 100 degrees regularly. From October to May, temperatures range from the thirties to the fifties.

Plan to include a stop at the **Alan Bible Visitor Center**, four miles northeast of Boulder City on Route 166 just past the junction with U.S. 93. Travel south from Las Vegas on Route 93/95 and stay on Route 93 at the split. The visitor center offers maps and information on services in the park.

You can also go to the park headquarters at the intersection of Nevada Highway and Wyoming Street in Boulder City or visit one of the many park ranger stations.

> **You can't get there from here.** The Shivwits Plateau can only be reached by unpaved roads from the north; check with park rangers for information on access.

> **Lake Mead information.** Write to: Superintendent, Lake Mead National Recreation Area, 601 Nevada Highway, Boulder City, NV 89005. The phone number is (702) 293-8907.

Reservations may be necessary for most lodging and many services in the summer. Campsites are available, for a fee, on a first-come first-served basis; some have time limits for stays. Each camp area includes picnic tables, grills, water, rest rooms, and a trailer sewage dump; no utility hookups are provided.

Backcountry camping is permitted along the shore on both lakes and in designated sites along unpaved backcountry roads.

Outside of the parks, you can find hotels, restaurants, and services in Las Vegas, Boulder City, Henderson, Laughlin, Searchlight, and Overton in Nevada; Bullhead City and Kingman in Arizona; and Needles in California.

Lake Mead Cruises

Several companies offer cruises all year long on Lake Mead near Hoover Dam.

The *Desert Princess* paddlewheel sails daily from the Lake Mead Resort Marina on Lakeshore Road between Las Vegas and the Hoover Dam. The Desert Princess, sister ship to the MS *Dixie II* on Lake Tahoe, has breakfast, sightseeing, and dinner/dance cruises priced from about $16 to $43. There are seven sailings daily, year-round. For information and reservations, call (702) 293-6180.

Animal Life in the Lake Mead Area

Living things have to be very hardy to survive in the temperature extremes of the desert and with an annual rainfall of less than six inches.

The creation of Lake Mead dramatically changed the ecology of the region, bringing waterbirds, fish, and aquatic plants. In the surrounding desert, more than a thousand bighorn sheep live along the mountain ridges; they are among the few desert animals active in the heat of the day. Other creatures include lizards, squirrels, rabbits, insects, and spiders.

The desert blooms year-round, but some of the flowers are so tiny that it is easy to miss them. A winter rain can cause a brief but glorious overnight bloom of wildflowers on the desert.

Fishing

The lake is a year-round bonanza for anglers. Check with park rangers or fishing guides.

In Lake Mead, the most sought-after fish is striped bass, which can reach 50 pounds and more. In Lake Mohave, especially in the upper reaches in Black Canyon, rainbow trout is the most popular. Other species include largemouth bass, channel catfish, black crappie, and bluegill.

Nevada and Arizona share jurisdiction over the two lakes. You must have a state fishing license to fish from shore. To fish from a boat, you must have a license from one state and a special-use stamp from the other. Licenses and stamps are available at most marinas.

Swimming

Both lakes are clear and clean for swimming. Water temperatures across most of the two lakes average about seventy-eight degrees in spring, summer, and fall. The coldest water is usually found in the northern portion of Lake Mohave.

Lifeguard beaches can be found in summer at Boulder Beach on Lake Mead and at Katherine Beach on Lake Mohave.

Boating

Boaters can get to some spots inaccessible to cars and can roam the entire 274 square miles of water of Lake Mead, including the narrow steep gorge of Iceberg Canyon.

Around the lake, many secluded coves are formed by fingers of the desert jutting out into the water; these are among the most popular campsites.

Sailboarding, a relatively new sport, is increasingly popular on the lake. Participants generally prefer near-shore areas that have stronger breezes.

There are six privately operated marinas along Lake Mead and three on Lake Mohave, each offering services and supplies year-round. Free public launching ramps and parking areas (parking limited to seven days) are found at each site.

Several companies offer boat tours, including a paddlewheel boat departing daily from the Lake Mead Marina. In summer, a boat tour through Boulder Canyon departs from Callville Bay every day.

On Lake Mohave, one-day raft trips are offered through the slow-moving waters of Black Canyon from Hoover Dam to Willow Beach.

Lake Mead
Courtesy of Las Vegas News Bureau

> **Water proofing.** Before going out on the water, call (702) 736-3854 or monitor marine radio channel 162.55 for National Weather Service forecasts. High winds can arrive suddenly, building up waves as high as six feet; lightning storms pose particular hazards to boats on open water. If you are caught in a storm, seek shelter in a protected cove.

> **Hot dogs.** Pets must always be leashed, and are prohibited from specified beaches and other public areas. Never leave a pet in a car; temperatures in a closed vehicle in the sun can reach 160 degrees.

Hiking

The best hiking months are October through May. Temperatures the rest of the year make for furnace-like conditions. You can explore on your own or join an escorted tour lead by naturalists. Always carry one gallon of water per person per day and let someone know where you are going and when you expect to return.

Health Considerations

The desert includes several species of dangerous animals, including rattlesnakes, scorpions, and Gila monster lizards. All of these will likely leave you alone if you do not disturb them. Wear sturdy boots to protect your feet.

A microscopic amoeba common to some hot springs can cause a rare infection that can become fatal; do not dive or submerse your head in springs and streams.

Oleander, a toxic plant, is common in non-wilderness areas, and hikers are advised not to eat unknown plants or drink water from ditches.

Lake Mead Resorts and Recreational Facilities

Callville Bay Resort. Callville Bay; (702) 565-8958. Snack bar, marina, houseboat rentals, small boat rentals, trailer village, RV sites, showers, laundry, auto/boat gas, dry boat storage, store.

Echo Bay Resort. Overton; (800) 752-9669, (702) 394-4000. Marina, restaurant/lounge, boat rentals, houseboat rentals, trailer village, RV sites, hotel, showers/laundry, auto/boat gas, store, dry boat storage.

Lake Mead Cruises. Boulder City; (702) 293-6180. Scheduled and charter sightseeing tours on the *Desert Princess* paddlewheel boat from Lake Mead Marina to Hoover Dam and back.

Lake Mead Resort. 322 Lakeshore Road, Boulder City; (702) 293-3484. Call (702) 293-2074 for lodging reservations only, or (800) 752-9669 for other reservations. Restaurant/lounge, marina, boat rentals, store, dry boat storage, boat gas, and motel.

Lakeshore Trailer Village. 268 Lakeshore Road, Boulder; (702) 293-2540. Trailer village with RV sites, showers, and laundry.

Las Vegas Bay Marina/Las Vegas Boat Harbor. Henderson; (702) 565-9111. Restaurant, lounge, marina, boat rentals, dry boat storage, store, gas.

Overton Beach Resort. Overton; (702) 394-4040. Snack bar, boat rentals, moorings, fuel dock, auto/boat gas, store, showers, laundry, trailer village, RV sites, dry boat storage, summer jet-ski rental.

Temple Bar Resort. Temple Bar, Arizona; (520) 767-3211. Reservations (800) 752-9669. Restaurant/lounge, motel, trailer village, dry boat storage, store, marina, boat rentals, showers, laundry, auto/boat gas, RV sites.

Canoe/Raft Services
Down River Outfitters. Boulder City; (702) 293-1190. Canoe/raft delivery and retrieval.

Jerkwater Canoe Co., Inc. Topock, Arizona; (520) 768-7753. Canoe delivery and retrieval.

Scuba Instruction
Lake Mead is a popular dive site because of its warm and clear waters. Special attractions include several wrecks as well as the remains of Callville and other submerged communities.

American Cactus Divers. Las Vegas; (702) 433-3483.
Blue Seas Scuba Center, Inc. Las Vegas; (702) 367-2822.
Colorado River Divers. Boulder City; (702) 293-6648.
Desert Divers Supply, Inc. Las Vegas; (702) 438-1000.
Water World Scuba Diving Center. Bullhead City, Arizona; (520) 763-5531.

Fishing Guides
Patrick Donoho. Las Vegas; (702) 451-4004.

Lake Mohave Resorts and Recreational Facilities
Black Canyon, Inc. Boulder City; (702) 293-3776. Raft tours from Hoover Dam to Willow Beach.

Cottonwood Cove Resort. Cottonwood Cove; (702) 297-1464. Cafe, marina, boat rentals, houseboat rentals, auto/boat gas, dry boat storage, store, showers, laundry, motel, trailer village, RV sites. Forever Resorts at Cottonwood Cove rents houseboats and deck cruisers. (702) 297-1005, (800) 255-5561.

Lake Mohave Resort. Bullhead City, Arizona; (520) 754-3245. Reservations (800) 752-9669. Restaurant/lounge, store, motel, auto/boat gas, marina, boat rentals, houseboat rentals, trailer village, RV sites, showers, laundry, dry boat storage.

Willow Beach Store. Willow Beach, Arizona. (520) 767-4747. Reservations (800) 845-3833. Boat rentals, auto/boat gas, store.

Border Town
Thirty miles south of Las Vegas on I-15 at the border with California lies the Primadonna empire. Basically a one-company town originally named Stateline but now renamed as Primm (and thus avoiding confusion with the other Stateline at the south end of Lake Tahoe), it has grown from a two-pump, twelve-room truck stop to a resort destination with almost 2,700 hotel rooms.

Primadonna Resort and Casino. A Victorian-style playground that has 661 rooms in a quartet of four-story buildings with a turn-of-the-century-style carnival theme. Visitors can take free rides on an authentic merry-go-round or a 100-foot Ferris wheel. There's also a bowling alley and a video arcade.

And in a more modern touch, visitors can cross over I-15 on a monorail that connects Primadonna to Whiskey Pete's. A recent renovation and expansion includes a new convention center and a retheming that emulates a private country club with a tie-in to the Primm Valley Golf Club, a pair of 18-hole championship courses four miles south across the border in California.

Buffalo Bill's Resort. A western-theme hotel and casino that has 1,243 rooms in two hotel towers. There's a Buffalo-shaped pool, waterslide, and Jacuzzi. Oh, and there's also the **Desperado**, which is claimed to be the world's tallest and fastest coaster—it is certainly the world's tallest and fastest roller coaster that passes through a gambling casino.

More about Desperado: The first lift takes about one minute to climb and 3.5 seconds to descend. During the nearly three-minute ride, cars reach speeds of close to ninety miles per hour and G-forces of close to 4.0. (By comparison, astronauts on the Space Shuttle feel a gravitational pull of 3.2 Gs.)

One of only three "magnum-type" coasters in the world, Desperado is 5,843 feet long with a lift height of 209 feet and a drop of 225 feet. The lift goes through the roof of the casino and then drops through a tunnel at top speed. It also passes through the porte cochere arrival area. Three points on the ride deliver near-zero gravity.

Turbo Drop takes twelve riders ensconsed in padded saddles and shoulder harnesses about 170 feet into the air where they will have a spectacular view of the desert and distant mountains for a moment before they plunge back to the ground at forty-five miles per hour, experiencing a negative-1-G feeling and then 4.5 Gs of force as they come to a stop via air brakes.

Nearby to the Desperado is the **Adventure Canyon Log Flume Ride**, the **Ghost Town Motion Simulator Theatres**, and a video arcade. Boarding areas for both the coaster and flume ride are inside the hotel.

Individual-ride tickets were priced at $6 in 2000; an all-day, all-ride wrist band costs $29. The rides are open daily from 11 A.M. to 7 P.M.

Also at Buffalo Bill's is the **Star of the Desert** arena, a 6,500-seat venue for entertainment from major concerts to boxing matches and rodeos.

Buffalo Bill's Hotel and Casino. (702) 386-7867 or (800) 386-7867.

Whiskey Pete's Hotel & Casino. In the mid-1950s, when nothing more than a lonely two-lane highway crossed the desert to Las Vegas, travelers would stop at the California–Nevada state line at a two-pump gas station run by a crusty old coot called "Whiskey Pete." He got his nickname because of a bootleg still he operated in a cave across the road from the station.

There are 777 rooms in an eighteen-story tower. The 700-seat showroom at the hotel regularly features headline acts.

For reservations at any of the three hotels, call (800) 386-7867.

The Fashion Outlet of Las Vegas opened the first phase of a massive mall connected to the Primadonna Resort in 1998. The mall has a 1920s urban seascape theme with re-creations of several famous waterfronts and a water ride.

Chapter 17
Laughlin

Everything's Up-to-Date in Laughlin

The burgeoning community of Laughlin is unique in Nevada in at least two respects. First, it is among the few major settlements that has no real history of its own other than as a camp for the construction of the Davis Dam. There wasn't even a rest stop there! Second, the place was named by and for its founder, who still operates a major casino there.

Laughlin is the most important settlement of the tri-state area, where Clark County, Nevada, Mohave County, Arizona, and San Bernardino County, California, come together. If something seems even stranger than usual for a Nevada gambling town, consider that almost nothing in Laughlin dates back more than about thirty years; everything you see has grown up around the Riverside Casino. In fact, most of the construction only dates as far back as the mid-1980s.

Today, there are about 11,000 rooms at nine hotels and two motels in Laughlin; a nearby Indian reservation has a hotel with 302 rooms. Across the river in gambling-free Bullhead City, Arizona, twenty-five small hotels and motels offer some 1,500 rooms.

Although some scientists believe that humans lived in the area as far back as 10,000 years ago, available evidence in the form of petroglyphs on the walls of canyons near Laughlin dates only some 4,000 or so years back. The first identified Indian tribe was the Patayan, who split into the Hualpai and Mojave tribes (*Patayan* is a Hualpai word meaning "ancient ones").

More than 100 Patayan campsites have been identified between Willow Beach near Hoover Dam, and Pyramid Canyon, the location of Davis Dam.

The Mojaves lived in the region for hundreds of years and were there when the Spanish claimed their land and when the Americans passed through and eventually came to settle. The first Europeans arrived in the sixteenth century when Spanish conquistadors led by Coronado came through on their quest for the mythical Seven Cities of Gold. Along the way, the Spanish found the Grand Canyon.

In the mid-nineteenth century, sternwheel steamboats from California chugged upstream as far as the present site of Hoover Dam bringing supplies and taking away minerals and other booty. In 1857, Lt. Edward Beale surveyed a trail from Fort Smith, Arkansas, to the Colorado River and established a fort near the present site of Bullhead.

Beale's other significant accomplishment was the deployment of a caravan of camels operating out of Fort Mohave. The camels were used to carry freight and mail in the desert, and were taken as far north in Nevada as the foothills of the Sierras. Today the camels are commemorated in a lighthearted way in the annual camel races in Virginia City near Reno.

Another Dam Site

The possibility of a dam across the Colorado River at Pyramid Canyon had been considered as far back as 1902, but work was not begun until after the completion of Hoover Dam some sixty-seven miles upstream.

Bullhead City in Arizona began as a construction camp for the Davis Dam, just as Boulder City was created for Hoover Dam. It received its name from a local landmark known as Bullhead Rock, now covered by the waters of the dam.

Laughlin was originally named South Pointe because of its location at the southernmost point of Nevada. It boasted a motel, bar, and a few other businesses to serve the construction workers. After the dam was completed, the motel was closed and most of the residents of Laughlin and Bullhead City left.

Don Laughlin, who had once owned the 101 Club casino in Las Vegas, came to the area in 1964. He purchased the shuttered motel along the river and rebuilt it as the **Riverside Resort**; he and his family lived in four of the motel rooms and rented out the other four. He added a small casino and restaurant.

According to local lore, the Postal Service gave Laughlin its name; others say the promoter volunteered it. Either way, from this very humble beginning, a new city was born. Today, Laughlin ranks third among Nevada resorts in gaming revenue, behind Las Vegas and Reno and ahead of Lake Tahoe. From 450 rooms in 1983, Laughlin now offers more than 10,000 rooms and boasts near-sellout conditions in the summer. In the winter off-season, the resort offers some of the best room rates anywhere; on one recent visit, two major hotels were offering rooms for $15 per night, and one gave the second night free.

Laughlin is different from Reno and Las Vegas in another way, with a real connection to the natural surroundings of the area. Among other things, most of its casinos are designed with windows that let in sunlight and views of the Colorado River flowing in front of the buildings.

As you descend into Laughlin from Highway 163, your first landmark is likely to be the steam plumes from the modern **Mohave Power Project** above town.

The Mohave Power Project has a total capacity of 1,580 megawatts from its two coal-fired steam turbine generators—about one-third the capacity of the massive Hoover Dam up the river. The generators receive their fuel from an underground river of its own: an eighteen-inch pipeline that brings a slurry of half coal and half water 275 miles from its source at a mine on the Navaho-Hopi Indian Reservation in Kayenta, Arizona.

The Laughlin airport, located across the river in Bullhead City, opened in 1991 with a 7,500-foot runway. America West Express provides daily scheduled service to and from Phoenix.
Bullhead City/Laughlin Airport. (520) 754-2134.
America West Express. (800) 235-9292.

Driving from Las Vegas to Laughlin

Driving from Las Vegas to Laughlin is a bit like taking a trip from Disneyland to Walt Disney World. What you leave and what you come to are pretty much the same; the interesting part is what you see along the way.

It's an interesting tour, though, and worth a day trip when you are ready to take a break from Las Vegas. Be sure to fill your gas tank and check your car's condition before heading out into the desert.

Take Interstate 93/95 south from Las Vegas through Henderson to the point where the roads split. I-93 heads to Boulder City and across the Hoover Dam and then south through Arizona; the direct route to Laughlin follows I-95, and we'll take that road.

Soon after the split, the barren desert is broken by electrical power lines that march across the landscape toward Las Vegas from Hoover Dam. You'll get a very real appreciation for the wildness of the desert that had to be crossed by the early settlers. On the broad, open desert between Nelson and Searchlight there are no houses or settlements at all. It is almost impossible to gauge the distance to the mountains that frame the desert because the land is so flat and there are no structures to give you a sense of perspective.

About four or five miles before Searchlight you'll come to some modern-day Wild West mining operations, made up mostly of ramshackle sheds and trailers. The signs say, "Guard on duty, don't trespass. You will be shot."

At **Searchlight**, you'll come to the first major crossroad since you left Boulder City some thirty-six miles back. Route 164 eastbound is a one-way path to Cottonwood Cove, a recreational area fourteen miles away on Lake Mohave in the Lake Mead National Recreational Area. Cottonwood includes a campground, boat rentals and launching services, and cabins.

Westbound Route 164 connects to I-15, which eventually makes its way to Los Angeles. We'll stay on I-95.

Searchlight is a town of one gas station, a small general store, a liquor store, and (of course) a small gambling parlor, the **Searchlight Nugget Casino.** There is some additional development, including a museum, a mile east on Route 164 toward Cottonwood Cove.

Searchlight received its name from a mining claim in the area, which was in turn named after a then-popular brand of matches. American composer Scott Joplin took note of the lively town with the "Searchlight Rag." Costume designer Edith Head grew up in Searchlight, and movie stars Rex Bell and Clara

LAUGHLIN

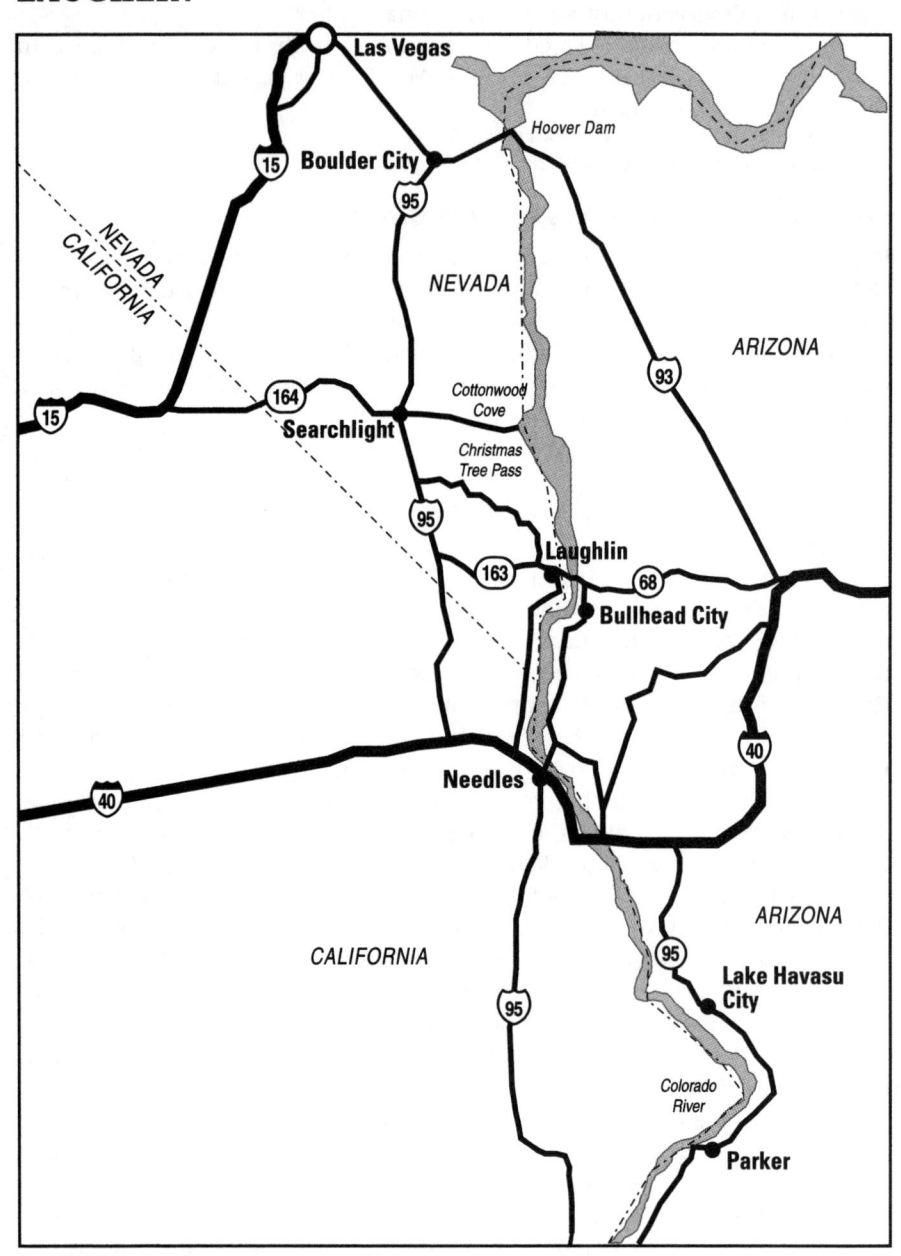

Bow had a ranch there in the 1930s before moving north and helping to launch the age of glamour in Las Vegas.

The next settlement is CalNevAri, named after the three state borders nearby. Even smaller than Searchlight, it nevertheless has a market, a part-time gas station . . . and a casino.

At this point we separate the men from the boys, the women from the girls, and the intrepid explorer from the white-knuckle driver. I'm talking about **Christmas Tree Pass**, an unpaved switchback road that cuts the corner from near CalNevAri to Grapevine Canyon just above Laughlin.

The road to Christmas Tree Pass branches off to the left about two miles past CalNevAri. In dry, clear weather the road should be passable in a passenger car; in wet conditions or snow, I'd recommend a four-wheel-drive vehicle or a resolution to come back another day.

The winding hard-packed dirt road gets narrower and narrower the further along you travel, becoming about a lane-and-a-half wide as you reach the top of the pass. Not that you are likely to meet any other cars on your expedition; I didn't pass another soul on my hour-long seventeen-mile trip. (No gas stations or emergency services, either.)

The road is marked by tiny white signs on the sides of the road that say designated route; resist the urge to follow the side roads off this side road unless you have a topographical map and an off-road vehicle.

At the very top of the pass—about nine miles along—the road suddenly turns into a one-lane switchback; go slowly, and honk your horn before you make the blind turn just in case there is another almost-lost soul ascending the pass.

Somewhere near the top you are likely to find a few forlorn desert bushes festooned with windblown Christmas ornaments; the pass has its name because of an old tradition apparently started by travelers through the pass.

On the down side of the pass you will enter into the Lake Mead Recreational Area, leading up to Lake Mohave. The roads in the park are even worse than the first half of the trip, although not quite as winding.

You'll pass some spectacular rock slide areas, including several mountains that seem to be made entirely of balanced boulders.

And then finally, you are in a valley and on a paved road. On your right is **Grapevine Canyon**, with its ancient petroglyphs. Just ahead is Route 163, at this point a four-lane highway zooming down to the Colorado River and Laughlin.

A direct trip from Las Vegas to Laughlin on Interstate 95 to Highway 163 is about 101 miles, and just under two hours in time. If you take Christmas Tree Pass, figure on just under three hours in total.

A good place to stop as soon as you enter Laughlin is the **Laughlin Visitors Bureau** at 1555 Casino Drive, just before the Riverside Casino. The office has a healthy supply of brochures, newspapers, and magazines. Call (702) 298-3022.

Casinos and Hotels in Laughlin

Don Laughlin's Riverside Resort Hotel & Casino

The start of it all, today offering 1,401 rooms, 830 RV spaces, a six-screen movie theater, five restaurants—and a casino.

Restaurants include the **Gourmet Room**, featuring Continental and American dishes from chateaubriand to rack of lamb to steak and lobster specials; open for dinner only. The **Prime Rib Room** offers beef carved at your table and an all-you-can-eat salad, potato, and dessert bar. The **Riverview Restaurant** is a twenty-four-

> **Laughlin Chamber of Commerce.** Box 2280, Laughlin, NV 89029; (702) 298-2214, (800) 227-5245. www.laughlinchamber.com.
> **Laughlin Visitor Center.** 1555 South Casino Drive, Laughlin, NV 89029; (702) 298-3321.

hour coffee shop. The **Buffet** offers breakfast, lunch, and dinner; on Friday night, seafood is the special, and Saturday and Sunday feature champagne brunches.

At the front entrance to the hotel is a showroom for part of Don Laughlin's classic car collection, augmented by cars on loan from the Imperial Palace collection in Las Vegas. Among the interesting vehicles is a 1935 Chrysler Imperial Airflow that was owned by Steve McQueen. It stands alongside a less impressive but even rarer 1908 Holsman Hi-Wheeler Run-a-Bout.

Recent additions include a thirty-four-lane bowling alley, expanded race and sports book, and a childcare center.

Across the river in Bullhead City, the Riverside runs the **River Queen Motel**, which includes a 600-space RV park; the two hotels are connected by twenty-four-hour ferry service.

The Riverside even has its own "luxury" cruise ship, a spiffed-up houseboat grandly dubbed the USS *Riverside*, that sails daily on seventy-five-minute cruises along the Colorado River to the Davis Dam.

Starring acts are featured at **Don's Celebrity Theatre**. For show information, call (702) 298-2535. Live country music is presented nightly in the Western Ballroom.

Rooms go for as low as $19, with weekends and holiday rates set as high as $105. Riverside Resort Hotel and Casino. 1650 Casino Drive; (702) 298-2535, (800) 227-3849. www.riversideresort.com.

Colorado Belle Hotel & Casino

Here's your basic 608-foot-long, six-deck Mississippi River gambling boat, only it's on the Colorado, and it has never gone and never will go anywhere. The hotel includes four huge environmentally safe (they don't work) smokestacks; at night, strobe lights make the faux paddlewheels appear to turn.

Within, the decorations are those of a turn-of-the-century New Orleans gambling (and probably more) house with excesses of red and bright brass. The high-ceilinged interior is made to look like the inside of a riverboat, with lots of red and gold furnishings.

There are 206 rooms in the "boat" and another 1,082 in a more conventional structure nearby.

Restaurants include the **Orleans Room**, the hotel's gourmet eatery, specializing in seafood, steaks, and pasta with a price range from about $10 to $20. **Mark Twain's Chicken and Ribs** features barbecued guess what, with entrees priced from about $8 to $15; also available are fried chicken and fish dishes. Open for dinner from 4 to 10 P.M.

Nearby are the **Mississippi Lounge & Seafood Bar** and the **Paddlewheel**, a twenty-four-hour coffee shop. The **Captain's Food Fare** offers a breakfast, lunch, and dinner buffet. You can also order main dishes from a menu on the wall and augment them with selections from the buffet bar.

The **Boiler Room Brew Pub** offers mesquite grilling as well as wood-fired pizza ovens. Specialties include "Drunkard Rib Eye Steak," herb-seasoned salmon, sandwiches, and desserts.

The Colorado Belle is owned by Mandalay Resort Group, parent company of Manadalay Bay, Luxor, and Circus Circus in Las Vegas. Room rates are generally in the range of about $40 to $100 but can be as low as $19 per night in the winter. The Colorado Belle Hotel/Casino. 2100 South Casino Drive; (702) 298-4000, (800) 477-4837. www.coloradobelle.com.

The Edgewater Hotel/Casino

Next door to the Colorado Belle is a corporate cousin, a 1,475-room budget behemoth also run by Mandalay Resort Group.

A blue neon waterfall cascades down the face of the building; inside, hand-painted Native American designs decorate many of the walls.

Restaurants include the **Hickory Pit Steak House**, open for dinner and serving steaks, seafood, chops, barbecued ribs, and chicken; the **Garden Room**, a twenty-four-hour coffee shop including a one-pound prime rib special; and the **Winner's Circle Deli**. The **Grand Buffet** is said to be Laughlin's largest buffet with a trio of ninety-foot serving lines.

Kokopelli's Lounge in the south casino area is named for a mythical Southwestern Indian flute player, an ancient bearer of good luck and health.

Room rates are generally in the range from about $19 to $40; in the winter, rates are as low as $16 per night. Call (702) 298-2453 or (800) 677-4837. www.edgewater-casino.com.

Flamingo Hilton Laughlin

A flashy Las Vegas–like resort with mirrors on the ceilings and lots of chrome in the casino, and 2,000 rooms in twin eighteen-story towers. As with other Hiltons in Nevada, there is a move toward accommodating young visitors; the Flamingo Funland carnival is open during the summer season.

Restaurants include **Alta Villa**, open evenings for fine Italian dining with prices ranging from about $16 to $30; closed Wednesday and Thursday. **Beef Barron** is a steak house open for dinner; fare includes prime rib from $9 to $14.

Casual eateries include the **Flamingo Diner**, a twenty-four-hour '50s-style diner.

The **Fruit Basket Buffet**, with an attractive window wall along the river, is open for breakfast, lunch, and dinner.

The Silver Bullet Showroom presents cabaret and lounge acts. An outdoor amphitheater on the river is used for major acts. And at the hotel's dock is *Celebration*, the largest tour boat in the area, with daily cruises for guests.

The Nevada Gold Museum on the first floor of the California Tower is home to what may be the world's largest collection of rare gaming memorabilia, valued at more than $2 million.

The hotel is owned by Park Place Entertainment. In late 2000, the hotel was due to open a huge ballroom for special events, concerts, and boxing.

Rates are as low as $17 in midweek in the off-season, higher on weekends. Flamingo Hilton—Laughlin. 1900 Casino Drive; (702) 298-5111, (800) 352-6464. www.hilton.com/hotels/BHCFLHH/index.html.

Golden Nugget Laughlin

An opulent tropical-theme resort, including an indoor rain forest and more ferns than a Los Angeles singles bar.

The Golden Nugget is the successor to the second casino opened in Laughlin. The Bobcat Club was opened in 1967 as a bar and sold in 1970 to be renamed as the Nevada Club and run as a hotel and casino. It was eventually purchased by Golden Nugget Corp., now known as Mirage Resorts.

The hotel itself is somewhat hidden by a large parking garage on Casino Drive. Visitors enter through an arcade adorned with animatronic singing birds into a tropical atrium, a miniature tribute to the greenery of the Mirage in Las Vegas. The hotel has 300 rooms.

Eateries include **Jane's Grill**, just off the casino floor and featuring a mesquite grill and wood-fired oven pizza. Offerings include pizza, burgers, and sandwiches priced from about $5 to $8.

The **River Cafe** is a twenty-four-hour diner. Its late-night special is steak and eggs for $2.45; breakfast specials include the "Four Deuces," $2.45 for two pancakes, two eggs, two strips of bacon, two sausages, and coffee. **The Buffet** is open for breakfast, lunch, and dinner.

In the back corner of the casino is **The Deli**, a hideaway with reasonably priced sandwiches, such as roast beef for $3 and pastrami or corned beef for $3.50. Pizza goes for $1 a slice. Dessert includes donuts, yogurt, and bear claws (the baked goods type).

Rates are as low as $25 in the winter, rising to as high as $55 for standard rooms. Holiday rates are higher. Golden Nugget—Laughlin Hotel and Casino. 2300 South Casino Drive; (702) 298-7111, (800) 950-7700. www.gnlaughlin.com.

River Palms Resort Hotel and Casino

The former Gold River Resort was reincarnated as the River Palms Resort in 1999. Built as a 1,003-room riverside box nearby the Emerald River Golf Course, it was designed to feel like being inside a mining camp. New owner Allen Paulson plans to recast the resort with a South Atlantic/Bermuda theme.

Restaurants include **Madeleine's Gourmet Room**. **Joey D's** is a moderately priced Italian restaurant. **River Palms Café** is a garden spot for breakfast, lunch, and dinner.

The **No Ka Oi Buffet** serves breakfast, lunch, and dinner.

In recent years, room rates at the Gold River were as low as $19 (with the second night free!) in the off-season; the new incarnation will likely be in the same bargain range. River Palms Resort. 2700 South Casino Drive; (702) 298-2242, (800) 835-7904. www.rvrpalm.com.

Harrah's Laughlin

A little bit of Mexico along the river, a 1,658-room outpost of the Harrah's chain set a bit apart from the rest of the casinos in a small canyon and featuring a small sandy beach along the river.

Restaurants include **William Fisk's** for steaks, seafood, and Continental cuisine in a Southwestern setting, open for dinner only. Steaks are priced from about $16 to $20; other offerings include veal, seafood, and broiled ahi. The very attractive room is decorated in white and gold painted wood, with a window view of the river.

The Monte Re Café, just off the casino floor, offers fine Mexican and American dishes for dinner. Fajitas, tacos, and such fare are priced from about $6 to $12. The **Fresh Market Square Buffet** serves breakfast, lunch, and dinner.

The Del Rio Beach Club rents one- and two-passenger jet-skis in season. Harrah's runs a free shuttle from Harrah's up to the Regency Casino, which is at the far end of the strip next to Laughlin's Riverside.

The Fiesta Showroom regularly rotates its shows. In mid-2000, the show was "10 Dragons Magic Show." Tickets were $15.95.

Another entertainment venue is the 3,000-seat Rio Vista Outdoor Amphitheater, where the likes of Kenny Rogers and the Beach Boys have performed. Shows take place only in the fall and spring.

Winter room rates are ordinarily priced from $19 to $140, with mini suites starting at $140. Harrah's Laughlin. 2900 South Casino Drive; (702) 298-4600, (800) 447-8700. www.harrahs.com/tour/tour_laughlin.html.

Pioneer Hotel and Gambling Hall

A Wild West–theme hotel with 414 rooms and riverfront suites and a swinging door entrance. The river facade features a huge neon cowboy known as River Rick. Eateries include **Granny's Gourmet Room** for fine dining; **Granny's Old-Fashioned Champagne Brunch** is served Sundays for $21.95; the **Boarding House Restaurant** offers menu items or buffet.

The casino has a smoky, dark Western feel; the cocktail waitresses wear costumes that are out of "Li'l Abner." The Pioneer is owned by the Sahara Corp. of Las Vegas.

Room rates range from about $23 in off-season to about $50. Pioneer Hotel and Gambling Hall. 2200 South Casino Drive; (702) 298-2442, (800) 634-3469. www.santafegaming.com/pio.

Ramada Express Hotel Casino

A 1,500-room railroad-theme hotel, including a full-sized train on a track that circles the property on the hillside a block away from the river. The Ramada Express is run by the Aztar Corporation, which also runs the Tropicana in Las Vegas.

The main gambling hall is set up like an old train barn with an arched roof. Old replicas of railroad signs and some old railroading equipment decorate the walls, from lines as archaic as the Tonopah Goldfield Railroad and the Goldfield Bullfrog Railroad Company. The train that circles the hotel is an unrealistic replica.

Eateries include **The Steakhouse** and **Passaggio Italian Gardens**, which offers pizza, pasta, and other Roman fare, and a $12.95 Sunday brunch. **Carnegie's** is a twenty-four-hour dining car, named after the nineteenth-century railroad man and industrialist.

The **Roundhouse Buffet** includes breakfast and a prime rib dinner, priced in 2000 at $4.25 and $7.95 respectively.

The showcase at the Ramada is the Pavilion Theater. For show information, call (800) 243-6846. In 1999, the hotel unveiled what it calls a permanent multimedia show in the Pavilion. "On the Wings of Eagles—A Tribute to American Heroes" is shown once an hour from 9 A.M. to 4 P.M., saluting American heroes from World War II to the present day.

Room rates in off-season are as low as $15, with weekend rates as high as $57. The Ramada Express. 2121 Casino Drive; (702) 298-4200, (800) 243-6846. www.ramadaexpress.com.

Outside of Laughlin

Avi Hotel/Casino. A 302-room hotel and casino on the Ft. Mohave Indian Reservation, fifteen miles south of Laughlin. The Avi (which means "loose change" in the Mojave language), includes a beach and marina on the river; a bridge connects the two sides of the reservation in Arizona and Nevada. The casino includes the Moon Shadow Grille restaurant as well as several fast food eateries and a cafe. Avi Hotel and Casino. 10000 AHA Macav Parkway, Laughlin; (702) 535-5555 or (800) 284-2946.

Laughlin Casinos, Hotels, and Motels

Basic room rates. Note that rates are subject to change and are likely to be higher during holiday periods and major events, and lower in slow periods.

$	$49 or less
$$	$50 to $99
$$$	$100 to $149
$$$$	$150 and more
♣	Casino/Hotel

Avi Hotel/Casino. ♣ 10000 Aha Macao Parkway. (702) 535-5555, (800) 284-2946. $–$$

Bay Shore Inn. 1955 West Casino Drive. (702) 299-9010. $

Best Western Riverside Resort Hotel & Casino. ♣ 1650 Casino Drive. (702) 298-2535, (800) 227-3849. $–$$

Colorado Belle Hotel & Casino. ♣ 2100 Casino Drive. (702) 298-4000, (800) 477-4837. $–$$

Edgewater Hotel & Casino. ♣ 2020 South Casino Drive. (702) 298-2453, (800) 677-4837. $–$$

Flamingo Hilton Laughlin. ♣ 1900 South Casino Drive. (702) 298-5111, (800) 352-6464. $–$$

River Palms Gold River Resort Hotel-Casino. ♣ 2700 South Casino Drive. (702) 298-2242, (800) 835-7904. $–$$$

Golden Nugget Laughlin. ♣ 2300 South Casino Drive. (702) 298-7111, (800) 950-7700. $–$$

Harrah's Casino Hotel. ♣ 2900 South Casino Drive. (702) 298-4600, (800) 447-8700. $–$$$

Pioneer Hotel & Gambling Hall. ♣ 2200 South Casino Drive. (702) 298-2442, (800) 634-3469. $–$$

Ramada Express Hotel/Casino. ♣ 2121 South Casino Drive. (702) 298-4200, (800) 243-6846. $–$$

Laughlin Buffets

Colorado Belle. Captain's Food Fair. (702) 298-4000. Breakfast $6, lunch $6, and dinner $6.49. Friday night seafood buffet $12.95.

Edgewater. Bountiful Buffet. (702) 298-2453. Breakfast $4.49, lunch $4.99, and dinner $6.49.

Flamingo Hilton. Fruit Basket Buffet. (702) 298-5111. Breakfast $3.99, lunch $4.99, and dinner $6.99. Sunday brunch $5.99.

Golden Nugget. The Bountiful Buffet. (702) 298-7111. Breakfast $3.99, lunch $4.99, and dinner $6.99.

Gold River. Opera House Buffet. (702) 298-2242. Breakfast $3.21, lunch $4.28, and dinner $6.99.

Harrah's. Fresh Market Square Buffet. (702) 298-4600. Breakfast $7.99, lunch $7.99, and dinner $8.99.

Pioneer. Boarding House Buffet. (702) 298-2442. Breakfast $4.95, dinner $6.95. On Friday night, there is a seafood buffet, for $12.95.

Ramada Express. The Roundhouse Buffet. (702) 298-4200. Breakfast $4.25, dinner $7.95.

Laughlin Area Attractions

Davis Dam. The second leg in man's reworking of the Colorado River for water control and power generation, the Davis Dam stops the Colorado's water and fills out Lake Mohave, a narrow sixty-seven-mile-long waterway that reaches upstream to Hoover Dam. The third dam on this portion of the Colorado is the Parker Dam eighty miles downstream; Lake Havasu backs up behind it.

The earth-filled Davis Dam is 200 feet tall, 151 feet above the streambed and not as large, nor as visually impressive as the Hoover Dam up the river. But it does have its own peculiar appeal. You are on your own to explore the outside and interior of the dam daily from 7:30 A.M. to 3:30 P.M.

Near the parking lot is an observation platform that gives a good view north up Lake Mohave, and south over the top of the dam and down into the valley with Laughlin and Bullhead City below. The gigantic 125-ton moving crane on the upper level is mounted on railroad tracks and is used to move equipment for the dam and generating plant. You can walk across the top of the dam and look down the sheer wall to the Colorado River below.

Lake Mohave is an after bay to regulate water releases from Hoover Dam. The main purpose of the Davis Dam is to regulate the water to be delivered to Mexico under the Mexican Water Treaty. Power production is a secondary benefit.

Visitors enter the dam via an elevator that drops down twelve stories within the structure. The first stop on the tour is the pre-computer age control room; it is all gauges and dials rather than electronic readouts, looking like something out of a Frankenstein movie. The plant has an installed capacity of 240,000 kilowatts produced by five vertical shaft generators.

Perhaps the most impressive part of the whole tour is the turbine gallery where you see the five gigantic rotating shafts of the turbines. The floor of the room rumbles with the power of the spinning machines.

The interior of the dam is cool and sterile, unnaturally clean. On the day of my tour in January, I was the only visitor inside the dam—even the automated control room was empty. As much as I enjoyed my solo tour, I was very relieved when the elevator deposited me back at the top of the dam.

For information, call (520) 754-3628.

Lake Mohave, built up behind the wall of Davis Dam, has 200 miles of shoreline reaching back upstream to the Hoover Dam at Boulder City. The waters are active with rainbow trout and bass.

Grapevine Canyon. To witness the petroglyphs at Grapevine Canyon, take Christmas Tree Pass road, off Highway 163 and about six miles west of Davis Dam. The gravel road runs into a flat valley dominated by sharp peaks, including Spirit Mountain, the most dominant hill. About two miles into the valley you will come to a spur road to the left, the entrance to the parking area for Grapevine Canyon. The walking trail leads several hundred feet to the mouth of the canyon.

Archaeologists believe there are three eras of art represented on the walls of the canyon, with the oldest about 600 to 800 years old and the most recent dating from about 150 to 200 years ago. Some of the oldest carvings may be below the present level of earth in the area, and others may have been eroded by water. The drawings seem to have some religious significance.

Colorado River Museum. An interesting, eclectic small collection of historical and household objects. The museum is located on the Arizona side of the river, toward Davis Dam; cross the Laughlin Bridge and make a left turn onto Highway 68 and get into the left lane to cross the road a half mile east.

Outside the museum is a small model of Don Laughlin's first casino, which opened in 1966 and brought South Pointe and Bullhead City back to life. Inside you'll find photographs of some of the old mines, including Oatman and the Tom Reed Gold Mine, a fabulous find that produced $13 million worth of gold between 1906 and 1931. Another display shows barbed wire from the 1880s.

Nearby is a steamboat anchor found in the Colorado River near Hardyville. When a steamboat approached a sandbar it would turn stern-to and send a small boat ahead with the anchor; the anchor would be sunk in the sand and then as the paddlewheel dug its way through the sand, the anchor chain would be winched in to pull the boat over the sandbar.

Katherine's Landing. A rich gold and silver strike was made here in 1900, on the Arizona side of the river three miles north of the present site of Davis Dam. The mine produced $12 million worth of preinflation gold in the four decades until it was closed down in 1942. Today, Katherine's Landing is a resort community and marina on Lake Mohave with boat slips, boat rentals, launch ramp, and sandy beaches with barbecues and picnic areas. (520) 754-3245.

Oatman. The town was born in 1906 as a gold mining tent camp; after tens of millions of dollars were extracted from the area, the town went bust in 1942 after Congress declared gold mining was no longer essential to the war effort.

At its height, the town had a population of more than 12,000 and featured its own local stock exchange. The scenery around Oatman has been used for a number of movies including *How the West Was Won*.

The ghost town and historic gold mining area includes museums, shops, and eateries. Gunfighters stage weekend showdowns on the town's main street, on historic Route 66, approximately thirty miles southeast of Laughlin.

London Bridge, English Village, and Lake Havasu. London Bridge did not fall down; it was taken apart stone by stone and shipped to Arizona where it is the centerpiece of a small British theme park. For information, call (520) 453-3444. Depending on whether you take backcountry roads or interstates, the distance is sixty-seven or ninety-seven miles, respectively; either way, it's about a two-hour drive to the southeast. (Highway route: east on State 68 to Kingman, Interstate 40 west 40 miles to Needles, south on State 95 to Lake Havasu City.)

Grand Canyon Caverns. About 100 miles east of Laughlin on Highway 66 between Kingman and Seligman, Arizona. Adults $9.50, children 4–12 $6.75. For information call (520) 422-3223.

Grand Canyon Railway. Steam engines from Williams, Arizona run from Memorial Day through September; vintage diesels work the line for the rest of the year. Trains depart at 10 A.M. and arrive at 12:15 P.M., heading back at 3:30 P.M. for a 5:45 P.M. arrival. Tickets range from about $50 to $155, depending on class. Packages including tours of the Grand Canyon and overnight accommodations are also available. For information call (800) 843-8724. *You will find a discount coupon in this book.*

Outdoor Recreation Near Laughlin
Golf

Emerald River Golf Course. 1155 West Casino Drive, Laughlin. (702) 298-0061. 18 holes.

Chaparral Country Club. 1260 Mohave Drive, Bullhead City, AZ. (520) 758-3939. 9 holes.

Riverview Golf Club. 2000 East Ramar Road, Bullhead City, AZ. (520) 763-1818. 9 holes.

Desert Lakes Golf Course. 5835 South Desert Lakes Drive., Fort Mohave, AZ. (520) 768-1000. 18 holes.

Colorado River Boat Tours

Laughlin River Tours. Fiesta Queen and Little Belle. Paddlewheel boats offer daily 90-minute tours of the Colorado River. Adults $11, children 4 to 12 $6. (702) 298-1047, (800) 228-9825.

USS *Riverside*. Daily excursions on the Colorado River from the Riverside Casino. $10 per person. (702) 298-2535, (800) 227-3849.

Colorado River Boat Rentals

Del Rio Beach Club, Harrah's. Wave runners and jet boats. (702) 298-6828.
New Horizons, Pioneer Hotel. Parasailing and wave runners. (702) 298-2442.
Splash Water Craft. Bullhead City. Wave runners. (520) 754-3101.

Driving from Laughlin to Las Vegas Through Arizona

We'll return to Las Vegas with a slightly longer tour that will take us east toward Kingman, Arizona, and then northwest in the valley alongside the Cerbat Mountains and then across the Hoover Dam and back into Nevada.

The trip totals about 140 miles and should take just under three hours.

Cross the Laughlin Bridge toward Bullhead City, and make an immediate left turn onto Highway 68 toward Kingman, Arizona. About 10 miles past the Colorado you will come to **Katherine Mine Road** on your left, which will take you down to the shores of Lake Mohave, the ruins of the once-fabulous gold mine there, and the town that grew up around it.

Gold and silver mining began in the Katherine and Union Pass areas in the mid-1860s, reaching a peak between 1900 and 1907. The mines were reopened in 1933 when the value of gold rose, but the mine structure was severely damaged by fire in 1934. Sporadic mining continued until 1943.

All that remains of the mine is a group of concrete pillars; deep below is a labyrinth of passages, now mostly flooded by Lake Mohave.

You'll cut through the first set of mountains on Union Pass at about 3,600 feet. The panorama of sharply peaked mountains on the Arizona side are much more spectacular than the ones you drove through coming down.

Once you are over the mountain pass you are into a mostly flat high desert plateau within a ring of mountains known as Golden Valley.

Kingman is where old Route 66, Route 93, and Route 68 all come together. Just short of Kingman, the road comes to a T at Interstate 93; head left to go north.

In the Cerbat Mountains to your right are dozens of small mining camps, some of which grew large enough to qualify as towns at their peak. The first you'll pass is **Cerbat**, which came into existence in the 1860s as a mining camp and had a mill, a smelter, a post office, school, stores, and saloons. Only a few sites remain now.

A few miles north on Interstate 93 brings you to a road to **Mineral Park**, located five miles northeast into the mountains. Now abandoned, it was the county seat from 1873 to 1887 and included a courthouse and jail, stores, hotel, saloons, assay offices, and two stagecoach stations.

I drove up Route 255 to Mineral Park. It had been raining in the valley, but as I climbed, it began to turn into snow and up above, the mountains were blanketed. The road ends in a box canyon and a mineral processing plant within barbed wire. On both sides of the road are capped pipes that sit over the top of former mine shafts. In the valleys are a few gigantic piles of tailings as tall as some of the mountains.

The next town of interest is **Chloride**, another mining boom town. A road leads directly to Chloride from I-93, but I chose to explore a very rough dirt road that led from Route 255 near Mineral Park; I almost did not make it. The back road is made of soft earth and the rain had turned the path into mud. Just to make things worse, the rough road is marked at several points with warnings about the possibility of flash flood areas. As with Christmas Tree Pass, I'd recommend against taking the back road in less than perfect weather.

Chloride sits four miles east of Grasshopper Junction, off I-93. It began in about 1863 with the discovery of the first silver mines in the area. By 1900 it had a population of 2,000, with more than seventy-five mines in operation including the Tennessee Schuykill, a large producer of gold, silver, copper, lead, and zinc. The post office is the oldest continuously operated station in Arizona, dating from 1871. A coach line known as the Butterfield Stage served Chloride from 1868 until 1919; the Santa Fe Railroad had a spur to Chloride from 1898 until 1935. The last of the mines were shuttered in 1944 when they were no longer profitable.

Today, though, some 350 hardy souls live on the hill. Each summer they cater to tourists who come to see the somewhat-preserved boom town. There are a couple of lean-to shacks, and a couple of shops, three cafes, two saloons, and the old post office to visit. The town celebrates Old Miners Day on the last Saturday of June, with a parade (at high noon, of course), plus music, dancing, melodramas, and gunfights. Vaudeville shows are performed on the first and third Saturdays of the month in the summer. For information, contact the Chloride Chamber of Commerce at (520) 565-2204.

Back on Interstate 93, there's a small community and gas station near Willow Beach, and then the road climbs up into the mountains again and then drops down through a series of spectacular switchback turns that eventually lead to the Hoover Dam. The road passes right over the top of the dam and into Boulder City.

Part III
Reno, Virginia City, and Lake Tahoe

Chapter 18
The Biggest Little Chapter in This Book: Reno

Econoguide 2001 Best Casino-Hotels in Reno-Sparks

★★★★	**Eldorado.**	*A classic fable of riches.*
★★★★★	**Harrah's.**	*Reborn as the class of downtown.*
★★★★	**John Ascuaga's Nugget, Sparks.**	*A quirky gem.*
★★★★★	**Peppermill.**	*The liveliest (and gaudiest) place in town.*
★★★★	**Reno Hilton.**	*A city within the city.*
★★★★	**Silver Legacy.**	*A theme park with slot machines.*
★★★	**Atlantis.**	*Still growing.*
★★	**Circus Circus.**	*Best-named casino in town.*
★★	**Comstock.**	*An old coin mine.*
★★★	**Flamingo Hilton.**	*Muted elegance.*
★	**Sands Regency.**	*Nothing to write home about.*

Welcome to Reno, also known as "The Biggest Little City in the World," whatever that means.

The title comes from the slogan on the famous arch that crosses Virginia Street in downtown Reno. Historians point to an early advertising campaign used to promote the Jeffries-Johnson heavyweight fight of 1910: "The Biggest Little City on the Map." The original arch was erected in 1927 honoring an exposition to mark the completion of the transcontinental highway system, which passed through Reno. The most recent update to the arch, an understated art deco design with 800 linear feet of neon and 1,600 light bulbs, was completed in 1987.

Reno has fought mightily against the decline of downtown with projects such as the Silver Legacy Resorts, improvements at Harrah's, a city-financed multiplex movie theater a block from South Virginia Street, and the closure of most of its downtown sawdust joints. It is still much more of a working-class place than Las Vegas, home of bowling competitions instead of computer expositions.

The glittery Peppermill is in the midst of a doubling in size, and Harrah's has bought up a whole chunk of downtown for an outdoor stage and expansion.

Winter is value season in Reno, which means rates at world-class hotel/casino and motel lodging are at their rock-bottom lowest except for the Christmas to New Year's period. And dining, whether it be a full-out breakfast buffet or a midnight snack, is more accessible and less expensive than at other winter resort destinations.

I love Reno most as a gateway to two of my favorite places: Lake Tahoe and Virginia City. I can stay in a city hotel, eat at casino restaurants, and be within ninety minutes of some of the best winter and summer activities in the country.

Reno and Lake Tahoe Climate

The climate in the Reno-Tahoe area can vary greatly by elevation and location. The overall climate is very arid; the Reno area receives very little precipitation, with an average of about 7.5 inches per year. Snowfall can vary greatly, from about six inches per month from December to February to measurements by the yard in some mountainous areas.

In January of 1997, all of the seasonal averages went out the window with a prodigious snowfall in the Sierras followed by rain; much of downtown Reno was flooded and both Route 50 west of Lake Tahoe and U.S. 395 south of Carson City were closed for several weeks because of slides and damage. Again in the winter of 1998–99, massive snowfalls buried the Sierras.

Although highways and major roads are plowed and sanded as necessary, many mountain passes are subject to closing because of poor visibility, ice, or blowing and drifting snow. At times, the use of snow tires and/or chains is mandatory. Drivers are generally advised to carry tire chains when crossing mountain passes in winter. Driving in the Sierra can be very dangerous at times during the winter, and motorists should use extreme caution, especially when heading down steep grades.

For road and weather information, call:

California Department of Transportation Road Reporting Service at (916) 445-7623.

Nevada Department of Transportation Road Reporting Service at (775) 793-1313. www.nvroads.com.

Nevada Weather Service at (702) 248-4800.

Reno-Sparks Convention & Visitors Authority at (800) 752-1177.

The area enjoys warm and dry days in spring, summer, and early fall, turning crisp though sunny for much of the winter. Nights turn cool year-round and sweaters or light jackets are usually appropriate even in summer. Sweaters and coats are needed in the winter. In ski season, ski clothing is acceptable in most casual restaurants and all casinos.

Reno/Sparks Average Temperatures

	Jan	Feb	Mar	Apr	May	Jun	Jul	Aug	Sep	Oct	Nov	Dec
High	45	50	54	63	70	79	89	87	81	70	56	48
Low	19	24	27	32	39	45	50	47	41	33	24	21

Mileage to Reno

Carson City	30	Heavenly Ski Resort	55
Elko	289	Incline Village	35
Fallon	60	Jackpot	406
Genoa	40	Las Vegas	440

Los Angeles	469	South Lake Tahoe	59
New York City	2,711	Sparks	3
Pyramid Lake	33	Squaw Valley USA	50
Sacramento	125	Truckee	30
Salt Lake City	526	Virginia City	24
San Francisco	229	Yosemite National Park	137

About Reno

The site of present-day Reno was settled about 1858 and was first known as Lake's Crossing. The town grew with the discovery of the Comstock Lode in nearby Virginia City. The railroad arrived in 1868, and the city was renamed for General Jesse Lee Reno. A native of Virginia, Reno was a popular military leader in the U.S. Civil War and before that in the Mexican War. He was killed as he led the Union Army's 9th Corps at South Mountain in 1862.

The city straddles the Truckee River, and civic leaders celebrate the revitalized downtown's Truckee River Walk with a festival in early June to begin the summer season and with a Christmas gala on the river in early December.

The early history of Reno, like Las Vegas, Carson City, and Genoa, was as a rest stop for travelers heading elsewhere. Many of the westward-bound settlers who chose a northern crossing of the Sierras followed the Humboldt-Carson trail; various branches of the trail crossed over at Carson Pass (north of Lake Tahoe) or a pathway through Truckee Meadows and over Donner Summit, named after the ill-fated 1846 winter expedition.

The wagon trains needed to find a place to cross the Truckee River, especially in the spring when the waters ran high, and several private entrepreneurs built toll bridges in the area. A young New Yorker named Myron Lake bought one of the bridges and opened an inn for the travelers; his bridge crossed the Truckee at the spot that is today the heart of Reno: First and Virginia Streets. Lake expanded his operations when he obtained the franchise to collect tolls on the Sierra Valley Road (now Virginia Street) and made his fortune with the boom that came with the discovery of the Comstock Lode in Virginia City.

Lake's Crossing, as the enterprise was known, came to control much of the land that would become Reno. In 1868, Lake made a business deal with the Central Pacific Railroad, which was pushing its tracks through the area. He gave the railroad sixty acres of land; the CP agreed to use the town site as a freight and passenger depot.

Very much like what would take place thirty-seven years later in Las Vegas, the railroad auctioned off 400 lots in May of 1868 and a town was born.

With its roots as a rough-and-tumble railroad city and trading post for the even-rougher mining men of Virginia City, Reno fulfilled the urgent demands of many of its clients. The red-light district was on Lake Street, and the gambling halls were semihidden on Douglas Alley.

Just as in Las Vegas, a power struggle over gambling, liquor, and prostitution took place just after World War I; the push to tone down what had become known as the "biggest little city in the world" eventually came to a vote in the 1923 election for mayor. E. E. Roberts, backed by some of the political and economic forces who had the most to gain, ran for office on a platform promis-

Reno's famous downtown arch
© *1995 Reno News Bureau*

ing to do away with or ignore all laws that affected "personal choice." He won easily and kept his word to close his eyes.

Reno, with its proximity to California, began to pick up a large trade in quickie divorces and marriages because of the liberal laws in Nevada. And the fact that there were other diversions in the town helped make it a very popular place with residents of the Golden State.

Of course, the Wild West had always been a place where social mores were . . . looser. So it was with legalities like divorce. Nevada had a law allowing almost immediate divorce for any citizen for a variety of reasons. And because Nevada had such a history of massive influxes for its various mining and railroad booms, citizenship was available to anyone living within its boundaries for at least six months.

The wealthy industrial class at the turn of the century realized that this combination offered a relatively easy way out of marriages; the procedure became a national affair when former showgirl Laura Corey moved to Reno for six months to initiate a "quickie" divorce from her philandering husband William Corey, the multimillionaire president of U.S. Steel in Pittsburgh. The publicity launched an industry in Reno.

The conservative establishment tried to reel in Nevada's wild-wheeling reputation with a ban on gambling in 1909—widely ignored—and a 1913 change in citizenship rules to twelve months. But an obvious decline in Reno's economy led to a 1915 repeal of the citizenship rule. In 1931, faced with competition from other states, including Arkansas and Arizona, Nevada dropped the residency requirement to six weeks and threw in legalized gambling for good measure. Reno's divorce industry was rejuvenated, with about 5,000 cases—about twenty a day—in 1931. (Some Reno hotels had "divorce specials" for the six-week stays.)

Reno's casinos, though they were now legal, seemed stuck in the mold of the dark, hidden, illegal enterprise they had once been. This began to change with the arrival of Raymond "Pappy" Smith and his sons Raymond Jr. and Harold; their Harolds Club on Virginia Street was the first "carpet joint" in Reno, an attempt to swap sin for fun as an image. The Smith family sold the casino in 1970 to Howard Hughes' Summa Corporation. It changed hands several times in the following years; in 1999 the property was purchased by Harrah's, which demolished the structure.

And there is life outside the casinos, including the gigantic National Bowling Stadium, with seventy-eight lanes and 1,200 seats. *See Chapter 20 for more details.*

> **Point of reference.** The Truckee River, which runs from Lake Tahoe to Pyramid Lake, travels from west to east as it passes through downtown Reno. Where the river and Virginia Street intersect is the zero point for the street numbering of the city. Fourth Street, for example, is called West Fourth Street west of Virginia and (you figured this out, right?) East Fourth Street east of Virginia.
>
> The north-south roads are similarly split: the main drag of Virginia Street is called North Virginia on the north side of the river and South Virginia on the south side. The higher the number, the farther away from the heart of downtown at the river.

About the Sierra Nevadas

The Sierra Nevada mountain range lies mostly in California, reaching into Nevada near Lake Tahoe.

Bounded on the north by a gap south of Lassen Peak and by the Cascade Range, and on the south by Tehachapi Pass, the range runs from northwest to southeast for about 400 miles in a forty- to eighty-mile-wide swath.

The tallest peak in the Sierra Nevadas is Mount Whitney, which at 14,494 feet is also the tallest peak in the lower forty-eight states.

According to geologists, the Sierra Nevadas are made up of a single block of the earth's crust tilted upward toward the east. The predominant rocks of the range are granite, other igneous rocks, and metamorphic slate. Great quantities of gold have been found embedded in quartz, while silver has been mined on the eastern slope.

Reno Casinos and Hotels

★★★ Atlantis Casino Resort

In the 1980s, there was only a small motel on the corner. Today the motel is still there, all but surrounded by one of Reno's largest and liveliest casinos, a place that seems to be constantly expanding.

Recent expansions include a twenty-seven-story tower with Jacuzzi suites. There's also a full-service health club with indoor and outdoor pools, and the city's only concierge tower. Expansion projects have changed the shape and configuration of the property every few years, including a skyway across South Virginia Street from the casino to the parking lot across the street.

The casino floor is tropic-themed with a waterfall and lots of greenery. Among the more attractive casinos in town, it's popular with locals who come for gambling and dining. The seven restaurants include Toucan Charlies and an upscale eatery called MonteVigna Italian Ristorante.

Atlantis Casino Resort. 3800 South Virginia Street; 982 rooms; (775) 825-4700, (800) 723-6500. www.atlantiscasino.com.

MUST-SEE ★★ Circus Circus Hotel/Casino

Yowzah, yowzah! It's Circus Circus, a smaller cousin of the Las Vegas original, but definitely a Reno must-see.

With 1,572 rooms, Circus Circus lost its title as downtown Reno's largest resort with the opening of the Silver Legacy next door; but in typical Nevada fashion, its owners have it their way anyhow: Circus Circus is partners with the Eldorado in ownership of the Silver Legacy and is connected to the new showplace by a second-floor walkway. And the place has been spiffed up a bit in recognition of its tony neighbor.

In any case, Circus Circus Reno is indisputably the World's Second Largest Hotel and Casino with a Circus and Midway, a few notches behind Circus Circus in Las Vegas. It's a lively low-roller haven that draws a lot of families to its combination of slots, video games, circus acts, and blackjack tables.

In recent years, the hotel's cheesy pink exterior was redone in whites with gold and green trim. Inside the public areas have been upgraded a bit with a "turn of the century European circus" theme.

Circus acts—including high-wire bicyclists, aerialists, gymnasts, and clowns—start at about 11:15 A.M. and continue until nearly midnight. The circus acts are introduced by a ringmaster and sometimes accompanied by a somewhat bored two-piece band. Each act is about eight to ten minutes long—the management doesn't want people to stay away from the tables too long.

The midway is a lure for children of all ages, offering coin toss, ring toss, shooting gallery, video arcade, face painting, and other such carnival entertainment. Concession stands offer food, drinks, and balloons.

Check out the shooting gallery that uses beams of light from the rifles; it's much better than your average mechanical ducks. We especially like the poor little canary atop the piano

Circus Circus, Reno

who will dance for you; hit the piano player in the behind and he'll provide the music.

And, of course, there is a casino, which is a pretty lively place at all hours. As you might expect, there seem to be a few families with the youngsters dispatched upstairs to the circus and carnival, while mom and dad are downstairs gambling the dinner money.

> **Send in the clown.** The landmark "Topsy the Clown" sign in front is 148 feet tall to the top of his lollipop, weighing in at 44.8 tons (about 90,000 pounds).

The circus performers, according to the hotel, constitute a minor league for the major shows, including Ringling Brothers and Barnum & Bailey Circus, the Moscow Circus, the Romanian State Circus, and other troupes.

The performers change regularly, but usually include trapeze artists, high-wire walkers, teeterboard acts, unicycle and trick bicycle performers, jugglers, and clown acts.

The **Courtyard Buffet** is an improvement over the former chowline that was served beneath a red-and-white striped circus big top. The buffet includes an omelet station and a Chinese exhibition kitchen.

The **Hickory Pit**, a dark brick wall room fairly well isolated from the casino floor, is open for dinner from 5 to 11 P.M. with entrees from about $10 to $20. Entrees on a recent visit included Steak Bourbon Street, flamed with bourbon and topped with shrimp scampi and Seafood Prima Vera Alfredo.

An interesting alternative is **Art Gecko's Southwest Bar & Grille**, with entrees from about $12 to $20; for reasons beyond me, within Gecko's is **Kokopelli's Sushi**.

Circus Circus Hotel/Casino. 500 North Sierra Street; 1,625 rooms; (775) 329-0711, (800) 648-5010.

★★ Comstock Hotel/Casino

An eclectic casino worth a visit. The upper levels of the casino feature Western scenes, including a robotic piano-playing couple named Lulabelle & Slim.

The casino floor includes a few real one-arm bandits (slot machines that point a six-shooter at the player), as well as a sprinkling of life-like dummies on the floor—some of which seem livelier than some of the players at the tables.

At the center of the casino is a stairway to **Amigo's Mexican Restaurant**, an inexpensive eatery that sweetens the offer with two-for-one margaritas and combination platters.

Or, you can take an escalator down through a simulated mining tunnel to the **Miner's Cafe**, a twenty-four-hour coffee shop.

Comstock Hotel/Casino. 200 West Second Street; 310 rooms; (775) 329-1880, (800) 648-4866.

MUST-SEE ★★★★ Eldorado Hotel/Casino

The Eldorado is a very attractive, very classy modern casino worth a visit. It has a collection of some of the better hotel restaurants in town.

In 1995, the hotel completed a major expansion and refurbishment that

> **Visitor Centers in Reno/Sparks.** For visitor information and room reservations, call (775) 827-7366 or (800) 367-7366. www.playreno.com
> Visitor centers are located at: Reno Cannon International Airport; Reno Downtown Visitors Center, 300 North Center Street, in the National Bowling Stadium; Reno-Sparks Convention Center, 4590 South Virginia Street; Sparks Downtown Visitors Center, Pyramid Way and Victorian Ave., Sparks.

> **Mud in your eye.** Coffees available at the Eldorado Coffee Company range in price from about $5 to $10 per pound and include products such as Ethiopian *Yergacheffe*, Mexican *Custepec*, Brazillian *Santos*, Guatemalan *Antigua* and Swiss water decaf. You can also order by calling (800) 648-5966.

included a snazzy upper lobby, a new tower with thirty-six super-suites for high rollers, a new show room, and convention center. It also made the most of its second-floor skyway connection to its corporate half-cousin, the Silver Legacy Casino, with a microbrewery, and a redone buffet that has regained the *Econoguide* ranking as the best feed-your-face eatery in town.

The 580-seat Eldorado Showroom features Broadway-style entertainment, six nights a week.

The Grand Plaza on the mezzanine level includes a fanciful fifty-foot marble and bronze "Fountain of Fortune," a trompe l'oeil sky dome, and a splashy restaurant, **Project Bistro 21**.

The lively casino includes what is billed as the world's largest roulette table, seating as many as forty people.

Let's eat our way through the Eldorado.

First stop, near the entrance, is **Choices**, an all-in-one "express cafe" food court. Among the stands in the attractive open room decorated with glass brick and tile off the casino floor are **Chinatown**, which offers entrees for $4 to $5, including lobster Cantonese and roast duck, and appetizers that include egg rolls and soup; **Little Italy**, offering pasta, pizza, and submarine sandwiches; **Virginia Deli**, with hot dogs, shrimp cocktail, and sandwich specialties; and the **American Kitchen**, featuring burgers, fried chicken, ham and eggs, and a steak and lobster special for about $10. The food court also offers a cheap shrimp cocktail with tiny, tiny shrimp. There's also the **Asian Noodle Kitchen** with some interesting options.

La Strada is a more formal room, serving dinner nightly from 5 P.M. Pizzas are prepared in a wood-fired brick oven. In addition to the basics, toppings include *pescatore* (fresh tomato, shrimp, scallops, clams, calamari with garlic and basil) for $9.95. Entrees range in price from about $22.

The nearby **Grill Steakhouse** has entrees in the range of $10 to $25. Interesting items include blackened rib steak with honey mustard and peppercorn, and spit-roasted leg of lamb.

And the attractions go on: be sure to stop at **Tivoli Gardens**, a high-scale food court decorated with overhead arbors and lots of brass with offerings from around the world. You'll know things are a bit different when you come to the elaborate coffee roaster at the entrance.

The selection of beans is made by the restaurant's executive chef, choosing premium arabica green coffee beans from the high altitudes of Central America, Africa, Indonesia, and Hawaii.

Depending on your age, sex, and degree of sweet tooth you may find the dessert carousel at Tivoli Gardens even more attractive than the cocktail waitresses who, just for the record, wear some of the skimpiest outfits in town.

Tivoli Gardens serves breakfast twenty-four hours a day. International specials, priced from about $5 to $12, are served from 11 A.M. to 3 A.M.

The **Chefs** buffet—one of the Econoguide bests—features American, Italian, Chinese, Mongolian, and Hispanic cuisine, prepared on grills and woks at the center of the dining area.

The **Brew Brothers** microbrewery is located on the south end of the skywalk linking the Eldorado to the Silver Legacy. Offerings, priced from about $6 to $8, include hot wings, onion rings, club sandwiches, pizzas, sausage, and baby back ribs. Brews we found on a recent (strictly research) trip included Eldorado Extra Pale Honey Ale, Big Dog Ale, Wild Card Wheat Ale, Gold Dollar Pale Ale, Redhead Amber Ale, Double Down Stout, and Brewmaster's Special.

The food is one of the best deals in town outside of the buffets and the greasy spoon specials at coffee shops. There's a happy hour most days from 3 to 6 P.M., with home brews selling for $1.25 a glass. They also produce a root beer.

The latest addition to the Eldorado's collection of restaurants is the **Bistro Roxy**, which is a Paris-style bistro with American influences; there are seven different settings including a "centuries-old" wine cellar, a turret to an old city wall, a Parisian-style bistro, an old-fashioned exhibition bakery, a European sidewalk cafe, and a Toulouse-Lautrec–inspired atrium bar. Specialties include spit-roasted pork loin and chicken, pan-seared Chilean sea bass, and fresh quail. Entrees range in price from about $15 to $26. The restaurant is open daily from 5 P.M.

Eldorado Hotel/Casino. 345 North Virginia Street; 800 rooms; (775) 786-5700, (800) 648-5966. www.eldoradoreno.com.

★★★ Flamingo Hilton Reno

An attractive, quality hotel, nice enough to almost forget for a while you are in a casino, the Flamingo Hilton offers 604 rooms, including 66 suites.

The hotel is actually located a block in from the Virginia Street strip but uses a street-level storefront (the former Paco's Casino) as a come-on to pedestrians. A series of escalators and a walkway connect you to the main hotel and casino.

The hotel draws its lineage back to the Primadonna. Next it became Del Webb's Sahara; then the Reno Hilton and when the former Bally's became the Reno Hilton it was renamed the Flamingo Hilton.

In 2000, the 1,200-seat showroom was home to Carnival of Wonders, a lively magic show. There is one show Sunday through Friday nights and two shows on Saturday nights; the theater is dark Tuesday. Tickets start at about $24.95, and children are welcomed for $12.95. Several combination packages that include the show plus a meal are available.

The premier restaurant is the **Top of the Flamingo**, which offers gorgeous views of the surrounding mountains. The eatery is paneled in dark wood like a private club, with gray carpet and chairs; an even more private dining area near the bar is available to large parties by reservation. High rollers and local regulars have their own locked liquor storage bins by the bar.

Open for dinner only, it is closed Tuesday. Offerings, priced from about $18 to $25, have included various steaks, swordfish, shrimp scampi, and roast rack of lamb. There's also a weekend champagne brunch with omelettes, eggs benedict, steak teriyaki, and ham.

An outpost of the Benihana Japanese steakhouse chain near the lobby is open nightly except Monday.

Other restaurants include the **Flamingo Room Buffet and Grill**, open twenty-four hours and serving a variety of fare, **Izzy's Deli**, and a selection of fast food outlets.

Standard rooms at the Flamingo Hilton are above average in quality; the suites on the top floor are quite impressive, but it is the Barron Suite, which includes two tubs and a large living room, that is most impressive. As in most Nevada casinos, the best rooms are generally reserved as comps for the high rollers.

Flamingo Hilton Reno. 255 North Sierra Street; 604 rooms; (775) 322-1111, (800) 648-4882. www.hilton.com.

MUST-SEE ★★★★★ Harrah's Casino/Hotel Reno

Harrah's has been reborn as the light of downtown. Several years of remake has extended into nearly every corner of the sprawling hotel and casino; all of the rooms have been redone, and the buffet has been reborn as one of Reno's best.

But the new star of South Virginia Street is The Plaza at Harrah's, a football field-sized open concert and special event center, lit up each night by an hourly music and laser light show.

A covered walkway begins at the base of the famous Reno Arch and leads into a rotunda entrance attached to the original casino. Strolling entertaineers and gourmet food carts mix among the guests.

The plaza occupies the former site of two venerable casinos, Harolds Club and the Nevada Club.

The history of Harrah's reaches back to 1946 when it was the first major casino of William Harrah and one of the classiest joints in town; he had previously run several tiny operations around Reno.

An outpost of the **Planet Hollywood** chain occupies the corner; memorabilia includes Tom Arnold's senior year high school yearbook and the model of the submarine used in *Hunt for Red October*.

Across Center Street on Virginia and connected by a skywalk is the Harrah's Sports Casino, which is a very lively smaller casino more oriented toward the sports bettor and the slot machine crowd; dealers are dressed in referee stripes.

Entertainment is presented in **Sammy's Showroom**, named after Sammy Davis Jr., who made more than 400 appearances there over twenty-two years.

Harrah's **Fresh Market Square Buffet**, features international service stations with offerings including Chinese, Italian, vegetarian, American, and other fare. Brunch is served daily from 8 A.M. to 2 P.M., and dinner nightly.

Café **Napa**, a twenty-four-hour coffee shop on the Skyway level of the hotel, offers California-themed entrees such as crab cakes with pesto hollandaise sauce; the Seafood Golden Gate, a bread bowl filled with smoked salmon, crabmeat, bay shrimp, avocado, and tomatoes, and Thai chicken or pork chops. Also within the restaurant is the Chinese Kitchen, offering Asian fare.

Harrah's Steak House is an award-winning restaurant, decorated in muted reds and hidden a floor below and a world away from the jingle-jangle of the casino. Specialties include rack of lamb with herb crust and pine nut–pinot noir sauce, and steak Diane. Dinner entrees range in price from about $18 to $25. Lunch is served 11 A.M. to 2:30 P.M. weekdays, and dinner is from 5 P.M. every day. Luncheon offerings are priced from about $9 to $14.

> **Seven-up.** Founder Bill Harrah had a gambler's view of the world. According to lore, he drank exactly seven cups of coffee each day and opened his first casino in 1937; he even managed to marry seven times. At one time, the Harrah's logo sported seven stars atop the seven letters of the company name.

The extensive dinner menu includes oyster, shrimp, and salmon appetizers and entrees priced from about $18 to $35.

Café Andreotti is open for dinner at 5 P.M. from Thursday through Monday nights. The kitchen is open to view and is worth a peek. For an appetizer, you can create your own pasta misto. Pastas include spaghetti, linguine, cheese tortellini, and cheese ravioli, and sauces include tomato basil, white wine, and red or white clam. Entrees are priced from about $8 to $15.

Room rates range from about $39 to $139, with seasonal specials often available.

Harrah's Entertainment owns and operates casinos under the Harrah's, Showboat, and Rio brands, including the sprawling Rio Suites in Las Vegas.

Harrah's Casino/Hotel Reno. 206 North Virginia Street; 974 rooms; (775) 786-3232, (800) 648-3773. www.harrahsreno.com.

★★★★★ **Peppermill Hotel/Casino** [MUST-SEE]

The Peppermill is a thoroughly modern assault on the senses, including a riot of purple, green, and pink neon, and electronic signboards like those at a sports stadium.

The Peppermill is a bit isolated from downtown—a few miles south; it is one of the more lively casinos in town. The now-sprawling complex had its beginnings in 1971 as a relatively humble coffee shop and restaurant built by two young contractors.

In late 1999, the Peppermill completed the first phase of a $300 million expansion that will eventually double the size of the resort to 2,234 rooms, eight themed restaurants, and a whole bunch of slot machines and gaming tables. As we go to press, the Peppermill's plans will make it the largest hotel-casino in northern Nevada.

The Peppermill bought out a movie theater, restaurant, and motel along Virginia Street to expand its property to forty acres overall.

The first phase of new construction added 100,000 square feet of casino space including a new sports book and high-limit playing area. Two new restaurants include a **Romanza**, an Italian showplace restaurant under a sky dome that changes from sunrise to sunset to starry sky, imported Italian marble and fabrics, and a surround-sound system with individual speakers recessed into each booth. At the center of the restaurant is a statue of the Roman emperor Antinous, surrounded by a pair of young maidens; the revolving statue is at the center of a special-effects show for diners. Circling the restaurant are Corinthian columns topped with real flames.

The former **Peppermill Island Buffet** has given its space to the expanding casino. A new, larger buffet was included in the expansion. The eatery is set within a rain forest, with four twenty-foot-wide waterfalls that are used as projection screens. Overhead the rumble of thunder and the flashes of a lightning storm mix with a liquid nitrogen fog.

The new buffet includes a daily seafood and Asian wok station, a southwestern section, an omelet and frittatas station, and a steak and carving table.

The former movie theater will be converted into a high-tech concert hall with 1,560 reclining seats; the hall will be used for concerts, theater, plays, and stage shows.

The **Food Court** includes several serving sections, including the **Italian Deli, American Diner, Chinese Wok**, and a **Mexican Taco Bar**, with offerings ranging from 99-cent tacos to shrimp scampi for $5 and Chinese offerings for $4 to $5.

Just off the hotel lobby, **The White Orchid**, open for dinner nightly, included in recent years dishes priced from about $20 to $40, with examples including elk loin with huckleberry sauce, abalone in tomato basil sauce, and pan-roasted chicken stuffed with wild mushroom mousse.

The Steak House replaced the venerable Le Moulin with a midrange menu. The **Coffee Shop** and **Cabana Café** provide additional dining options.

Peppermill Hotel/Casino. 2707 South Virginia Street; 1,070 rooms; (775) 826-2121, (800) 648-6992. www.peppermillcasinos.com.

▰MUST-SEE▰ ★★★★ Reno Hilton

A city within a city, with 2,001 rooms, bowling alley, movie theater, golf driving range, video arcade, shopping mall . . . and a casino.

Out front is the **Ultimate Rush Thrill Ride**, a sky tower where up to three riders are suspended from a 185-foot tower and then launched out into space on a cable. And they get to pay for the privilege, about $25 per person.

Downstairs is a pair of high-tech movie theaters showing first-run and art features. (The back sections of the theaters include love seats for those who are amorously inclined or who are generally more used to watching movies in the comfort of their living rooms or beds.)

The shopping arcade includes a broad selection of stylish shops and tourist magnets, as well as the large **Fun Quest Arcade**, and fast food offerings. Outside you can find **Hilton Bay Aqua Golf** on Lake Hilton, an artificial pond created during the excavation for the hotel. Using floating golf balls, players can

The Biggest Little Chapter in This Book: Reno 211

test their swings on 100-, 150-, and 200-yard holes and hope to win prizes and free trips. Club rental is free with the purchase of two buckets; the unusual course is open from 7 A.M. to 2 A.M.

There is also one of the largest hotel health clubs we have seen, along with five indoor and three outdoor tennis courts. There are fifty lanes for bowling, too.

The expanded **Sports and Race Book** includes state-of-the-art electronics in an attractive corner of the casino. There are small TV screens at each table as well as larger ones up on the wall. Hanging from the ceiling are some experimental and acrobatic airplanes and a Rutan canard-wing plane. At **Johnny Rockets** on the floor of the sprawling casino, the waiters and waitresses sing along with the oldies issuing forth from the jukebox. The food, of course, is good ol' American burgers, fries, and malts.

Most of the hotel's restaurants are located on Restaurant Row, a semiprivate alcove off the casino floor.

The premier Italian restaurant at the Hilton is **Andiamo**, an elegant place with lots of space between the tables and leather chairs. Appealing appetizers include *scampi alla livornese* (jumbo shrimp sautéed in olive oil with garlic, shallots, white wine butter sauce, and diced peppers) for $6.95. Entrees, priced from about $8 to $24, include *ravioli di gamberi* (raviolis filled with bay shrimp, fresh salmon mousse, and zucchini served in a light creamy tomato sauce) and *tournedos al bardolino* (two petite filets mignons sautéed with mushrooms, rosemary, and garlic in bardolino red sauce). You can finish off the meal with dessert and espresso or cappuccino, available plain or spiked with anisette or brandy.

The **Reno Hilton Steak House** features an English Tudor manor house setting. Light fare includes an open-faced smoked salmon and cream cheese bagel with potato salad or cole slaw, and croissant cordon bleu. Steaks range from about $16 to $25. Desserts include homemade ice creams and sherbets with toppings including chocolate Kahlúa sauce, hot brandied fruits, vanilla hazelnut sauce, and butterscotch rum.

Asiana is a high-tone noodle shop and restaurant fusing Asian ingredients and California cuisine; it is open for dinner only. There's also **Chevys Fresh Mex**, a twenty-four-hour Mexican food outlet.

The **Grand Canyon Buffet** is a Southwestern-theme eatery set in a stone mountain lodge setting with attractive, subdued lighting; it is open for breakfast, lunch, and dinner.

Entertainment at the Reno Hilton centers on the **Hilton Theater**, the hotel's

> **Parking lots.** The Reno Hilton welcomes RV vehicles to park in a special camperland area, with rates of about $15 per night. There are spaces for 286 RVs.

> **Goin' to the chapel.** The Reno Hilton has an attractive wedding chapel for those who feel the urge or need for nuptials. Among the most unusual ceremonies performed there was the marriage of a pair of llamas who were in town for a rather sizeable convention of llama lovers. For humans, emergency wedding cakes, gowns, and suits are available at stores in the shopping arcade.

premier showroom, with 2,000 seats. Production shows including *Cats*, The Moscow Circus, and *Spellbound* and entertainers including Frank Sinatra, Liza Minelli, and Randy Travis have appeared here in addition to, would you believe, Dr. Ruth Westheimer? (We can only imagine the floor show.) The theater has one of the biggest showroom stages in the world. An interesting sidelight is the fact that when the showroom was constructed along with the hotel in 1978, the stage was built around a large mock-up of a jet plane that was used in the original long-running musical show at the hotel. The prop is so big—and the stage area so huge—that the plane was still there years later.

Nearby is the 250-seat **Improv Comedy Club**, a showcase for up-and-coming comics. There's music nightly at the **Confetti Cabaret** except Monday.

Reno Hilton. 2500 East Second Street; 2,001 rooms; (775) 789-2000, (800) 648-5080. www.renohilton.net.

★ Sands Regency Hotel/Casino

An older hotel-casino a few blocks off Virginia Street, the Sands is a strange jumble of slot machines, gaming tables, hotel desks, and donut counters. There's even a Baskin Robbins ice cream stand directly opposite the registration desk.

The matriarch of the founding Cladianos family is honored with **Antonia's**, serving a breakfast and dinner buffet.

There's a branch of the **Tony Roma's** chain, offering ribs for about $8 to $14 and boneless chicken. Appetizers include potato skins and chicken wings. Special offers include a $7.77 ribs-and-barbecued-chicken combo, and an all-you-can-eat Cajun or Carolina honey ribs dinner served Tuesday nights.

Other franchise eateries at the Sands Regency include **Blimpies**, **Pizza Hut**, and **Arby's**.

The **Palm Court** is a twenty-four-hour coffee shop. Offerings in recent years included a one-pound T-bone steak for $7.99, steak and lobster for $8.99, prime rib for $5.99, and chicken fingers for $3.99.

Sands Regency Hotel/Casino. 345 North Arlington Avenue; 1,000 rooms; (775) 348-2200, (800) 648-3553. www.sandsregency.com.

MUST-SEE ★★★★ Silver Legacy Resort Casino

The new class of downtown Reno is the Silver Legacy, which is the first Vegas-like theme park gambling mall in northern Nevada.

The project occupies two city blocks in downtown Reno, with a skywalk linking it to its corporate partners Circus Circus Hotel/Casino on the north and the Eldorado Hotel/Casino on the south.

The hotel's exterior facade of storefronts re-creates Reno of the 1890s and early 1900s. Three hotel towers in a "Y" shape add 1,720 guest rooms. One of the buildings is Reno's tallest hotel/casino tower at thirty-seven stories.

The 85,000-square-foot casino, with 2,300 slot machines and ninety table games, lies beneath a 180-foot-diameter dome. Rising from the gaming floor is a huge automated mining machine of steel and brass, with a special effects light and sound show including thunder and lightning; the show occurs every hour on the hour between 9 A.M. and 1 A.M. The machine seems to produce coins that cascade into a giant pavilion at its base. Actors perform mining tasks on the machines during the day.

An expanded "Legend of the Legacy Laser Show" is presented several times of the day; it tells the fable of the Silver Legacy with strobes, lights, smoke, fog, and Tchaikovsky's "1812 Overture."

The whole place is supposed to be the legacy of the mythical silver baron Sam Fairchild. According to the modern marketing department's myth, "Old Silver" Sam discovered a deep vein of blue quartz ore beneath the depths of what is now the Silver Legacy casino. The story goes on: he searched for a famous European engineer to design an automated mining machine. He commissioned the mining machine now seen under the dome of the casino, constructed from gleaming steel and iodized brass—continuously in motion with ore wagons, pumping bellows, and steam engines.

> **Hot tickets.** The mahogany ticket booth located on the Silver Legacy casino's mezzanine level—transformed into a cappuccino stand—was brought to Reno from its former location at a classic theater in St. Louis.

To support the story, the hotel is decorated with antique treasures including an authentic Wells Fargo stagecoach on the mezzanine level, antique cash registers, and a collection of antique model planes, trains, and automobiles.

The hotel lobby includes a display of some of the pieces from the famed **Mackay Silver Collection** of the University of Nevada, Reno. The silver is part of the 1,300-piece silver service that once belonged to John W. Mackay, the famous silver baron of Virginia City. The pieces loaned to the Silver Legacy include a thirty-six-inch candelabra that weighs more than 500 ounces and can hold twenty-eight candles.

The collection began in 1876 when Mackay shipped a half ton of Comstock silver to Tiffany & Company in New York and commissioned the company to make the elaborate service for his wife, Marie Louise—it took 200 men two years to finish the job. When it was completed, Mackay purchased the dies so the pattern could not be duplicated; he apparently destroyed them because they have never been found.

Restaurants at the Silver Legacy include **Sterling's Seafood Steakhouse, Fairchild's Oyster Bar, The Victorian Buffet,** Sweetwater Café, and **The Legacy Deli Exchange**.

The menu at Sterling's includes spicy roast chicken for about $10, red pepper linguine for $9, and medallions of filet mignon for $18.

In addition to a fresh shellfish bar, Fairchild's Oyster Bar offers seafood pan roasts. The Sweetwater twenty-four-hour coffee shop has Chinese and American specialties, with entrees from about $6 to $12.

The Victorian Buffet is an attractive, open room with a view of the upper level of the mining works and good quality but uninspired food.

Silver Legacy Resort Casino. 407 North Virginia Street; (775) 329-4777. www.silverlegacy.com.

Other Hotels and Casinos in Reno

Cal-Neva Virginian Casino. Earplugs are optional at this adult playroom. Some of the slots are built into colorful but-not-all-that realistic mockups of trains and western buildings. There's a somewhat interesting collection of old railway signs scattered about.

Food is served from a dining car lunch cart or at the **Top Deck** coffee shop (featuring a twenty-four-hour prime rib special at $4.95 or ham and eggs for ninety-nine cents) or the **Copper Ledge** restaurant.

The club announced a 775-space "Parking Stadium" across the street on Center Street; the garage will be connected to the casino by a skywalk.

Cal-Neva Virginian Casino, East Second and North Virginia Streets; 323-1046.

Fitzgerald's Casino-Hotel. The wearing of the green can become a bit wearing in this little piece of Ireland in Reno. The mirrored ceilings add to the visual overload.

But for a touch of the blarney, if not the bizarre, be sure to visit the "Lucky Forest" on the second floor. There has got to be something here that will improve your luck at the tables: four-leaf clovers, rabbit's feet, horseshoe, a wishing well, Asian gods—if there's a good luck charm not represented here, we'd like to know about it.

Fitzgerald's, located in the heart of downtown in the shadow of the Virginia Street arch, is named after Lincoln Fitzgerald, another of the early casino developers of Reno.

Fitzgerald's Casino-Hotel, 255 North Virginia Street; 351 rooms; (775) 785-3300, (800) 648-5022. www.fitzgeralds.com.

Liberty Belle Saloon & Restaurant. The place features a private collection of antique slot machines, old wagons, and other unusual items of historical note. The grandfather of the restaurant's owner, Charles Fey, is credited with inventing the first modern slot machine, the Liberty Bell, in 1898.

Liberty Belle Saloon & Restaurant, 4250 South Virginia Street; (775) 825-1776. www.libertybellereno.com.

Riverboat Hotel & Casino. Relatively quiet, small, and ordinary.

Riverboat Hotel & Casino, 34 West Second Street; 297 rooms; (775) 323-8877.

Gone Bust?

A somewhat bizarre plan for a hotel and casino based on the Beverly Hillbillies may have gone bust. Jethro's Beverly Hillbillies Mansion and Casino, complete with a fire-spitting oil derrick and an All You Can Et Buffet featuring two-pound Jethro hot dogs on Ellie May's buns, apparently fell apart for lack of financing.

The front man for the $175 million, 391-room project was Max Baer Jr., who played Jethro on the 1960s TV series *The Beverly Hillbillies*.

About Sparks

Sparks was Nevada's "Instant City," going from zero to 1,500 residents in 1904 when it was created out of swampland by the Southern Pacific Railroad.

The Golden Spike that united the westward and eastward tracks across the continent had been driven in 1870. Just thirty years later, railroad engineers decided to straighten out some of the railroad lines in Northern Nevada to eliminate treacherous curves and steep grades. As part of that effort, the Southern Pacific decided to abandon its former division point in Wadsworth near Pyramid Lake and move its operations south about thirty miles to a new site in the Truckee Meadows.

The previous owner of the railroad, the Central Pacific, had bypassed the area below Reno because of the swamplands. But the Southern Pacific decided to make its own dry land; it used its trains to haul in thousands of carloads of rock and dirt for four years to build a base for track and a huge roundhouse that could hold forty-one engines.

The summer of 1904 saw the massive migration of workers, families, houses, and belongings from Wadsworth to the new town; all of the railroad equipment was also moved. By the fall, Wadsworth was all but empty and the new town—complete with a library, hotel, store, and boarding houses—was open for business.

In 1905, the settlement was officially named the city of Sparks in honor of Governor John Sparks. In 1907, Sparks became the home of the Mallet, the largest steam engine ever built; it was used to haul long trains over the Sierras into the Sacramento Valley of California.

Until deep into the twentieth century, Sparks was a railroad company town. The old roundhouse and most of the other trappings of the railroad are gone, but the history of Sparks lives on in **Victorian Square** downtown, a restored turn-of-the-century center.

History and railroad buffs should make a stop at the **Sparks Heritage Foundation & Museum**, located at 814–820 Victorian Avenue in Victorian Square. The two unpretentious connected buildings include a fascinating but helter-skelter collection of railroad and community memorabilia. How about a mechanical device from about 1900 used to punch initials in hat bands to help owners keep track of their chapeaus?

You'll find a complete turn-of-the-century barber shop, railroad uniforms and equipment, and household furnishings. There is a collection of very old front pages—would you believe a New York paper's report of the death of George Washington on January 4, 1800?

A section of the museum features some of the fixtures from the Perry's Grocery Store as they appeared in 1918. In the back room is a collection of items from an old railroad station master's office, including a telegraph key. One of the photos on the wall shows an incredible snow scene on Donner Summit with a Central Pacific Railroad locomotive up against a wall of snow in 1889.

The free museum is open from 11 A.M. to 4 P.M. daily, and from 1 to 4 P.M. weekends. Closed Monday; call (775) 355-1144 for information.

Across the square from the museum is the **Sparks Visitor Center** set within a replica of the original Southern Pacific Depot in Sparks. Pulled up at the station is a 1907 Southern Pacific ten-wheeler Baldwin Steam Locomotive, which had been used in and around Reno on branch lines. You can walk into the driver's compartment, an old-style affair where the engineer had to lean out the side of the cab to the left or the right to see around the big boiler.

Next in line is a Houston Club Car, constructed by the Pullman Company in 1911 and converted to an executive car in 1929 for the private use of a division superintendent of the Southern Pacific; it includes a parlor, several bedrooms, and a small kitchen. The end of the small train is a period caboose, complete with a cupola for observation and a stove for cooking and eating.

The **Sparks Tourist Information Office** near the Railroad Museum is open Monday through Friday from 8 A.M. to 5 P.M.

The revival of the eight-block **Victorian Square** area includes a fourteen-screen, 3,200-seat theater complex and a 702-space parking garage.

The **Wild Island** entertainment complex is open daily from May to October and includes a water park with water slides, a tide pool, and rafting. Next door is Adventure Golf, a 36-hole miniature golf course and ice-skating facility. Call (775) 359-2927 for information. Tickets in 2000 were $16.95 for visitors forty-eight inches and taller, and $12.95 for those beneath the barrier. Thirty-six holes of golf sells for $5.50, and $4.50 for 18 holes. Tickets for the raceway were $2.50 to $4.25.

Sparks is home to the Sparks Indian Rodeo in September.

A valued addition to Sparks, on Victorian Square, is a microbrewery and restaurant known as the **Great Basin Brewing Co.** The pleasant little pub, home to jazz and other music from time to time, offers a range of beers, including Nevada Hold, Wild Horse Ale, Ichthyosaur Pale Ale, and Jackpot Porter. There are also seasonal special brews that in the past have included Kringle Cranberry, Outlaw Oatmeal Stout, McClary's Irish Red, Chilebeso Jalapeño Ale, and Ruby Mountain Red. Pints are priced at about $2.75, but we like the idea of ordering a row of 75-cent four-ounce samplers and trying them all.

The pub also offers burgers, sausages, sandwiches, and other nibbling food. Great Basin Brewing Co., on Victorian Square; (775) 355-7711.

Hotels and Casinos in Sparks

MUST-SEE ★★★★ John Ascuaga's Nugget

By now you should have guessed that my favorite hotels and casinos are those with a bit of quirkiness and individuality. By those criteria, John Ascuaga's Nugget qualifies as a must-see in the Reno Valley.

The large hotel and casino complex is actually located in Sparks, a small town that is within sight of Reno, just east of downtown. The place definitely caters to large bus tours, but it is certainly a step up from most of the downtown houses. A major addition to the casino was completed in 1997, with a second tower that added 802 new rooms and a new restaurant.

The hotel's large parking garage is among the more attractive homes for autos we have visited, and includes a huge video arcade at its skywalk entrance to the hotel.

The dear departed Liberace used to make his stage entrance at the Nugget riding on the back of Bertha the elephant; the animal made her own stage debut, appearing on "The Steve Allen Show" in 1963 and "Hollywood Palace." Bertha, alas, died in 1999 and her coworker Angel was packed off to a zoo.

Then there is the **Golden Rooster**, which may be the only member of its species ever to serve time in a federal lockup. The story is this: in 1958, the Nugget was preparing to open a new restaurant called the Golden Rooster and it was decided to decorate the place with an unusual work of art: a solid gold statue of a rooster.

Seven months after it went on display inside a fortified glass case, officials of the U.S. Treasury Department charged the Nugget with violation of the Gold Reserve Act, which made it unlawful for a private individual to possess more than fifty ounces of gold. Legal skirmishes continued until 1960 when the hotel was formally presented with a complaint titled "United States of America vs. One Solid Gold Object in the Form of a Rooster." The statue was confiscated; the Nugget's offer to put up bail was denied.

> **One-man show.** The Nugget has been owned and operated by John Ascuaga since 1960, an unusual one-man history in Nevada gaming.

> **Fishy business.** Be sure to check out the large salt water aquarium that sits behind the bar at Trader Dick's. The tank is home to more than a hundred exotic fish, including clown, grouper, damsel, yellow tang, and lion fish.

Two years of captivity for the golden bird followed, until a jury trial was held in 1962; the government was unable to counter the arguments of the Nugget and art critics that the statue was a work of art, and the rooster was sprung and returned to its perch at the restaurant. In 1987, the Golden Rooster Room was closed, but the bird eventually received a new place of honor behind the registration desk of the hotel. The 18-karat solid gold statue weighs 206.3 troy ounces (14.1 pounds).

An interesting eatery is **Orozkos**, named for the Pyrenees mountain hamlet in northern Spain where the Ascuaga family originated. Specialties include Basque dishes, paella, mesquite-broiled steaks, pasta, and pizza.

The Rotisserie combines a buffet and a la carte menu. A glassed-in rotisserie cooks chickens near the entryway. Tuesday nights feature chocolate fantasies.

Trader Dick's, a dark, lush tropical garden setting with palm fronds and grass thatching sits just off the main casino floor, serving South Sea and Polynesian lunch Monday through Friday and dinner every night. A prix-fixe dinner is available for $16.95; specialties range from about $9.50 to $20. A soup and salad bar is offered for $4.95. At the center of the room is a large Chinese smoke oven used to prepare spareribs, chicken, and pork menu items.

The **Steak House** serves steaks; lots of them. A sign outside its entrance tracks steaks served since 1956. As 2000 began, the counter had crossed over the four million marker. Steak, seafood, and Italian entrees are priced from $15 to $20.

At the far end of the casino are a few other casual eateries. The **Farm House** is a coffee shop-like establishment, offering omelettes and pancakes for breakfast, a range of sandwiches and salads for lunch, and dinner specials, including fried deep-sea scallops and ranch-hand beef stew.

Nearby is **John's Oyster Bar**, which carries a bit of a nautical theme that includes a ship's mast and yardarm overhead. Specialties include lobster surprise salad (topped with a remoulade sauce of mayonnaise, mustard, gherkins, chervil, tarragon, and capers with a touch of chablis).

The **General Store** is a dimly lit, open-space coffee shop with attractive ceiling fans. Specialties include deep-fried catfish and nuggets of tenderloin (chunks of filet mignon breaded, seasoned, and fried).

Outside the General Store are gold scales used at the U.S. Mint in Carson City from about 1875 until the mint closed in 1893. Millions in gold and silver crossed its plates; it is claimed the scale is accurate enough to weigh a postage stamp.

John Ascuaga's Nugget. 1100 Nugget Avenue, Sparks; 1,500 rooms; (775) 356-3300, (800) 648-1177. www.janugget.com.

Smaller Casinos in Sparks

A smaller, unusual Sparks joint worth checking out is **Baldini's Sports Casino**. This is not a place for the claustrophobic; in fact, it feels as if you have descended directly into the innards of a slot machine. There's a country-western dance floor and nearly free food.

Baldini's is located at 865 South Rock Boulevard; (775) 358-0116.

Across Victorian Road from the Nugget is the **Treasury Club**, a very unexceptional little slot club catering mostly to locals. And then there is the **Mint Casino**, a mint green box of slots.

The **Silver Club** on Victorian Avenue is an attractive, high-ceilinged place, quieter and smaller than the Nugget but with some amenities of its own. Restaurants include **Victoria's Steak House** where entrees run from about $10 to $15, including prime rib, scampi ala romano, and seafood fettucine. The sports bar on the second floor known as **Rails**.

Reno Casinos, Hotels, and Motels

Basic room rates. Note that rates are subject to change and are likely to be higher during holiday periods and major events, and lower in slow periods.

$	$49 or less
$$	$50 to $99
$$$	$100 to $149
$$$$	$150 and more
♣	Casino/Hotel

Adventure Inn and Wedding Chapel. 3575 South Virginia Street. (775) 828-9000, (800) 937-1436. $–$$$$

Airport Plaza Hotel. 1981 Terminal Way. (775) 348-6370, (800) 648-3525. $$–$$$$

Americana Inn. 340 Lake Street. (775) 786-4422. $–$$

Aspen Motel. 495 Lake Street. (775) 329-6011, (800) 367-7366. $–$$

Atlantis Hotel Casino. ♣ 3800 South Virginia Street. (775) 825-4700, (800) 723-6500. $–$$$$

The Biggest Little Chapter in This Book: Reno 219

Best Value Inn. 844 South Virginia Street. (775) 786-6700. **$-$$**
Best Western Daniel's Motor Lodge/Casino District. 375 North Sierra Street. (775) 329-1351, (800) 337-7210. **$$-$$$**
Bonanza Motor Inn. 215 West Fourth Street. (775) 322-8632, (800) 808-3303. **$-$$$**
Cabana Motel. 370 West Street. (775) 786-2977. **$-$$**
Capri Motel. 895 North Virginia Street. (775) 323-8398. **$-$$**
Carriage Inn. 690 West Fourth Street. (775) 329-8848. **$$**
Castaway Inn. 525 West Second Street. (775) 329-2555. **$$$-$$$$**
Center Lodge. 200 South Center Street. (775) 329-9000. **$-$$**
Circus Circus Hotel Casino. ♣ 500 North Sierra Street. (775) 329-0711, (800) 648-5010. **$-$$**
City Center Motel. 365 West Street. (775) 323-8880. **$-$$**
Coach Inn. 500 North Center Street. (775) 323-3222. **$-$$**
Colonial Inn Hotel and Casino. ♣ 250 North Arlington Avenue. (775) 322-3838, (800) 336-7366. **$-$$$**
Colonial Motor Inn. 232 West Street. (775) 786-5038, (800) 255-7366. **$-$$$**
Comstock Hotel and Casino. ♣ 200 West Second Street. (775) 329-1880, (800) 648-4866. **$-$$**
Crest Inn. 525 West Fourth Street. (775) 329-0808, (800) 367-7366. **$-$$$**
Days Inn. 701 East Seventh Street. (775) 786-4070, (800) 448-4555. **$-$$$**
Donner Inn Motel. 720 West Fourth Street. (775) 323-1851. **$**
Downtowner Motor Lodge. 150 Stevenson Street. (775) 322-1188. **$**
Easy 8 Motel. 255 West Fifth Street. (775) 322-4588. **$**
El Cortez Hotel. 239 West Second Street. (775) 322-9161. **$-$$**
El Lobo Motel. 1659 North Virginia Street. (775) 323-8309. **$**
El Patio Motel. 3495 South Virginia Street. (775) 825-6666. **$**
El Ray Motel. 330 North Arlington, (775) 329-6669. **$-$$$**
Eldorado Hotel/Casino. ♣ 345 North Virginia Street. (775) 786-5700, (800) 648-5966. **$-$$$$**
Executive Inn. 205 South Sierra Street. (775) 786-4050. **$$**
Fireside Inn. 205 East Fourth. 786-1666, (800) 367-7366. **$-$$$**
Fitzgerald's Casino/Hotel. ♣ 255 North Virginia Street. (775) 785-3300, (800) 648-5022. **$-$$$$**
Flamingo Hilton Reno. ♣ 255 North Sierra Street. (775) 322-1111, (800) 648-4882. **$$-$$$$**
Flamingo Motel. 520 North Center Street. (775) 323-3202. **$-$$**
Gatekeeper Inn. 221 West Fifth Street. (775) 786-3500, (800) 822-3504. **$-$$**
Gateway Inn. 1275 Stardust Street. (775) 747-4220. **$-$$$**
Gold Dust West Casino. ♣ 444 Vine Street. (775) 323-2211, (800) 438-9378. **$-$$**
Gold Key Motel. 445 Lake Street. (775) 323-0731, (800) 648-3744. **$**
Golden West Motor Lodge. 530 North Virginia Street. (775) 329-2192. **$**
Harrah's Reno Casino/Hotel. ♣ 219 North Center Street. (775) 786-3232, (800) 648-3773. **$$-$$$**

Holiday Inn-Downtown/Diamond's Casino. ♣ 1000 East Sixth Street. (775) 786-5151, (800) 465-4329. $$-$$$
Horseshoe Motel. 490 Lake Street. (775) 786-5968. $
In-Town Motel. 260 West Fourth Street. (775) 323-1421. $-$$
Keno Motel No. 1. 322 North Arlington Avenue. (775) 322-6281. $
Keno Motel No. 2. 331 West Street. (775) 322-4146. $
La Quinta Inn. 4001 Market Street. (775) 348-6100, (800) 531-5900. $$
La Quinta Inn Northwest Tech Center Inn and Suites. 7101 Cascade Valley. (775) 360-1200, (800) 531-5900. $$
Lakemill Lodge. 200 Mill Street. (775) 786-1500. $-$$
Lido Inn. 280 West Fourth Street. (775) 322-3822. $
Mardi Gras Motor Lodge. 200 West Fourth Street. (775) 329-7470. $
Mark Twain Motel. 2201 South Virginia Street. (775) 826-2101. $
Kay Martin Lodge. 6950 South Virginia Street. (775) 853-6504. $-$$
Midtown Motel. 611 West Second Street. (775) 323-7178. $
Miner's Inn. 1651 North Virginia Street. (775) 329-3464, (800) 626-1900. $-$$
Monte Carlo Motel. 500 North Virginia Street. (775) 329-2010. $-$$
Motel 500. 500 South Center Street. (775) 786-2777. $
Motel 6 Reno Convention Center. 1901 South Virginia Street. (775) 827-0255. $
Motel 6 Reno Events Center. 866 North Wells Avenue. (775) 786-9852, (800) 466-8356. $
Motel 6 Reno West. 1400 Stardust Street. (775) 747-7390, (800) 466-8356. $
National 9 Inn. 645 South Virginia Street. (775) 323-5411. $-$$
Nevada Inn. 330 East Second Street. (775) 323-1005, (800) 999-9686. $-$$
Olympic Apartment Hotel. 195 West Second Street. (775) 323-0726. $-$$
Ox-Bow Motor Lodge. 941 South Virginia Street. (775) 786-3777. $-$$
Oxford Motel. 111 Lake Street. (775) 786-3170, (800) 648-3044. $-$$
Park Villa Apartments Motel. 61 South Park Street. (775) 322-7396. $-$$
Peppermill Hotel Casino. ♣ 2707 South Virginia Street. (775) 826-2121, (800) 648-6992. $-$$$
Pioneer Inn Hotel/Casino. ♣ 221 South Virginia Street. (775) 324-7777, (800) 648-5468. $-$$
Plaza Resort Club. 121 West Street. (775) 786-2200, (800) 648-5990. $$-$$$
Ponderosa Hotel. 515 South Virginia Street. (775) 786-6820, (800) 228-6820. $-$$
Ponderosa Motel. 595 Lake Street. (775) 786-3070. $-$$
Ramada Vacation Suites at Reno. 140 Court Street. (775) 329-4251, (800) 634-6981. $$
Ranch Motel. 7400 South Virginia Street. (775) 851-1129. $
Rancho Sierra Motel. 411 West Fourth Street. (775) 786-6277. $-$$
Reno Best Inns and Suites. 1885 South Virginia Street. (775) 329-1001, (800) 626-1900. $$

Reno 8 Motel. 1113 East Fourth Street. (775) 786-6828. $
Reno Hilton. 2500 East Second Street. (775) 789-2000, (800) 648-5080. $$–$$$
Reno Riviera Hotel & Lounge. 395 West First Street. (775) 329-9348, (800) 367-7366. $$$–$$$$
Reno Royal Park N Walk Motel. 350 West Street. (775) 323-4477. $–$$
Reno Travelodge Central. 2050 Market Street. (775) 786-2500, (800) 648-3800. $–$$$
Reno Travelodge Downtown. 655 West Fourth Street. (775) 329-3451, (800) 578-7878. $–$$
Riverboat Hotel & Casino. ♣ 34 West Second Street. (775) 323-8877, (800) 888-5525. $–$$
Sage Motel. 411 Lake Street. (775) 329-4083. $–$$
Sandman Motel. 1755 East Fourth Street. (775) 322-0385. $$$
Sands Regency Hotel/Casino. ♣ 345 North Arlington Avenue. (775) 348-2200, (800) 648-3553. $–$$$$
Savoy Motor Lodge. 705 North Virginia Street. (775) 322-4477. $–$$
Seasons Inn. 495 West Street. (775) 322-6000, (800) 322-8588. $–$$$
7/11 Motor Lodge. 465 West Second Street. (775) 348-8898. $
777 Motel. 777 South Virginia Street. (775) 786-0405. $–$$
Shamrock Inn. 505 North Center Street. (775) 786-5182. $–$$
Showboat Inn. 660 North Virginia Street. (775) 786-4032, (800) 648-3960. $–$$$
Silver Dollar Motor Lodge. 817 North Virginia Street. (775) 323-6875. $–$$
Silver Legacy Hotel Casino Resort. ♣ 407 North Virginia Street. (775) 785-9051, (800) 687-8733. $–$$$
Stardust Lodge. 455 North Arlington Avenue. (775) 322-5641. $–$$
Sundance Motel. 850 North Virginia Street. (775) 329-9248. $–$$
Sundowner Hotel Casino. ♣ 450 North Arlington. (775) 786-7050, (800) 648-5490. $–$$$
Super 8 Motel. 5851 South Virginia Street. (775) 825-2940, (800) 800-8000. $
Town House Motor Lodge. 303 West Second Street. (775) 323-1821, (800) 438-5660. $–$$
Town View Motor Lodge. 131 West Third Street. (775) 329-1560. $
TownSite Motel. 250 West Commercial Row. (775) 322-0345. $
Truckee River Lodge. 501 West First Street. (775) 786-8888, (800) 635-8950. $–$$$$
University Inn. 1001 North Virginia Street. (775) 323-0321, (800) 352-6464. $–$$
Uptown Motel. 570 North Virginia Street. (775) 323-8906. $–$$
Vagabond Inn. 3131 South Virginia Street. (775) 825-7134, (800) 522-1555. $–$$
White Court Motel. 465 Evans Avenue. (775) 329-1957. $–$$
Wonder Lodge. 430 Lake Street. (775) 786-6840, (800) 454-0303. $–$$

Sparks Casinos, Hotels, and Motels

Listed here are rates for basic double rooms. Note that rates are subject to change and are likely to be higher during holiday periods and major events, and lower in slow periods.

$	$49 or less
$$	$50 to $99
$$$	$100 to $149
$$$$	$150 and more
♣	Casino/Hotel

McCarran House Inn. 55 East Nugget Avenue. (775) 358-6900, (800) 548-5798. $–$$

John Ascuaga's Nugget. ♣ 1100 Nugget Avenue. (775) 356-3300, (800) 648-1177. $–$$

Pony Express Lodge. 2406 Prater Way. (775) 358-7110. $–$$

Safari Motel. 1800 Victorian Avenue. (775) 358-6443. $–$$

Silver Club Hotel/Casino. ♣ 1040 Victorian Avenue. (775) 358-4771, (800) 905-7774. $–$$

Sixpence Inn. 1901 South Virginia. (775) 827-0255. $–$$

Sunrise Motel. 210 Victorian Avenue. (775) 358-7010. $–$$

Thunderbird Resort Club. ♣ 200 Nichols Boulevard. (775) 359-1141, (800) 821-4912. $–$$

Victorian Inn. 1555 Victorian Avenue. (775) 331-3203, (800) 367-7366. $–$$

Wagon Train Motel. 1662 Victorian Avenue. (775) 358-0468. $–$$

Western Village Inn & Casino. ♣ 815 East Nichols Boulevard. (775) 331-1069, (800) 648-1170. $

Windsor Inn. 60 East Victorian Avenue. (775) 356-7770, (800) 547-0106. $–$$

Local Bus Service

RTC/Citifare. For information on bus service, call (775) 348-7433.

Long-Distance Bus Service

Airport Mini Bus. Airport, Reno, and Lake Tahoe. (775) 323-3727, (800) 235-5466.
Bell Limo Service. Airport, Reno, and Tahoe. (775) 786-3700, (800) 235-5466.
Greyhound Lines West. Reno. (775) 322-2970, (800) 231-2222.
Sierra Nevada Gray Line. Daily ski shuttle to Alpine Meadows, Squaw Valley, and Northstar-at-Tahoe. (775) 329-1147, (800) 822-6009.
Tahoe Casino Express. Scheduled service from Reno Airport to South Lake Tahoe. (775) 785-2424, (800) 446-6128.

Car Rentals in Reno

Advantage Rent-a-Car. 5301 Longley Lane; (775) 825-9191, (800) 777-5500.
Alamo Rent a Car. 1120 Terminal Way; (775) 323-8306, (800) 327-9633.
Avis Rent a Car. Airport; (775) 785-2727, (800) 331-1212.
Budget Car & Truck Rental. (775) 785-2690, (800) 527-0700.
Dollar Rent a Car. Airport; (775) 348-2800, (800) 800-4000.
Enterprise Rent-a-Car. Airport; (775) 329-3773, (800) 325-8007.
Hertz Rent a Car. Airport; (775) 785-2554, (800) 654-3131.
National Car Rental. (775) 785-2756, (800) 227-7368.
Thrifty Car Rental. 2697 Mill Street; (775) 329-0096, (800) 873-0377.

Chapter 19
Eating Your Way Through Reno-Sparks

Econoguide 2001: Best Casino Buffets in Reno-Sparks
★★★★ **Toucan Charlie's.** Atlantis
★★★★ **Chef's Buffet.** Eldorado
★★★★ **Fresh Market Square Buffet.** Harrah's
★★★★ **Rotisserie.** John Ascuaga's Nugget
★★★★ **Island Buffet.** Peppermill
★★★★ **Victorian Buffet.** Silver Legacy

Econoguide 2001: Best Casino Restaurants in Reno-Sparks
★★★★ **Harrah's Steak House.** Harrah's
★★★★ **Peppermill Steak House.** Peppermill
★★★★ **Orozco.** John Ascuaga's Nugget
★★★★ **Cafe Andreotti.** Harrah's Reno
★★★★ **Ristorante La Strada.** Eldorado

Reno-Sparks Buffets

Atlantis.★★★★ Toucan Charlie's. (775) 824-4433. Eight specialty stations, including wood-fired meats, Mongolian BBQ grill, Chinese wok, and Asian exhibition kitchen. Breakfast 7:30 to 10:30 A.M.; lunch 11 A.M. to 3 P.M.; and dinner 4:30 to 10 P.M. Seafood buffet Friday and Saturday. Sunday brunch 8:30 A.M. to 3 P.M. Prices range from $5.99 for weekday breakfast to $18.99 for Friday and Saturday night dinner.

Baldini's. Triple Crown International Buffet. (775) 358-0116. Breakfast weekdays 7 to 10 A.M., $3.99; lunch 11 A.M. to 3:30 P.M., $5.99; and dinner 4 to 10 P.M., $6.99. Weekend champagne brunch 9 A.M. to 3 P.M., $6.99.

Bonanza. Branding Iron Cafe. (775) 323-2724. Lunch 11 A.M. to 2 P.M., $5.95; dinner 4:30 to 10 P.M., $7.97. Friday and Saturday dinner, $8.95. Sunday brunch 8 A.M. to 2 P.M., $7.95.

Circus Circus. Courtyard Buffet. (775) 329-0711. Breakfast 7 to 11 A.M., $5.49; lunch 11 A.M. to 4 P.M., $6.49; and dinner 4 to 11 P.M., $8.99. Weekend brunch 7 A.M. to 4 P.M., $8.99. Friday and Saturday dinner $12.99.

Eldorado. ★★★★ Chef's Buffet. (775) 786-5700. Breakfast 7:45 to 11 A.M., $5.99; lunch 11 A.M. to 2 P.M., $6.49; and dinner 4 to 10 P.M., $8.99. Friday seafood buffet, $18.99. Saturday brunch 7:45 A.M. to 2 P.M., $7.99; Saturday dinner $13.99; Sunday champagne brunch 7:45 A.M. to 2 P.M., $8.99; Sunday dinner $9.99.

Fitzgerald's. The Lord Fitzgerald's Feast. (775) 785-3300. 7 to 11 A.M., $4.99; lunch 11:30 A.M. to 1:30 P.M., $5.99; and dinner 4 to 9 P.M., $7.77.

Flamingo Hilton. Top of the Hilton Buffet. (775) 322-1111. Weekend buffets, $7.95. Sunday champagne brunch at Top of the Flamingo, 9 A.M. to 2 P.M., $15.99.

Harrah's. ★★★★ Fresh Market Square Buffet. (775) 786-3232. Weekday brunch 7:30 to 11 A.M., $6.99; weekday dinner 4 to 10 P.M., $9.29. Weekend brunch 8 A.M. to 3 P.M., $9.29. Saturday dinner 4 to 10 P.M., $9.29. Saturday seafood buffet dinner $16.99.

John Ascuaga's Nugget. ★★★★ Rotisserie. (775) 358-3300. Lunch Monday through Saturday 11 A.M. to 2 P.M., $7.50. Dinner 5 to 10 P.M., Sunday and Monday $10.50 to $13.50, Tuesday through Thursday, $10.50 to $12.95, and Friday and Saturday, $16.95. Weekend brunch 8:30 A.M. to 2 P.M., $10.95.

Peppermill. ★★★★ Island Buffet. (775) 826-2121. Breakfast weekdays 7:30 to 11 A.M., $7.99; lunch weekdays 11 A.M. to 3 P.M., $9.99; and dinner Sunday through Thursday 4:30 to 10 P.M., $14.99. Saturday brunch 7:30 A.M. to 3 P.M., $7.99. Sunday brunch 7:30 A.M. to 3 P.M., $15.99. Friday seafood buffet dinner, 4:30 to 10:30 P.M., $24.95. Saturday 4:30 to 10:30 P.M., $22.99.

Reno Hilton. ★★★★ Grand Canyon Buffet. (775) 789-2000. Breakfast weekdays 7 to 10:30 A.M., $6.49; lunch 11:30 A.M. to 2 P.M., $6.99; and dinner 5 to 9 P.M., $9.95. Weekend brunch, $7.99.

Sands Regency. Antonia's. (775) 348-2200. Weekends only, $4.99.

Silver Legacy. ★★★★ Victorian Buffet. (775) 329-4777. Breakfast, $5.49; lunch, $6.49; and prime rib dinner Sunday through Friday, $8.99. Saturday night, $9.99. Saturday brunch, $8.49. Friday seafood buffet 4:30 to 10 P.M., $13.99, and International Saturday 4:30 to 10 P.M., $13.99. Sunday Brunch 9 A.M. to 2 P.M., $8.99.

A Selection of Reno's Best Restaurants Outside the Casinos

(Be sure to also see restaurant descriptions in the hotel listings in Chapter 18.)

American

Adele's Restaurant. Valley Bank Plaza, 425 South Virginia Street; (775) 333-6503. Also, 1112 North Carson; (775) 882-3353. Lunch and dinner. Reservations suggested.

Brew Brothers at the Eldorado. ★★★★ Fourth and Virginia Streets, (775) 786-5700.

Famous Murphy's Restaurant Grill and Oyster Bar. 3127 South Virginia Street; (775) 827-4111. The Grill serves sandwiches, burgers, salads, scampi, pan roasts, pasta, steamers, oysters, chowder, hot rocks, and more for lunch and dinner. The dining room serves steak, pasta, chicken, and seafood specialties. Lunch and dinner daily. Reservations suggested.

Johnny Rockets at the Reno Hilton.★★ 2500 East Second Street. (775) 789-2000.

Liberty Belle Saloon & Restaurant. 4250 South Virginia Street; (775) 825-1776. Prime rib, chicken, and salads in a venerable local favorite decorated with area antiques. Lunch weekdays, dinner daily.

Midtowne Market and Dinner House.★★★ 121 Vesta Street. (775) 323-7711. Warehouse decor and atmosphere, with a deli and bakery on premises. Loud and lots of fun.

Rapscallions Seafood House & Bar.★★★ 1555 South Wells Avenue. (775) 323-1211. Where Reno's movers and shakers take clients to lunch.

Asian

Asian Garden. Plumb & Virginia Streets; (775) 825-5510.

Formosa Restaurant. 5089 South McCarran Boulevard, Smithridge Plaza; (775) 827-0222. Authentic Chinese cuisine.

Ichiban Japanese Steak House. 210 North Sierra Street; (775) 323-5550. Teppanyaki cooking in a garden setting; Chopstix Restaurant at same location offers Japanese, Chinese, and Korean fare. Lunch weekdays, dinner nightly.

Kyoto. 915 West Moana Lane; (775) 825-9686.

Pho 777 Vietnamese Noodle Restaurant.★★★ 201 East Second Street. (775) 323-7777. Outstanding soups.

Rickshaw Paddy.★★ 4944 South Virginia Street. (775) 828-2335. Asian dishes with an Irish accent, reflecting backgrounds of the two owners. Good food at fair prices.

Seoul Restaurant.★★★ 1999 South Virginia Street. (775) 829-2115.

Delicatessen

Chicago Express Deli and Restaurant. Days Inn Hotel, Seventh and Wells; (775) 333-0922. An informal luncheon delicatessen that transforms to a dinner house featuring pastas, lasagna, and other Italian specialties.

Paolo's Deli. 921 West Moana Lane; (775) 827-3860. Italian specialties for lunch and dinner.

French

The Crown Point.★★ Main Street. (Highway 342), Gold Hill; (775) 847-0111. Built in 1859 within the Gold Hill Hotel. The stone structure is Nevada's oldest hotel. Lavish accommodations with period antiques.

German

Bavarian World. 595 Valley Road at East Sixth Street; (775) 323-7646. Pork roast, sauerbraten, Alpine cuisine from schnitzel to *schweinebraten*, and famous rye bread. Open daily for breakfast, lunch, *und* dinner.

Galena Forest Inn. 17025 Mount Rose Highway; (775) 849-2100. Six miles up Mount Rose Highway. Alpine cuisine combining Swiss, Austrian, northern

Italian, French, and German specialties. A local classic, under new ownership in 2000 and receiving rave reviews. Dinner is served Wednesday through Sunday from 5 P.M. Reservations suggested.

Indian
Sapna Indian Restaurant. 3374 Kietzke at Moana Lane; (775) 829-1537. *masala dosa*, vegetarian and meat curries, *mouglai*, *biriyani*, and *thalli* specialties. Lunch and dinner daily; closed Sunday.

Italian
Coco Pazzo. 3446 Lakeside Drive; (775) 829-9449. Traditional and specialty Italian cooking for lunch and dinner.

Siri's. ★★ 1565 South Virginia Street. (775) 786-9907. A Reno institution, with three generations of the Siri family in attendance. Huge portions and reasonable prices for Northern Italian fare.

La Vecchia. ★★ 3501 South Virginia Street. (775) 825-1113. Northern Italian chefs prepare traditional favorites plus house specials like duck salad with radicchio and white truffle salad.

Mexican
Eatos Burritos. 1420 South Wells Avenue; (775) 786-8500.

La Cabana. 668 Greenbrae Drive, Sparks. (775) 358-8333. Home-style fare, including some dishes not found on most Mexican menus. One of the best deals in town.

La Pinata. 1575 Vassar. (775) 323-3210. A long-time local favorite.

Natural and Vegetarian Food
Anthony's Dandelion Deli. 1170 South Wells Avenue; (775) 322-6100. Natural food, vegetarian, and gourmet specialties for lunch.

Blue Heron. 1091 South Virginia; (775) 786-4110. Vegetarian and macrobiotic cuisine, fresh breads, microbrewed and all-natural wines. Lunch daily, dinner weekends.

Einstein's Quantum Café. 6135 South Virginia Street. (775) 829-6611. Outstanding vegetarian fare, a Reno favorite.

Wild Oats Community Market. 5695 South Virginia Street. (775) 829-8666.

Southwestern
Café Soleil. ★★ 4796 Caughlin Parkway. (775) 828-6444. Nouvelle Southwestern cuisine, like *chipotle* chicken mole. A favorite with Reno's business community who come for the food, the exhibition kitchen, and views of the city lights.

Chili's Grill & Bar. 5090 Smithridge Drive; (775) 829-7775. Chili, fajitas, ribs, and margaritas.

Thai
Cafe de Thai. 3314 South McCarran and Mira Loma; (775) 829-8424.

The Basque Influence

The Basques, an adventuresome people with origins in the Pyrenees Mountains of France and Spain, came to Nevada in a circuitous route that began with migration to Argentina, where they worked as shepherds. Many thousands moved north in the 1850s, lured by the California Gold Rush, and some then came over the Sierra Nevadas eastward to work in the mines of the Comstock and elsewhere in Nevada.

There are still remnants of the once-thriving Basque culture in and around Reno, including festivals and restaurants. Most Basque eateries are decidedly informal, serving dishes family-style. You will likely be served at a large table with strangers in a boisterous atmosphere; Basque restaurants are not the place for a romantic getaway, but they are a lot of fun and a lot of food for a reasonable price—usually in the range of $10 to $20 for a complete dinner.

A local favorite is the **Santa Fe Hotel**, at 235 Lake Street, next to Harrah's. The restaurant, closed for several years, reopened in early 2000. Open every day for lunch and dinner. (775) 323-1891.

One of the best in the area is the **Carson Valley Bar and Restaurant**, 1029 Riverview Avenue at the country club two miles south of Gardnerville, or about ten minutes south of Carson City on I-395. (775) 265-3715. Platters of two kinds of meat, one usually steak, plus pasta, vegetables, and dessert are served at long tables; the food keeps coming until everyone is stuffed. Open daily except Tuesday.

Louis' Basque Corner★, at 301 East Fourth Street, features Basque cuisine such as *tripas callos,* chicken, oxtails, shrimp, and *tonque à la basquaise, paella, lapin chasseur* (hunter's rabbit), and *veau panne* (breaded veal), served family-style. A local institution; the quality of the food is sometimes inconsistent. Lunch Tuesday through Saturday from 11:30 A.M. to 2:30 P.M. Dinner nightly from 5 to 9:30 P.M. (775) 323-7203.

Chapter 20
Reno-Sparks Area Attractions

Like Las Vegas, Reno is a lot more than casinos, showrooms, and restaurants. Here is a listing of the more interesting museums and entertainment areas, as well as sports and outdoor activities.

Be sure to also check listings in this book for Carson City, Virginia City, and Lake Tahoe. Information about ski areas at Mount Rose, Incline Village, South Lake Tahoe, and North Lake Tahoe, as well as other winter sports, including sledding, skating, and snowmobiling can be found in the section about Lake Tahoe.

Area codes. In 1999, Nevada was split into two telephone area codes for the first time. Most of the state outside of the Las Vegas, Boulder City, and Laughlin area was placed in the (775) area code.
Here is the split:
(702): Las Vegas, North Las Vegas, Henderson, Boulder City, Laughlin, most of Clark County
(775): Reno, Sparks, Carson City, remainder of state

National Bowling Stadium

The National Bowling Stadium is the visual counterpoint to the dome on the Silver Legacy in downtown Reno; instead of the beeps and whirls of slot machines and the cheers and groans of the craps tables, beneath the stadium's silver dome is the rumble and crash of a whole lot of bowling.

This is one heck of an alley, with seventy-eight tournament-level lanes.

Some 82,500 bowlers participated in the American Bowling Congress championship tournament that ran from February through July of 1998; the ABC is due to return to Reno in 2001 and 2004. The Women's International Bowling Congress will hold its championship tournament in Reno again in 2000 and 2003, drawing another 85,000 or so keglers to town.

The stadium offers permanent seating capacity for 1,200. The video scoring system at the stadium includes the longest rear-projection, high-definition video display in the world, at 450 feet in length. The Bowlervision II scoring system in the spectator section does more than keep score; visitors can order drinks and food from the monitor.

> **Reno-Sparks Convention and Visitors Authority.** 4590 South Virginia Street, Reno, NV 89502; (775) 827-7600, (775) 827-7366, or (800) 367-7366.
> **Reno-Sparks Indian Colony Tribal Council.** 98 Colony Road, Reno, NV 89502; (775) 329-2936.
> **Sparks Chamber of Commerce.** 831 Victorian Avenue, Sparks, NV 89431; (775) 358-1976.
> **Virginia City Chamber of Commerce.** V&T Railroad Car, C Street, Virginia City, NV 89440; (775) 847-0311.
> **Nevada Department of Wildlife.** Box 10678, Reno, NV 89520; (775) 688-1500.
> **Pyramid Lake Fisheries.** Star Route, Sutcliffe, NV 89510; (775) 476-0500.
> **Bureau of Land Management.** Box 12000, Reno, NV 89520; (775) 785-6402.

The bowling lanes are not available for public use; they are reserved for tournaments. Admission is free to many tourneys, but some events may sell tickets.

The stadium pro shop includes a fully functioning bowling lane so that shoppers can try out equipment before they buy. An instant replay video system allows you to watch yourself in action with new equipment.

The focal point of the stadium is its giant silver ball, decorated on the outside with 15,000 feet of fiber-optic lights that wash it with color at night. Within the ball is a 177-seat movie theater with an Iwerks 70mm projection system and a forty-two-foot-wide by thirty-one-foot-tall wraparound screen.

Kicks, a dance club with a small restaurant, is also located within.

Museums

Wilbur May Center. A museum, arboretum, botanical garden, and a fabulous assortment of animal trophies and other items from the personal collection of Wilbur May, the son of the founder of the department store chain that bears his name. May was a traveler of great renown in the 1920s and '30s, making some forty trips around the world.

The Living Room section of the museum includes some of May's own paintings, collections, and a recording of May's greatest hit, "Pass a Piece of Pizza Please," a song he wrote together with comic Jerry Colona. The collection of artifacts he collected includes a shrunken head, an elephant's ear, and other trophies. An indoor arboretum includes a three-story waterfall and a hands-on science room dubbed the Sensorium.

The museum is located in Washoe County's Rancho San Rafael Park, 1502 Washington Street in Reno. Admission is $5.50 for adults and $4.50 for seniors and children younger than 12. Hours vary; call (775) 785-5961 for information about the museum and (775) 785-4153 for arboretum schedules.

Next door to the May Museum is the **Great Basin Adventure** theme park, designed for children ages 2 to 12. Included are mining exhibits, gold panning, petting zoo, a dinosaur park, and more. Open weekends from Memorial Day to the end of the school year from 10 A.M. to 5 P.M. on Saturday and noon to 5 p.m. on Sunday. Open daily in summer through Labor Day from 10 A.M. to 5 P.M., Sundays from noon to 5 P.M. Call (775) 785-4319 for information. Adult admission is $3.50; children ages 3 to 12, $2.50.

Nevada Museum of Art. An eclectic collection of modern and fine art, located at 160 W. Liberty Street. The collection of the E. L. Wiegand Gallery focuses on the art of the Great Basin region, and nineteenth and twentieth century American art. Open Tuesday, Wednesday, and Friday from 10 A.M. to 4 P.M., Thursday from 10 A.M. to 7 P.M., and Saturday and Sunday from noon to 4 P.M. Admission is $5 for adults, and $3 for students and seniors, and $1 for children ages 6 to 12. Call (775) 329-3333 for information.

Nevada State Historical Society Museum. A well-stocked and attractively presented collection of Indian artifacts, mining devices, and other elements of the Silver State's history, from prehistoric times to the Wild West to modern days. A research library includes many priceless manuscripts, records, maps, and other historical data. The gift shop is the answer to a history buff's prayer.

Located on the University of Nevada-Reno campus at 1650 North Virginia Street near U.S. 395. Open Monday through Saturday from 10 A.M. to 5 P.M. Admission is $2 for adults; children younger than 18 are free. Call (775) 688-1190 for information.

Fleischmann Planetarium. Next to the Historical Society Museum on the University of Nevada at Reno campus. A stargazer's fantasy: a fascinating planetarium show, there are films, a display of meteorites, and scheduled use of telescopes. The planetarium presents a number of theme shows, including a Halloween special and coverage of planetary events that include the passage of comets and planets.

The SkyDome 8/70 uses extra-large film and special audio effects to present spectacular movies, including *Seasons* and *Africa the Serengeti*. Planetarium shows admission for adults is $6; children younger than 13 and seniors older than 60, $4. Call (775) 784-4811 for hours. *You will find a discount in the coupon section of this book.*

W. M. Keck Museum, Mackay School of Mines. If a mining museum is what you're looking for, here is a fine example: an incredible collection of mineral wealth from Nevada, including gold and silver from the Comstock, as well as copper, lead, and other rocks that shaped the state. The collection was originally endowed by John Mackay, one of the men who made a fabulous fortune in the early days of Virginia City. On the UNR campus, within the Mackay Mining School. Call the school for hours and information at (775) 784-6052.

National Automobile Museum. A spectacular collection of just some of the more than 1,000 vintage vehicles owned by casino developer William Harrah. Most of the cars were auctioned off after Harrah's death (some were bought for the equally spectacular and quirky collection at the Imperial Palace in Las Vegas); about 200 were given to a foundation set up by his heirs. The collection was moved into an attractive new building downtown in 1989; the architecture of the building is reminiscent of some of the chrome boats within.

A tour begins with a twenty-minute multimedia presentation that includes some of the actual cars from the exhibit; visitors then enter the museum through a re-created antique gas station.

Mill and Lake streets. Open every day but Christmas. Open Monday through Saturday from 9:30 A.M. to 5:30 P.M. and Sunday from 10 A.M. to 4 P.M. Adult tickets $7.50, seniors $6.50, and children ages 6 to 18, $2.50. Call (775) 333-9300 for hours.

Amusement Parks

Kiddie Playland at Idlewild Park is a small play area with trains, a merry-go-round, swimming pool, and rides. Call 329-6008 for hours and rates.

Wild Island Family Adventure in Sparks offers a wave pool, water slides, and other wet entertainment in warm weather. Also at Wild Island is **Adventure Golf**, a 36-hole miniature golf course, open year-round, weather permitting. Also at the park are three go-cart raceways and the **Tut's Tomb** video game arcade. 250 Wild Island Court (north from Sparks Boulevard exit of I-80). Call (775) 331-9453 for operating days. Admission is $16.95 for visitors forty-eight inches and taller, and $12.95 for those beneath that height. Children younger than 3 free. Open Memorial Day through Labor Day weekends.

Performing Arts and Theater Groups

Nevada Festival Ballet. (775) 785-7915.
   Nevada Opera Association. (775) 786-4046.
   Reno Little Theater. (775) 331-1877.
   Reno Philharmonic Association. (775) 323-6393.
   Sierra Arts Foundation. (775) 329-2787. www.sierra-arts.org.
   UNR Performing Arts Series. (775) 784-6847. www.unr.edu\artscalendar.

Major Hotel Showrooms

Flamingo Hilton. (775) 785-7080.
   Harrah's Reno. (775) 786-3232; (800) 427-7247.
   John Ascuaga's Nugget. (775) 356-3304; (800) 648-1177.
   Reno Hilton. 789-2285; (800) 648-3568.

Nightclubs

Baldini's. 865 South Rock Boulevard, Sparks; (775) 358-0116.
   Cantina Los Tres Hombres. 7111 South Virginia Street; (775) 852-0202.
   Just for Laughs Comedy Club. Reno Hilton, 2500 East Second Street; (775) 789-2285.
   Confetti's. 50 East Grove Street. (775) 829-9477.
   The Cube Bar at the Peppermill. 2702 South Virginia Street. (775) 826-2121.
   The Garage in the Reno Hilton. 2500 East Second Street. (775) 789-2000.
   Reno Live Dance Club Complex. 45 West Second Street. (775) 825-5500.
   Vintage Court Bar at Harrah's Reno. 219 Center Street. (775) 786-3232.

Zoos and Animal Preserves

Animal Ark. (775) 969-3111. 1265 Deer Lodge Road, Red Rock. Closed in winter.
   Sierra Safari Zoo. 10200 North Virginia Street, Reno; (775) 677-1101. A small private zoo, about 10 miles north of Reno on Highway 395 at Red Rock. More than 200 animals representing 40 species. Admission: adult $5; children 2–12, $3. Open 10 A.M. to 5 P.M. daily, April 1 to October 31.

Chapter 21
The Great Outdoors in Reno-Sparks

Golf Courses

Most Reno-area courses are open year-round or close to it; courses north and south may be closed in the winter. Call for hours and fees. Listed yardage is for championship or men's course.

Brookside Municipal Golf Course. 700 South Rock Boulevard, Sparks; (775) 856-6009. 9 holes. Par 35; 2,882 yards. Year-round. $9.50.

Lakeridge Golf Course. 1200 Razorback Drive, Reno; (775) 825-2200. 18 holes. Par 71; 6,703 yards on championship course designed by Robert Trent Jones. Year-round. Summer rates April 1 through October 31, $70 with cart Monday through Thursday; $75 Friday through Sunday.

Northgate Golf Club. 111 Clubhouse Drive, Reno; (775) 747-7577. 18 holes. Par 72; 6,966 yards. Year-round except December 15 through January 31. Summer rates April 1 through October 31, $58 with cart.

Rosewood Lakes. 6800 Pembroke Drive, Reno; (775) 857-2892. 18 holes. Par 72; 6,693 yards. Year-round. Summer non-resident greens $33; cart fee $11.

Sierra Sage Golf Course. 6355 Silver Lake Road, Reno; (775) 972-1564. 18 holes. Par 71; 6,623 yards. Year-round. Summer, $25; with cart, $36.

Washoe County Golf Course. 2601 S. Arlington Avenue, Reno; (775) 828-6640. 18 holes. Par 72; 6,695 yards. Year-round. Summer $19; winter $17. Carts $11. Built by the WPA in the 1930s.

Wildcreek Golf Course. 3500 Sullivan Lane, Sparks; (775) 673-3100. 18 holes. Par 72; 6,932 yards. Year-round. Summer rates April 1 through October 31, $53 with cart.

Hunting Information

Contact the Department of Wildlife, P.O. Box 10678, Reno, NV 89520; or call (775) 688-1500. Information is also available at most sporting goods stores.

Tennis Courts

Lakeridge Tennis Club. (775) 827-3300.

Reno Hilton. (775) 789-2145.

Reno Parks & Recreation Department. (775) 334-2262.
Reno YMCA. (775) 329-1311.
City of Sparks Parks and Recreation Department. (775) 353-2376.
Washoe County Parks Department. (775) 785-4849.

Parks and Recreation

City of Sparks Parks and Recreation. (775) 353-2376.
　Nevada State Parks Division. (775) 687-4384. www.state.nv.us\stparks\.
　Reno City Parks and Recreation. (775) 334-2262.
　Sparks Family YMCA. (775) 685-9622.
　United States Forest Service/Toiyabe National Forest. (775) 331-6441.
　Washoe County Parks and Recreation. (775) 785-4849.

RENO

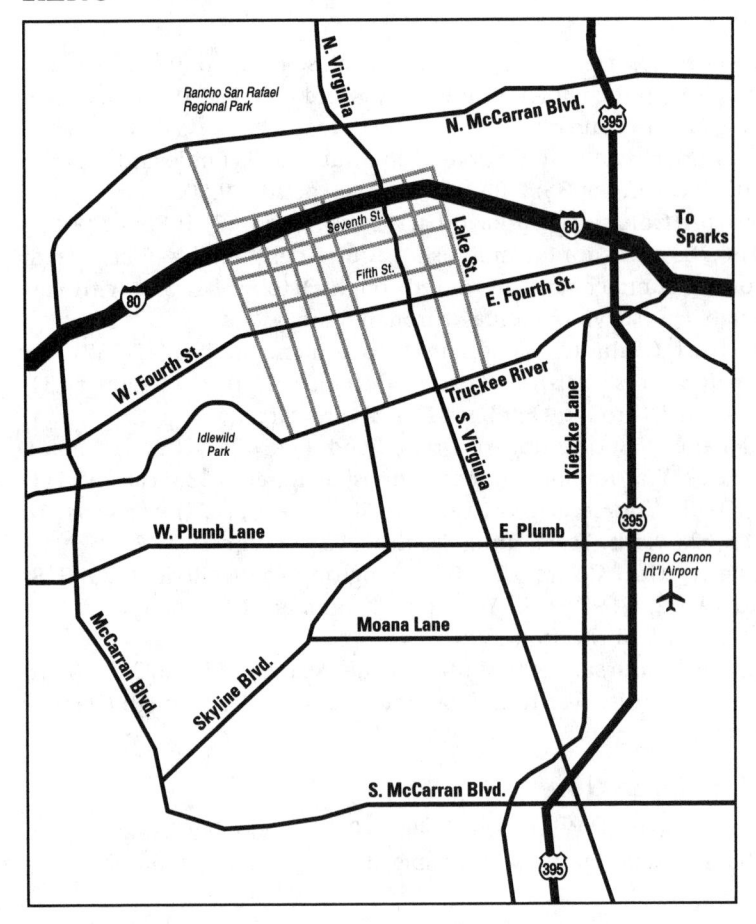

Chapter 22
Shopping and Getting Married

Shopping Malls
Meadowood Mall
Located off South Virginia Street near the intersection with South McCarran Boulevard, past the Reno Cannon International Airport and the Reno-Sparks Convention Center. Open Monday through Friday 10 A.M. through 9 P.M.; Saturday 10 A.M. to 7 P.M.; Sunday 11 A.M. to 6 P.M. (775) 827-8450.

Citifare bus service is available from the following points to Meadowood: Downtown (Fourth and Center Streets), City Station in Sparks on C Street between Ninth and Tenth, the Atlantis Casino on Virginia Street, and The Peppermill on Virginia Street.

Meadowood Mall has more than a hundred stores, including Macy's Reno, said to be the largest single department store in the state.

Department Stores: JC Penney, Macy's, Sears.

Arts, Crafts, Hobbies, and Toys: Disney Store, World of Toys, The Sharper Image.

Athletic Wear and Sporting Goods: Champs, Copeland's Sports, Eddie Bauer, Foot Locker, Lady Foot Locker, Track 'n Trail.

Children's Clothing and Shoes: Boardriders Club, Champs Sports, Eddie Baeuer, Foot Locker, Lady Foot Locker, Speedo Authentic Fitness, The Walking Company.

Electronics, Music, and Video: Electronic Boutique; Radio Shack, Waldensoftware.

Luggage: Eddie Bauer.

Men's Fashions and Shoes: Champs, Copeland's Sports, Eddie Bauer, Florsheim Shoes, Foot Locker, The Gap, Mr. Rags, Miller's Outpost, Pacific Sunwear, Structure.

Women's Fashions and Shoes: Ann Taylor, Casual Corner, Contempo Casuals, Copeland's Sports, Eagles Nest, Eddie Bauer, Express, The Gap, Guess, The Icing, Lady Foot Locker, Lane Bryant, Miller's Outpost, Motherhood Maternity, Naturalizer, Nine West, Pacific Sunwear, Victoria's Secret, Wilson's The Leather Experts.

Park Lane Mall

At the southeast corner of South Virginia Street and Plumb Lane. Open weekdays 10 A.M. to 8 P.M.; Saturday from 10 A.M. to 7 P.M.; and Sunday from 11 A.M. to 6 P.M. (775) 825-9452. More than ninety stores.

Department Stores: Gottschalks.

Women's Clothing: Claire's Boutique, Frederick's of Hollywood, Modern Woman, Rave.

Men's Clothing: Jeans West.

Family Apparel: Hat Haven, T-Shirts Plus, Wilson's Suede and Leather.

Shoes: Foot Locker, Guys and Dolls Boots, Huston's Shoes, Huston's Youngland, Payless ShoeSource.

Toys, Hobbies, and Entertainment: Game Force, Kay Bee Toy, Mirabelli's Music City, Radio Shack, Waldensoftware.

Gifts, Cards, and Books: Crystal Island, Spencer Gifts, Tinder Box, Waldenbooks.

Jewelry: Crescent Jewelers, Gordon's Jewelers, Precision Diamonds, Time Square, Zales.

Airport Square

Located on E. Plumb Lane off Highway 395, this is a bustling shopping center with more than two dozen specialty stores, including the **Sierra Trading Post** catalog outlet store. Outdoor clothing and equipment by Columbia, New Balance, Nike, Kelty, The North Face, and the like. (775) 828-8050.

More Shopping

In recent years, malls have proliferated north, south, and west of S. Virginia Street near Meadowood Mall. Here you'll find national discount stores as well as upscale shops, bookstores including Barnes & Noble and Borders, and small restaurants.

Shopping in Sparks

Greenbrae Shopping Center

Greenbrae Drive and Pyramid Way. Thirty-five stores, with everything from groceries to fabrics and crafts.

Silver State Plaza

McCarran Boulevard and East Prater Way. Forty-two stores.

Shopping in South Lake Tahoe and Stateline

A few miles over the border into California is a stretch of factory outlet stores offering clothing, accessories, and household items.

Factory Stores at the Y

Intersection of Highways 50 and 89, South Lake Tahoe. (At the point where Highway 50 continues on toward the California Coast and Highway 89 heads up along the western shore of Lake Tahoe.) The California number is (530) 541-

8314. Stores include Bass Shoes, Geoffrey Beene, Great Outdoor Clothing Outlet, Home Again, Pfaltzgraff, Sierra Shirts, and Van Heusen.

Mikasa Factory Store
2011 Lake Tahoe Boulevard, South Lake Tahoe; (916) 541-7412.

Oneida Factory Store
2016 Lake Tahoe Boulevard, South Lake Tahoe; (916) 541-0826.

Casino Shopping Arcades
Caesar's, Harrah's, and Harvey's all have a few specialty shops on the premises.

Caesar's Tahoe has the largest arcade, which includes shops such as Hot Cha Cha, Paper and Gold, and Neighbors Bookstore.

Among Harrah's Tahoe shops are Addi Gallery, The Harley-Davidson Shop, and Extended Play.

Harvey's shops run the merchandise gamut from the Heavenly Sport Shop to Harvey's Flower Shop.

Shopping in Truckee
Tahoe-Truckee Factory Stores
I-80 to 12047 Donner Pass Road. Bass Shoes, Big Dog, Dansk, Fragrance Outlet, Gorham, Home Again, Izod, L'egg's/Hanes/Bali, Van Heusen, Superstar Video.

Getting Hitched
Marriage licenses are issued to males and females 18 or older. Both must appear before the County Clerk. The marriage license fee is $35 and may be obtained at the Marriage Bureau in the courthouse. Legal identification with proof of birth date is required, such as a certified copy of the birth certificate, a valid driver's license, identification from the Department of Motor Vehicles, or a passport. No witness is necessary to obtain a license.

Courthouse Locations: Washoe County Clerk's Office, corner South Virginia and Court Streets, P.O. Box 11130, Reno, NV 89520; (775) 328-3275. Hours: 8 A.M. to midnight, daily. Fee: $35.

Civil Marriages: Civil marriages in Reno and Sparks are performed by the Commissioner of Civil Marriages, 195 South Sierra Street, Reno, NV 89501; (775) 328-3461. Fee: $35. No appointment is necessary.

In Incline Village/Crystal Bay, civil marriages are performed by the Incline Village Justice of the Peace, 865 Tahoe Boulevard. Open 9 A.M. to 6 P.M. Wednesday through Sunday. Fee: $35. An appointment is necessary.

All Nevada license fees must be paid in cash.

Wedding Chapels in Reno, Sparks, and Nearby
Adventure Inn. (775) 828-2436, (800) 937-1436.
  Candlelight Wedding Chapel. (775) 786-5355.
  Chapel of the Bells. (775) 323-1375, (800) 872-2933.

Church of the Ponderosa. (775) 831-0691.
Heart of Reno Chapel. (775) 786-6882.
Incline Village/Crystal Bay Cal-Neva Lodge. (775) 832-4000.
Lakeside Community Church. (775) 826-0566
Nugget Hotel Wedding Chapel. (775) 356-3300 ext. 3480, (800) 648-1177.
Park Wedding Chapel. (775) 323-1770.
Reno Hilton Wedding Chapel. (775) 322-5353, (800) 255-1771.
Silver Bells Wedding Chapel. (775) 322-0420, (800) 221-9336.
Starlite Wedding Chapel. (775) 786-4949.
Unity Church of Reno. (775) 747-2207.
White Lace & Promises Wedding Chapel. (775) 786-7020, (800) 613-0348.

Chapter 23
Drive, He Said: Eight Trips from Reno and Lake Tahoe

Econoguide 2001 Best Driving Trips from Reno and Lake Tahoe

★★★★ Lake Tahoe
    Emerald Bay
    Heavenly
    Incline Village
    Squaw Valley

★★★★ Pyramid Lake
★★★★ Virginia City

I. A Mirage in the Desert: North to Pyramid Lake
Trip 1: Pyramid Lake

Reno
Pyramid Lake

A spectacular sea in the desert, **Pyramid Lake** is unlike any body of water in the world. Named for the distinctive rock formation that rises from its waters, Pyramid Lake is the largest remnant of a giant inland sea that once covered more than 8,000 square miles. Ancient petroglyphs depicting Paiute Indian life line the hills surrounding the lake, and its Anahoe Island (closed to the public) is a sanctuary for beautiful pelicans.

    The lake is about twenty-five miles from Reno. Take I-80 east to the Pyramid Way exit, near John Ascuaga's Nugget. The four-lane Pyramid Way (Nevada Route 445) crosses through the northeast quadrant of Sparks, then narrows to two lanes and continues on as the Pyramid Highway to Pyramid Lake. The road meanders through what is mostly range land, although it's being developed at a rapid pace. There's a wild horse refuge adjacent to the road near the lake.

    As you cross the mostly barren desert toward the lake, the area to the east includes the former Rocketdyne test sites, where the rocket engines for the lunar lander were built and tested in the 1960s.

    Eventually, you enter into the **Pyramid Lake Indian Reservation**, past the ruins of Pyramid City, a silver mining boom camp of the 1870s. The Pyramid

Lake Indian Reservation was created in 1859 in an effort to contain the Paiute. You can pick up fishing permits at the Pyramid Lake Store just after you enter the reservation; just past the store the road makes a sharp turn and you will have your first glimpse of the lake below. Eventually you will come to a pull-off with the view most visitors come for: Frémont's Pyramid.

There is no paved road that circles the lake, so you'll have to decide whether to continue up the western shore through Sutcliffe, or go southeast to Nixon on Route 446.

The Paiute tribe operates a fish hatchery for Pyramid Lake cutthroat trout and *cui-ui* at **Sutcliffe**, and informal tours are usually available. Call (775) 476-0500 for information.

The road to Nixon meets up with Route 447 north, which follows the eastern shore of the lake from a distance. You will be rewarded with some starkly beautiful scenery, but you'll have to double back, unless you want to go the very, very long way around; there's hardly a settlement for hours in any direction.

Pyramid Lake is a remnant of ancient Lake Lahontan, which covered some 8,450 square miles in western Nevada at the time of the Ice Age. In caves and rock shelters along the shores of the lake, explorers have found evidence of a prehistoric people who had a well-developed community life.

John C. Frémont came upon the lake on January 10, 1844, and named it for the pyramid-shaped island just off the east shore. Just south of the pyramid is Anahoe Island, which was established as a national wildlife refuge in 1913; today it is one of the largest white pelican nesting grounds in North America.

The road comes to a T near the shoreline of the lake, with Highway 445 continuing north a short distance to Sutcliffe, and 446 turning south along the shoreline of the lake toward Nixon. You might want to go north for a short distance to get a good view of the pyramid across the lake before turning back and descending to the lake on 446.

The shoreline features all kinds of strange rock formations; the first big formation you come to as you head toward Nixon is Indian Head. It looks more like a stone castle as you approach it, but as you look back over your shoulder while heading away, you can see a small outcropping of rock near the top and figure out where the rock gets its name.

If you take Route 447 south from Nixon toward Wadsworth along the Truckee River you can pick up Interstate 80 west back to Sparks and Reno. As you drop down on Route 447 you will be driving through the area of the **Pyramid Lake War of 1860.**

Although early relations between explorer John Frémont and the Paiutes at Pyramid Lake were peaceful, the increasing influx of whites created by the Comstock Bonanza brought problems. In May of 1860, several whites were found killed near Williams Station on the Carson River east of Carson City; the circumstances of their deaths were never fully explained, and historians say the attack may have been made in retribution for the kidnapping and rape of several Indian women just before. Nevertheless, an "army" of more than a hundred volunteers was gathered.

Drive, He Said: Eight Trips from Reno and Lake Tahoe 241

The men arrived at Wadsworth, about fifteen miles south of Pyramid Lake, on May 12, 1860, and marched into a trap set by the Paiutes; more than half of the men were killed. The battle began with an ambush north of Nixon and continued along the plateau almost to the present site of Wadsworth. More white men died than in any prior white-Indian engagement in the Far West.

A second, larger army of nearly 1,000 came back to the lake on June 2 and this time prevailed over the natives, killing 160 of them. Several hundred

RENO, VIRGINIA CITY, AND LAKE TAHOE

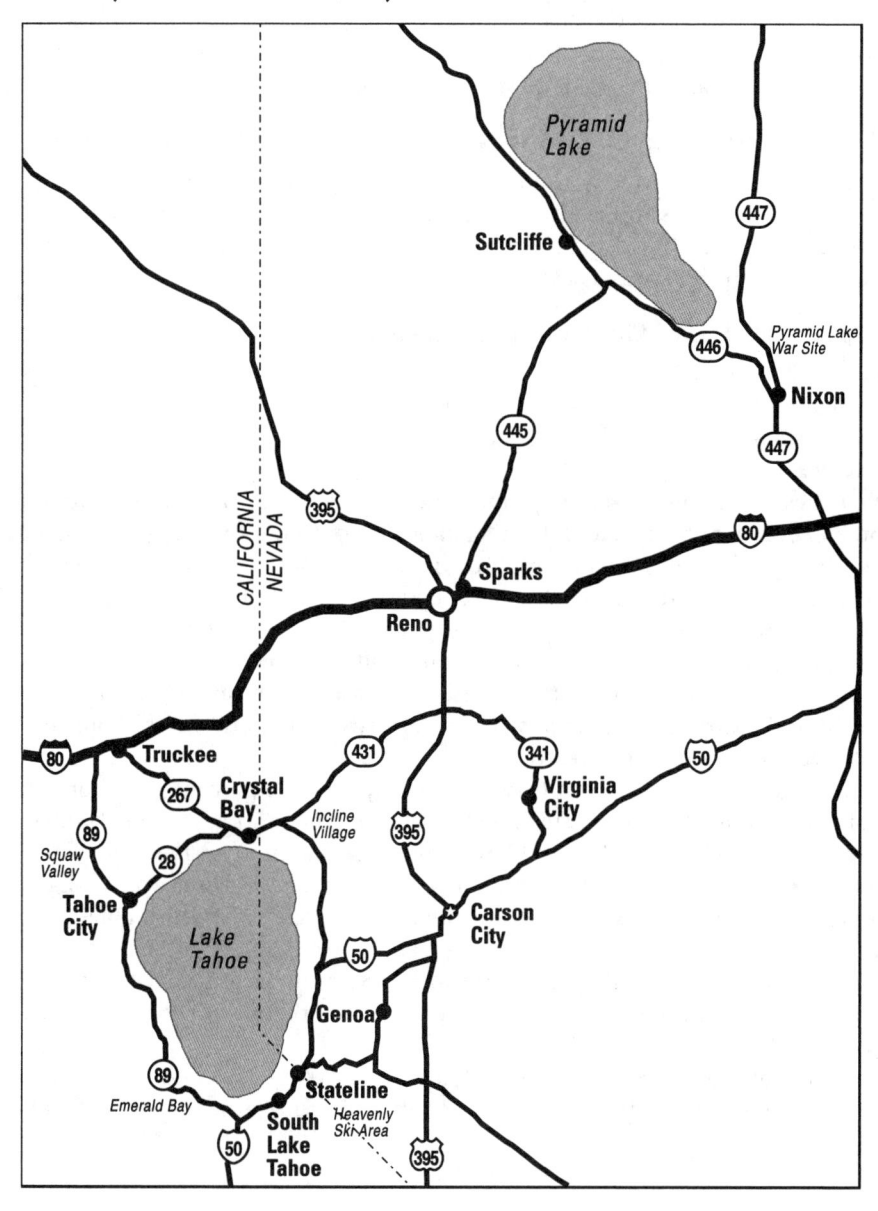

braves fought long enough to allow their women, children, and elders to escape. A forced peace treaty was negotiated ending the "war."

About a half mile further down past the historic marker for the Pyramid Lake War, you will come to the Numana Hatchery Visitors Center, which is operated by the Pyramid Lake Fisheries and the Pyramid Lake Paiute Tribe in cooperation with the Bureau of Indian Affairs. It is open daily from 9 to 11 A.M. and 1 to 3 P.M.

If you're up for a full day of exploring, you can continue on Route 447 past Interstate 80 to Silver Springs and pick up Route 50 west, which enters into the south end of the Comstock silver mining area and into Carson City. At Carson City you can head back north to Reno on Interstate 395 or cross the front range of the Sierra Nevadas on Route 50 to Lake Tahoe.

II. The Jewel in the Mountains: South to Lake Tahoe

From Reno and Carson City there are three passages through the front range of the Sierra Nevadas to Lake Tahoe. All are spectacular, and each has its own appeal. Any road will be fine in summer and early fall; winter conditions can make driving treacherous as can spring melts and refreezes.

Trip 2: The Easy Way to South Lake Tahoe

Reno	Zephyr Cove
Glenbrook	Edgewood
Spooner Summit	Stateline
Cave Rock	

The easiest, and *almost* weatherproof route from Reno to Lake Tahoe is across Spooner Summit at midlake. Take Interstate 395 south out of Reno past Carson City for thirty-five miles and then turn right onto Route 50 toward the face of the mountains. From there it's ten miles up and over Spooner Summit at 7,146 feet and down to the lake; continue twenty-five miles farther south through the Cave Rock Tunnel, Zephyr Cove, and Edgewood to Stateline.

Except in the worst of weather, these roads are kept clear of snow and ice and are well patrolled. The trip is about sixty-two miles, and takes about seventy-five minutes in good weather.

The first climb from Carson City on Highway 50 is a 6 percent grade for five or six miles, one of the most sustained climbs on a major road in this country.

On a stormy January day, each twist and turn in the road revealed a new winter sight. There was a blizzard underway at the top of distant peaks, light snow on the pass, huge snowbanks in the canyons, and even a few blue holes in the clouds overhead.

There's not much of a descent after Spooner Summit before you come to the alpine level of Lake Tahoe. On my stormy-day visit, there were wind-whipped waves on the lake.

At the bottom of the grade where Route 50 meets the lake and turns south toward Stateline is **Glenbrook**, once the center of the logging industry that all but denuded the hills for miles around to serve the needs of the Comstock Mines and Virginia City. It was also the location of the first large, fancy hotel on the lake, the Glenbrook House.

Lumbering and logging operations in Glenbrook began in 1861. By 1872, consolidation of flume systems in and around Clear Creek Canyon made it possible to float lumber and logs from **Spooner Summit** to Carson City and to eliminate wagon hauling over the narrow and treacherous mountain roads. A small rail line ran from Glenbrook to Spooner Summit and the top of the flume.

Logging began first on the east shore of the lake and moved across the west shore later where the trees were logged and dropped by flumes into the lake and then towed across by a tugboat to the mill at Glenbrook.

Depletion of the timber at Lake Tahoe and the slowdown of mining in the Comstock ended lumbering in the area in 1898, after the Glenbrook operation had taken 750 million board feet of lumber and 500,000 cords of wood from the Tahoe Basin forest.

The highway takes a short detour at **Cave Rock** and passes through a pair of tunnels through a gigantic volcanic rock. Cave Rock had been a place of religious significance to the native Washoes, who believed that the cave at the site was the home of an avenging Giant of the Sierras. Much of the cave was destroyed with the construction of the road at the turn of the century.

Tahoe Tessie, the supposed mysterious monster of the deep, is said to live in an underwater cavern beneath the cave—that is, when she is not on vacation at Loch Ness.

By the way, there have been enough reported sightings of an unusual creature in the waters of Lake Tahoe to have drawn some scientific interest; some scientists believe the "monster" may be a large lake sturgeon, a particularly ugly fish known to have existed in area waters. In 1888, a seven-foot sturgeon was caught at Pyramid Lake above Reno; Pyramid Lake is connected to Lake Tahoe by the Truckee River.

Put aside your preconceptions of the aesthetic merits of California versus Nevada and consider the fact that while there are many communities and developments on the western side of the lake, the east shore in Nevada from Glenbrook north to Incline Village is mostly untouched.

The ten-mile gap was preserved mostly through the acquisitive career of a most eccentric millionaire, Capt. George Whittell Jr. Today, Whittell's **Thunderbird Lodge** near Sand Harbor sits on 143 acres of land, the last vestige of what once was a sprawling empire that covered more than 32,000 acres and more than fourteen miles of Lake Tahoe's East Shore. At one time Whittell owned one-sixth of the entire Tahoe Basin.

Most of his property today is within Nevada's **Lake Tahoe State Park** and the latter-day planned community of **Incline Village**.

Whittell, born into a wealthy San Francisco family that built a fortune during the Gold Rush, blazed the path followed later by strange characters Howard Hughes and Michael Jackson. His sprawling estate included a menagerie of exotic animals; some of the creatures made appearances at wild parties he put on for Hollywood stars and other celebrities.

According to newspaper reports of the time, Whittell was once seen leading a pack of dogs in a chase of naked guests. And he was sued several times by guests who claimed injuries from his pet tigers and lions. In 1930, he lost a lawsuit by a San Francisco woman who accused him of having her horsewhipped at a party in San Francisco.

The landscaping around the rustic stone main house was intricate, including an artificial waterfall and a pair of private lighthouses. Along the lake was a 150-foot-long boat house blasted out of the bedrock; it was home to his fifty-six-foot-long chrome-and-mahogany speedboat, the Thunderbird, powered by four 400 hp engines.

Beneath it all is a 500-foot-long rock-lined tunnel from Thunderbird Lodge to the boat house and the outlying **Card House**; the entrance to the tunnel from the Card House was hidden behind the wall of a shower.

Other oddities include large speakers he used to broadcast warnings to uninvited boaters, and microphones installed in the guest and servant rooms to eavesdrop on conversations.

Near the end of his life he fought a losing battle against tax claims, and in the late 1960s the state of Nevada purchased 5,300 acres of his Tahoe estate for $3 million. He also made donations of much of his land to the University of Nevada, a local hospital, and for a South Shore high school. Whittell died in 1969 at the age of eighty-seven, leaving most of his estate to animal welfare groups. His last words were reportedly, "I shall come back as a lion."

Zephyr Cove draws its name from the winds that often sweep across the lake. In summertime, the beach, marina, and stables are popular attractions; the glass-bottom MS *Dixie* paddlewheel is based there. In the winter, it is a take-off point for snowmobile tours, sleigh rides, and cross-country ski trails.

Pull in at the **Visitors Center** and the **Tahoe Douglas Chamber of Commerce**, which is just past Zephyr Cove on the mountain side of the road, to mine a treasure load of brochures, coupons, and maps.

Things have changed greatly in **Edgewood**, a residential community just outside of Stateline. In the 1860s, it was the site of **Friday's Station**, a waystation on the Pony Express route established by Friday Burke and Big Jim Small; it was the home station of "Pony Bob" Haslam, one of the most famous of the Express riders. The toll booth in front of Friday's Station was one of the most profitable such franchises at the height of the reverse migration from California to the Comstock, bringing in as much as $1,500 per day.

The Pony Express was a privately owned and operated courier service, sort of the Federal Express of its day. The service, which charged $5 per ounce for letters, stretched from St. Joseph, Missouri, to Sacramento, California. There were about seventy-five way stations where horses were swapped. As famous as is the Pony Service, it is interesting to note that it lasted less than two years, put out of business by the transcontinental railroad and the telegraph.

The restored Friday's Station Inn—now a private residence—still stands across the highway from today's watering hole, the Edgewood Golf Course. The golf resort is considered one of the top public courses in the country.

Next stop is **Stateline**.

Trip 3: To the Top of the Lake and Down the Eastern Shore

Reno *Ponderosa Ranch*
Mount Rose *Sand Harbor Beach*
Incline Village *Stateline*
Crystal Bay

The views keep getting better and better as you follow the switchbacks on Mount Rose Highway. This is the most direct route to the north end of Lake Tahoe, and a slower, scenic route to the eastern shore and the south end of the lake.

Take Interstate 395 south from Reno about eleven miles to the intersection with Highway 431 and 341. (If you turn left onto Route 341, you will climb Geiger Grade into Virginia City; see Trip 6 for details on that must-see tour.) Instead, turn right onto Highway 431 toward the imposing face of the mountains.

At the intersection of Interstate 395 and the Mount Rose Highway and a bit further up the approach road to the mountains, you will find several places where you can buy snow chains for your car if necessary. You can also rent ski equipment, tubes, and snowboards before you get to the ski areas. Ski reports can be heard on several radio stations in the area, including 590 AM.

The Mount Rose Highway presents a twenty-five-mile, twist-and-turn climb up Mount Rose. The road reaches an altitude of 8,911 feet; **Mount Rose** itself continues to a summit elevation of 10,338 feet.

The road includes several switchbacks hanging out into space and very few guardrails. If you have a little bit of nerve and a decent car with a good set of tires, and most important, dry pavement, the Mount Rose Highway is quite an exciting approach to the north end of the lake.

Near the top of the highway, just before you get to the Mount Rose ski area, sneak a peak back to your left for a view that extends all the way north to Reno and south toward Carson City.

Now, try to put yourself back in the days before there were cars and a paved road. Imagine what it was like to lay out this trail through the tall trees and along the mountain ridges. And then think about what it was like to go up the trail by foot, by horse, or by wagon.

Galena Creek Park, on the slopes of the mountain, includes picnic areas, hiking trails, and other facilities for summer and winter recreation. The park is run by the Washoe County Department of Parks & Recreation; call (775) 785-4849 for information.

Mount Rose is named after Jacob Rose, who exploited diggings in Gold Canyon and brought a large crew of Chinese workers to the area in 1856 to build a water ditch.

A bit further on is the **Mount Rose/Slide Mountain** ski area. The two facilities, which combined into a single resort a decade ago, has the region's high-

> **Reno-Sparks Convention & Visitors Authority Information Center.** (800) 367-7366.
> www.playreno.com.

est base elevation at 8,250 feet, which is a pretty good guarantor of dependable snow. There is a 1,450 foot vertical drop with twenty-seven trails served by a half dozen lifts. Call (775) 849-0704 for information.

At the highest point on the road is a turnoff to the left to **Mount Rose Campground**. The road begins a gradual descent and about six miles later you will enter **Incline Village** at the northeast corner of Lake Tahoe.

At Incline Village, bear left onto State 28 south for fourteen miles to where it joins with Route 50 south into Stateline.

Incline Village was wilderness until the mid-1800s when loggers began using its timber to shore up the rich silver mines of Virginia City some twenty miles away on the other side of the easternmost mountain range. The mountainsides were stripped of nearly all hardwood, and the sawdust and debris from sawmills choked many of the creeks, all but destroying the trout population of Lake Tahoe for decades.

On the mountain at Incline Village, behind the Ponderosa Ranch, lie the remnants of the **Great Incline of the Sierra Nevada**. Completed in 1880, this 4,000-foot-long lift was constructed by the Sierra Nevada Wood and Lumber Company. A steam-powered cable railway pulled cordwood and lumber 1,800 feet up the double tracks to the top on canted cars.

At the top, the wood was automatically dumped into a V-flume and tumbled down to the Washoe Valley where it was loaded onto wagons for use in the mines of the Comstock. At the height of the enterprise, 300 cords of wood a day were moved from the mill at what is now **Mill Creek**.

Just a few years after it was completed, the railway pulled free of its moorings and fell down the mountain, leaving scars on trees and rocks that can still be seen. The bull wheels of the railway can be seen at **Spatz Restaurant** near the **Diamond Peak Ski Area**.

A small settlement was established in 1884, but the area did not gain much attention until 1927 when the first casino was built in **Crystal Bay**.

The **Cal-Neva Lodge** at Crystal Bay is famous for its swimming pool, which sits atop the state border, allowing swimmers to start in California and end up in Nevada where there is, of course, a casino. The hotel, which claims lake views from each of its 200 rooms, also includes the **Frank Sinatra Celebrity Showroom**. Sinatra was at one time a part owner of the lodge, a regular gathering place for the Rat Pack.

The wood paneled Indian Room, on the non-casino California side of the resort, is like a time capsule of the 1940s. A stone hearth that has a roaring fire sits on the state line, surrounded by a collection of old photographs and Indian artifacts, including a pair of life-sized Hopi Kachina dolls.

Room rates range from $79 to $279, higher for chalets and suites, depending on season and day of week. Packages with ski tickets are also available in the winter.

The resort is located at 2 Stateline Rd., Crystal Bay, NV. For information, call (800) 225-6382 or (775) 832-4000. www.calnevaresort.com.

Nearby, off Reservoir Drive, is the **Crystal Bay Fire Lookout**, which offers a spectacular view of the lake from the north shore. To drive to the lookout tower, follow Reservoir Road, which lies between the Tahoe Biltmore Casino and the former Tahoe Mariner Casino; turn right at the firehouse and climb the hill to the U.S. Forest Service road and proceed to the parking lot.

The development of the area for condominiums and homes also began in the 1960s and included a spectacular 18-hole championship golf course designed by Robert Trent Jones Sr. and the development of Ski Incline. The ski area, greatly expanded, is now known as Diamond Peak.

Other major construction included what is now the **Hyatt Regency Lake Tahoe Resort and Casino**, a second golf course, beach facilities, and the Lakeside Tennis Resort.

By the way, Crystal Bay was not named after the clear waters of Lake Tahoe, but rather after lumberman George Iweis Crystal who owned much of the area in the 1860s.

In the summer, special events at Incline Village include the **Shakespeare at Sand Harbor** festival, with plays presented from the end of July through August. Call (775) 832-1616 for information.

The **Ponderosa Ranch**, the mythical setting of the Cartwright family made famous in the *Bonanza* television series, has been brought to life in Incline Village in a mix of original artifacts from the show and re-creations in a historic setting along the shores of Lake Tahoe at an elevation of 6,350 feet.

The main attraction is the Cartwright home, the actual set used to film interior scenes with Ben Cartwright and his three sons, Hoss, Little Joe, and Adam. Visitors are taken on a guided tour, which includes antique furnishings and Hop Sing's kitchen, where the table is all set for Ben and his boys.

Just outside the home is a Western theme park, including a general store, gambling hall, old-time photo parlor, and numerous shops. Other attractions include a shooting gallery, antique autos, one of the country's largest collections of farm and ranch equipment, a Western memorabilia museum, and an 1870 church where old-fashioned weddings are celebrated. Children can visit a petting farm, gold panning slough, and Hoss' Mystery Mine.

Each morning from Memorial Day to Labor Day, visitors are invited to take the Haywagon Breakfast Ride, a tour that climbs through a rich pine forest to a scenic point high above Lake Tahoe. There an all-you-can-eat breakfast of scrambled eggs, sausage, pancakes, juice, and coffee is provided.

More than 300,000 people annually visit the Ponderosa Ranch. The admission rate for adults is about $9.50, and about $5.50 for children ages 5

> **Reruns.** The original *Bonanza* series ran for thirteen years on network television in the United States and has been seen in 85 other countries. It was the first major series to be regularly broadcast in color, making use of the area for many of its settings.

to 11. Admission is $1 higher for adults in peak season from Memorial Day to Labor Day weekend. The Haywagon Breakfast Ride is an additional $2 per person. Hours are 9:30 A.M. until 5 P.M. daily from mid-April to October. The Ponderosa Ranch is located at 100 Ponderosa Ranch Road, Incline Village, NV 89451, off Highway 28. For information, call (775) 831-0691.

Sand Harbor Beach State Recreational Area, about five miles south of Incline Village, offers a small but pretty sand beach on an inlet of Lake Tahoe. Rocks are piled on top of each other reaching out into the lake like little jetties. The beach sits at the base of an almost sheer cliff mountainside. In summer, there is an entrance fee of $2; the charge to launch a boat is $5.

Follow the outlines of the lake toward **Spooner Lake** where you will meet up with Route 50. Swimming is not recommended in Spooner Lake because of harmless but annoying leeches. Continue on Route 50 south through the Cave Rock Tunnel to Zephyr Cove and into Stateline.

The regular traffic to and from the Mount Rose ski area and the top of the lake and other points in California to Reno will keep the roads clear except in the worst weather, but the mountain crossing here is twice as long as the one at Spooner Summit in midlake. The trip is about sixty-six miles, and takes about ninety minutes in good weather.

Trip 4: Driving the Route of the Pony Express

Reno   *Kingsbury Grade*
Genoa   *Stateline*

My favorite approach to South Lake Tahoe is a piece of cake in good weather, a white knuckle trip in ordinary winter weather, and impossible in a storm. But what a ride!

Take Interstate 395 out of Reno past Carson City for 46 miles (eleven miles past the point where Route 50 branches off). Just past the tiny Douglas County Airport, look for the signs to the historic settlement of **Genoa**; turn right toward the wall of mountains.

Genoa was the first permanent settlement in Nevada. It was established by one of Brigham Young's traders in 1849 and was originally called **Mormon Station**. It was located at the base of the front range of the Sierra Nevadas in a meadow fed by a small creek that came down from the mountains. At the station, the trader sold supplies—brought all the way from Salt Lake City—to travelers who were preparing to go up and over the mountains westward to California.

For a short time, the little outpost was the most important point between Salt Lake City and Placerville, on the road to San Francisco. In 1854, Mormon Station was renamed as Genoa (pronounced jin-no'-ah) and became the seat of government of Carson County of the Utah Territory. In 1857, most of the Mormons were recalled to Salt Lake City to bolster Brigham Young in a confrontation against federal troops over local government; they mostly abandoned their settlement in place.

In 1857, the history of the area changed dramatically with the discovery of gold in a placer deposit—in the runout of a stream—on what was to become known as Gold Creek, a tributary of the Carson River near the village now known as Gold Hill. Significant amounts of gold in rock outcroppings were found in January of 1859 a bit to the north on Sun Mountain, sparking a gold rush; the boom took off when miners realized that the "blue mud" that stood in the way of the gold and was treated as a nuisance actually contained significant amounts of silver.

The result was a reverse migration, with many miners returning across the Sierra Nevadas from California, through Genoa, and on to the Gold Creek area. For a while, the **Johnson Cutoff Trail** (now known as the Pioneer Trail above the present location of Stateline, at the southern end of Lake Tahoe) became the most heavily traveled highway in the West. That same year the first territorial legislature met in Genoa in 1859 and drafted a demand to separate the region from the Utah Territory.

Most of the town, including the original Mormon Fort, was destroyed by fire in 1910. There's a small display in the **Genoa Courthouse Museum** on Main Street. The building served as the justice center from 1865 through 1916, and as a school from 1916 through 1956. It is open daily from mid-May to mid-October; call (775) 782-4325 for information.

Displays at the Courthouse include the Buckaroo Room with ranching and farming items from the early nineteenth century, including snowshoes for a horse. A blacksmith shop, located in the former jail, includes tools and a bellows that once belonged to Colonel John Reese, the founder of Genoa. A period classroom includes old maps, textbooks, and furniture.

Late each September, Genoa presents the **Candy Dance**, a fundraising weekend that dates back to 1919 when a group of local women raised funds for gas streetlights with a "social." Today the **Candy Dance Ball**, held in the Town Hall, raises money to pay the town's expenses—including some of those same old lights. For information on events, call the Genoa Town Board at (775) 782-8696.

There are nearly thirty buildings on the National Register of Historic Places in the tiny settlement, including the **Genoa Saloon**, said to be Nevada's oldest bar.

On nearby State 206 (Foothill Road) is **Mormon Station Historic State Park**, with a museum and restored trading post open from about May 1 to October 15. Call (775) 782-2590 for information.

At Genoa, turn left and follow the base of the mountains on Foothill Road until you come to Route 207 (Kingsbury Grade). **Kingsbury Grade** was built about 1860 as the route of the Pony Express; it was also the principal path for the Bonanza traffic from the west to Virginia City.

Head west up and over Daggett Pass (elevation 7,334 feet) and then descend into Stateline through Haines Canyon, dropping about 3,000 feet over six miles. This path should take a bit less than two hours.

The Kingsbury Grade is a shorter but somewhat more treacherous pass over the front range than Route 50 over the Spooner Summit.

You'll proceed up an incredible set of switchbacks on a two-lane highway with what looks like a dangerously frail guardrail between you and the abyss. At some points, you can see three or four stepped levels of the road above or below.

Trip 5: Into the Olympic Valley and Donner Lake

Reno
Kings Beach
Tahoe Vista
Carnelian Bay
Tahoe City
Alpine Meadows

Squaw Valley
Truckee
Donner Lake
Verdi
Boomtown

Take Interstate 395 south from Reno about eleven miles to the intersection with Highway 431 and 341. Turn right onto Highway 431 toward the imposing face of the mountains and go up and over the summit.

Kings Beach, across the border into California, sits at the absolute "top" of the lake and affords a spectacular view down its length. On a clear day—and there are many—you will be able to see the Heavenly ski resort twenty-two miles away, towering over the casinos of Stateline. Kings Beach, which includes some lovely beaches and marinas for boating and other water sports, was self-named by Joe King, a gambler who supposedly won the property in a poker game in 1925.

Just past Kings Beach, Route 267 branches off toward Truckee. At that intersection is a popular snowmobiling course on the nine-hole Old Brockway Golf Course.

Skiers and tourists can take a six-mile sidetrip on Route 267 to explore **Northstar-at-Tahoe**, a resort complex that includes a ski area, golf course, stables, and more. Northstar is a serious ski hill with a 2,200-foot vertical drop.

The next settlement westward around the lake is **Tahoe Vista**, which overlooks Agate Bay. It was named after a spectacular hotel of the early 1900s, which sat up on a hill overlooking the lake. Tahoe Vista was also one of the first subdivisions on the lake in 1911, a period when speculators almost succeeded in ruining the pristine wilderness forever. In a strange turn of fate, Tahoe Vista's subdivision may have failed because of the notoriety attached to one of its first land buyers, Miss Cherry de St. Maurice, an infamous Sacramento madam.

Although much land was sold in small lots, the region's wilderness was preserved in part by the stock market crash and the Great Depression, which caused many of the purchase contracts to go unpaid in the 1930s.

Carnelian Bay takes its name from the reddish semiprecious stones known as carnelian, which were found on its beach by the Whitney Survey party in the 1860s. An early establishment there was Dr. Bourne's Hygenic Establishment, a health resort later renamed as the Carnelian Springs Sanatoria. Dr. Bourne also tried to rename Lake Tahoe as Lake Sanatoria, an attempt which thankfully failed.

Tahoe City was established as a lumbering

> **Someone has to do it.**
> Yes, that really is a U.S. Coast Guard station just north of Tahoe City at Lake Forest Park. Because of its size and the fact that it is an interstate navigable waterway, the whole of the lake falls under the supervision of the federal Coast Guard in what must be one of the most desirable assignments in the service.

camp and as a port for freight traffic on the lake. Today it sits at the northern end of man's intrusion on the lake's beauty.

A small city of about 5,000 year-round Tahoe City is built at the site of a dam first built across the mouth of the Truckee River, the only outlet from Lake Tahoe. The passage over the river is known as the **Fanny Bridge**; it supposedly draws its name from the outstretched posteriors of those leaning over the railing to gawk at cutthroat trout below. Alongside the bridge is the **Gatekeeper's Cabin and Museum,** which includes artifacts of the early days of Lake Tahoe development, items from ancient Indian history, and items from the 1960 Winter Olympics held at nearby Squaw Valley. The cabin was used from about 1909 until it was destroyed by fire in 1978; the museum occupies an exact replica built by the North Lake Tahoe Historical Society. Call (530) 583-1762 for information.

The dam was first built in 1870 as part of a plan to drain some of the lake's waters to San Francisco through a tunnel to be bored through the Sierras. This was before environmental concerns, of course, but the tunnel was never built. One result of the damming of the outlet, though, was to raise the level of the lake by several feet, changing its outlines in many places.

There were actually several efforts to drain the lake for the use of San Francisco, including a proposal in 1900 to construct a system that would divert from 30 million to 100 million gallons of Tahoe water per day. A second plan in 1903 called for a tunnel under the Sierras to send the water into the Rubicon branch of the American River, which leads into San Francisco. The final—and almost successful effort—was supported by the U.S. Reclamation Service and would have sent the water into the dry Nevada desert for irrigation and power needs. Luckily, bureaucracy stalled the plan when the chief forester for the Department of Agriculture held up the project for years on something close to environmental objections.

In 1871, the Grand Central Hotel was opened at Tahoe City, setting a new level of luxury at the lake. The completion of a narrow-gauge spur railroad in 1900 from Tahoe City to Truckee, where the transcontinental main line passed, established the area as an important gateway to Lake Tahoe.

The Big Tree in the center of town is a big tree, celebrated as a landmark and town Christmas Tree for more than a century. The **Watson Cabin Living Museum** is within a small, authentic Lake Tahoe cabin. Nearby are several small shopping areas, the Boatworks Mall, the Roundhouse Mall, and the Lighthouse Shopping Center.

To go to Alpine Meadows and Squaw Valley, turn left onto Highway 89 at Tahoe City and enter the Olympic Valley.

On your left about six miles up the road you will come to the **Alpine Meadows** ski area. Though not as well known or anywhere near as large as Heavenly to the south or Squaw Valley just north over the mountain range, Alpine Meadows is still one big hill full of snow that has about a hundred runs.

A few miles farther along on Route 89 is the approach road to **Squaw Valley** with its Tower of Nations and the Olympic rings, a remnant of the VIII Winter Olympic Games held here in 1960.

The ski resort, with thirty-three lifts, including a 150-passenger gondola and more than a hundred runs, is set in a bowl of mountains that include KT-22 at 8,200 feet, Emigrant Peak at 8,700 feet, Squaw Peak at 8,900 feet, and Granite Chief at 9,050 feet.

Summer activities include arts and writers conferences and a world-class golf course.

After it leaves Squaw Valley, Route 89 meets up with Interstate 80, just west of Truckee.

Truckee presents an interesting freeze-frame of the Wild Old West in its historic downtown. Like much of Nevada, it grew as a rest stop—first as a point on the Emigrant Trail westward, then when the Transcontinental Railway passed through in 1868, and then in early twentieth century when the Lincoln Highway opened up the pass to transcontinental cars and trucks.

More than a hundred of the structures in and around Commercial Row date from the nineteenth century, and at least one—the Truckee Hotel—date from Truckee's boom lumber and railroading time in 1871. The 36-room **Truckee Hotel** was completely restored a few years back, with its Victorian parlor and marble fireplace as a centerpiece. Most of the rooms are "European," which means the bathroom is down the hall; the eight with private baths sport clawfoot tubs. Another important industry was ice harvesting. Cakes of ice were cut from rivers and lakes and stored in warehouses; Truckee ice was shipped east and west for hundreds of miles by railroad until the 1920s. Truckee ice was considered a delicacy in San Francisco.

Canopied wooden walkways are maintained in some of the sections. Jibboom Street, one street in from Commercial, was the active red-light district of Truckee and also houses the Truckee Jail, in use from 1875 until 1964. The streets are not quite as redolent of history as Virginia City, but worth a visit if you're on the north end of the lake.

The town received its name in honor of a Paiute Indian guide who helped a party migrating west across the Sierras; Truckee was a chief and father of Winnemucca. The westward party named the lake they found Mountain Lake; it was named Truckee's Lake in 1846 when the ill-fated Donner Party was stranded there for the winter.

Sites to see in downtown Truckee include the famed **Rocking Stone**, a seventeen-ton boulder that was balanced atop a larger rock and was used by ancient Indians as much as 15,000 years ago as a place to grind meal and by later generations as a ceremonial location. Though first thought to be a natural occurrence, more recent studies have concluded that the upper stone may have been chiseled to serve the purpose of a grinding place thousands of years ago. The stone was enclosed within a tower in 1893, and again in the 1950s; it has been cemented into a fixed position for safety's sake.

A plaque on Front Street records the actions of the **601**, a vigilante group from the Wild West days. Across Commercial Row is the **Southern Pacific Depot**, which dates to 1896.

From Truckee, you can head east back to Reno or take a short jog about four miles west on Donner Pass Road to **Donner Lake** and the Donner Memorial State Park.

Drive, He Said: Eight Trips from Reno and Lake Tahoe

The story of the Donner Party is one of the most famous tragedies of the American cultural consciousness.

The Donners and the Reeds made up the largest family groups among the eighty-seven emigrants who left Sangamon County, Illinois, in 1846 for California.

> **Park information.** For information on California State Parks and advance reservations at some facilities, call (800) 444-7275.

Under the leadership of George Donner, they made a series of bad decisions and mistakes in choosing trails across the Great Salt Lake in Utah and then the Sierra Nevadas. They were trapped by unusually heavy snows in the mountains above Reno in October and were forced to camp for the winter at a small lake about thirteen miles northwest of Lake Tahoe. They ran out of food and other supplies, and some of the members of the group resorted to cannibalism to survive—those few who would talk about their experience afterward claimed they ate only those who had died naturally from the harsh conditions.

When spring finally arrived, forty-seven of the eighty-seven emigrants were eventually brought to California by rescue parties, traveling over what is now known as Donner Pass.

A memorial and museum about the ill-fated Donner Party expedition is located at **Donner Memorial State Park.** The park includes the Emigrant Monument with a statue representing the Donner party atop a twenty-two-foot-high pedestal; the pedestal represents the depth of snow recorded in and around the lake that terrible winter of 1846–47.

The park is a strange mix of pleasant surroundings and awful memories, a sense of history and a connection to the present in the form of Interstate 80, which passes by a few hundred feet away with a steady stream of trucks.

But if you walk down the little trail that leads from the museum, you enter into a much quieter place, an area that hints at the terrifying loneliness of this place in 1846. You'll come to a large house-size rock bearing a plaque that reads, "The face of this rock formed the north end and the fireplace of the Murphy cabin. General Stephen W. Kearny on June 22, 1847, buried under the middle of the cabin the bodies found in the vicinity." There is a listing of several dozen names, including seven Donners.

Kearny, by the way, went on to become commander of the Army of the West in the Mexican War and served as military commander of California.

The small **Emigrant Museum** at the park is open year-round and includes a selection of books about the Donner Party and the area; the campgrounds are open from Memorial Day into October. Admission to the museum is $2 for adults and $1 for children ages 6 to 17. Call (530) 582-7892 for information.

As you head east back into Nevada toward Reno, you will pass through the former logging boomtown of **Verdi.** The town grew in the early 1860s around a logging mill that cut wood for railroad ties for the Central Pacific Railroad and a bridge across the Truckee. The settlement was named in honor of Italian opera composer Giuseppe Verdi, who was at his peak of fame at the time. Verdi is claimed by some to be the site of the first train robbery in the West. Bandits held up a CP train in 1870, making off with some $40,000 in payroll money for the Yellow Jacket mine. The robbers were eventually collared in mine shafts on nearby Peavine Peak above the town; all but $3,000 of the cash was recovered.

The town was kept alive as a rest stop on U.S. 40, and later moved a bit east to serve Interstate 80; the area is now known as **Boomtown**.

The **Boomtown Hotel Casino**, just off the interstate, is a K-mart of a casino including an indoor miniature carousel and an arcade with 100 games. A new seven-story tower added 200 rooms for a total of 522; the addition also includes a large Silver Screen buffet room.

Other features at Boomtown include a forty-seat **Dynamic Motion Theater**, a Ferris wheel, an indoor 18-hole miniature golf course, and an indoor swimming pool. The Laughing Lady animatronic greeter at the entrance to the casino cracks Western jokes and puns for the visitors.

Call (775) 345-6000, (800) 648-3790 for information.

A round trip from Reno over Mount Rose to Crystal Bay and through the Olympic Valley should take about three hours.

III. The Mines of the Bonanza
Trip 6: Frozen in Time

Reno	Silver City
Virginia City	Carson City
Gold Hill	

Follow I-395 south out of Reno and drive to its intersection with Highway 431 and 341, about 10 miles from downtown Reno. Turn left onto Route 341 and begin the slow but steady climb up Geiger Grade into Virginia City.

When you finally make it up the hill, you will find yourself in **Virginia City** itself; there is no mistaking where you are, either. Every Western movie ever made included a Hollywood version of this place. *See Chapter 24 for more details about Virginia City.*

After you've visited the wonders of Virginia City, continue on Route 341 to the point where it splits: take the right fork, marked as Route 342, to see the ruins of **Gold Hill** and **Silver City**, two of the mining outposts of the time. The road will soon join up with Route 341 again, which will eventually come to a T at Route 50. Make a right turn, west.

Route 50 will come to another T, at Interstate 395. Head south for a short jog to explore **Carson City**, or head north for the rapid return to Reno.

On your way back to Reno, you may want to branch off the interstate at Route 429 to visit the historic **Bowers Mansion**, constructed by one of the discoverers of the Comstock Lode, Lemuel Sanford Bowers. Bowers' new wife Eilley Orrum spent what was at the time a fortune—at least $200,000—on building and furnishing the house in 1864. Her husband, though, did not live to enjoy the house much, dying of miner's lung disease in 1868; by that time, too, the Gold Hill mine had gone bust and there was not much money left for Mrs. Bowers; she tried running the mansion as a hotel and resort but eventually saw it sold at public auction. The home is closed from November through

April. Admission is $3 for adults and $2 for children 12 and younger. For information on the mansion, call (775) 849-0201.

The trip from Reno to Virginia City takes about forty-five minutes. To make the full tour from Reno to Virginia City, continuing on to Gold Hill and to I-395 at Carson City before returning to Reno, allow about two hours. Add extra time to visit Virginia City, Carson City, and the Bowers Mansion.

IV. North from Stateline

The western side of the lake offers some of the most spectacular waterside views and the older, more historic communities. Much of the development of the west shore came from California money, with San Francisco's high society setting up camp along the lake.

Trip 7: North Along the Western Shore

Stateline	*Meeks Bay*
Bijou	*Rubicon Bay*
Camp Richardson	*Sugar Pine Point State Park*
Tallac Historic Site	*Homewood*
Fallen Leaf Lake	*Idlewild*
Emerald Bay	*Tahoe City*

West of Stateline on the California side is the little community of **Bijou**. It draws its name from a lovely little beach along the lake; don't look for the strand, though: it's gone. In 1910, the lake's level was raised by the construction of a dam at its outlet near Tahoe City, and the beach was drowned.

Bijou now includes two marinas, including the home of the *Tahoe Queen* paddlewheel, which makes cruises year-round.

The **Osgood Toll House** near Rufus Allen Boulevard is the oldest building in Lake Tahoe. Dating to 1859, it once served as a tollhouse on the Bonanza Route near Meyers; it was moved to the city for preservation.

Along the mountain side of Route 50 is a city park that includes the **Lake Tahoe Arts Center** and the **Lake Tahoe Historical Society Museum**. The museum includes old photographs of the valley; for information, call (530) 541-5458.

Back on Route 50 at the very base of the lake is **Al Tahoe**, a turn-of-the-century subdivision of cottages and campgrounds. It draws its unusual name from developer Al Sprague who named his hotel and the land around it after himself and the lake. A small beach meets the water.

Continue on Route 50 to the Y where Route 50 continues westward toward Sacramento and Route 89 heads in a northerly direction around the lake as far as Tahoe City and from there to Truckee and Donner Pass. Bear right onto 89, and the trappings of the tourist zone fall away quickly.

Camp Richardson, the first settlement you'll come across as you head north on Emerald Bay Road, was established in the 1880s as a logging camp; a narrow-gauge steam railroad line ran from the site. It later became an early resort along the shores of Lake Tahoe. Today it offers a large campground, marina, and horse stables.

Just past the camp is the **Tallac Historic Site**, a U.S. Forest Service Preserve that includes the sites of nearly a dozen former grand residences and the location of the fabled Tallac Hotel. The Tallac, opulent for its turn-of-the-century time, was known as the "Saratoga of the Pacific." The **Tallac Point House** was built in the 1870s; in 1880, it was taken over by Elias "Lucky" Baldwin, who expanded it into a luxurious resort that included a ballroom with a spring-mounted dance floor and croquet and tennis courts; guests could also take steamer excursions from the hotel. The hotel was torn down in 1916.

Among the estates open to the public at Tallac are the **Baldwin, Pope** and **Valhalla** estates. The Pope estate dates to 1894. It was expanded in 1899 to become one of the most spectacular in the area; it now serves as the visitors center for Tallac. The Baldwin home was built in 1921 by Dextra Baldwin, granddaughter of Lucky Baldwin. The Valhalla estate dates from 1924; it is used for community events. Special events held at the site include a Renaissance Festival each June and a Native American Festival in August. For information, call the Tallac Historic Site at (530) 541-5227.

The **Kiva Beach Recreation Area** offers one of the nicest beaches on the lake, set in a nearly untouched pine grove. The U.S. Forest Service Visitors Center on Kiva Beach Road offers trail guides and an interesting display about the geology and wildlife of the region. Nearby is an outdoor amphitheater where slide shows and other presentations are made in summer.

Several short interpretive trails branch off from the visitors center at Kiva. They include the **Rainbow Trail** that leads through a mountain meadow to the **Stream Profile Chamber** where you can look through an underwater window into a salmon spawning pool. The **Lake of the Sky Trail** descends to the lakeshore, while the **Trail of the Washoe** climbs a small section of the hill across the road from the visitors center.

Across the road is **Mount Tallac**, at 9,735 feet, the tallest mountain directly on the lake itself. On the northeast face of the mountain is a cross-shaped indentation that is known as the "Snowcross" when filled with the snows of winter.

If it weren't for the overshadowing glories of Lake Tahoe, **Fallen Leaf Lake** might be world famous as a spectacular alpine lake in the Sierra Nevadas. As it is, this is a side trip well worth taking on a tour of the California side.

Fallen Leaf Lake is three miles long and a mile wide, with depths up to 418 feet. The Fallen Leaf Lodge and surrounding cabins, dating back to the 1910s, are now privately owned. A boathouse and marina are opposite the lodge, and the lake is a prime fishing area. Hiking trails—some of them quite isolated—lead into some even more remote and smaller lakes, including Azure and Heather.

There are two resorts and marinas and several campgrounds at the lake, as well as the trailheads of a number of hiking trails that lead into the Desolation Wilderness. One of the private homes along the lake was used in the film, *The Bodyguard*.

The lake, at 6,377 feet, is about 100 feet higher than Lake Tahoe. The waters are fairly cold for swimming most of the year, warming up to a tolerable level by the end of summer. The lake is open to fishing year-round.

Drive, He Said: Eight Trips from Reno and Lake Tahoe

To reach the lake, turn left onto Fallen Leaf Lake Road. The lake lies at the end of the road, about five miles in; it may not be accessible in winter.

There's an even more remote set of lakes on the mountainside above: **Upper Angora Lake** and **Lower Angora Lake**. They draw their names from a flock of Angora goats tended by a man named Nathan Gilmore around the turn of the nineteenth century. Today you will find the **Angora Lake Resort**. There are a few cabins for rent; call (530) 541-2092 for information.

To reach Angora Lakes, start on Fallen Leaf Lake Road and take the first left and then the first right. You will come to the Angora Fire Lookout at 7,290 feet; continue on the dirt road until you come to a parking lot. A half-mile trail continues to the resort.

Heaven's gate. The state has a gate across the road just short of Emerald Bay that closes off Route 89 when the danger of snow avalanches or rockslides is high, or when the road is actually blocked. If the road is closed, there is no real alternative other than to backtrack and take Route 50 around the eastern side of the lake.

Information about trails in the Fallen Leaf Lake area can be found at the visitors center on Highway 89 near Fallen Leaf Lake Road. Call (530) 573-2674.

North of Tallac, the road begins to twist and climb, finally revealing the spectacular **Cascade Lake** and even-more spectacular **Emerald Bay**.

Cascade Lake, on the mountain side of the road, was the setting for several well-loved motion pictures, including *Rose Marie* with Nelson Eddy and Jeanette McDonald. The lake is named for White Cloud Falls at its southwest corner; mountain streams plunge 100 feet into the lake. The falls are usually at their fullest in the spring as the snow melts; in winter, the stream and the lake itself are often frozen. Visitors to the lake have included writers Mark Twain, John Muir, and John Steinbeck.

You'll know you've reached Emerald Bay when you hear a collective "Wow" from everyone in your car; it's an automatic reaction to one of the most spectacular sights in the West. The road approaches the southern edge of the bay and then circles 180 degrees around it; there are several spots to stop and take a picture.

In the mouth of the bay is tiny Fannette Island, the only island in the lake; it holds a tiny one-room "tea house" built in the 1930s by the owner of the Vikingsholm estate during another of the periodic tourist booms around the lake.

If you can take your eyes away from the view of the bay to the right, look to the left to see the foothills of Desolation Wilderness, some 60,000 acres of, well, desolate wilderness. Several rough roads and hiking trails lead off into the hills. They are not for amateurs and often inaccessible in winter; check with park rangers for conditions.

At the north end of the bay is a parking lot at the head of a steep mile-long trail that descends to the shoreline of the lake and **Vikingsholm**, another treasure of the Tahoe Valley. The thirty-eight-room stone structure, built in 1929 by Lora Josephine Moore Knight, a wealthy socialite, is a replica of a 1,200-

Forewarned. Pay attention to weather forecasts in the winter and spring, especially if you must cross one of the mountain passes. Rain at the "lower" elevations of Lake Tahoe or Reno may well be heavy snow in the passes. Highway 431 and Route 207 are regularly shut down in the winter because of storms. And Route 89 on the west shore of the lake is closed so often there are permanent barriers that can be swung across the road to stop traffic at Emerald Bay.

Much of Route 89 on the California side and Routes 207 and 431 in Nevada have no guardrails to block the spectacular view—and the tremendous drop to the rocks below.

year-old Viking castle. Actually, Mrs. Knight had planned to bring back fabulous antiquities from Norway and Sweden, but the Scandinavian governments declined to allow them to be removed and instead expensive replicas were made.

Some 200 workmen were brought to Lake Tahoe in the spring of 1929, and the house was completed by summer's end. The estimated cost of Vikingsholm, in 1929 dollars, was $500,000.

There are two towers with turrets; part of the building is covered, in Viking style, with sod roofs that bloom with wildflowers in the spring. Inside, the castle is filled with antique and reproduction furnishings from Norway and other Scandinavian countries. The beams in the ceiling of the living room are intricately carved with dragon heads.

Vikingsholm is now managed by the state, and tours are conducted in summer months, generally from July 1 to Labor Day. There is a $3 admission fee for adults and $2 for children. For information, call (530) 525-7277.

The Rubicon Trail, a four-mile hiking path, connects to the **D. L. Bliss State Park** at the north end of the lake in **Meeks Bay**. Some tour boats pull up at a dock near the castle; private boats can also approach from the lake.

The state park includes 1,237 acres of forests and a sand beach at **Rubicon Bay**. Naturalist programs are offered in the summer, and the park is open from mid-June through mid-September. There is a daily use fee. In the summer, parking is extremely limited at Bliss Park, with only twenty-five $5 day passes sold per day; the lot is usually filled by 10 A.M. For information, call (530) 525-7277.

A trail within Bliss Park leads to **Balancing Rock**, a 130-ton boulder resting on a small pedestal.

The 2,000-acre **Sugar Pine Point State Park** runs from Sugar Pine Point on the lake across the highway and up General Creek into Desolation Wilderness and the Tahoe National Forest. The park includes many majestic sugar pines, some as tall as 200 feet. Down near the lake is the Ehrman Mansion, a 1903 estate that was one of the social centers of the West Shore in the Roaring '20s. The rock and wood estate was the summer cottage of Isaias Hellman a businessman who was to become president of Wells Fargo Nevada National Bank. It was sold to the California State Park System in 1965, which today conducts tours in the summer. For information call (530) 525-7982.

Summer hiking trails, including the Dolder Nature Trail, become nordic ski trails in the winter.

The **Homewood Ski Area** extends to within feet of the highway at Homewood, with a marina on the lake side of the road. North of the ski area is a seaplane base for tourist flights and charters.

Idlewild, just below Tahoe City, was developed in the 1890s as a colony of the well-to-do from San Francisco.

Just south of the Idlewild, you'll pass the imposing stone walls of **Fleur du Lac** (Flower of the Lake), built in 1939 for wealthy industrialist Henry Kaiser. There was a fabulous stone mansion surrounded by six cottages intended for the heads of Kaiser's six companies. Kaiser got his start with a road paving business and went on to participate in the construction of the Boulder (now Hoover) Dam, the Grand Coulee Dam, and the San Francisco–Oakland Bridge. His Kaiser Industries included steelmaking, construction, and auto making.

Fleur du Lac was used as the site of much of the location filming for *Godfather II* in the 1970s. Many of the original buildings are now gone, replaced by privately owned condominiums.

We're now at **Tahoe City**. From here you can continue across the top of the lake and back to Reno on the Mount Rose Highway, or go northwest to Truckee and Donner Lake and then east to Reno.

Trip 8: Eastward Ho!
The Great Bonanza Road from California

Meyers   Stateline
Pioneer Trail

Although our modern movie-shaped perceptions put the emphasis on the great westward rush of settlers, personified by the Donner Party tragedy of 1846–47, the process reversed for a while in the 1860s with the discovery of silver in and around Virginia City.

The present Route 50 brought back thousands of miners and merchants from Sacramento and Placerville, California. The road follows the south fork of the American River for part of its route and then descends from the mountains into Meyers. From there it heads north to near the present site of South Lake Tahoe and adjoining Stateline, Nevada. Also from Meyers, though, is the Pioneer Trail, also known as the Placerville-Carson Road, which stays above the shoreline of the lake and heads for the front range of the Sierra Nevadas.

We'll start our short tour from Meyers and head toward South Lake Tahoe and Stateline. If you're coming from Stateline, we'd suggest you follow Route 50 along the lake west to Meyers and then double back.

Meyers was settled in 1851 and included the **Yank's Station** trading post, named for owner Ephraim "Yank" Clement. About ten years later, Yank's Station became an important remount point for Pony Express riders.

Today, Meyers is a popular winter sports area with cross-country ski trails in and around Echo Lake; several companies run snowmobile tours to the mountain meadows.

Coming from California, the **Pioneer Trail** bears off to the right at Yank's Station, about six miles before the Y where Route 89 heads north around the lake and Route 50 turns toward Stateline. At the peak of the eastward return from California to Virginia City about 1864, this section of the trail was said to be the busiest road in the West. Thousands of would-be miners and workers crossed above Lake Tahoe on foot, by stagecoach, or by horse. Each day some 300 tons of cargo was pulled along the narrow dirt or corduroy wood roads. There were many inns and other way stations; the location of many of them are marked with wooden pegs or signs.

Among the inns along the road, near where Cold Creek crosses the road, was the Sierra House. This inn was supposedly frequented by the infamous highway robbers Black Bart and Jack Bell, among others.

The completion in 1869 of the transcontinental railroad farther to the north through Truckee and across Donner Summit ended most of the slow traffic on the Pioneer Trail.

Chapter 24
Virginia City: A Side Trip Back in Time

A century ago, Virginia City went from desolation to the richest place on earth and then back to desolation in the course of a few decades.

Today it is a living ghost town, a museum in place, and one of our favorite places to visit and dream. There are few places on Earth that, by their mere existence, speak so eloquently of their history.

As you stand on C Street in Virginia City and feel the mass of Mount Davidson over your shoulder, you may think you are on solid ground, but in fact you are perched atop a near-hollow shell. Millions of tons of rock have been removed from beneath your feet and the hills around you are honeycombed with 750 miles of tunnel.

The Carson Valley Rest Stop

Like many of the settlements described in this book, the Carson Valley began as a rest stop. Thousands of emigrants seeking their riches in the 1840s Gold Rush of California passed through northern Nevada, and many of them stopped for provisions or spent the winter in the valley before making the treacherous crossing of the Sierras.

While they were in the area, some of the would-be California gold-seekers explored a bit on the eastern side of the mountains. In July of 1849, Abner Blackburn and the members of a Mormon wagon train spent some time on the banks of the Carson River; Blackburn found a few specks of gold in his pan near the present-day town of Dayton, but it was not enough to make the travelers stay.

In the coming few years there were small discoveries among wagon trains waiting for the snows to melt in the mountain passes. One group panned its way up a small stream that flowed into the Carson River; they optimistically named the waterway Gold Creek. On June 1, 1850, one of the men discovered a gold nugget at an isolated rock formation now known as Devil's Gate.

During the following decade, many small finds were made, including, according to the legend, a major discovery in Gold Canyon by brothers Allen and Hosea Grosh. Unfortunately, both brothers died—one from blood poisoning because of an accident and the other as the result of severe frostbite suffered on a crossing of the Sierras on a trip to California to raise money for a new mine.

This brings us, then, to scrappy miners Pat McLaughlin, Peter O'Reilly, and their grabby neighbor Henry Comstock. They began to mine the area at the head of Six Mile Canyon in 1859, grinding the rock in search of gold and casting aside the black rock that got in the way.

Early gold miners complained about the sticky blue-gray mud that fouled their picks, clothing, and shovels. It wasn't gold; some thought it was low-value lead. McLaughlin, O'Reilly, and the other miners, who had been earning about $876 per ton for gold-bearing ore stopped complaining when the mud was assayed and discovered to be silver ore, worth $2,000 to $3,000 per ton. The Comstock Lode had been found.

Getting to Virginia City

I-395 South ends about 10 miles south of Reno and becomes a two-lane highway; continue until you come to a traffic light at the intersection of two of the most interesting roads most drivers will ever experience: Highway 341 and 431. Head left to Virginia City on 341 or right to Lake Tahoe.

Virginia City sits at 6,200 feet; Route 341 follows the Geiger Grade, which twists back and forth for thirteen miles to its highest point of 6,799 feet before descending slightly as you reach the town. The trip is a total of twenty-three miles from Reno.

As you drive up the twisting and turning Geiger Grade to Virginia City, think about how the miners and the suppliers brought their equipment and logs up the grade, and how they brought their silver and gold ore back down. Take advantage of some of the turnoffs on the drive up; from some of the higher points you can see the remains of the original Geiger Trail, which was even steeper and more twisty than the road you are negotiating in the relative comfort of your car.

The Old Geiger Grade was constructed by Davison M. Geiger and John H. Tilton in 1862, and served as the most direct connection between the Comstock Lode and the Truckee Meadows until it was replaced by the present paved highway in 1936. Concord stages, mud wagons, and ten-mule "freighters" carried thousands of passengers and millions of dollars in precious cargo across this section of the Virginia Range.

In addition to the unpredictable winds, snow, and landslides, this area was also popular with highwaymen. A marker near the top of the grade points out the location of the descriptively named **Dead Man's Point** and **Robbers Roost**.

Just after you cross the summit of Geiger Peak, you will find a marker on your left for **Louse Town**. Near its location was a station established in 1860 on Geiger and Tilton's new toll road from Truckee Meadows.

Around Louse Town—what a picture that name paints—was a large population of teamsters, stock, and sheep men. The steep hillside area included the

Virginia City: A Side Trip Back in Time

first Virginia City railroad surveys, a race track, a trap shooting range, and other amenities.

As you drive up the Geiger Grade, you will be assaulted by sign after sign proclaiming your approach to something known as the "Suicide Table" at the **Delta Saloon**. It sounds a lot more sinister than it really is: the Suicide Table is an 1860 faro table that apparently was the source of lost fortunes for three of its owners, each of whom killed himself.

When you reach the town itself, find a parking space—a lot easier in the winter than the summer, when you may have to use an outlying lot—and walk to C Street. One good place to start is the privately run **Visitor Center**, which, in addition to selling knickknacks, continuously shows an interesting video about Virginia City made a few years back as a promotional effort.

A City Above and a World Below

Mark Twain, under his real name of Samuel Clemens, worked for a while as a reporter for the *Territorial Enterprise*. Years later he wrote about the town: "Virginia was a busy city of streets and houses above ground. Under it was another busy city, down in the bowels of the earth, where a great population of men thronged in and out among an intricate maze of tunnels and drifts, flitting hither and thither under a winking sparkle of lights, and over their heads towered a vast web of interlocking timbers that held the walls of the gutted Comstock apart."

The money-making engine for Virginia City was the fabled Comstock Lode, a two-and-a-half-mile deposit that paid out some $500 million in silver and $700 million in gold. About 20 million tons of ore were brought out of the 750 miles of workings.

Discovered in 1859, the Comstock Lode began a wild twenty-year boom that helped bring Nevada into Statehood in 1864, contributed funds to the Union Army, and helped build San Francisco. There were seven major mines, several of which can be seen from C Street.

Dying to get in. Just below town is the Virginia City Cemetery. According to legend, there were eighty-eight violent deaths before someone spoiled it all by dying of natural causes.

Insert peg A into slot B. Several years into the boom, a German engineer named Philip Deidesheimer invented the square-set method of timbering that supported the crumbling rock and enabled shafts to be dug to depths of more than 3,000 feet.

The timbering of the mine had another effect: the near denuding of the forests for miles around. In fact, the search for more wood to timber the mines of Virginia City and Gold Hill extended over the Sierra Nevada. One of the more ambitious engineering schemes of the day took place in what is now known as Incline Village, at the north end of Lake Tahoe. There, a lumber company built a primitive tramway that lifted logs up the side of a mountain to a flume where they were tumbled back down to waiting wagons that transported them to Virginia City.

At boom time, it's said that Virginia City was home to 40,000 people, 100 saloons, six breweries, fifty dry goods stores, four banks, and five newspapers.

> **Bright lights, big city.** When Ben Cartwright sent "the boys" to town for supplies or adventure in the television series *Bonanza*, he was sending them over the mountain ranges into Virginia City. A re-creation of the Ponderosa Ranch can be found in Incline Village at the north end of Lake Tahoe.

> **Namesake.** Virginia City got its name from one of the first miners, James Finney, nicknamed "Old Virginny" after the state of his birth. Returning from a revelry, he supposedly dropped and broke a bottle of booze. Instead of crying over spilt whiskey, he christened the tent city on the slopes of Mount Davidson "Old Virginny Town" in his own honor.

The local payroll reached $500,000 a month. Restaurants imported lobsters, raw oysters, champagne, caviar, and other fineries from San Francisco; the wives of the mine owners furnished their homes with European crystal and wore Parisian gowns.

According to one of the many versions of the discovery of the riches in the hills and valleys south of Reno, miners Pat McLaughlin and Peter O'Reilly discovered a small quantity of gold-bearing rock at the head of Six-Mile Canyon in 1859. Henry Comstock, another prospector, made a loud but dubious claim that the men were trespassing on his property, and the lucky-then-unlucky miners settled the dispute by giving Comstock a neighboring piece of land. It was there that the gigantic Lode was first found, and its riches were named after him and not its unfortunate discoverers.

By the 1880s, though, most of the riches had been extracted, with the profits taken to San Francisco, New York, or overseas. In fact, between 1880 and 1890, the population of all of Nevada declined by 25 percent, and between 1890 and 1900 still further. Nevada's mining boom reignited about 1900 with the discovery of gold and silver in the center of the state at Tonopah and Goldfield; those fields led in great part to the development of Las Vegas as a railroad town.

The decline of the boom towns on the western and northwestern side of the state continued, though. Virginia City probably would have completely disappeared were it not for the birth of the tourist industry in the second half of the twentieth century.

Almost Everything You Wanted to Know About Mining

Dan DeQuille, whose real name was William Wright, headed west from Ohio with the news of the silver discoveries in the Comstock Lode. Failing as a miner, he became a journalist and in 1862 joined the staff of the *Territorial Enterprise* in Virginia City. In that same year, the newspaper also hired Sam Clemens (later to gain fame as Mark Twain) for a brief stint. In 1875, Clemens persuaded Wright to publish his remembrances of the wild times in Virginia City. Wright's book was called *The Big Bonanza*, and it paints a vivid picture of the difficulties and rewards of the time.

As rich as the Comstock Lode was, the Hollywood myth of miners carving out huge chunks of gold or silver rarely happened. Instead, there were tiny flakes of precious metal embedded in quartz or other rocks. There was much hard work involved in extracting the wealth. The first test of the worth of a piece of ore was usually done on the spot.

The results of the test in a vessel known as a "horn" were generally enough to tell the miner whether to load up a larger sample and bring it into town to an assayer's office. There, a determination would be made of the value of the ore by the ton.

> If a specimen of ore was supposed to contain silver, it was pulverized in the same way as gold-bearing quartz, then was placed in the horn, and the lighter matter it contained washed out. . . . The heavy residuum was then washed from the horn into a matrass (a flask of annealed glass, with a narrow neck and a broad bottom). Nitric acid was then poured into the matrass until the matter to be tested was covered, when the flask was suspended over the flame of a candle or lamp and boiled until the fumes escaping (which are for a time red) came off white.
>
> When the contents of the matrass had been allowed to cool and settle, the liquid portion was poured off into a vial of clear, thin glass, called a test-tube. A few drops of a strong solution of common salt was now poured into the test-tube. If the ore . . . contained silver, the contents of the test-tube would at once assume a milky hue.

Anyone who has worked in a darkroom has worked with the same basic set of chemicals, by the way. What the test produced was a silver salt, which is the basis of photographic film and paper. In fact, some miners would take the test tube out into the desert sun for a few minutes and observe the effect of strong light on the solution: if there was silver in the salt solution, the liquid would turn purplish-black.

Virginia City: History Underfoot

Stop for a moment in Virginia City and absorb the history that surrounds you. The old buildings with their wooden walkways on C Street mostly date from about 1875, the year when fire nearly wiped out the town, destroying more than 2,000 structures. After the Great Fire, the entire town was rebuilt within six months, so strong was the faith that the underground riches would continue forever. Of course, this did not happen, but there was just enough activity in the mines to keep the town alive.

In 1875, 30,000 people lived in town. The Fourth Ward School, built in 1876 and still standing, was one of the first commercial buildings west of the Mississippi that had indoor plumbing. The six-story International Hotel had the West's first elevator, which they named a "rising room."

As befits a wild place with a lot of money, Virginia City quickly became home to celebrities, Shakespearean plays, opium dens, newspapers, competing fire companies, police precincts, and a red-light district.

The Combination Mine was the deepest mine in the region, going down 3,262 feet—half the way to sea level. These deep mines did suffer from a significant problem, that of flooding from underground springs. To make things

> **Pool's gold.** The Brunswick Ledge, a rich ore body about a mile east of the Comstock Lode, probably received its name in honor of the billiard tables in the back rooms of several of the bars in Virginia City.

even more difficult, the water was often hot and sulphurous. Mine owners were forced to install huge pumps such as the Cornish pump at the Union Mine, which had a forty-five-foot flywheel and a pump rod that extended 2,500 feet down the shaft and could lift more than 1 million gallons of water to the surface each day.

The grandest scheme for removing the water from the mines, though, was that of businessman Adolph Sutro who came from Prussia in 1850 in search of wealth in California. He amassed his first fortune in retail and real estate ventures in San Francisco, but he was drawn to Virginia City in 1860. He ran a successful reduction mill at Dayton.

Sutro saw the problems of ventilation and removal of water from the deep mines and came up with the idea of a deep tunnel that would run from three miles east of Dayton near the Carson River under the base of the mountains to link up with the mines of Virginia City. Mine operators would only have to drain their operations to the Sutro Tunnel and not to the surface. He expanded his concept to include the use of the tunnel as an emergency evacuation route for miners and as an underground transportation system that would bring the ore from the various mines to mills at the mouth of the tunnel.

It took more than eight years to secure all the various permits and permissions, as well as financing, for the project. He even had to obtain a special act of Congress, the Sutro Tunnel Act of 1866, which granted him the land and the right to charge royalties to companies using the tunnel. Investors came from as far away as England and Germany.

Construction of the 3.8-mile tunnel began on October 19, 1869; it was July 8, 1878 when the tunnel connected with the Savage Mine at the 1,640-foot level. However, by the time the tunnel was completed, most of the major mines had gone far deeper than that. The tunnel did serve its original purpose as a means of getting some of the water out of the tunnels, but little more. Sutro eventually returned to California where he made more money in real estate and even served a term as mayor of San Francisco, from 1895 to 1897.

The **Ponderosa Saloon**, established in 1873, has some of its walls lined with old flume boards from the Virginia and Gold Hill Water Company. Iron pipes brought water from the High Sierras down across the Washoe Valley and up to a reservoir five miles from town. From there, wooden flumes brought water to Virginia City. The original system was used until 1957.

The Ponderosa Saloon is located in the former site of the Bank of California, established in 1864. Within the saloon you can walk into the old bank vault; the Bank of California provided much of the capital for the early growth of the Comstock mines. Much of the billion dollars in earnings passed through the doors to be stored in the vault, which is lined from ceiling to floor with half-inch steel plate; the outside walls are two feet thick.

On October 25, 1927, the Bank of California was robbed of $32,000. The robbers were eventually caught, but much of the loot was never recovered and is supposedly hidden in the hills around Six Mile Canyon.

At the back of the Ponderosa is a hoisting cage salvaged from one of the many mines in the area. There are some rather unique safety features in the upper frame. The weight of the cage hanging on the flat woven steel cable would turn the safety to the flat side; if the cable should break, the theory was that the safety would roll outward, sinking the gear teeth into the wooden guide beams on the side of the shaft and stopping the cage from plunging to the bottom.

One of the greatest dangers of the mines was the extremely fast ascent and descent of the cages. The waist-high fencing on the cage was installed to protect miners from being injured or killed by banging into the sharp rock on the sides of the shaft.

You can visit a portion of the **Ponderosa Mine** from the back of the Ponderosa Saloon on South C Street. The mine tour at the Ponderosa is a walking tour into a portion of the 1869 Best and Belcher Mine and goes about 300 feet deep into the underground works. Admission to the twenty-five-minute tour is about $4 for adults, $1.50 for children, or $8.50 for a family of two adults and children younger than 12. Tours are available year-round from 10 A.M. to 4:30 P.M.; open weekends only in winter. For information, call (775) 847-0757.

A few steps past the back room of the Ponderosa puts you into the abandoned Best and Belcher mine. The mine closed for the first time in 1863 during the Civil War; the Bank of California built its office at the location, and about 1874 the mine was reopened when a higher grade of ore was found. In 1917 the owners closed the mine and walked away, leaving tools, dynamite, and rail cars in place.

The tour heads 377 feet straight back into the mountainside, in year-round temperatures of fifty to sixty degrees; off to the sides of the horizontal stope are several 200-foot-deep shafts. A single miner would be lowered to the bottom of the shaft in a bucket; he would fill the same bucket with ore, which would be lifted back up. At the end of his shift he would use the same bucket to ride back up—as our guide pointed out, the miner at the bottom would work hard to make sure he remained good friends with the man at the top.

Among major problems for miners was the lack of oxygen or the pressure of methane gas. The mines were lit by candlelight and the fixtures also included hooks to hold caged canaries to serve as early warning devices. Mules were commonly used in the mines. Some of the animals spent their entire lives underground; they were bred and born without ever seeing the sun. In fact they were not allowed to come up to daylight for fear that they would be blinded.

About twenty-five men worked in the mine at a time, making about twelve feet of progress per day.

Deep into the tour, at a point where the stope ends at a wooden platform covering a 500-foot-deep shaft, the guide may turn out the electric lights to

> **Hands off.** Children can enter the casinos and saloons of Virginia City, but as in other parts of Nevada they must stay away from the gaming devices.

> **Low finance.** In 1869, John Mackay and James Fair bought an interest in the failing Hale and Norcross mines. Joined by James Flood and William O'Brien, a pair of San Francisco saloon-keepers turned stockbrokers, they bought the barren Consolidated Virginia Mine in 1872 for about $50,000.
>
> They sunk an even deeper shaft and eventually struck the "Big Bonanza" 1,167 feet down. That one lode brought out $135 million in ore; in today's money that is worth more than $2 billion.
>
> Mackay went on to lay the first Trans-Atlantic and Pacific telegraphic cable for a company competing against Western Union. Fair became a U.S. Senator from the new state of Nevada. O'Brien and Flood spent their money.

show you the scene by candlelight . . . and then blow out the candle to plunge you into the darkest darkness you are ever likely to experience. Because pumping is no longer performed in the tunnels, water has risen about halfway up the 500-foot-deep shaft.

The **Chollar Mine** at South F Street at D Street is open for half-hour walking tours from mid-May through the end of October from 10 A.M. to 4 P.M. Visitors can also pan for gold. Admission is about $4 for adults and $1 for children ages 5 to 14. Panning costs an extra $5. For information, call (775) 847-0155.

The front window of the **Red Garter** saloon celebrates the famous gift made by "Barbara," one of the most sought-after ladies of the night, to her new husband.

The inscription on the window reads, "To Judge Orville Hardison from his loving wife Barbara on the occasion of her retirement and our marriage, July 23, 1893." The gift came from Barbara's personal collection of business tools: a .41-caliber ivory-handle Colt Derringer, a bone-handled dagger, and her red garter.

We suspect you will be unable to resist the insistent come-ons for the Suicide Table at the **Delta Saloon.** While you are there, check out the old nickelodeon at the back of the saloon, which features "Grandpa's Pin-Up Girls in 3D." The Delta also includes a great collection of old coin-operated devices, including a gypsy fortune teller and an Electric Traveling Crane that can scoop up candy and trinkets.

The Delta was the first saloon rebuilt after the disastrous fire of 1875. Of the 100 saloons—that's no mistake, 100—in Virginia City, the Delta was the most famous because of its gaming room where a significant portion of the riches of the Bonanza was gambled away in games of Rocky Mountain (a variation of blackjack) or another card game known as faro.

Directly opposite the Delta Saloon on C Street is a small monument constructed from pieces of ore from every Nevada county. It was erected in 1958 commemorating the 100th anniversary of the discovery of silver.

The *Territorial Enterprise* **Museum** on C Street commemorates the famous newspaper of the same name, as well as some of its most famous employees, including Samuel Clemens (Mark Twain) and Dan DeQuille. The *Enterprise* was Nevada's first newspaper and most celebrated in the Old West. Founded at Genoa in 1858, it was moved to Virginia City in 1859. The paper suspended publication in 1916 but was revived in 1952.

The **Crystal Bar** on C Street first opened in 1871; it has remained in one family since 1909. The original crystal chandeliers and mirrors arrived at San Francisco by ship from France and were sent by railroad to Virginia City. During Prohibition, the Crystal Bar was officially converted to an ice cream parlor; unofficially, it continued as a speakeasy.

At the top end of C Street is the **Fourth Ward School**, built in 1875. The cut stone foundation is anchored in solid granite from Mount Davidson. The four-story structure was built to accommodate 1,025 students in fourteen classrooms and two study halls. The last grammar and high school students to use the school were members of the Class of 1936. After sitting dormant for many years, it was restored by the Nevada State Museum and includes a fascinating exhibit about the history of the Comstock, including models of the mines and their works. The museum, at the end of C Street on the way out of town toward Gold Hill, is open from May to November. For information, call (775) 847-0975.

The modern-day Virginia City High School, home of the "Muckers" football team, is down in the valley below the town.

For a decidedly offbeat view of old Virginia City, you might want to check out the **Julia Bulette Red Light Museum** on C Street. (The sign out front warns that the exhibit is not for the "faint of heart.") We didn't see anyone being carried out on stretchers, but we did see an exhibit not often seen in museums: opium pipes and other drug paraphernalia, slightly risqué (by today's standards) French postcards, and leftovers from the local brothels were among the items on display. Open daily at noon until 7 P.M. or later. For information, call (775) 847-9394.

The **Virginia and Truckee Railroad** was built to serve the needs of the mines in 1869. The first track linked Virginia City to Carson City; in 1872, the line was connected to Reno, thirty miles north, directly linking Virginia City to the transcontinental line from the East to San Francisco on the West Coast.

At its height, as many as forty-five trains a day arrived and departed from Virginia City. Think about that number: that's several an hour, day and night.

Work began in April of 1868, with more than 1,000 mostly Chinese workmen working on parts of the line spread from Virginia City to Carson City; the rails were tied together and the first train ran on November 12 of that year. The line had an almost immediate effect, dropping the cost of supplies brought into the mining area and reducing the freight for the ore moving out; the lowered cost made some of the marginal mines more profitable and extended the boom.

The distance to Carson City was only twenty-one miles, but it was a very dif-

> **Citizen Hearst.** George Hearst, the father of newspaper magnate William Randolph Hearst, started the family fortune as a stockbroker in Virginia City. He claimed that his fortune was built entirely on commissions from the sale of stock and that he never had any direct involvement in Comstock shares.

ficult distance to traverse. The tracks dropped about 1,600 feet over thirteen miles, making twenty complete circles and crossing a huge wooden trestle at Crown Point.

By 1938, traffic had diminished so much that the link to the state capital was discontinued, and in 1950 the last train was run to Reno. Parts of the line were rebuilt and restored in 1976 for the tourist trade, and the railroad takes visitors on an interesting circuit through the mining areas in the summer months, pulled by a real steam engine.

The thirty-five-minute trips go from the V & T depot on F Street past the Chollar Mine and through Tunnel Number 4 to Gold Hill and back; passengers can get off the train at Gold Hill and catch a later trip back to Virginia City. Trains run from the end of May through late September. Fares are about $4.50 for adults and $2.25 for children; an all-day pass is $9. For information, call (775) 847-0380.

In 1952, the celebrated *Territorial Enterprise* newspaper was purchased by former New York society columnist Lucius Beebe and his associate Charles Clegg. They came to town in great Eastern style, running the paper until 1961. Among the changes they brought to Virginia City were their ornately decorated railroad cars.

The **Nevada Gambling Museum** is a small display of slot machines—some of them playable for free, and one of the few chances for children to lay hands on a slot machine, even though they can't win any money—as well as guns, knives, and weapons, cheating devices, and rare photos and gambling artifacts. The museum is within the Palace Emporium Mall, 20 C Street, across from the Delta Parking Lot in the center of town. Open year-round from 10 A.M. to 5 P.M. For information, call (775) 847-9022.

And now we come to one of the stranger elements of today's Virginia City: the **International Camel Races.**

It all began with the little-known fact that camels were used in some parts of the Wild West as pack animals; there was even a U.S. Army Camel Corps. They were brought to the Comstock to carry salt and general supplies in the early, disorganized days of mining. Once the major mines were functioning and the Virginia & Truckee Railroad was the main freight carrier, the camels—not known as particularly affectionate pets—were turned loose in the hills and eventually disappeared.

In the 1950s, though, in the tradition of Mark Twain, Dan DeQuille, and other tongue-in-cheek writers for the paper, the *Territorial Enterprise* published a totally fabricated account of the result of a great camel race. In 1960, a race was held for real in a challenge that reached to San Francisco, with movie director John Huston winning the first race on a camel borrowed from the San Francisco Zoo. Quite logically, ostrich races were added in 1962.

Traditionally, the camel races are held on the weekend after Labor Day in Virginia City in an arena east of F Street, and in mid-May in Alice Springs, Australia, sister city to Virginia City.

Other unusual events in Virginia City include the **Ferrari Club of America Hill Climb** and apparently unrelated World Championship **Outhouse Races** and **Privy Parade**, all held in October of each year. In November and December, Virginia City celebrates **Christmas on the Comstock**. And in March there is the **World Championship Mountain Oyster Fry**. (If you don't know what a mountain oyster is, be sure to ask before you take a bite. Or, ask the emasculated bull cowering in the brush.)

The **Virginia & Truckee Railroad** train ticket window and the **Virginia City Chamber of Commerce** are located within a bright yellow rail car on C Street. V & T Car No. 13 is said to be the only railroad car ever designed expressly for transportation of precious metals, built in 1874 for the Virginia & Truckee and used until 1939 to transport millions of dollars in silver and gold from Virginia City to the mint at Carson City and to the Southern Pacific Railroad at Reno. For information on events, contact the chamber at (775) 847-0311.

Off the Beaten Track in Virginia City

Virginia City is laid out in an above-ground mirror of the squareset timbering that holds up the mines below ground. The main streets run north and south and are labeled from "A" (highest up on Mount Davidson) to "F" Street down in the valley. Cross streets run east and west and carry names, many drawn from those of the founders or wealthy landowners of early days.

The main commercial district, described above, runs along C Street; many of the once-grand mansions were built on "Millionaire's Row" on B Street up the mountain while some of the workers lived down below. Some of the upper homes managed to escape the 1875 fire.

Start your tour at the south end of town on B Street at **The Castle**. This local must-see is a snapshot of how the world came to Virginia City when it was at its peak. Built from 1863 to 1868 for Robert Graves, the superintendent of the Empire Mine, the sixteen-room mansion was designed to look like a castle in Normandy and was furnished with the best money could buy. Furnishings include a 600-year-old Heidelberg sideboard, crystal chandeliers from Czechoslovakia, and elegant wallpaper from France. It is even more amazing when you consider that virtually everything in The Castle was sent by boat from Europe around the Horn to San Francisco and then overland through the Sierra Nevadas and into Virginia City.

The Castle was above the fire, and most of the original furnishings are still intact; it is open for tours from May to November.

At 158 South B is the **A. M. Cole Mansion**, a classic Victorian built in 1887 for a successful pharmacist. Nearby at 130 South B is the **Water Company**

Building, constructed in 1875 for the offices of the Virginia City and Gold Hill Water Company.

Providing drinking water to the burgeoning city at the top of the mountain was a difficult matter; what little ground water there was available quickly became fouled by runoff from the mines and in any case there was nowhere near enough for 40,000 residents.

The solution was yet another gargantuan project for Virginia City, a system that imported water nearly twenty miles from Hobart Creek near Lake Tahoe, eight miles across Washoe Valley and back up a 1,500-foot climb over the mountains to Virginia City. Almost immediately the water supply was insufficient, and so the wooden pipes and sluiceways were extended another eight miles to Marlette Lake high up in the Sierra Nevadas.

Our tour continues on to the **Storey County Courthouse**, built in 1877 to replace an earlier building destroyed by the fire. The Victorian-style courthouse is still open and used for government offices. Take a close look at the statue of Justice. What's wrong with the picture? Justice is not blindfolded, and the scales are in balance. It could be sloppy work; then again, it may be a message from the past.

The next building of note is **Piper's Opera House**. Every decent Western boom town had to have an opera house; in fact the miners and upper class of Virginia City probably received a richer diet of culture than do modern Americans. John Piper's wooden structure—the third in a succession of theaters he built on the Comstock—was completed in 1885 and featured carpeted floors, hanging balconies, and a spring-mounted dance floor. Performances ranged from Shakespearean plays to Italian operas to dog fights. Great actors and performers seen at Piper's included Edwin Booth, Harry Houdini, Lillie Langtry, John Philip Sousa, and Buffalo Bill Cody. Inside are the raked stage and elegant proscenium boxes, along with some of the original scenery. The opera house is open for tours afternoons in the spring and summer on an irregular schedule; for information, call (775) 847-0433.

Three different **International Hotels** once stood on a single spot just below Piper's Opera House. The first hotel, a fourteen-room wood structure, was built in 1860 and dismantled in 1863. The second, a 100-room, four-story brick building was destroyed by the Great Fire of 1875. The third and grandest International Hotel opened its doors in March of 1877 with 160 rooms on six floors, complete with hot and cold running water, steam heat, gas lighting, and the first hydraulic elevator in Nevada. The hotel was destroyed by fire in 1914 and was not rebuilt because of the Comstock's decline.

Past the courthouse is the **Knights of Pythias Hall**, built in 1876. Next door is the **Miners Union Hall**, organized in 1863 as the first such protective association for miners; among its accomplishments was the negotiation of a munificent minimum daily wage of $4; the Union Hall offered the rough and tough miners a ballroom, library, and chess room.

As you face the Union Hall, look up the mountain and to the right to see the **Orphir Pit**, the site of the original gold strike.

Virginia City: A Side Trip Back in Time

Climb up to A Street; from here we will head back to the south. At 6 South A Street is the Victorian home built for George Hanning, a prosperous Virginia City merchant.

Here you'll find a marker near where the Great Fire began early in the morning of October 26, 1875, when a coal oil lamp was knocked over in Crazy Kate's boarding house. Strong winds spread the flames, and supplies of blasting powder in and around the mines made the blaze much worse. In all, thirty-three blocks of structures were leveled. Losses included St. Mary's in the Mountains Catholic Church, the Storey County Court House, Piper's Opera House, the International Hotel, and city offices of most of Virginia City's business district. The offices and hoisting works of nearby mines were also destroyed.

The marker is near a small hose house that was part of a new hydrant system put into place after the fire. The system is still in use today.

There are two short streets above A Street with a commanding view of the valley. At 66 Howard Street is the **King Mansion**, a castle-like structure built in 1861 for George King, secretary of the Virginia & Truckee Railroad.

Now we drop down below the C Street commercial district. The former red-light district was located on D Street, just below the Silver Dollar Hotel on D Street between Union and Sutton Streets.

According to legend, the queen of lower Virginia City was Julia Bulette. Some of the grand stories about her—which may or may not be true—said that she was at the center of Virginia City's cultural establishment with her own box at the opera and drove around town in a formal horse-drawn brougham with her own crest on the door. The tourist guides will tell you she also sold her charms for as much as $1,000 per night. They'll say she was a favorite of the miners and had a mine named after her; the railroaders put her name on a V & T car, and she was named an honorary member of Fire Engine Company No. 1. Perhaps.

An undisputed fact is that on the morning of January 20, 1867, Bulette was found brutally murdered in her bed; a chest full of valuable jewelry and other possessions *may* have been missing. Many of the men of the town—including the firemen—showed up for her funeral, and again for the trial and eventual hanging of the accused murderer, a Frenchman named Jean Millain.

Bulette's house was located on D Street at Union directly above the V & T depot and freight yards. Look up over the slot machines in the Ponderosa Saloon for a rosey painting of Ms. Bulette. Moving southward you will come to the **Mackay Mansion** at 129 D Street, originally built as the office for the Gould & Curry Mine, which had its shaft across the street; after the Great Fire of 1875, mining millionaire John Mackay took over the building as his home. For information, call (775) 847-0173. *You'll find a discount coupon in this book.*

Continue south to the **Savage Mansion** at 146 D Street; this building had a similar history, with the offices of the Savage Mine on the ground floor and the residence of the mine manager on the upper two levels.

Near the south end of D Street, below the Fourth Ward School, is the **Chollar Mansion**, built in 1883 as an office and residence for the Chollar-Potosi Mining Company.

Drop down one more row to E Street to the famed **St. Mary's in the Mountains** church. The Victorian Gothic structure was rebuilt after the Great Fire; according to legend, Silver King John Mackay paid for the reconstruction after he had convinced the priest to send his parishioners to help save the mine buildings and let the church burn. Within the church is a display of history. A railroad tunnel for the V & T once ran in front of the church to the depot at the end of the line.

On F Street at Union at the bottom of town is **St. Mary's Hospital,** built in 1875 with much of the funding from Mackay; the former Chinatown, a community of almost 2,000 people, was located in front of the hospital. St. Mary's is now an arts center.

Surrounding Towns

As you drive out of Virginia City toward Carson City, you will come to Gold Hill, site of other major discoveries. There are remains of former mines on the left and right as you traverse the switchbacks, including one of the sharpest S-turns you will experience, alongside a mountain side that has been completely dug away in modern-day pit mining.

Gold Hill, just outside Virginia City, was the actual location where the Comstock Lode was first found. By 1865, just six years after the first strike, Gold Hill had three foundries, two banks, two newspapers, and several thousand residents; the population peaked at 9,000. The mines, though, petered out in the 1870s, and Gold Hill became a ghost town in the first half of the twentieth century. Since then, there have been sporadic attempts to bring out ore using modern methods, the most recent ending in 1983.

You'll see some old workings and hoisting wheels in and around the **Gold Hills Hotel and Saloon.** The 1859 stone and brick building was the first hotel in the Comstock and the oldest hostelry in the state. Restored to something approaching its boom town finest, it is once again open for guests.

A nearby marker is on the site of the first recorded claim in the Comstock Lode. Across from the saloon is the site of the Gold Hill Brewery.

Silver City

Silver City was another mining town on the Comstock, and the location of the toll booth for the locally famed **Devil's Gate Toll Road** that led up the winding canyon from Dayton and Carson City to Virginia City.

But for an accident of history, the story of the Comstock Lode might have centered on Silver City instead of Virginia City up the road. The brothers Allen and Hosea Grosh discovered silver here in 1856, but both died in 1857 before their ore was assayed.

Below Silver City is the former location of McCone's Foundries, first established in 1862 at John Town two miles southeast in Gold Canyon. After two years, the operation was moved to Silver City. A fire on May 15, 1872, left nothing standing but the walls. McCone then bought the Fulton Foundry in Virginia

City and made it the largest in the state employing 110 men at its peak. All the early castings of the Virginia & Truckee Railway were manufactured at Fulton's.

Henry Comstock, who horned his way into history with a cut of the fabulous lode that now bears his name, operated a store in Silver City for a short while after he sold his claim (for a paltry $10,000); he went broke when the mines petered out, and left for new boomtowns in Montana, eventually committing suicide in 1870.

Dayton

Dayton, at the location where the Gold Canyon empties into the Carson River, was a rest stop for travelers on their way to California and a Pony Express Station. A permanent settlement and a tent trading post were established about 1851, just after Genoa was founded; the area was at first named Chinatown because of the Chinese railroad workers who populated the area. After the gold discoveries on the other side of the range, the community was renamed as Dayton and, with a population of about 2,500, was considered as a site for the state capital before it ended up a few miles west in Carson City.

Adolph Sutro lived in Dayton and operated a stamp mill there to serve mining interests. It was in Dayton where Sutro located the exit for his fantastic tunnel into the Comstock Lode to drain water and remove the ore; there were great hopes when the Sutro Tunnel was being planned and constructed, but the boom never came.

Dayton has the oldest cemetery in the state, with tombstones recording the names of many of the pioneers mentioned in this book, including James "Old Virginny" Finney, who gave Virginia City its name.

After a hundred years of decline, Dayton was once again a glittering boom town for a short time in 1960 when Hollywood came to town to film *The Misfits*, with stars including Marilyn Monroe and Clark Gable.

Accommodations in the Virginia City Area

Remember: you're looking for historical ambiance and realism, right? You are not going to find the opulence of a Caesars Palace or the big-city hotel amenities of a Reno Hilton here in the hills. You will, though, find old-time bed-and-breakfasts, inns, and an antique hotel or two. (If you must have more modern facilities, continue on down the hill to Carson City.)

For general information about Virginia City, call (775) 847-0311.

Chollar Mansion. A bed-and-breakfast within the former mansion and office built in 1861 for a mine superintendent. The hotel includes rooms decorated with Victorian-era furnishings, an arched vault that once stored millions of dollars worth of silver and gold bullion, and the paymaster's booth. The guest library includes a large collection of books on Virginia City and the surrounding area. Rooms range from about $75 to $110 for a double; there is also a guest cottage available for $125. 565 South D Street, Virginia City; (775) 847-9777.

Gold Hill Hotel and Crown Point Restaurant. Nevada's oldest operating hotel, this Victorian country inn was built in 1859, less than a mile down the canyon from Virginia City in Gold Hill. There are fifteen refurbished guest rooms, four with private fireplaces; a separate building offers three kitchen suites. The hotel's Great Room features a massive open hearth stone fireplace. Room rates range from about $50 to $125. 1540 Main Street, Gold Hill; (775) 847-0111.

Comstock Lodge. A motel-like lodge just outside of downtown, with room rates of about $50 to $80 for a double. 875 South C Street, Virginia City; (775) 847-0233.

Sugar Loaf Motel. 416 South C Street. Rates from $40 to $100. (775) 847-0551.

Virginia City Motel. Open year-round. Room rates range from about $48 to $65. 675 C Street, Virginia City; (775) 847-0444.

Chapter 25
Carson City: A Capital Before There Was a State

Like the state for which it serves as capital, Carson City is a bit unusual. To begin with, it is one of the smallest capitals in the nation, with just 53,000 or so residents.

The site of Carson City lay in the Eagle Valley on the Overland Trail, over which stages and the Pony Express crossed the Sierras on the south side of Lake Tahoe en route to Sacramento, California. Once again, here is the story of a city—a state capital, even—that grew from a rest stop.

The commercial founder of Carson City was Abraham Curry, a businessman from Ithaca, New York, who arrived in Eagle Valley in 1858, just a year before the discovery of the Comstock Lode. Curry sought his riches as a merchant, buying an existing ranch and trading post to serve both the emigrants heading to California and, as it turned out, gold-seekers coming the other direction to the Comstock.

Though the idea of Nevada as a state was still a rather remote dream, Curry immediately began to develop the site as a future capital, even calling the "downtown" of his hardscrabble sand empire Capitol Square. He named the developing town Carson City after the famed guide Kit Carson, who was still alive at the time.

In addition to his skill as a merchant, Curry proved to be an able politician. He promoted his town site at every opportunity and also struck an alliance with the territorial governor, James Nye, another refugee from New York. The first territorial government was centered in Carson City, and in 1864 when statehood was granted, it became the capital.

Among his other activities, Curry served as the warden of the first territorial prison—inmates constructed many of the early sandstone buildings that make up the core of the city today. In 1865, the federal government ordered the construction of a branch of the U.S. Mint in Carson City to convert some of the gold and silver into the coinage of the realm, and Curry built the structure to house it and served as its first superintendent.

Carson City, along with much of the western part of the state, went into decline about 1880 as the Comstock Lode petered out. The population of Reno

> **Little big man.** The famed mountain guide and trapper Kit Carson was born in 1809 in Missouri. He was a little guy, never topping five-foot, six-inches in height. Carson's father was killed by a falling tree limb when the boy was just nine, and when he was fifteen his mother apprenticed him to a saddler and harness maker. There he met some of the early adventurers heading west; he talked his way into one of the lowliest jobs on the wagon train—that of cavy boy, the driver of the spare mules and oxen.
>
> He went on to demonstrate his prowess as a frontiersman, and he was hired by John C. Frémont as a guide for expeditions in 1842 and 1843, including a midwinter crossing of the high Sierra Nevadas. He went on to great fame during the Mexican War.

> **Map your course.** Stop at the cartographic mother lode in the State Department of Transportation at 1263 South Stewart (Room 206) where you can purchase a full range of official maps of almost every description. For information, call (775) 888-7000.

did not recover to its 1880 level of about 7,500 until about 1960.

Touring Carson City

Stop at the Carson City Convention and Visitors Bureau at 1900 South Carson Street, (775) 687-7410, to pick up a touring map for the capital. More than twenty stops on the tour are "talking houses" that broadcast to car radios and portable radios on the AM band at 1020, 1040, 1060, or 1080 frequencies.

The **Nevada State Museum** is a small but rich collection of artifacts and displays that tell the story of Nevada from prehistoric times to the current day. The museum is housed in the old Carson City Mint Building, where the mint operated from 1870 to 1893 and produced nearly 60 million coins, including the famous Carson City silver dollar. All told, the Carson City mint struck $49,274,434.30 in coinage.

The sandstone blocks for the building were quarried at a nearby prison. Out front is a time capsule that was put in place on October 31, 1964, for the centennial of Nevada, and to remain sealed until the year 2064.

As you enter the museum, one of the first major exhibits is the original coin press, a six-ton apparatus manufactured by Morgan and Orr of Philadelphia. On February 11, 1870, the big press struck its first coin, an 1870 silver dollar.

Up to 175 tons of pressure was required to strike a gold double eagle. The intense strain soon caused a crack to develop in the arch of the press; the foundry at the shops of the Virginia & Truckee Railroad in Carson City cast a new three-ton iron arch in 1878 to repair the press. In 1899 the press was dismantled and shipped to the Philadelphia mint. It was rebuilt in 1930 to work with an electric motor and was transferred to the San Francisco mint in 1945 where it operated for ten more years. When that mint closed, the press was saved from the scrap heap and returned to its first home as part of the Nevada State Museum. In 1964, the coin press was loaned to the Denver mint for three years to help alleviate a national shortage of coins.

The press is still used occasionally to stamp out commemorative bronze and silver coins sold at the museum's gift shop.

Another fascinating exhibit displays the exquisite silver service of the U.S. *Nevada*, commissioned in 1916. The plates and serving pieces were a gift from the State of Nevada to its battleship namesake, fashioned from 5,000 ounces of silver. In World War II, the *Nevada* served off the Aleutians and then stood off the coast of France during the Normandy landing of D-day, its fourteen-inch guns pounding the shore. The *Nevada* ended its life a bit ignominiously, serving as a target ship for an atomic bomb test at the Bikini Atoll; the silver service was removed first. According to Naval records, though, even the atomic bomb could not sink her and the Navy scuttled the ship.

An exhibit on the geology of Nevada includes the skeleton of an *imperial mammuthus* (a North American woolly mammoth) that died about 17,000 years ago in Nevada's Black Rock Desert; it is the largest such skeleton on exhibit in America. Nearby is the skeleton of an early horse, *equus pacificus*, a large Ice Age horse about 25,500 years old and recovered from near Pyramid Lake.

Carson City Chamber of Commerce. 1900 South Carson Street, Suite 100, Carson City, NV 89701; (775) 882-1565.

Carson City Convention and Visitors Bureau. 1900 South Carson Street, Suite 200, Carson City, NV 89701; (775) 687-7410 or (800) 638-2321. www.carson-city.org.

Carson Valley Chamber of Commerce and Visitors Authority. 1512 Highway 395, No. 1, Gardnerville, NV 89410-7814; (775) 782-8144 or (800) 727-7677.

Greater Reno–Sparks Chamber of Commerce. 133 North Sierra Street, Reno, NV 89503; (775) 686-3030.

The well-stocked book section in the gift shop is worth some serious browsing. At the time of a recent visit, the nearby rotating exhibit was devoted to the Chinese influence on Nevada, including some beautiful clothing and artifacts brought to America by Asian railroad and mine workers.

The Environmental Gallery teaches about the animal and plant life of the state, from dinosaurs to today; the Earth Science Gallery explains the complex geology that formed not only the gold and silver deposits of Nevada but also the dramatic mountain ranges and deserts. Also on display is an impressive collection of artifacts of ancient Native American cultures.

The last exhibit is a recreation of one of the mines of the Comstock, so well done that some visitors may suffer from claustrophobia. Along the low-ceiling path you will step into a "Dillon Box," a mine cage used to lower men into the deep shafts. The floors of the "mine" include pieces of old rails, which were actually wood covered with metal straps; displays include mine faces made up of actual ore.

The museum is located at 600 North Carson Street and is open every day from 8:30 A.M. to 4:30 P.M. Admission is $3 for adults; $2.50 for seniors; children younger than 18 are admitted free. For information, call (775) 687-4810.

Another essential stop on the tour of Carson City is the **State Capitol** on Carson Street between Second and Musser Streets. The stone building, first

> **Safer that way.** In Nevada, the legislature is very much a part-time job, in session (except for emergencies) only for a few months at the beginning of odd-numbered years. There are only sixty-three legislators—twenty-one senators and forty-two members of assembly, the fourth-smallest state legislature in the nation. (Representatives are paid just $130 per day for a sixty-day session, too.) We might all be better off if the U.S. Congress was to adopt such semi-retirement.

erected in 1871 and expanded in 1915, is distinctive for its huge log rafters within. It is set in a four-block, elm-shaded park—Abraham Curry's Capitol Square. The governor maintains his office in the building, but the original legislative and Supreme Court chambers are used for exhibits, including an amazing museum of official and unofficial state items on the second floor.

There is a strange mix of buildings as you move on to the **Legislative Building**, which is open to the public interested in seeing the Assembly and Senate. For information, call (775) 684-6800.

The legislative mall includes statues of Kit Carson, Adolph Sutro, and Abraham Curry.

The **Nevada Supreme Court** is located at 201 South Carson Street and is jarringly modern in this old city. Completed in 1992, the building is sometimes used to house exhibits on state history. Oral arguments are open to the public during the session from September to June; for information, call (775) 684-1755. The Supreme Court also meets in Las Vegas, on the other side of the state, for part of its schedule.

Just outside Carson City and before the point where Highway 50 and Interstate 395 split is the office of the **Carson Ranger District of the U.S. Forest Service**. You can stop in for a wilderness permit or obtain information on hiking trails in the area. It is also a good place to check on road conditions and weather forecasts. The ranger station is open weekdays from 8 A.M. to 4:30 P.M.

Railroad buffs and children of all ages are not going to want to miss the **Nevada State Railroad Museum**, which mostly commemorates the Virginia & Truckee Railroad. The V & T rail line running from Virginia City to Carson City was completed in 1869 and the tracks were extended north to Reno in 1872 where they met the transcontinental lines.

At the museum, there are engines, passenger cars, railroad construction equipment, and a display of model railroad cars that is definitely a cut above the old Lionel set you had as a kid.

In the summer season, you can take a short ride around the museum property on an old engine. The museum, located south of Carson City on I-395 at Fairview Drive, is open daily from 8:30 A.M. to 4:30 P.M. Admission is $2 for adults; children younger than 18 are free. For information, call (775) 687-6953.

Next door to the railroad museum is the **Carson City Visitor Center** and the **Chamber of Commerce**. An old Prairie Schooner wagon sits outside.

The **Stewart Indian Cultural Center** is located at 5366 Snyder Avenue on the campus of the former Stewart Indian School. Exhibits include displays on tribes of the Great Basin, including the Washoe, Paiute, and Shoshone, and irreplaceable photographs taken by E. S. Curtis, who lived with more than eighty western tribes from 1898 to 1928. A trading post offers arts and crafts. The museum is open daily from 9 A.M. to 4 P.M. and is free. For information, call (775) 882-6969.

A more current attraction in an old place is **The Children's Museum of Northern Nevada**, located in the Carson City Civic Auditorium at 813 North Carson Street. In the summer, the museum is open daily from 10 A.M. to 4:30 P.M. weekdays and until 5:30 P.M. on weekends; it is closed Sunday the rest of the year. Admission is $3 for adults and $2 for children ages 3 to 14. For information, call (775) 884-2226.

The **Brewery Arts Center** celebrates the arts, not beer, although it is located within the former site of the Carson Brewing Company at King and Division Streets. The building was constructed in 1864 and was operated as a brewery more or less continually until 1948; it then became the printing plant for the Nevada *Appeal*, the state's older continuously published daily newspaper. It became the center of Carson City's cultural arts in 1975, offering art exhibits and sponsoring performances in the area. For information, call (775) 883-1976.

Mills Park, located on Highway 50 East at Saliman Street, features a miniature train ride, the Pony Express Pavilion, swimming, tennis, and the like.

Yes, There Are Casinos

You cannot compare the gambling establishments of Carson City with those of Las Vegas or Reno, or even with the historically interesting slot palaces of Virginia City. But you can make a bet of almost any description.

The **Nugget** is definitely a casino for the hardcore. How else to describe a place that was nearly packed with locals at noon on a drizzly Friday? At the time of our visit, the Nugget offered an eminently forgettable buffet that offered several varieties of indeterminate meat, poultry, and fish-like substances, tired salads, and scary Jell-O. 507 North Carson Street.

The historical award goes to the **Ormsby House** at 600 South Carson Street, which had its birth in 1859, the same year as the discovery of the Comstock Lode. It was established by Major William Ormsby, a buddy of Abraham Curry (and in whose name the county was named). A major renovation was undertaken in recent years and the casino and hotel reopened in 1995.

A newer casino is **Carson Station** farther south at 900 South Carson Street. For information, call (775) 883-0900.

Carson City Casinos, Hotels, and Motels

Listed here are rates for basic double rooms. Note that rates are subject to change and are likely to be higher during holiday periods and major events, and lower in slow periods.

$	$49 or less
$$	$50 to $99
$$$	$100 to $149
$$$$	$150 and more
♣	Casino/Hotel

Best Western Carson Station Hotel/Casino. ♣ 900 South Carson Street. (775) 883-0900, (800) 528-1234. $–$$

Best Western Trailside Inn. 1300 North Carson Street. (775) 883-7300, (800) 528-1234. $–$$

Bliss Mansion B&B. 710 Robinson. (775) 887-8988, (800) 320-0627. $$$$

Carson City Inn. 1930 North Carson Street. (775) 882-1785. $–$$

Carson Motor Lodge. 1421 North Carson Street. (775) 882-3572. $

City Center Motel. 800 North Carson Street. (775) 882-5535, (800) 338-7760. $–$$

Days Inn. 3103 North Carson Street. (775) 883-3343, (800) 329-7466. $–$$$

Deer Run Ranch B & B. 5440 Eastlake Boulevard. (775) 882-3643. $$–$$$

Desert Hills Motel. 1010 South Carson Street. (775) 882-1932. $–$$

Downtowner Motor Inn. 801 North Carson Street. (775) 882-1333, (800) 364-4908. $–$$$

Frontier Motel. 1718 North Carson Street. (775) 882-1377. $–$$$

Hardman House Motor Inn. 917 North Carson Street. (775) 882-7744, (800) 626-0793. $–$$$

Mill House Inn. 3251 South Carson Street. (775) 882-2715. $–$$

Motel 6. 2749 South Carson Street. (775) 885-7710, (800) 466-8356. $

Nugget Motel. 651 North Stewart Street. (775) 882-7711, (800) 948-9111. $–$$

Ormsby House Hotel. ♣ 600 South Carson Street. (775) 882-1890, (800) 662-1890. $–$$$$

Pioneer Motel. 907 South Carson Street. (775) 882-3046, (800) 882-3046. $–$$

Plaza Motel. 805 South Plaza Street. (775) 882-1518. $–$$

Round House Inn. 1400 North Carson Street. (775) 882-3446. $–$$

St. Charles Executive Suites. 310 South Carson Street. (775) 882-1887. $–$$

Silver Queen Inn. 201 West Caroline. (775) 882-5534. $

Super 8 Motel. 2829 South Carson Street. (775) 883-7800, (800) 800-8000. $–$$

Westerner Inn. 555 North Stewart Street. (775) 883-6565. $–$$

Chapter 26
Lake Tahoe: Mountain Shangri-La

Econoguide 2001: Best Casinos and Hotels Around Lake Tahoe
★★★★ **Caesars Tahoe**
★★★★ **Harrah's Casino Hotel Lake Tahoe**
★★★★ **Hyatt Regency Lake Tahoe Resort & Casino.** Incline Village
★★★★ **Harvey's Resort Hotel/Casino**
★★★★ **Resort at Squaw Creek.** Squaw Valley

Econoguide 2001: Best Restaurants Around Lake Tahoe
★★★★ **Le Petit Pier.**
★★★★ **Llewellyn's.** Harvey's Lake Tahoe
★★★★ **Empress Court.** Caesars Tahoe
★★★★ **Summit Room.** Harrah's Lake Tahoe
★★★★ **Friday's Station.** Harrah's Lake Tahoe
★★★★ **Scusa!** South Lake Tahoe
★★★★ **Glissandi.** Resort at Squaw Creek

Econoguide 2001: Best Casino Buffets in Lake Tahoe
★★★ **Roman Feast.** Caesars Tahoe
(Note: in past years, the **Forest Buffet** at Harrah's Lake Tahoe has held a place on this list; that eatery was under reconstruction in 2000.)

A Heavenly Emerald

As a travel writer and journalist, I have been to many spectacular places around the world, but on a stressful day at the keyboard, my mind regularly drifts back to a view of Lake Tahoe from Emerald Bay, with the Heavenly ski area towering over the casinos of Stateline.

Lake Tahoe is, without argument, one of the most breathtaking places on earth, and its natural beauty is complemented—for the most part—by resorts and developments to suit most tastes.

The lake was formed by the rise and fall of faults about 5 million to 10 million years ago, which created a deep valley; then about 2 million years ago, lava flowing from the Mount Pluto volcano on the north shore blocked the north-

> **Over and under.** The U.S. Bureau of Reclamation controls the top 6.1 feet of Lake Tahoe as a reservoir. The water is claimed to be 99.9 percent pure. The lake contains an estimated 39.75 trillion gallons of water, enough to cover the entire state of California to a depth of fourteen inches.

eastern outlet of the basin. Geologists say the initial height of Lake Tahoe was 600 feet higher than its present level.

Today the lake itself covers the Nevada-California border, fifty-nine miles southwest of Reno and 100 miles northeast of Sacramento. Lake Tahoe has a surface area of about 192 square miles, a circumference of seventy-two miles, and contains some nine trillion gallons of water.

At twelve miles wide and twenty-two miles long, it is the largest alpine lake, the third deepest lake in North America, and the tenth deepest in the world, with an average depth of 989 feet and 1,645 feet at its lowest point; at its bottom, the lake is ninety-two feet below the level of Carson City on the other side of the Sierra range in Nevada.

The lake is fed by sixty-three streams, but only one waterway—the Truckee River—flows out; it goes through Reno and on to Pyramid Lake. As such, Lake Tahoe is one of the few major bodies of water in North America that does not eventually empty into the ocean.

The surface of Lake Tahoe is more than a mile above sea level, at 6,227 feet. During times of drought, the surface of the lake can drop below the outlet to the Truckee and become a self-contained lake.

In the summer, the top twelve feet of the lake warms to as much as sixty-eight degrees. In winter months, and in the lower depths of the lake, the temperature remains at a constant—and life-threatening—thirty-nine degrees. However, the lake is not known to have ever frozen over because of the constant turnover of water from the bottom to the surface; Emerald Bay has frozen, though, in especially cold winters, most recently in 1989.

The highest peak rising directly from the shoreline is Mount Tallac at 9,735 feet. The highest point in the basin is Freel Peak at 10,881 feet.

The exact source of the name "Tahoe" is a bit obscure. In any case, the spectacular body of water has held many names during the years. When explorer John C. Frémont, accompanied by famed guide Kit Carson, came to the lake on February 14, 1844, he named it Lake Bonpland, after a French botanist who had been with him on earlier explorations. But mapmaker Charles Preuss wrote it down as Mountain Lake.

Despite all this, it was commonly referred to as Frémont Lake until 1852 when California Governor John Bigler led a party to the area to rescue some snowbound travelers; the lake was renamed as Lake Bigler at the time.

But again, other names were applied to the still-remote area, including Truckee Lake and Maheon Lake. When the Civil War broke out, the politically correct on the Union side sought to strike Bigler's name from the lake because of his supposed Southern sympathies. It was at this time that the word "Tahoe" was proposed, supposedly meaning "high water." There was little historical support for the meaning of the word, but it nevertheless stuck; some suggest the word is actually a corruption of the Spanish word "tajo," pronounced ta-ho and meaning a "cut."

Just to make things difficult, the State of California went ahead and entered into its laws an official designation of the waterway as Lake Bigler, a name that was not officially withdrawn until 1945.

Mileage to South Lake Tahoe

Las Vegas	468
Reno	59
Sacramento	100
San Francisco	198
Virginia City	50

Lake Tahoe Average Temperatures

	Jan	Feb	Mar	Apr	May	Jun	Jul	Aug	Sep	Oct	Nov	Dec
High	36	39	44	50	60	69	79	80	70	51	47	40
Low	16	18	21	26	32	37	43	42	37	31	24	20

Like No Other Nevada Casinos

If you are going to Nevada to gamble, there is not a lot of difference between the major resorts of Stateline, Reno, or Las Vegas. They all have slot machines and blackjack tables and myriad other ways to lose your money. Several of the major resorts offer stage shows and headliner acts—admittedly, the stars are bigger and production shows more lavish in Las Vegas. The best of the restaurants in Stateline, Reno, and Las Vegas are all satisfying.

But what you get in Lake Tahoe that you get nowhere else is the combination of the excitement of the casinos and all they offer, with the tremendous range of outdoor activities available in the Tahoe Basin. Here are just a few: downhill skiing, cross-country skiing, ice skating, sleigh rides, sledding, dogsled rides, snowmobiling, horseback riding, and indoor and heated outdoor pool swimming in the winter; waterskiing, lake and pool swimming, hiking, camping, horseback riding, hot-air-ballooning, boating, and cruises in the summer, spring, and fall.

Caesars Tahoe is the most showily opulent Las Vegas–like casino in town; Harvey's displays the most understated class, and Harrah's is usually the liveliest place in town. The Horizon and Bills' Casino make up the low rent district.

Getting to Lake Tahoe from Reno

Lake Tahoe is an easy drive from Reno, less than an hour to Crystal Bay and about ninety minutes to South Lake Tahoe. *See the section on Driving Trips from Reno for guided tours from Reno to the lake.*

Several bus and shuttle companies offer scheduled and on-demand service from Reno to South Lake Tahoe. **Tahoe Casino Express** has eighteen departures in each direction, charging about $17 per person, $30 round-trip.

Coming from Sacramento, the primary road to South Lake Tahoe is U.S. 50, and to the north end of the lake Interstate 80. Massive snows followed by rainstorms in January of 1997 resulted in closure of U.S. 50 west of Stateline for sev-

> **Econoguide alert.** You'll find most of the major fast-food chains on the California side, along with a large assortment of factory outlets and discount stores. You will also find cheaper ski rental and equipment stores past the entrance to the Heavenly resort toward California.

> **White stuff.** Snowfall at alpine skiing elevations averages 300 to 500 inches per year. At the lake level, the average is about 125 inches. At high elevations, it has been known to snow in any month of the year. On December 28, 1992, snow began to fall at South Lake Tahoe, eventually reaching rates of up to six inches per hour. During the next forty-eight hours, the ski resort received more than nine feet of snow, one of the largest recorded snowfalls ever.

eral weeks in the heart of the season, forcing drivers to take more northern or southern routes.

For information on road conditions in California, call (800) 427-7623 in the state or (916) 445-7623 from other states; for Nevada conditions call (775) 785-2260 or (775) 782-9900.

Air Travel

More than 2 million passengers pass through the Reno Cannon International Airport each year, and in winter months about 25 percent of all travelers are destined for Lake Tahoe.

Several commuter airlines offer service from points in California to the small Lake Tahoe Airport near South Lake Tahoe.

Hotels and Casinos in South Lake Tahoe

The state border runs through Lake Tahoe, dividing it so that about one-third is in Nevada and the remainder in California and demarking the line between two rather different cultures.

The Nevada communities of Crystal Bay, Incline Village, and Stateline each feature small-scale versions of Reno or Las Vegas casino resorts, with all that entails: gambling, glitzy shows, buffets, and fine dining. The largest collection of casinos can be found in Stateline, along both sides of a half-mile stretch of Highway 50. The very last casinos sit just short of the border between California and Nevada.

On the other side of the border, the hotels in California must find different lures. They generally go for high luxury or low price; either way, they do not have casinos to subsidize the room rates.

Tahoe resorts are generally more expensive than their equivalents in Reno and some Las Vegas resorts, partly because of the additional appeal of winter and summer recreation.

High-season in Lake Tahoe is generally from mid-June into September. Low-season is April and May, and November into early December. New Year's and Christmas are busy times. The "shoulder" or middle season is February and March, when ski and winter sports enthusiasts sell out the hotel on weekends.

★★★★ Harvey's Resort Hotel/Casino

It pretty much all started here. Harvey Gross moved to South Lake Tahoe about 1940 to operate a meat company. In 1944, he opened Harvey's Wagon Wheel

Lake Tahoe: Mountain Shangri-La 287

Saloon & Gambling Hall in Stateline on Highway 50. It was a one-room log cabin with a six-stool lunch counter and the only twenty-four-hour gas pump between Placerville, California, and Carson City on the other side of the Sierra Nevadas. Oh, and it also included three slot machines and a pair of blackjack tables.

They made them a deal. Among films made in and around Lake Tahoe are *Indian Love Call*, starring Jeannette McDonald, *The Godfather*, and *The Bodyguard*.

From that humble beginning, Harvey and his wife Llewellyn helped build Stateline into a year-round resort; one early winter they joined with Tahoe residents in shoveling out Echo Summit before the state of California committed heavy equipment to the task.

Harvey's has undergone several stages of expansion, with its two main towers rising in the 1960s and 1980. (In 1980, an extortionist's bomb blew a five-story hole in the hotel tower.)

Today, Harvey's occupies the catbird seat in Stateline with some of the best views of the lake from its towers and restaurants. The attractive lobby is a floor away from the casino, and nicely insulated; it is possible to forget there is a world of blinking lights, bouncing coins, and shuffling cards.

Rest assured, though, there is a full-featured casino at Harvey's, including the Land of the Giants, five seven-foot-tall slot machines against the wall between the California Bar and Sage Room. Harvey's has a Vegas-sized casino, at 88,000 square feet, offering 2,300 slot machines, 121 table games that include blackjack, red dog, fast action hold 'em, poker, pai gow, baccarat, craps, and roulette, plus a race and sports book. The cocktail waitresses glide by in (skimpy) black velvet.

The 740 rooms and suites are among the nicest in Lake Tahoe. The prime Lake Suites include a Jacuzzi, private lakeview balcony, two color TVs, and a marble bath and dressing area. Hotel facilities include a heated outdoor swimming pool, health club, wedding chapel, and four tennis courts. Room rates range from about $95 to $170; suites range from $179 per night. The hotel regularly offers special packages, including breakfast and dinner and a show, priced as low as $69 per night on non-holiday fall and winter weekdays.

Just slightly less adventuresome are arcade challenges such as the four-seat Namco Endurance Championship Race, which permits head-to-head motorcycle racing. Nearby is a Galaxy Force machine, a moving fighter-pilot simulator.

At the rear of the arcade is a shooting gallery with a room full of animated Smurf-like creatures; the targets may be a bit too realistic for the tastes of some parents. More traditional amusements include a wide variety of video games and a skee-ball bowling alley.

Restaurants at Harvey's include the **Seafood Grotto**, a somewhat ordinary room that has windows opened toward the slot machines. Lunch sandwiches and salads range from $7 to $11 and include the Clipper Salad (greens with shrimp, crabmeat, avocado, asparagus, cucumber, tomato, and onion).

Dinner entrees range from about $10 to $25 and include spinach fettuccine *pescatore, cioppino,* a Pacific clambake for two (lobster, prawns, chicken, corn on the cob, and potatoes steamed with wine and herbs), broiled New York steak teriyaki, and bouillabaisse Marseilles.

At **Llewellyn's**, a stunning rooftop restaurant that has wraparound windows, you'll find dishes such as mesquite-broiled quail with creamy polenta and wild rice; salmon *involtini*, stuffed with asparagus, leeks, and carrots wrapped in phyllo dough with sun-dried tomato butter; and lamb Gilroy, in caramelized garlic with couscous and ratatouille.

Llewellyn's is open for lunch Wednesday through Saturday from 11:30 A.M. to 2:30 P.M., and for dinner daily. A champagne brunch is offered Sundays from 10 A.M. to 2 P.M.

El Vaquero is a pleasant den-like setting decorated in Santa Fe reds and blacks; don't back into the cacti in the dark. Specialties include enchiladas Acapulco (flour tortillas filled with your choice of shrimp or crabmeat or both, covered with ranchera sauce and covered with melted cheeses and sour cream) For lunch, offerings include sautéed red snapper topped with a tomatillo sauce and served with black beans. Open for dinner every night, and for lunch from Wednesday to Sunday, El Vaquero also offers karaoke parties in the lounge Friday and Saturday at 10 P.M.

The Carriage House is an attractive twenty-four-hour coffee shop that offers a variety of standard offerings, plus a special breakfast and lunch on-the-run deal for skiers and travelers: you get an egg or pancake breakfast and leave the restaurant with a box lunch of fried chicken or ham and cheese sandwich along with fresh fruit, cookie, and granola bar.

The **Garden Buffet** offers a selection of buffets.

The **Sage Room** steak house, open for dinner from 6 P.M., features entrees including peppercorn steak filet mignon with sauce béarnaise; roast duckling "bigarrade" (Long Island duckling topped with an orange sauce and flambéed with Grand Marnier). Other unusual offerings include honey rabbit sausage lasagne and venison grand *veneur* with melted Brie cheese.

Harvey's **Peak Lounge**, a small room alongside Llewellyn's, offers light fare including chilled prawns or crab, minted split pea soup with lobster, vanilla soufflé, and hot spiced wine.

A pedestrian underpass connects Harvey's to Harrah's across the road.

Harvey's Resort/Hotel Casino. Highway 50, at Stateline; (775) 588-2411, (800) 427-8397. www.harveys-tahoe.com.

Bill's Lake Tahoe Casino

This is a high-fun, low-roller joint, the self-proclaimed "Quarter Capital of Nevada." Bill's, which is part of the same company that owns the next-door Harrah's Casino, has gone out of its way to encourage its young staff of dealers and attendants to be friendly to its crowd of skiers, summer vacationers, and party-goers. The serious gamblers are elsewhere.

They even encourage the taking of photographs on the casino floor.

Bill's Lake Tahoe Casino. Highway 50, Stateline; (775) 588-2455.

★★★★ Harrah's Casino Hotel Lake Tahoe

Harrah's is one of the class acts of South Lake Tahoe. The eighteen-story, 534-room hotel begins with some of the most beautiful views of the mountains and the lake and also includes a domed swimming pool and an indoor family fun center. By Nevada standards, Harrah's is one of the more understated and elegant hotels in town.

The lobby is decorated like an alpine lodge, with slate tile floors and Persian rugs, wood and brass, a natural stone fireplace, and a waterfall. A small **Warner Brothers Studio Store** is just off the registration lobby.

A large L-shaped casino, it is relatively muted compared to some of the other casinos in town. Harrah's draws a lively mix of skiers, lake visitors, and gamblers. It offers a set of nice restaurants tucked away from the casino floor.

Guests staying at the nicely appointed rooms have access to a dome-covered swimming pool and spa and health clubs.

Room rates at Harrah's start at about $109 per night in the off-season; the hotel runs a number of special promotions throughout the year, including midweek and weekend packages. Also available are ski packages in conjunction with Heavenly, Kirkwood, Sierra-at-Tahoe, or Northstar ski resorts, and golfing packages with the Dayton Valley Golf Course.

Value season runs from January 1 to mid-June and from mid-September through mid-December, with room rates starting at about $119 (higher on weekends). The summer season occupies the middle of the year, with rooms starting at about $179 in midweek.

Harrah's **Family Fun Center**, located on the lower level of the hotel, is a smoke- and alcohol-free indoor playground that includes two levels of slides, ball pools, climbing areas, and games of skill, including video games, skee-ball, and air hockey. The play area is open to midnight or later.

The **PlayPal** indoor playground for young children includes a two-story plastic obstacle course with tunnels, ball bins, ladders, slides, and moonwalks.

Nearby is the **Zone Hunter** virtual reality game, in which contestants wear a headset with video and audio simulation of a futuristic hunting adventure. Players can enter the zone alone, or compete against a second contestant. Each round costs $3.

The exquisite **Summit Room** is on the sixteenth and seventeenth floors, not quite the summit of the High Sierras, but still a highly recommended gourmet experience for dinner; reservations are necessary. The two-story win-

> **Payment due.**
> Some casinos will advertise their "overdue" jackpots on progressive machines, giving the implication that your chances of winning are higher if you play on one of them. Actually—assuming as you must that the machines are honest—the chances of winning on an overdue machine are the same if it has been ten years since it has paid off or if the machine just paid off five minutes ago.
>
> Think of it this way: if you flip an honest quarter forty-nine times and it somehow comes up heads every time, the odds of it coming up tails on the fiftieth toss are still 50-50.

dows offer spectacular views. The restaurant is located in the former site of the Star Suite, one of Harrah's private luxury suites for high rollers.

Among entrees at the Summit on one of my visits were grilled ono with soba noodles and tamarind-ginger glaze, individual prime Wellington with truffle-Madeira sauce, and sautéed veal loin with Apple Hill–Calvados confit. Desserts include a sinful Grand Marnier soufflé, individual baked Alaskas, and a chocolate "piano" with white chocolate mousse. The chef's selection dinner is about $60 per person without wine, and $90 with wine.

Another fine restaurant is **Friday's Station Steak & Seafood Grill** on the eighteenth floor. Named after a famous stop on the Pony Express near Stateline, Nevada, it offers views of Lake Tahoe and the Sierras matched only by the food.

A favorite appetizer at Friday's Station is blackened shrimp; we're also partial to the roasted elephant garlic, or the grilled artichoke. Entrees range from about $8.50 to $50. On one visit entrees included aged steaks and chops with choice of sauces, including Jack Daniel's whiskey, teriyaki, béarnaise, salsa fresca, and green peppercorn with grappa. Salmon dishes are offered poached in chardonnay, pistachio-crusted with lemon-wine butter, or blackened with fried ginger. Prime rib is offered in big, bigger, and gigantic servings. And you can also order a steakhouse combination with chicken, salmon, shrimp, and other dishes. If you have room for dessert, consider Roasted Banana Decadence or white chocolate cheesecake with dark chocolate chunks.

A budget-priced showplace is the **American River Café** on the lower level. The very attractive eatery is set amongst redwood trees and a babbling brook. Specialties include maple-glazed barbecued baby back ribs, Hangtown fried oyster omelet, and 49'er tailgater chili. You'd hardly know about the mayhem going on next door in the Family Fun Center or upstairs on the casino floor.

Harrah's, Lake Tahoe

Lake Tahoe: Mountain Shangri-La 291

The **North Beach Deli** offers San Francisco decor and specialties, including pasta, submarine sandwiches, espresso, and desserts twenty-four hours a day. Entrees start at about $7; sandwiches are about $6. One of the specialties is San Francisco Bay dilled bay shrimp with lettuce and tomato on sourdough baguette. Skiers and travelers can order sandwiches to go.

The **Forest Restaurant**, home to the casino's buffet, was closed for remodeling in early 2000.

The 800-seat **South Shore Room** has been the home of regular headline entertainment, including Hollywood and Broadway-theme productions. In the summer season, the stage is held by big-name performers.

Harrah's Casino Hotel Lake Tahoe. Highway 50, Stateline; (775) 588-6611, (800) 648-3773. www.harrahstahoe.com.

★★★★ Caesars Tahoe

Smaller than the Las Vegas landmark and considerably less opulent, Caesars Tahoe nevertheless carries through with its Roman theme pretty well. Among the touches of Vegas transported to the lake is the legion of cocktail waitresses in off-the-shoulder togas.

Many of the 440 suites and rooms offer circular bathtubs for those who like to bathe in the round. Other facilities include an indoor pool, health spa, racquetball, and tennis courts. Room rates range from about $89 to $225; suites go from about $300 to $650 per night.

The casino is attractive but a bit cramped. Top headliners perform in the 1,600-seat Circus Maximus Showroom. There is live music and dancing at Nero's 2000 Nightclub.

In an attempt to attract "Generation X" to the casinos, the **Planet Hollywood** restaurant is open every day from 11 A.M. to 2 A.M. The restaurant's grand opening included some of the restaurant chain's celebrity owners such as Bruce Willis and Arnold Schwarzenegger.

The exterior of the restaurant is adorned with a huge set of Hollywood-style sunglasses. Memorabilia on display at the restaurant include Mel Gibson's motorcycle from *Lethal Weapon III*, Arnie's cyborg from *Terminator II*, the gambling dice from *Indecent Proposal*, Don Johnson's pants from *Miami Vice*, and Freddy's shirt, as worn by *Nightmare on Elm Street* actor Robert Englund.

The toniest Chinese restaurant in town is the **Empress Court**, a small, dimly lit elegant room decorated in Oriental blues and reds with gold accents. Specialties include sautéed scallops and shrimp in black bean sauce, crispy sesame chicken with lemon sauce, ginger beef with pineapple, crystal prawns with glazed walnuts, and slowly roasted imperial Peking duck.

The **Broiler Room** is an unusual cubbyhole with dark brick walls and dim candelabras and sconces. Menu items include New York steak, veal piccata, and T-bone steak. Seafood specialties include Spanish gambas (jumbo prawns marinated in olive oil and herbs, broiled, and served with garlic croutons and sauce Catalan).

Also on the menu is a selection of spicy creole foods made from recipes that come from the famed K-Paul's Louisiana Kitchen in New Orleans. Offerings

> **He'll be back.**
> According to publicists for Caesars Tahoe, Arnold Schwarzenegger hit a $500 jackpot at a $1 slot machine while posing for photographers at the grand opening of Planet Hollywood. They claim it was strictly a matter of luck.

include Louisiana seafood gumbo, K-Paul's favorite blackened prawns, and jambalaya with plump shrimp and spicy Andouille sausage.

More simple repasts are available at the **Café Roma** or, believe it or not, at the only **Subway** sandwich outlet I've ever seen set amidst Roman columns and statues of fallen emperors.

Caesars Tahoe. Highway 50, Stateline; (775) 588-3515, (800) 648-3353.

Horizon Casino Resort

A very lively and busy casino with a big collection of nickel slots; we'd recommend dark glasses. The mirrored ceiling makes you feel like you're inside a huge powder room turned sideways.

Back in the '60s, when the place was the Sahara Tahoe, the King played and stayed here. The Presley Suite is available for rent for special functions.

There are 520 rooms and suites, many with lakeview balconies. Facilities include a large outdoor pool and hot tubs. Winter room rates start at about $69 during the week and about $89 on weekends and reach to about $149.

Entertainment, featuring headline acts, is presented in the 1,200-seat **Grande Lake Theatre**. Shows and revues are offered in the 200-seat **Golden Cabaret**, and there is live music nightly in the **Aspen Lounge**.

Josh's restaurant, a rather ordinary setting, offers lobster and steak specials, prime rib, and other Nevada steakhouse fare. An enticing addition is the **Tahoe Mountain Brewery**, a trendy microbrewery pub.

Horizon Casino Resort. Highway 50, Stateline; (775) 588-6211, (800) 648-3322.

Lakeside Inn & Casino

A small casino and hotel a bit off the main drag at the base of Kingsbury Grade, with 124 motel units. Room rates range from about $69 to $129.

Lakeside Inn & Casino. 168 U.S. 50, Stateline; (775) 588-7777.

★★★ Embassy Suites Resort

An all-suites hotel with 400 rooms, just across the state line into California, the Embassy Suites Resorts shares some of its facilities with its corporate and physical neighbor, Harrah's.

The resort offers an indoor pool, whirlpool spa, and workout room.

Entertainment is presented at the **Turtles Sports Bar & Dance Emporium**, where you can also get a bite to eat. Other restaurants include **Zackary's**, **Pasquale's**, and **Julie's Deli**.

And guess what? No casino. That is, unless you want to walk a few feet into Nevada.

Room rates run from about $100 to $200 across the seasons; lower-priced packages are offered at slow times.

Embassy Suites Resort. Highway 50, South Lake Tahoe, CA; (916) 544-5400, (800) 362-2779. www.embassy-suites.com

★★★ Ridge Tahoe Resort
Tucked away on the Kingsbury Grade and just above the Stagecoach Lodge of Heavenly ski resort, the Ridge offers guests their own private ten-passenger gondolas to take them to the lodge for a day of skiing. Other amenities include an indoor/outdoor pool, tennis and racquetball courts, and a health club.
   The Ridge Tahoe Resort. Stateline; (775) 588-3553, (800) 334-1600.

South Lake Tahoe Casino Buffets
Caesars Tahoe. ★★★ Roman Feast. (775) 588-3515. Brunch 7 A.M. to 3 P.M., $7.99 weekdays, $9.99 Saturday and Sunday. Dinner Sunday to Thursday 3 to 9 P.M., $11.99. Friday seafood buffet 3 to 10 P.M., $17.99. Saturday steak buffet 3 to 10 P.M., $17.99.
   Harrah's. Forest Buffet was under renovation in mid-2000. (775) 588-6611.
   Harvey's. ★★★ Garden Buffet. (775) 588-2411. Breakfast weekdays 7 to 11 A.M., $5.95; Saturday brunch 9 A.M. to 2:30 P.M., $9.75. Sunday seafood brunch 7 A.M. to 2:30 P.M., $12.50. Dinner Monday through Thursday 5 to 9 P.M., $10.95. Sunday dinner 5 to 9 P.M., $12.95. Friday and Saturday seafood buffet, $19.95.
   Horizon. LeGrande Buffet. (775) 588-6211. Dinner Sunday to Thursday 5:30 to 9:30 P.M., $10.95. Dinner Friday and Saturday 5 to 10 P.M., $12.95. Sunday brunch 9 A.M. to 2 P.M., $9.95.

Restaurants in South Lake Tahoe and Stateline
As befits a year-round vacation playground, the south end of Lake Tahoe is well supplied with a wide variety of restaurants. Following are some of the more interesting eateries outside of the casinos.
   The Beacon. 1900 Jamison Beach Road, Camp Richardson; (530) 541-0630. Lunch and dinner. Burgers and sandwiches for lunch on the beach. Dinner entrees include rosemary chicken, bourbon New York steak, and macadamia nut prawns priced from about $15 to $25.
   The Brewery. 3542 Highway 50; (530) 544-2739. Lunch and dinner. A microbrewery and pub. Brews include local specialties Needle Peak Ale, Alpine Amber, and Bad Ass Ale; munchies include beer-steamed shrimp.
   Cafe Fiore. 1169 Ski Run Boulevard; (530) 541-2908. Breakfast, lunch, and dinner.
   Cantina Los Tres Hombres. 765 Emerald Bay Road; (530) 544-1233. Lunch and dinner. An ambitious menu of Mexican and Southwestern specialties from steak, chicken, and shrimp *fajitas* to *chile colorado* in mild red chile sauce and *chile verde* in green chiles. Entrees range from about $8 to $16. The bar serves at least seven unusual Margarita concoctions.
   The Dory's Oar. ★★★ 1041 Fremont Avenue; (530) 541-6603. A little bit of Cape Cod on the lake, featuring Maine lobster, Chesapeake Bay crabs, and fish from both coasts.
   The Eagles' Nest. 472 Needle Peak Road; (775) 588-3245. Lunch and dinner. Restaurant and jazz club with live performances most weekends. A lively

eatery with entrees in the range of about $13 to $22, with entrees including steak, lamb chops, and venison.

Emerald Palace. 871 Emerald Bay Road; (530) 544-2421. Lunch and dinner. An ambitious Chinese menu, from unusual soups such as Spinach Bean Cake, Chicken Corn, and Shrimp Sizzling Rice, to a full range of standard and exotic beef, seafood, chicken, pork, and vegetable dishes, priced from about $5 to $10.

Fresh Ketch. 2433 Venice, Tahoe Keys Marina; (530) 541-5683. Lunch and dinner. Oysters to smoked salmon, sashimi to burgers, chowder to filet mignon. Entrees priced from about $7 to $23.

Grand Central Pizza. 2229 Highway 50; (530) 544-1308. Lunch and dinner. Basic to fancy pizza, from spaghetti to lasagna.

The Greenhouse. ★★★ 4140 Cedar Avenue; (530) 541-5800. Dinner. Salads, escargots, veal piccata, chicken cordon bleu, tournedos of lamb, and roast duckling a l'orange, with entrees priced from about $12 to $35.

Nepheles. ★★★ 1169 Ski Run Boulevard; (530) 544-8130. Lunch and dinner. "Creative California Cuisine." Appetizers include seafood cheesecake, and swordfish egg rolls. Entrees, priced from about $10 to $25, include baked fresh ahi in Asian peanut sauce, wild boar in prunes and cabbage and topped with orange apricot brandy sauce, and chicken teriyaki.

Rojo's. Highway 50 and San Francisco Avenue; (530) 541-4960. In an atmosphere described as "rustic old Tahoe." Lunch and dinner. Steaks, burgers, ribs, and Italian offerings, priced from about $10 to $15.

Samurai. 2588 Highway 50; (530) 542-0300. Dinner. Sushi, teriyaki, tempura, and *nabemono* grilled beef or seafood, priced from about $11 to $25.

Sato. 3436 Highway 50; (530) 541-3769. Dinner. Japanese fare from a full range of sushi dishes to tempura and teriyaki entrees, priced from about $8 to $14. Sato's Love Boat is a special sampler dinner that includes California roll, sushi, tempura, teriyaki, and soup, priced at about $18 per person.

Scusa! ★★★★ 1142 Ski Run Boulevard; (530) 542-0100. Dinner. From unusual pizzas such as a pie with smoked chicken, Andouille sausage, cilantro, and mozzarella to stuffed eggplant, seared sea scallops Mediterranean, and chicken piccata, priced from about $10 to $20.

Tep's Villa Roma. ★★ 3450 Highway 50; (530) 541-8227. Dinner. Serious Italian fare, including all of the usual suspects such as all sorts of pasta dishes, a full range of shrimp, veal, steak, and chicken offerings, and more. Entrees, priced from about $9 to $17, include a salad bar.

Water Wheel South. Crescent V Shopping Center; (775) 588-0555. Dinner. Chinese fare, from about $5 to $13. Chef's specialties include beggar's chicken and Peking duck at about $24.

Hotels and Casinos in North Lake Tahoe
★★ Cal-Neva Lodge, Crystal Bay

Famous for its swimming pool, which sits atop the state border. Swimmers can start in California and end up in Nevada where there is, of course, a casino.

There are 200 rooms, including lake-view rooms and suites, chalets with fire-

Lake Tahoe: Mountain Shangri-La

places, and celebrity cabins that include rooms where Marilyn Monroe or Frank Sinatra slept. In the winter, standard rooms start at $109; the same room in the summer goes for $139. A VIP chalet in the winter starts at $199, rising to as much as $279 in prime summer weeks.

Early guests included mobster Pretty Boy Floyd. During Prohibition, the Cal-Neva was one of the most famous speakeasies in the country. Later on, the hotel was owned by singer Frank Sinatra and was one of the gathering places for the "Rat Pack" Hollywood crowd during the 1960s.

The hotel's main room is the impressive Indian Room, with vaulted ceiling and huge beams and a rock fireplace split by the state line. The room includes a display on the Washoe tribe, as well as antique hunting trophies from the lake region. As befits a casino, the room is open twenty-four hours a day.

Cal-Neva Lodge. Crystal Bay; (775) 832-4000, (800) 225-6382. www.calnevaresort.com.

★★★★ Hyatt Regency Lake Tahoe Resort & Casino, Incline Village

A 458-room, four-star resort with mountain- and lake-view rooms and suites, as well as twenty-four lakeside cottages on the hotel's private beach. Other amenities include a health club, outdoor heated pool and jet spa. Camp Hyatt is for kids ages 3 to 12.

Restaurants include the **Lone Eagle Grill** and the **Sierra Cafe** with breakfast, lunch, and dinner buffets as well as coffee shop service.

Room rates start at about $180, with lakeside cottages going for about $1,200; winter specials drop well below those levels.

Hyatt Regency Lake Tahoe Resort & Casino. Country Club Drive and Lakeshore Drive, Incline Village; (775) 832-1234, (800) 553-3288.

Tahoe Biltmore Lodge & Casino, Incline Village

A big old-style hotel, with a group of small wooden motel units along the lake. Room rates range from about $49 to $149. 5 Highway 28, Incline Village; (775) 831-0660, (800) 245-8667. www.tahoebiltmore.com.

★★★★ Resort at Squaw Creek, Squaw Valley

A spectacular resort set in and among the trails at Squaw Creek with ski-in/out access, cross-country trails, golf course, three swimming pools, four spas, tennis center, horseback riding, and more. There are 405 rooms, including 204 suites. Rates range from about $300 to $1,900.

Restaurants at the resort include **Glissandi** for elegant French cuisine; **Cascades**, an all-day eatery with buffet and a la carte offerings; **Ristorante Montagna**, with Italian pasta and other specialties; the **Bullwhackers** pub and steak house; the **Sun Plaza Deck** barbecue wagon for lunch; and the **Sweet Potatoes Deli.**

Resort at Squaw Creek. Olympic Valley, CA; (530) 583-6300, (800) 327-3353. www.squawcreek.com.

North Lake Tahoe Restaurants

Bacchi's Inn. Italian and seafood specialties priced from about $11 to $40, including fettuccine a la Romana, spaghetti Caruso with chicken livers and mushrooms, veal piccante tenderloin, Italian barbecue spare ribs, and beef a la Stroganoff. Dinners include hors d'oeuvres, minestrone soup, salad, and pasta. Lake Forest, northeast of Tahoe City; (530) 583-3324.

Boulevard Cafe & Trattoria. ★★ Classic northern Italian fare, including *osso bucco di vitello con Gremolada* (braised veal shanks with vegetables, garlic and herbs), *anatra al Forno all Ciliege* (roast duck with balsamic vinegar and sun-dried cherry glaze), and *conchiglie con spinaci e salsicce* (pasta shells stuffed with spinach, sausage, and ricotta cheese). Prices range from about $14 to $26. 6731 North Lake Boulevard, Tahoe Vista; (530) 546-7213.

Captain Jon's Seafood. ★★ Entrees include oysters Florentine (baked Malpeque oysters on a bed of spinach topped with Brie cheese), filet mignon Roquefort broiled and served in a cognac, demiglace, and Roquefort sauce, and angel hair pasta in white cream sauce with scallops and prawns. Open for lunch and dinner in summer, and dinner only in winter; prices range from about $18 to $23. 7220 North Lake Boulevard, Tahoe Vista; (530) 546-4819.

Jason's Saloon & Grille. An interesting mix of seafood, chicken, steak, and burgers, including Bayou shrimp, Louisiana chicken, baby back ribs, and a Russian burger (with horseradish cream sauce and bacon). Entrees range from about $12 to $18. 8338 North Lake Boulevard, Kings Beach; (530) 546-3315.

Lakehouse Pizza. Not just pizza, they say: Polish pirushki stuffed with peppers, mushrooms, olives, tomatoes, onions, and sauce; Italian calzone; American Salad . . . and pizza. 120 Grove Street, Tahoe City; (530) 583-2222.

Las Panchitas. A full range of Mexican specialties that include tacos, enchiladas, burritos, chili, and tostadas. Dinners, priced from about $9 to $15, include steak Ranchero, and *achiote* halibut served on black beans. North Lake Boulevard, Kings Beach; (530) 546-4539.

Le Petit Pier. Tahoe's most popular French restaurant with charming decor and terrific food. Entrees include lavender honey-glazed duck, Chilean sea bass, and Pheasant Souvaroff, with prices from about $22 to $30. 7252 North Lake Boulevard, Tahoe Vista. (530) 546-4464.

Mofo's Pizza. New York–style pizza from basic to unusual, such as clam and garlic, spinach, and vegetarian. Also offered are sandwiches, calzones, lasagna, and a salad bar. Christmas Tree Village, Incline Village; (775) 831-4999.

Old European Restaurant. From sauerbraten to *kassler rippchen* (smoked pork loin) to Vienna *schnitzel* garnie, priced from about $14 to $20. Specialties include chateaubriand for two for $45. Highway 89 north of Tahoe City; (530) 583-3102.

Soule Domain Restaurant. ★★★ Gourmet dining in a log cabin, across from the Tahoe Biltmore Casino. Appetizers include garlic raviolis, wild shiitake mushrooms, and soft-shell crabs. Entrees, priced from about $16 to $23, include sea scallops poached in champagne with kiwi and papaya cream sauce, fresh pasta with lobster, prawns, and scallops in lemon garlic butter, and curried cashew chicken with snow peas and teriyaki sauce. Stateline Road, Crystal Bay; (530) 546-7529.

Yama Sushi & Robata Grill. A wide range of the real thing: from more than two dozen types of sushi to *gyoza* dumplings to *robatayaki* skewers of asparagus, eggplant, quail eggs, beef tongue, salmon, and a dozen more. Entrees, priced from about $10 to $25, include tempura, sashimi, and *udon* soups. 950 North Lake Boulevard, Tahoe City; (530) 583-9262.

Lake Tahoe Region Hotels and Accommodations

Listed here are rates for basic double rooms. Note that rates are subject to change and are likely to be higher during holiday periods and major events, and lower in slow periods.

$	$49 or less	$$	$50 to $99
$$$	$100 to $149	$$$$	$150 and more
♣	Casino/Hotel		

Northern Lake Tahoe Casino-Hotels and Motels

Cal Neva Resort. ♣ 2 Stateline Road, Crystal Bay. (775) 832-4000, (800) 225-6382. $$-$$$$ www.calnevaresort.com.

Club Tahoe Resort. 914 Northwood Boulevard, Incline Village. (775) 831-5750, (800) 731-6222. $$$-$$$$

Crystal Bay Motel. 24 Highway 28, Crystal Bay. (775) 831-0287. $-$$

Haus Bavaria B&B. 593 North Dyer Circle, Incline Village. (775) 831-6122, (800) 553-3288. $$-$$$ www.hausbavaria.com.

Hyatt Regency Lake Tahoe Resort & Casino. ♣ 111 Country Club Drive at Lakeshore Boulevard, Incline Village. (775) 832-1234, (800) 233-1234. $$-$$$$ www.hyattahoe.com.

Inn at Incline & Condos. 1003 Tahoe Boulevard, Incline Village. (775) 831-1052, (800) 824-6391. $$-$$$

Lakeside Tennis & Ski Resort. 955 Tahoe Boulevard, Incline Village. (775) 831-5300 (800) 821-4912. $$-$$$

Tahoe Biltmore Lodge & Casino. ♣ Highway 28, Crystal Bay. (775) 831-0660, (800) 245-8667. $-$$ www.tahoebiltmore.com.

Vacation Station. 110 Country Club Drive, Incline Village. (775) 831-3664, (800) 841-7443. $$-$$$$ www.vacationstation.net.

North Lake Tahoe Condominium Brokers

A Bella Properties. Incline Village. (775) 831-5335. $$$-$$$$

Ann Nichols & Company. Crystal Bay. (775) 831-0625. $$$-$$$$

B.R.A.T. Realty Management. Incline Village. (775) 831-3318, (800) 869-8308. $$-$$$$

Coldwell Banker/Incline Village Realty. Incline Village. (775) 831-4800, (800) 572-5009. $$-$$$$ www.2ctahoe.com/incline

ERA Tahoe North Realty. Incline Village. (775) 831-1169. $$-$$$$

> **North Lake Tahoe Resort Association.** Box 5578, Tahoe City, CA 95730; (530) 583-3494, (800) 824-6348. www.tahoefun.org.

Forrest Pines Rental Agency. Incline Village. (775) 831-1307, (800) 458-2463. $$–$$$$
Incline Tahoe Realty. Incline Village. (775) 831-9000, (800) 843-9399. $$–$$$$
Incline Village Sales Company. Incline Village. (775) 831-3349, (800) 831-3304. $$–$$$$
Omni Properties. Incline Village. (775) 832-3003, (800) 338-4884. $$$–$$$$ www.inclinevillage.com.
Tanager Realty. Incline Village. (775) 831-0752, (800) 333-7454. $$$–$$$$
Vacation Tahoe. Incline Village. (775) 831-6700, (800) 822-8282. $$–$$$$
Wheeler Associates. Incline Village. (775) 831-8333, (800) 654-2755. $$–$$$$

South Lake Tahoe Hotels and Motels

Caesar's Tahoe. ♣ Stateline. (775) 588-3515, (800) 648-3353. $$$–$$$$
Harrah's Lake Tahoe Hotel Casino. ♣ Stateline. (775) 588-6611, (800) 427-7247. $$$–$$$$ www.harrahstahoe.com.
Harvey's Resort Hotel & Casino. ♣ Stateline. (775) 588-2411, (800) 553-1022. $$–$$$$ www.harveys-tahoe.com.
Horizon Casino Resort. ♣ Stateline. (775) 588-6211, (800) 648-3322. $$–$$$
Lakeside Inn & Casino. ♣ Kingsbury Grade, Stateline. (775) 588-7777, (800) 624-7980. $$–$$$
The Ridge Sierra. 265 Quaking Aspen, Stateline. (775) 588-5565, (800) 821-4912. $$$–$$$$

> **Incline Village/Crystal Bay Visitor and Convention Bureau.** 969 Tahoe Boulevard, Incline Village, NV 89451; (775) 832-1606 or (800) 468-2463. www.gotahoe.com.
>
> **North Lake Tahoe Chamber of Commerce.** 950 North Lake Boulevard Suite 3, Tahoe City, CA 96145. (530) 581-6900, (800) 824-6348. www.tahoe-4-u.com.
>
> **Lake Tahoe Visitors Authority.** 1156 Ski Run Boulevard, South Lake Tahoe, CA 96151; (530) 544-5050 or (800) 288-2463.

The Ridge Tahoe. 400 Ridge Club Drive, Stateline. (775) 588-3553, (800) 334-1600. $$$–$$$$
Zephyr Cove Resort. 760 Highway 50, Zephyr Cove. (775) 588-6644. $–$$$$

South Lake Tahoe Condominium Brokers

Lake Tahoe Accommodations. Stateline. (800) 544-3234. $$–$$$$
Lake Village Vacation Condos. Zephyr Cove. (775) 588-2481, (800) 242-5387. $$$–$$$$ www.tahoe-estates.com.
PineWild Condominiums. Zephyr Cove. (775) 588-2790, (800) 822-2790. $$$$
Resort Properties. Stateline. (775) 588-3300. $$–$$$$
Selective Accommodations. Stateline. (775) 588-8258, (800) 242-5387. $$–$$$$
Tahoe Management Company. South Lake Tahoe. (775) 588-4504, (888) 624-3887. $$

Cabins and Campgrounds
Carney's Cabins. (530) 542-3361.
>   Carson Valley Inn RV Park. (775) 782-9711.
>   Echo Creek Ranch. (530) 544-5397, (800) 462-5397.
>   Inn at Heavenly Reservation Bureau. (916) 544-4244, (800) 692-2246.
>   KOA Campground. (530) 577-3693.
>   Lakeside RV Park. (775) 588-4220.
>   Michelsen Vacation Rentals. (775) 588-4811, (800) 568-2463.
>   Pine Cone Resort. (775) 588-6561.
>   Richardson's Resort. (530) 541-1801, (800) 544-1801.
>   Sorensen's Resort. (530) 694-2203, (800) 423-9949.
>   Tahoe Keys Resort. (530) 544-5397, (800) 698-2463.
>   Walley's Hot Springs Resort. (800) 628-7831.
>   Zephyr Cove Lodge and Campground. (775) 588-6644.

Cruises Around the Lake

MS *Dixie II*. A new version of a Lake Tahoe classic, making 1½- to 3½-hour cruises to Emerald Bay (about $20 for adults and $5 for children) and summer sunset dinner and dance cruises (about $45, including dinner). The ship is based at the Zephyr Cove Marina, four miles north of Stateline on Route 50. The glass-bottom sternwheeler can accommodate 350 passengers. There's also a summer champagne brunch, at $25 for adults and $9 for children.

Passengers on the *Dixie* can also watch *The Sunken Treasures of Lake Tahoe*, a video presented on each cruise; cameras show underwater canyons, ancient petrified forests hidden by the lake, the sheer vertical cliffs of Rubicon Bay and the scuttled Steamer Tahoe, 500 feet below the surface of Glenbrook Bay.

The boat runs year-round, weather permitting. Free shuttle service is offered from South Lake Tahoe, Carson City, Reno, or the north shore of the lake. Call (775) 588-3508 or (775) 882-0786. www.tahoedixie.com. *You will find a discount in the coupon section of this book.*

Tahoe Queen. Daily cruises vary from one during the winter to several for the remainder of the year. The 500-passenger glass-bottom paddlewheeler travels to Emerald Bay. $18 for adults, $8 for children. There's also a dinner cruise in season, at $46.75 for adults and $29.75 for children. Call (530) 541-3364 or (800) 238-2463 for information. www.hornblower.com.

Woodwind. A large trimaran sailing vessel, it makes day cruises (for about $20 for adults and $10 for children) and sunset champagne cruises (about $22 for adults) from May to October. Call (775) 588-3000 for information. www.sailwoodwind.com.

Getting Around in Lake Tahoe
Airports
Tahoe Valley Airport. South Lake Tahoe, CA; (530) 543-1259.
>   Truckee-Tahoe Airport. Truckee, CA; (530) 587-4119. Private aviation.
>   Carson Airport. Carson City, NV; (775) 884-1163. Private aviation.
>   Douglas County Airport. Minden, NV; (775) 782-8277. Charter service.

Car Rental

Avis Rent a Car. Caesars Tahoe, Stateline; (775) 588-4450. South Lake Tahoe; (530) 542-5710. Nationwide; (800) 331-1212.
    Enterprise Rent-a-Car. Horizon Casino Resort, Stateline; (775) 586-1077.
    Hertz Rent a Car. 1875 Lake Tahoe Boulevard (530) 542-4804. Nationwide; (800) 654-3131.
    Tahoe Rent-a-Car. Tahoe Valley Motel, South Lake Tahoe; (530) 544-4500.

Road and Weather Information

California Highway Conditions. (916) 445-7623, (800) 427-7623.
    California Highway Patrol. (916) 657-7261.
    Nevada Highway Patrol. (775) 793-1313.

Bus Service

Five Star Enterprises Limo Service. Airport to Reno and North Lake Tahoe; (530) 587-7651, (800) 782-4707.
    Greyhound Lines West. South Lake Tahoe; (530) 544-2351. Truckee; (916) 587-3822.
    STAGE (South Lake Tahoe Area Ground Express). South Lake Tahoe area; (530) 573-2080.

Ski Area Shuttle Buses

The following ski areas provide shuttle services; call for schedules and pickup locations:
    Alpine Meadows. (530) 583-4232.
    Diamond Peak. (775) 832-1177.
    Northstar. (530) 562-2248.
    Squaw Valley. (530) 583-6985, ext. 7182.
    Sugar Bowl. (530) 426-3651.
    Mount Rose. (775) 849-0704.

Lake Tahoe Health

Altitude Sickness. Feeling a bit faint, tired, nauseated, headachy, or short of breath? Having trouble sleeping, or does the fabulous spread of a casino buffet hold no particular appeal? You may be suffering from altitude sickness. Lake Tahoe sits at about 6,235 feet above sea level; if you have come from an east or west coast city, you are living more than a mile higher than ordinary.
    The cure is to avoid overexertion, get plenty of rest, and drink plenty of fluids. You also should eat lightly and cut down on alcohol consumption. The ultimate cure is time: your body should adjust within two or three days.
    If your symptoms are especially severe, or if they don't seem to pass, you should see a doctor. Persons with heart conditions or high blood pressure should check with their doctor at home before heading for the mountains.
    Frostbite. It gets very cold up in the hills. Wear warm, layered, dry clothing, including hats and gloves; avoid alcohol and take indoor breaks.

Frostbite occurs when the water in your body cells literally freezes. Superficial frostbite usually involves the fingertips, ears, nose, toes, and cheeks; symptoms include a burning sensation, tingling, or numbness and a whitish discoloration of the skin. Deep frostbite is a more serious condition and can result in the death of the cells and open wounds susceptible to infection.

If you develop frostbite, find warm shelter immediately. *Do not* rub frostbitten skin; instead, immerse the affected parts of the body in *lukewarm* (not hot) water. If the skin does not return to its normal color, or if blistering, swelling, pain, or numbness develops, seek medical attention.

Hypothermia. This serious condition results when the body's core (internal) temperature drops below the normal range of about 98.6 degrees. Left untreated, hypothermia can lead to organ malfunction, damage, and eventual death. Symptoms include fatigue, mood changes, and impaired motor skills.

Sunburn. Ultraviolet rays in the mountains are about five times as strong as at sea level. Use a sunscreen with a rating of at least 20, including PABA; lip balms with PABA or zinc oxide are also suggested. Wear UV-blocking sunglasses.

If you receive a sunburn, apply cool compresses and if your doctor approves, take aspirin for pain and Benadryl to relieve itching. Blisters are a sign of a second-degree burn. Do not pop blisters, and stay out of the sun to avoid further damage. You should see a doctor for any facial blisters or blisters with cloudy liquid, or for severe pain.

Indian Reservations and Councils

Western Nevada is home to many Native American councils; many operate businesses and cultural exhibits.

Battle Mountain Band Council. 35 Mountainview Drive, #138–13, Battle Mountain, NV 89820. (775) 635-2004.

Carson Indian Community Council. 2900 South Curry Street Carson City, NV 89701 (775) 833-6459.

Duck Valley Shoshone-Paiute Tribes. P.O. Box 219, Owyhee, NV 89832. (775) 757-3211.

Duckwater Shoshone Tribe. P.O. Box 140068, Duckwater, NV 89314. (775) 863-0227.

Elko Band Council. 511 Sunset Street, Elko, NV 89801. (775) 738-8889.

Ely Shoshone Tribe. 16 Shoshone Circle, Ely, NV 89301. (775) 289-3013.

Fallon Paiute Shoshone Tribe. 8955 Mission Road, P.O. Box 1650, Fallon, NV 89406. (775) 423-6075.

Fort McDermitt Indian Reservation. P.O. Box 457, McDermitt, NV 89421. (775) 532-8259.

Moapa Tribal Store. P.O. Box 340, Moapa, NV 89025. (775) 865-2787.

Pyramid Lake Paiute Tribe. P.O. Box 256, Nixon, NV 89424. (775) 574-1000.

Reno-Sparks Indian Colony. 98 Colony Road, Reno, NV 89502. (775) 329-2936.

Stewart Indian Museum. 5366 Snyder Avenue, Carson City, NV 89701. (775) 882-1808.

LAKE TAHOE

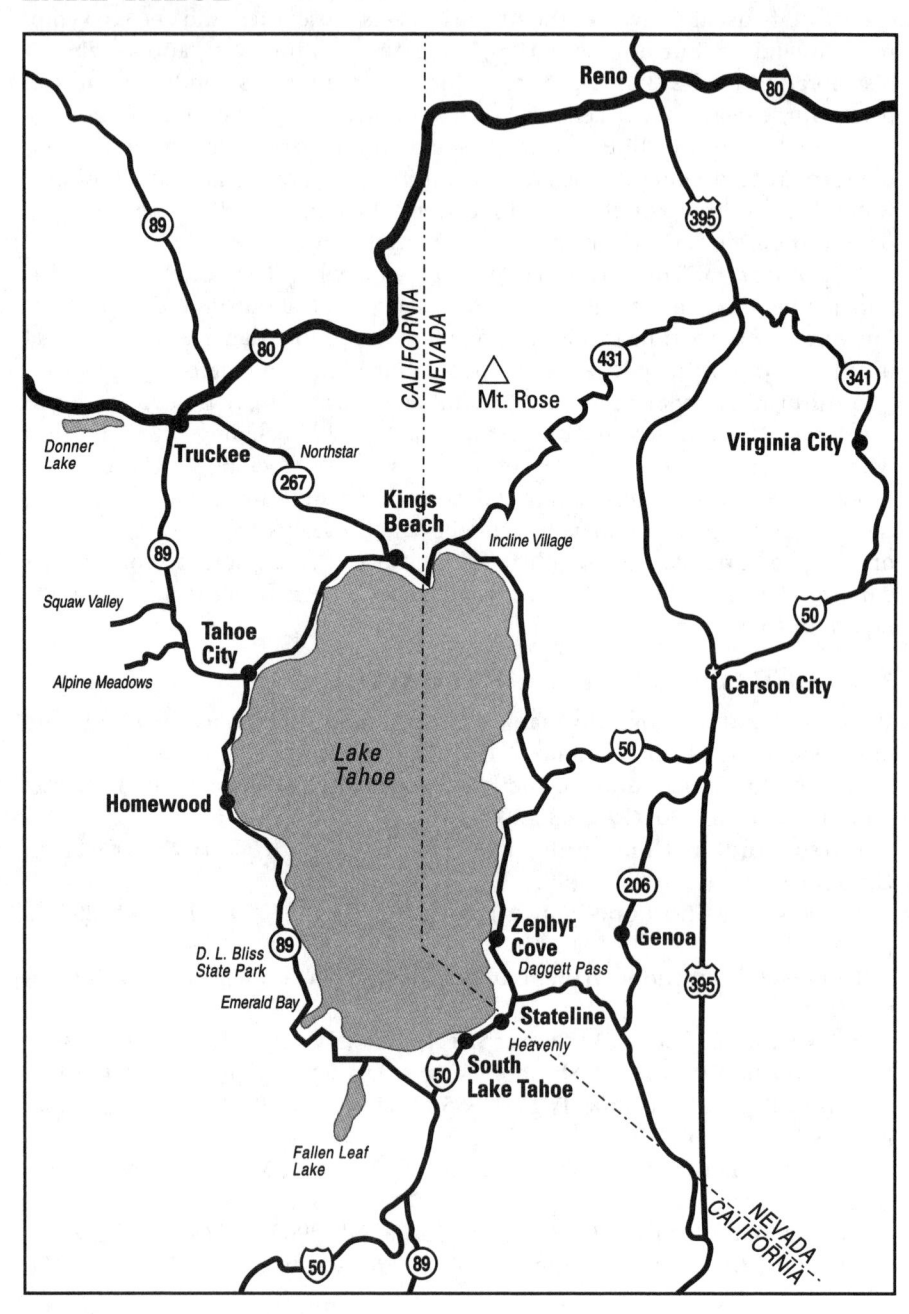

Chapter 27
Winter Sports in the Lake Tahoe Region

Econoguide 2001: Best Ski Areas in the Lake Tahoe Region
★★★★★ Heavenly
★★★★★ Squaw Valley USA
★★★★ Royal Gorge Cross-Country Ski Area

We don't know of many places more breathtaking than Lake Tahoe, especially when seen from the top of a spectacular snow-packed plunge. And there aren't many groups of more than a dozen world-class ski resorts that lie within a one- to two-hour drive from a full-feature city like Reno. Add in the attraction of gambling casinos, restaurants, and showrooms of Reno and Lake Tahoe and you've got a wintertime bet worth making.

If you're in Reno for a casino visit or a business stop, it is a very simple matter to rent a car or take a shuttle bus down to Lake Tahoe and take in a day's skiing; if you are staying at Lake Tahoe, it is equally easy to take a break from the slopes to drive north to Reno to see the big city.

The Queen of South Lake Tahoe ski areas is Heavenly, a massive resort whose lower slopes can be seen from Stateline/South Lake Tahoe, and from much of the lake itself.

Ruling over the north end of the lake area is Squaw Valley USA, site of the 1960 Winter Olympics.

The Lake Tahoe ski season typically runs from about November through mid-April. Many of the major areas now have snowmaking capability.

Multi-Area Ski Passes

If you are planning to spend several days skiing in and around Lake Tahoe, you might want to consider purchasing an interchangeable ski pass.

One interesting option in recent years has been the Ski Lake Tahoe pass, which offers five- or six-day lift tickets to five of Tahoe's premier resorts: Alpine Meadows, Northstar-at-Tahoe, Heavenly, Kirkwood, and Squaw Valley USA. With a Tahoe North pass, you can enjoy three to six days of skiing at Alpine

Meadows, Boreal, Diamond Peak, Mount Rose, Northstar-at-Tahoe, Ski Homewood, Squaw Valley, or Sugar Bowl.

For information on the pass, contact one of the participating resorts, or call (800) 824-6348.

Ski Resort	Distance from Reno (miles)	Vertical Drop (feet)
Alpine Meadows	50	1,800
Boreal Ridge	42	1,500
Diamond Peak	35	1,840
Donner Ski Ranch	46	1,750
Heavenly	55	3,500
Kirkwood	90	2,000
Mount Rose	22	1,440
Northstar-at-Tahoe	40	2,280
Sierra-at-Tahoe	75	2,212
Ski Homewood	50	1,650
Squaw Valley USA	45	2,850
Sugar Bowl	44	1,500
Tahoe Donner	38	1,600

Lake Tahoe Ski Areas

★★★★★ Heavenly

Skiers get to see sights that many of the rest of the flatlanders miss. Though I have been to many of the most spectacular ski areas of the world, Heavenly took my breath away.

Heavenly opened in 1955 with one chair lift and a small hut on U.S. Forest Service land. Today, it includes twenty-seven lifts, six day lodges, 4,800 acres of terrain, 700 acres of snowmaking, and parts of two states. The resort is part of American Skiing Company, along with Steamboat in Colorado, Killington and Mount Snow in Vermont, Sugarloaf and Sunday River in Maine, and other resorts.

As overwhelming as Heavenly is today, it is on the verge of a major expansion and improvement that will literally change its face. During the coming decade, Heavenly will gain a new gondola with a portal from the heart of Stateline, NV; seven new lifts; two new on-mountain lodges; new trails on the Nevada side of the mountain; and an extensive remodeling of base facilities.

Engineering of the new gondola was also begun, with construction expected in the next few years. With the gondola, the ski resort will be more closely tied to the town of Stateline, creating immediate resort access for guests of approximately thirty hotels, motels, and casino resorts, with more than 7,000 beds.

The accompanying area redevelopment project focuses on a two-mile stretch of Highway 50, which comprises what is now considered downtown South Lake Tahoe and the Stateline commercial-core area. Once completed, the area will be the focus of visitor activity on the South Shore, featuring shopping, increased lake access and watercraft activities, and direct access to the Heavenly ski resort.

In any case, what you see today from the road in South Lake Tahoe or Stateline is perhaps one-third of just one face of the mountain. Sixteen of its lifts

Skiing above Lake Tahoe at Heavenly

lie in California, and nine are in Nevada, including the resort's famous aerial tramway, one high-speed six-seat chair, three high-speed quads, eight triples, seven doubles, and seven surface tows. The tram runs from the base lodge on the California side, 1,700 feet up the mountain at an average angle of more than forty-five degrees; a restaurant awaits at the upper tram base.

The hill, impressive as it is, is a decidedly intermediate area. There are eighty-two runs—20 percent novice, 47 percent intermediate, and 33 percent advanced/expert. Among the skiable areas is the Mott Canyon Trail, one of the steepest in America.

The vertical drop is 3,500 feet, with the top elevation at 10,040 feet. The base elevation in California is at 6,540 feet, and in Nevada it is at 7,200 feet. The longest mountain descent is five and a half miles.

Heavenly receives an average annual snowfall of 340 inches, and in recent years has put down an additional 120 inches of machine-made snow. The season usually runs from mid-November through early May. Area hotels usually offer packages based on three seasons, running from least crowded to busiest.

Value season runs from just after Thanksgiving to just before Christmas, or approximately November 29 to December 17. Regular season includes Thanksgiving and January through the end of March, except for the President's Week holiday. Holiday Season runs from Christmas through New Year's, plus President's Week in mid-February.

The **Monument Peak Restaurant** is located at the top of the Heavenly Aerial Tram, 2,000 feet above Lake Tahoe. It's an unusually sophisticated (tablecloths and silverware!) restaurant for a ski resort, especially for one where many of the visitors are wearing boots. The restaurant serves an interesting mix of Italian and Oriental cuisine, salads and sandwiches, as well as spectacular vistas.

Non-skiers who ride the tramway up the hill are also welcome. Lunch is available daily, and dinner is available during the summer.

Facts and Figures on Lake Tahoe Skiing

*(N-I-A is Novice-Intermediate-Advanced)

★★★★★ Heavenly

P.O. Box 2180, Stateline, NV 89449; Information: (775) 586-7000. Reservations: (800) 243-2836. www.skiheavenly.com

Vertical	Summit	Lifts	Rating (N-I-A)*
3,500	10,040	27	20-45-35

Longest trail: 5.5 miles. Lifts: 1 tram, 1 high-speed six-seater, 5 high-speed quads, 8 triples, 5 doubles, and 7 surface tows. Complimentary shuttle throughout South Lake Tahoe. Location: South Lake Tahoe, on the California/Nevada border, 55 miles southwest of Reno and 180 miles east of San Francisco.

1999–2000 rates: Full-day $55 adults, $44 youth (13–18), $25 children (6 to 12), $25 seniors. Half-day, $38 adults, $33 youth, $15 children.

★★★★ Alpine Meadows

P.O. Box 5279 Tahoe City, CA 96145; Information (530) 583-4232; (800) 441-4423. Snowphone: (530) 581-8374. www.skialpine.com.

Vertical	Summit	Lifts	Rating (N-I-A)*
1,800	8,637	12	25-40-35

Longest trail: 2.5 miles. Base: 6,840 feet. Lifts: 1 high-speed six-seater, 1 high-speed quad, 4 triples, 5 double chairs, and 1 surface lift. Call for information on daily and multiple-day tickets and interchangeable multiple-day tickets for other North and South Lake Tahoe areas. Complimentary shuttle bus from South Lake Tahoe/Stateline and from North Shore of Lake Tahoe. Location: 6 miles northwest of Tahoe City on State Route 89.

Right outside the base lodge are two high-speed quad lifts, accessing two mountain peaks and six open bowls.

Alpine Meadows claims the longest season in the Tahoe region, usually from mid-November through the end of May, and even later.

1999–2000 rates: $50 adults, $38 teens, $10 children, $28 seniors (65–69), six and younger and 70 and older, $6.

★★ Boreal Ridge

P.O. Box 39, Truckee, CA 96160; (530) 426-3666.

Vertical	Summit	Lifts	Rating (N-I-A)*
500	7,700	9	30-55-15

Longest trail: 1 mile. Base: 7,200 feet. Lifts:1 high-speed quad, 1 quad, 3 triples, and 4 doubles. Location: At the top of Donner Summit, 10 miles west of Truckee, 90 miles east of Sacramento.

Boreal and Soda Springs are part of the POWDR Corporation, which also owns the Alpine Meadows Ski Area near Lake Tahoe, and the Park City Ski Area near Salt Lake City, Utah.

1999–2000 rates: $31 adults, $10 juniors, $15 seniors. Night tickets, $20 adults, $10 juniors, $11 seniors.

★★★ Diamond Peak

1210 Ski Way, Incline Village, NV 89451; Information: (775) 832-1177. Snowphone: (775) 831-3211. www.diamondpeak.com.

Vertical	Summit	Lifts	Rating (N-I-A)*
1,840	8,540	6	18-49-33

Longest trail: 2.5 miles. Base: 6,700 feet. Lifts: 3 quads, 3 doubles. Free shuttle service within Incline Village. Pickup by reservation for groups of 10 or more from Reno or South Lake Tahoe. Location: Northeast shore of Lake Tahoe in Incline Village. Diamond Peak is directly above Incline Village.

1999–2000 rates: $38 adults, $31 teens (13–18), $14 children, $21 seniors, younger than 4 and older than 70, free.

★★ Homewood Mountain Resort

Homewood, CA; (530) 525-2992. www.skihomewood.com.

Vertical	Summit	Lifts	Rating (N-I-A)*
1,650	7,880	8	15-50-35

Longest run: 2 miles. Base: 6,230 feet. Lifts: 1 quad, 2 triples, 1 double chair, 4 surface lifts. Location: on Highway 89 along the west shore of Lake Tahoe, 6 miles south of Tahoe City and 19 miles north of South Lake Tahoe.

1999–2000 rates: $38 adults, $25 juniors, $9 youth and seniors. Half-day $28 adult, $19 junior, $8 youth, $7 senior.

★★★★ Kirkwood Ski Resort

Kirkwood, CA; Information: (209) 258-6000. Snowphone: (209) 258-3000. Reservations: (209) 258-7000, (800) 967-7500. www.skikirkwood.com.

Vertical	Summit	Lifts	Rating (N-I-A)*
2,000	9,800	12	15-50-35

Longest trail: 2.5 miles. Lifts: 1 quad, 7 triples, 2 doubles, and 2 surface lifts. Shuttle from major South Lake Tahoe resorts. Location: 35 miles south of South Lake Tahoe, Highway 88 at Carson Pass. Take Highway 89 south to 88 west.

Kirkwood sits in a spectacular alpine meadow valley. The views from the summit extend into the central valley of California. The resort has its own small village at the base, including some condominiums.

The 2,300 acres of skiable terrain includes 65 runs, wide trails, steep chutes, and open bowls. The base elevation of 7,800 feet is the highest in northern California, and the natural snow magnet attracts an average of 450 inches each year, allowing Kirkwood to sometimes stay open as late as July 4.

1999–2000 rates: $46 adults, $36 juniors, $10 children, $23 seniors. Younger than 5, free. Age 70 and older, $10.

★★★ Mount Rose

22222 Mount Rose Highway, Reno; (775) 849-0704. www.skirose.com.

Vertical	Summit	Lifts	Rating (N-I-A)*
1,440	9,700	5	30-35-35

Longest trail: 2.5 miles. Base: 8,260 feet. Lifts: 2 quads, 3 triples. Location: 22 miles southwest of Reno, on State Route 431, 11 miles from Incline Village.

The nearest of the Lake Tahoe ski areas to Reno, the high base elevation makes good conditions likely even into the spring. The area offers a morning half-day ticket, which might allow a bit of skiing on your departure day.

1999–2000 rates: $42 adults, $35 teens, $10 children, $21 seniors (60 and older.) Half-day $34 adult, $30 teen, $10 child, and $17 senior.

★★★★ Northstar-at-Tahoe

P.O. Box 129, Truckee, CA 96160; Information: (530) 562-1010. Snowphone: (530) 562-1330. Reservations: (800) 466-6784. www.skinorthstar.com.

Vertical	Summit	Lifts	Rating (N-I-A)*
2,280	8,610	13	25-50-25

Longest trail: 2.9 miles. Base: 6,330 feet. Lifts: 1 gondola, 4 high-speed quads, 2 triples, 2 doubles, 4 surface tows. Interchangeable tickets with other Lake Tahoe resorts available. Complimentary shuttle bus between Incline Village/Kings Beach and Northstar. Reno airport pickup for groups. Shuttle to South Lake Tahoe runs twice weekly. Location: 40 miles southwest of Reno on California Highway 267 and 196 miles northeast of San Francisco.

New development on the "backside" of Mount Pluto opened up 200 more acres, including tree skiing. An unusual program at Northstar-at-Tahoe is the "Ski with the Legends" program, which offers special clinics with world-class skiers, including former members of the U.S., Austrian, and Yugoslav ski teams.

1999–2000 rates: $49 adults, $39 young adults (22 and younger), $10 children, $25 seniors (65–69). Age 70 and older, $5.

★★★★ Sierra at Tahoe

1111 Sierra-at-Tahoe Road, Twin Bridges, CA; Information: (530) 659-7453. Snowphone: (530) 659-7475. www.sierratahoe.com.

Vertical	Summit	Lifts	Rating (N-I-A)*
2,212	8,852	12	25-50-25

Longest trail: 2.5 miles. Base: 6,640 feet. Lifts: 3 high-speed quads, 1 triple, 5 doubles, 3 surface tows. Complimentary shuttle bus from South Lake Tahoe/Stateline casino area. Location: 12 miles west of South Lake Tahoe on Highway 50, 72 miles west of Reno.

The 2,000 acres of terrain feature 44 trails, including heart-stopping fall line plunges on the West Bowl. This area was formerly Sierra Ski Ranch.

1999–2000 rates: $46 adults, $36 young adults, $8 children, $25 seniors. Age 70 and older, $8.

★★★★★ Squaw Valley USA

Squaw Valley, CA; Information: (530) 583-6985. Snowphone: (530) 583-6955. Reservations: (800) 545-4350. www.squaw.com.

Vertical	Summit	Lifts	Rating (N-I-A)*
2,850	9,050	28	25-45-30

Longest trail: 3.5 miles. Base: 6,200 feet. Lifts: 1 115-passenger tram, 1 28-person funitel, 2 six-passenger chairs, 4 high-speed quads, 1 quad, 8 triples, 7 doubles, 3 surface tows, 1 six-person pulse lift.

Squaw Valley USA is one of only two places in America where you can point your skis down a slope once zoomed by the Olympians. (The other place is

Whiteface Mountain near Lake Placid, New York. In 2002, several ski areas near Salt Lake City will add the same honor.)

Founded in 1949 amidst 8,000 acres of wilderness preserve in the California High Sierra, Squaw Valley was the site of the VIII Olympic Winter Games in 1960. The Squaw games were the first Winter Games to be televised.

The Olympics propelled Squaw Valley onto the world stage and helped fuel the growth of skiing in America. In 1960, the resort had four double chairs and a rope tow; today there are thirty lifts, including a 150-passenger cable car and a high-tech funitel tram, and an automated "pulse lift" that connects the two mid-mountain lodges.

You're in for a bit of a shock—a pleasant one for most of us—when you look at the trail map for Squaw Valley USA. Since most of the area consists of expansive open bowls, there aren't really "trails," especially in the sense that Eastern skiers are used to. Pay attention to the rating that is assigned to the chairlifts to see what kind of terrain they serve; then head down the hill on a bowl that seems appropriate to your skiing style. In some parts of the resort you'll find the easiest way down the hill marked with signs.

The fact is that the wide-open bowls and the consistent deep snow at Squaw Valley generally make it possible to ski one notch above normal—accomplished novices will be able to cruise intermediate bowls, and dedicated intermediates should be able to try out some of the black diamond terrain. If you get in over your head, there is plenty of room to traverse the fall line.

Shuttle services from various North Lake Tahoe and South Lake Tahoe locations. Location: fifty miles west of Reno, 200 miles east of San Francisco.

1999–2000 rates: $52 adults, $26 teens, $5 children, $26 seniors. Age 76 and older, free. Half-day for adults, $35.

> **Skiing museum.** Way back when, cross-country skiing and snowshoeing were not sports but means of transportation. The **Western American SkiSport Museum** is located at the Boreal Ski Area and includes displays on Pioneer days, the mining era, and the 1960 Winter Olympics. The museum is open from mid-June to mid-March. For information, call (530) 426-3313.

★★ Sugar Bowl
Norden, CA; (530) 426-3651. www.skisugarbowl.com.

Vertical	Summit	Lifts	Rating (N-I-A)*
1,500	8,383	13	17-43-40

Longest trail: 2 miles. Base: 6,883 feet. Lifts: 1 four-person gondola, 3 high-speed quads, 4 quads, 3 doubles, 2 surface tows. Location: Donner Summit near Soda Springs, 44 miles from Reno.

1999–2000 rates: $48 adults, $39 young adults, $10 juniors ($5 with helmet), $24 seniors. Age 70 and older, free.

Tahoe Donner
Truckee, CA; (530) 587-9444. www.tahoedonner.com.

Vertical	Summit	Lifts	Rating (N-I-A)*
600	7,350	3	40-60-0

Longest trail: 1 mile. Base 6,750 feet. Lifts: 1 quad, 1 double, 1 surface tow. Location: west of Truckee.
1999–2000 rates: $26 adults, $12 juniors, $12 seniors.

Children's Ski Programs

Alpine Meadows. Snow School for children ages 4 to 6.
Boreal. Animal Crackers Children's Ski School for children 4 to 10.
Diamond Peak. Bee Ferrato's Child Ski Center for ages 7 to 12.
Heavenly. L'il Angels for children 3½ to 8. Junior Mountain Adventure for children 8 to 12.
Homewood. Ski and Play for children ages 4 to 12.
Kirkwood. Mighty Mountain for children 4 to 12.
Northstar. Ski Cubs for children 3 to 6 is an introduction to snow sports. Children 4 to 6 can enter Super Ski Cubs. Experienced young skiers from ages 5 to 12 can enter StarKids.
Squaw Valley. Children's World at Papoose for children 3 to 12.
Sugar Bowl. PowderKids is for children 6 to 12. For the youngest visitor, there's the Sugar Bears Child Care program.

Lake Tahoe Region Cross-Country Ski Areas

Cross-Country Ski Area	Distance from Reno (miles)	Trail (kilometers)
Diamond Peak	35	35
Kirkwood	90	80
Lakeview	45	65
Northstar-at-Tahoe	40	65
Royal Gorge	45	328
Spooner Lake	40	101
Squaw Creek Nordic	45	30
Tahoe Donner	38	94

Cross-Country Ski Resorts

Diamond Peak Cross-Country. ★★★ Five miles up the Mount Rose Highway from Incline Village. (775) 832-1177. 35 kilometers of groomed trails. Adults $14, children 6–12, and seniors 60–69, $10. Children 5 and younger and seniors 70 and older free. Half-day: $10 adults/$6 children and seniors. Younger than 5 and older than 70, free. Twilight ticket from 3 until 4:30 P.M. $6. Snowshoe rental and trail pass, $20.

Kirkwood. ★★★ Highway 88 at Kirkwood Meadows, 30 miles south of Lake Tahoe. (209) 258-7248. 80 kilometers of groomed trails. Adults $16, children $5. Half-day: $13 adult, $3 child. Rentals: $16 adult, $10 child.

Northstar-at-Tahoe Cross-Country & Telemark Center. ★★★ Eight miles south of Truckee off Highway 267 on Northstar Drive. (530) 583-3653. 65 kilometers of groomed trails. Adults $19, children $11. Half-day: $11/$9. Rentals: $19/$15.

Royal Gorge Cross-Country Ski Area. ★★★★ Soda Springs/Norden exit off Interstate 80 near Donner Summit, Soda Springs, CA. Van Norden Trailhead is one mile east on Highway 40 near the Sugar Bowl Ski Resort. (530) 426-3871, (800) 500-3871. www.royalgorge.com.

Eighty-eight trails, 328 kilometers of track. That's not a typographical error: Royal Gorge claims it is North America's largest cross-country ski resort and the world's largest groomed track system with eighty-eight trails spread across 9,000 acres with two hotels, four cafes, a day lodge, and ten warming huts. There are even four surface tows in steep areas.

In a typical season, the area at 7,000 feet in the Sierras receives about 600 inches of snow; just to be on the safe side, though, snowmaking covers 15 kilometers.

The Wilderness Lodge is tucked into the track system, offering meals, food, and lodging. The smaller Rainbow Lodge dates to the 1920s and is set along a bend in the Yuba River.

Royal Gorge typically operates from mid-November to mid-April. Adults weekday $17.50, weekend $21.50. Youth (13–16), $8.50. Children (12 and younger), free. Half-day: $13.50 to $16.50. Rentals: $17.50/$11.50.

Spooner Lake Cross-County Ski Area. ★★★★ North of the junction of U.S. 50 and Highway 28 at the parking lot for Lake Tahoe–Nevada State Park. (775) 749-5349. Snow conditions: 887-8844. 101 kilometers of groomed trails. Adults $15; students (16–22), $9; children $3; seniors $5. Half-day: $11/$9/$3/$5. Rentals: $15/$4.

Tahoe Donner Cross-Country. ★★★ Donner State Park exit from Interstate 80, one half-mile east on Donner Pass Road to left turn on Northwoods Boulevard. (530) 587-9484. 94 kilometers of groomed trails. Adults $17, children $9, seniors $14. Half-day: $13/$7/$11. Ages 10 and younger, 70 and older, free. Rentals: $17/$9.

Smaller Cross-Country Areas

Bijou. South Lake Tahoe; (530) 542-6056. 4 kilometers open terrain, all beginner.

Camp Richardson. Hwy. 89, South Lake Tahoe; (530) 541-1801. 35-kilometers groomed trails.

Eagle Mountain Nordic. (530) 389-2254. 75-kilometers marked groomed trails.

Granlibakken. Hwy. 89, Tahoe City; (530) 573-2600. 7.5 kilometers to Page Meadow.

Hope Valley Cross-Country at Sorensen's Resort. Highway 88 in Hope Valley, (530) 694-2266, (800) 423-9949. 51-kilometers marked trails, 10-kilometers groomed.

J & M Winter Sports. Highway 50 at Meyers, CA; (530) 577-2121.

Lake Tahoe Basin. (530) 573-2600. Various trails maintained by the U.S. Forest Service.

Squaw Creek Cross-Country Ski Area. Olympic Valley, CA; (530) 583-6300. 18 kilometers of track.

Sunset Ranch. Tahoe Airport Highway 50, South Lake Tahoe; (530) 541-9001.

Tahoe Nordic Center. Tahoe City, CA; (530) 583-9858. 12 trails, 65 kilometers of track.

U.S. Forest Service Trails. Contact Forest Service for Sno-Park and wilderness permits, snow conditions, and trail safety information at (530) 573-2600.

Ski Shuttles

Ski shuttle services allow you to sample more than one mountain without the need to check into a new hotel or rent a car.

Tahoe Casino Express. More than a dozen daily departures from Reno Cannon Airport to South Lake Tahoe. (775) 785-2424, (800) 446-6128. $17, one-way; $30, round-trip.

Daily shuttle bus service by Gray Line to **Squaw Valley USA** leaves from major hotels in Reno and Sparks between about 7 and 8 A.M. and arrives between 9 and 9:30 A.M. Round-trip tickets, including an all-day lift pass, were about $47 for adults; ticket/lift passes for children 12 and younger were $25.

You can get in a half-day afternoon at **Mount Rose** every day but Monday with a Gray Line shuttle that leaves from Sparks and Reno hotels between 10 and 10:45 A.M., arriving between 11:30 A.M. and noon. Adult round-trip tickets plus the half-day lift ticket for Mount Rose are $29.

All shuttles leave the slopes at 4:30 P.M. and arrive in the Reno area between about 5:30 and 6:30 P.M.

Gray Line also offers shuttle service from South Lake Tahoe hotels to Squaw Valley, seven days a week with pickups beginning at 7 A.M. Fares from South Lake Tahoe to Squaw Valley, $52; from South Lake Tahoe to Heavenly, $56.

Call Sierra Nevada Stage Lines/Gray Line Tours at (775) 331-1147 or (800) 822-6009.

Diamond Peak. Free shuttle service within Incline Village and Crystal Bay and Kings Beach. (775) 832-1177.

Heavenly. Free shuttle service within South Lake Tahoe. (775) 586-7000.

Kirkwood. Shuttle from major South Lake Tahoe properties. (209) 258-6000.

Northstar-at-Tahoe. Free shuttle service between Incline Village, Kings Beach, Tahoe City, and Truckee daily. (530) 562-2248.

Sierra-at-Tahoe. Free shuttle between South Lake Tahoe and Stateline. (530) 659-7453.

Squaw Valley USA. Free shuttle service from North and South Lake Tahoe properties. (530) 583-6985.

In addition, the Truckee North Tahoe Transportation Management Association publishes a complete schedule of North Tahoe/Truckee public transportation and ski area shuttle services, including those for **Alpine Meadows** and **Squaw Valley USA.** To obtain the schedule, call (530) 581-3922.

Snowmobiling

There are few places where snowmobiling has a more spectacular perch than high up in the mountain meadows above Lake Tahoe. There are quite a few companies renting machines and offering trail rides. No experience is necessary; outfits will offer training and will even rent out cold-weather boots, jumpers, and parkas. Some of the companies offer two-person machines.

Rates for two-hour tours range from about $70 for a single rider to about $90 for a two-person sled. Here are some of the best companies:

Eagle Ridge Snowmobile Outfitters. Tours on some 200 miles of groomed trails in the Tahoe National Forest north of Truckee. Riders get to visit some extremely remote areas, including Treasure Mountain, the Sierra Buttes, and Lakes Basin. The company also offers two- and three-day overnight tours. Incline Village, NV; (530) 546-0132, (775) 831-7600.

J & M Winter Sports. Highway 50 at Meyers, CA (three miles south of Lake Tahoe Airport); (530) 577-1813.

Mountain Lake Adventures. Tours to Mount Watson, the highest point on the North Shore. South Lake Tahoe, CA; (530) 546-4280, (775) 831-4202.

Northstar-at-Tahoe. Two-hour tours around the edges of the downhill and cross-country ski trail system. Moonlight tours to the lookout atop Mount Watson are also offered. Truckee, CA; (530) 562-1010.

Reindeer Lodge Snowmobile. (775) 849-9902.

United States Forest Service. Snowmobiling is open in most National Forest lands within the Lake Tahoe Basin, provided there are at least six inches of snow on the ground. Recommended areas include Spooner Summit, Hell Hole, and Blue Lakes Road in Hope Valley. Contact U.S. Forest Service for maps. (530) 573-2600.

Zephyr Cove Snowmobile Center. A range of tours, including two-hour guided trips running from Thanksgiving through mid-April that reach the ridge line on the Nevada side of the lake, some 9,000 feet above sea level. Three-hour tours for experienced riders are also available. Parkas, bibs, gloves, and boots are available for rental; required helmets are free. 760 Highway 50, Zephyr Cove, NV; (775) 588-3833.

Snow Play Areas

The California Department of Parks requires purchase and display of a permit to use Sno-Park parking areas during the season. Permits may be obtained at many sporting goods stores, ski rental and snowmobile shops, automobile clubs, and the South Lake Tahoe Chamber of Commerce.

You don't need a lot of facilities to go sledding—a patch of snow and a saucer, sled, or cardboard box will do—but some places are nicer than others. Here are some designated sledding spots in the Lake Tahoe region.

Blackwood Canyon Sno-Park. Off Highway 89, three miles south of Tahoe City. (530) 573-2600. Bring your own equipment; there is a $3 day fee.

Boreal Ski Area. Ten miles west of Truckee, off I-80 in Donner Pass; (530) 426-3666. Snow play area with two groomed slopes; plastic disk use only. $10 fee includes rental. Open weekends and holidays.

Emigrant Gap. Laing Road, off I-80, 10 miles west of Soda Springs on the south side of the freeway. Bring your own equipment.

Granlibakken Ski Area. Off Highway 89 in Tahoe City. (530) 581-7333. Hill for saucers only; $4 day use fee. Saucers available for rent for $3.

Hansen's Resort. 1360 Ski Run Boulevard, South Lake Tahoe, CA; (530) 544-3361. $6 per hour per person, including sled or tube. The area includes some bobsled-like banked runs.

Heavenly. There are several toboggan and sled hills where you can rent equipment and use the hills on the road leading to Heavenly on Ski Run Boulevard on the California side.

Incline Village. On the driving range next to the Chateau. Bring your own equipment.

Mount Rose. Undeveloped and very steep area eight miles up Mount Rose Highway (Highway 431). Bring your own equipment.

Northstar-at-Tahoe. Northstar Drive off Highway 267. (530) 562-2248. Tubing hill with lift and groomed slope. Must use equipment provided. $13 for unlimited runs.

North Tahoe Regional Park. At the end of National Avenue in Tahoe Vista, CA; (530) 546-6115. Snow hill for toboggans, saucers, and inner tubes. No charge for play area; equipment rentals available for about $3.

Sorenson's Resort. Hope Valley off Highway 88, just east of junction with Highway 89. (530) 694-2203.

Spooner Summit. Highway 28, off Highway 50. West side of Highway 28, about 9 miles south of Incline Village where two roads come together. Steep hill; bring your own equipment.

Tahoe City. Off Highway 89, south of Fanny Bridge. Bring your own equipment.

Tahoe Vista. North Tahoe Regional Park snow play area. Turn left at top of National Avenue, off Highway 28. $3 parking.

Truckee. Donner Pass Road, central Truckee. Bring your own equipment.

If you choose to go sledding in an "unofficial" area be sure to follow commonsense rules. For example, never sled alone. Don't sled onto bodies of water or across roads or trails.

Sleigh Rides/Horseback Riding

Borges Sleigh Ride. U.S. 50 at Lake Parkway, South Lake Tahoe. (775) 588-2953, (800) 726-7433. 35-minute rides daily when snow conditions permit. Call for prices.

Northstar Stables. At Northstar, seven miles south of Truckee off Highway 267. (530) 562-2036. 30-minute rides daily when conditions permit. Call for prices.

Ice Skating

Resort at Squaw Creek. (530) 583-6300. Ice Skating Pavilion and Sports Activity Center at Squaw Valley. Rental shop. Open Thanksgiving to spring.

Squaw Valley USA. (530) 581-7246. Olympic-sized outdoor ice rink at the High Camp Bath and Tennis Club. Rental shop and lessons. Open year-round.

Chapter 28
Warm Weather and Year-Round Activities in the Lake Tahoe Region

South Lake Tahoe Attractions

Please call the numbers listed for hours of operation, ticket prices, and fees.

Heavenly Aerial Tram. Heavenly Ski Resort, South Lake Tahoe, CA; Summer: (916) 544-6263; Winter: (775) 586-7000. Dinner reservations: (775) 586-7000 ext. 6347. Available for sightseeing trips and for dinner at the mountainside restaurant. In the summer, hiking tours are conducted from the top of the tram.

Tours, led by a Lake Tahoe trail guide, are offered daily at 11 A.M. and 1 P.M.

In summer, the tram operates Monday through Saturday from 10 A.M. to 9 P.M., and on Sundays from 9 A.M. to 9 P.M. Summer rates are $12.50 for adults, and $9.50 for children 12 and younger. The **Monument Peak Restaurant** at the top of the tram is open for lunch from 11 A.M. to 2:30 P.M. Monday through Saturday, and for dinner daily from 5 to 9 P.M. A tram/lunch combo is offered from 10 A.M. to 2 P.M. for $18.95 for adults.

For information on the tram and restaurant, call (775) 586-7000. For dinner reservations, call (530) 544-6263.

Lake Tahoe Historical Society Museum. 3058 Lake Tahoe Boulevard, South Lake Tahoe, CA; (530) 541-5458.

U.S. Forest Service Lake Tahoe Visitor Center. Highway 89, South Lake Tahoe, CA; (530) 573-2600; (530) 573-2674. Mid-June to Labor Day, 8 A.M. to 5:30 P.M.; September, 8 A.M. to 4:30 P.M.; open weekends only during October and from Memorial Day through mid-June. Interpretive center, stream profile chamber.

Washoe Indian Cultural Foundation Exhibit. McGonagle Estate, Tallac Historic Estates, Highway 89, South Lake Tahoe, CA; (530) 573-2600.

Emerald Bay State Park. Highway 89, South Lake Tahoe, CA; (530) 525-7277. If you've got a camera, this is the place to take it for breathtaking views of Lake Tahoe; if you didn't bring a camera, buy one and bring it here.

Within the park is **Vikingsholm Castle** at the head of the bay near Eagle Falls and Creek. Tours are offered June through September, 10 A.M. to 4 P.M. Emerald Bay State Park, Highway 89, Emerald Bay, CA; (530) 525-7277.

D. L. Bliss State Park. Highway 89, South Lake Tahoe, CA; (530) 525-7277.

Ehrman Mansion. Sugar Pine Point State Park, Highway 89, Tahoma, CA; (530) 525-7982. Tours 11 A.M. to 4 P.M. July through September.

Gatekeeper's Log Cabin Museum. 130 West Lake Boulevard, Tahoe City, CA; (530) 583-1762.

Donner State Park. Highway 40, Truckee, CA; (530) 582-7892. Memorial to the ill-fated Donner Party of 1846. Open Memorial Day to mid-October, weather permitting.

Ponderosa Ranch. Highway 28, Incline Village, NV; (775) 831-0691. Open from May through October, 9:30 A.M. to 5 P.M. Site of some of the scenes of television's *Bonanza* series. *See more details in Chapter 23.*

Water Sports and Cruises
South Shore Boat Rentals and Marinas

Action Watersports of Tahoe. (530) 831-4386. Boating and parasailing.

Camp Richardson Marina. Highway 89, South Lake Tahoe, CA; (530) 542-6570.

Cave Rock. Cave Rock, NV; (775) 831-0494.

Emerald Bay Kayak Tours/Tahoe Whitewater Tours. Tahoe City, CA; (530) 581-2441. Guided kayak tours of Emerald Bay, Sand Harbor, and other spots. Raft tours on American, Carson, and Truckee rivers.

Kayak Tahoe. (530) 544-2011.

Lakeside Marina. End of Park Avenue, South Lake Tahoe, CA; (530) 541-6626.

O.A.R.S. Inc. (800) 346-6277.

River Adventures & More. (800) 466-7238.

Ski Run Marina. 900 Ski Run Boulevard, South Lake Tahoe, CA; (530) 544-0200.

Sunsports. 1018 Herbert Avenue, South Lake Tahoe, CA; (530) 541-6000. Kayak rentals and river rafting.

Tahoe Keys Boat Rental. Tahoe Keys Marina, South Lake Tahoe, CA; (530) 544-8888.

Tributary Whitewater Tours. (530) 346-6812, (800) 672-3846. Guided whitewater trips. www.whitewatertours.com.

Truckee River Raft Rentals. (530) 583-0123.

Whitewater Connection. (530) 622-6446, (800) 336-7238.

Zephyr Cove Resort & Marina. Boating and snowmobiling. 760 Highway 50, Zephyr Cove, NV; (775) 588-3833.

North Shore Boat Rentals and Marinas

Homewood High & Dry. Homewood, CA; (530) 525-5966.

Lighthouse Watersports Center. Tahoe City; (916) 583-6000. Jet skiing, paddle boats, canoes, and more.

North Tahoe Marina. Tahoe Vista; (530) 546-8248. Boat rentals and fishing charters.

Sand Harbor. Sand Harbor; (775) 831-0494.

Tahoe Paddle & Oar. Kings Beach; (530) 581-3029. Canoe and kayak rentals.

Tahoe Whitewater Tours. Tahoe City; (530) 581-2441. Guided tours of Emerald Bay and area rivers.

Cruises

Tahoe Queen. Boats depart from the Ski Run Marina in South Lake Tahoe. (530) 541-3364; (800) 238-2463. www.tahoequeen.com. Scheduled cruises to Emerald Bay, including dinner-dance cruise. Ski shuttle cruises run Tuesday through Friday.

Emerald Bay cruises are $16. Three-hour dinner-dance cruises on Saturday nights are priced at about $40 for adults ($18 without dinner), and $27.50 for children ($9 without dinner).

MS *Dixie II* Cruises. Year-round cruises from Zephyr Cove, NV, along the South Shore and to Emerald Bay on a paddlewheeler that has a glass bottom window. You'll find more details on the cruise schedule in Chapter 26 of this book. For information, call (775) 588-3508. www.tahoedixie2.com. *You will find a discount in the coupon section of this book.*

The *Dixie II* replaced the original Tahoe paddlewheeler, which took to the lake in 1972; the new vessel was built in Wisconsin and then separated into four sections and transported 2,000 miles by trailers. A major hurdle for this trip was Cave Rock Tunnel, four miles north of Zephyr Cove. A 275-foot-long rig inched through the curved tunnel with two inches of clearance on either side; the pieces were finally assembled at Zephyr Cove and the *Dixie II* was launched in May of 1994.

North Tahoe Cruises. Departs from Tahoe Yacht Harbor, Tahoe City, CA; (916) 583-0141. Year-round cruises on the *Sunrunner.*

Woodwind Sailing Cruises. Departs from Zephyr Cove, NV; (775) 588-3000. Five departures a day, including a sunset champagne cruise each night on a forty-one-foot glass-bottom catamaran. You'll find more details on the cruise schedule in Chapter 26 of this book. www.sailwoodwind.com.

Fishing

All of Lake Tahoe and most of the hundreds of smaller backcountry lakes are open for fishing year-round. Certain exceptions apply to tributaries of Lake Tahoe on both the California and Nevada sides—obtain a copy of fishing regulations from sporting goods stores in the area.

Federal and state authorities regulate fishing activities in Lake Tahoe, surrounding lakes, and tributaries. For a full set of rules, contact the California Department of Fish & Game at (530) 227-2244 or the Nevada Division of Wildlife at (775) 688-1500.

We hope you fancy trout: there are at least six variants of that fish in the rivers and lakes of the Tahoe Basin: Brook, Brown, Cutthroat, Golden, Mackinaw, and Rainbow. Golden Trout are scarce and likely to be found only in the most remote, high mountain lakes. Lake Tahoe also has Kokanee Salmon.

Fishing in Lake Tahoe is allowed from one hour before sunrise until two hours after sunset; hours for other bodies of water are similar. Most areas impose a limit of five trout, with stricter limits on scarce Mackinaw and Golden Trout.

Lake Tahoe. Locals advise getting out into the deep water on a boat; if you do fish from the shore, the best spots are where the bottom falls off sharply, including Cave Rock on the east shore and Rubicon Point on the west.

Fallen Leaf Lake. Deep waters offer the most promise; fishing within 250 feet of the dam at the northwest corner of the lake is forbidden.

Echo Lakes. Shore fishing from the dam is a good bet.

Blue Lakes. High mountain lakes at more than 8,000 feet, about twelve miles south of the Tahoe Basin, off Highway 88. Locals recommend fishing from the dams.

Carson River, West Fork. A popular fishing area, south of Lake Tahoe along Highway 88 and Blue Lakes Road. **Carson River, East Fork.** Closed to fishing above Carson Falls. From Hangman's Bridge south of Markleeville to the Nevada line, there are size limits in effect.

Truckee River. Fishing is prohibited in and around the dam at Lake Tahoe, with other restrictions applied at various times of the year.

Here are some fishing services and resorts catering to anglers:

Caples Lake Resort. Highway 88, Kirkwood, CA; (209) 258-8888.

First Strike Sportfishing. (530) 577-5065.

Kingfish Guide Service. Homewood; (530) 525-5360.

Mac-a-Tac Charters. Tahoe Vista; (530) 546-2500.

The Sportsman. South Lake Tahoe, CA; (530) 542-3474.

Tahoe Sportfishing Company. Ski Run Marina, South Lake Tahoe, CA; (530) 541-5448, (800) 696-7797.

Truckee River Outfitters. Truckee; (530) 582-0900.

Parks, Campgrounds, and Beaches

Camp Richardson. Highway 89, South Lake Tahoe, CA; (530) 541-1801.

Davis Creek Park. Highway 395 to Bowers Mansion exit. (775) 849-0684. Twenty miles south of Reno. Sites for tents and trailers. Fishing. Open all year.

D. L. Bliss State Park. Highway 89, north of Emerald Bay; (916) 525-7277.

Echo Lakes. Echo Chalet, a privately leased U.S. Forest Service resort. Echo Summit Road off Highway 50; (916) 659-7207.

Emerald Bay State Park. Highway 89, Emerald Bay; (916) 525-7277.

Grover Hot Springs State Park. Highway 89 South, 3 miles west of Markleeville, CA; (530) 694-2248.

Lake Tahoe Nevada State Parks. (775) 831-0494.

Mount Rose Campground. Route 431; (800) 280-2267. Twenty miles southwest of Reno on the slopes of Mount Rose. Twenty-four sites for tents and trailers up to sixteen feet. Elevation 8,900 feet. Open July to mid-September.

South Lake Tahoe Parks & Recreation Department. (530) 542-6055.

Sugar Pine Point State Park. Highway 89; (530) 525-7982.

U.S. Forest Service, Lake Tahoe Basin. (530) 573-2600.

Warrior Point Beach. Route 445, past Sutcliffe nine miles to the end of the pavement; (775) 476-1155. Forty miles north of Reno. Permits for fishing and camping available.

Washoe Lake State Park. Highway 395, Washoe Lake State Park exit; (775) 687-4319. Twenty-five miles south of Reno. Twenty-five sites for tents and trailers up to thirty feet. Equestrian area, swimming, fishing, boat launch.

Hiking Trails

The star among stars in hiking trails along Lake Tahoe is the **Tahoe Rim Trail**, a hiking and horseback riding trail through National Forest lands surrounding Lake Tahoe. Built entirely with donations and volunteer labor, 138 miles of a planned 150-mile circle have been completed, including fifty miles of the existing Pacific Crest Trail. (The current gaps lie near Tahoe City, and across Mount Rose and above Incline Village.) The trail passes high mountain lakes, streams, and meadows and offers views from as high as 10,000 feet at Freel Peak and Alpine Meadows. The trail does not exceed a 10 percent grade and is suitable for beginner through advanced hiking. Camping is allowed along the trail.

Tahoe Vista Trails at Heavenly

The Heavenly ski resort offers guided tours and marked trails that lead off from the top of its tram, which operates year-round. It's a good way to take the easy way up to the 8,250-foot mark, and the three main trails offer a moderate challenge with spectacular rewards.

The Tahoe Vista Trail traverses a ridge line high above the lake. The longest trail is a 2.1-mile hike to the Fremont Camp, up a series of switchbacks to the 9,000-foot level. The camp was established by Kit Carson and Colonel John C. Frémont in February 1844 when they became the first nonnatives to see the Lake.

A second trail leads to Snowshoe Ridge, named after John A. "Snowshoe" Thompson, Tahoe's earliest known skier. Thompson became a legend in the Sierra by carrying mail in the 1860s on a route that led from Placerville, California, to Genoa, Nevada, on the east side of the Sierra Nevadas.

Neumann Point is named in remembrance of Terry Neumann, a Heavenly ski instructor who was killed in a huge avalanche at this location in 1974.

Guided tours from the top of the tram leave at 11 A.M. and 1 P.M. in the summer and are free to riders on the tram. Also offered is a Sunday brunch ticket that includes the tram ride and a meal at the Monument Peak Restaurant.

East Shore Trails

Rim Trail South. Take the hint from the name: this is a southerly walk along the top of the Lake Tahoe world, a strenuous jaunt of about twenty-one miles that reaches up to 10,778 feet at its highest point.

The trail begins behind the Nevada Department of Transport building at the Spooner Summit Rest Area on Highway 50. If the views of Lake Tahoe to the west and the Carson Valley to the east from the Rim Trail aren't enough for you, branches of the trail head off to even more isolated peaks, including Duane Bliss Peak, South Camp Peak, and Genoa Peak.

Rim Trail North. A slightly less challenging eighteen-mile hike that begins about half a mile up Route 50 from the junction with Route 28. There's a small parking area at the trailhead.

This wooded trail reaches to about 8,000 feet as it heads north. Just before Snow Peak, the trail comes to a fork. The left fork switchbacks down a steep slope to Marlette Lake, while the right fork leads to Tunnel Creek Road.

Nevada Lake Tahoe State Park. On the East Shore, off Highway 28. Trail to Sand Harbor, Marlette Lake, and the upper elevations of the Carson Range. Access from Spooner Lake at the intersection of Highways 50 and 28. For information, call (775) 831-0494 or (530) 573-2600.

Marlette Lake. A five-mile uphill jaunt of moderate challenge through North Canyon to Marlette Lake. To get to the trail, park at the Spooner Lake Trailhead in Lake Tahoe Nevada State Park, northwest of the junction of Highways 50 and 28; a parking fee is charged in season.

North Shore/Mount Rose Trails

Mount Rose Wilderness. A recent addition to the protected wilderness around Lake Tahoe, it includes the land at the northeast corner of Lake Tahoe above Incline Village. For information and maps, contact the Carson Ranger District in Carson City at (775) 882-2766.

Mount Rose Trail. A view to the north of Reno and to the southwest of the Tahoe Basin from the 10,778-foot summit. A five-mile hike of moderate difficulty, the trail begins one mile south of the summit on Highway 431 (Mount Rose Highway). The trail crosses a high mountain meadow before making a final two-mile switchback ascent to the ridge.

South Shore/Mount Rose Trails

Mount Tallac Trail. The Big Kahuna of the southern end of the Tahoe Basin, a difficult nine-mile ascent to a view worth 10,000 words of description. The trail begins on a fairly easy level, heading for Floating Island Lake and Cathedral Lake. The trail turns steep and difficult past Cathedral Lake for the final five miles to the top of Tallac at 9,735 feet.

The trailhead can be found on Highway 89, about three-and-a-half miles north of South Lake Tahoe. The road to the parking area is across the road from the entrance to Baldwin Beach.

Kirkwood. Highway 88 at Carson Pass; (209) 258-6000. Along the south shore, 8,000 acres with trails for all abilities. Passes high country lakes and streams with access to Pacific Crest and Mormon Emigrant Trails.

Meiss Lake Country. (530) 573-2600. U.S. Forest Service land south of South Lake Tahoe, CA. The trails encompass 10,000 acres at intermediate and advanced levels and pass several high country lakes. Access off Highway 89, five miles south of Highway 50 in Meyers, CA.

Pope-Baldwin Recreation Area. (530) 573-2600. The Fallen Leaf Trail System leads to the south shore of Fallen Leaf Lake. Access from the U.S. Forest Service Lake Tahoe Visitors Center on Highway 89.

Glen Alpine Trail Head. Several hikes of moderate to strenuous challenge depart from this trailhead off Fallen Leaf Lake Road, which itself branches off of Highway 89 three miles north of South Lake Tahoe. This is a slightly less strenuous six-mile path to the top of Mount Tallac.

Half Moon and Alta Morris Lakes. A moderate trail of about five miles.

Lake Aloha. A six-mile hike that includes a high mountain meadow, three alpine lakes, and a small waterfall.

Tallac Historic Site. An easy, half-mile walk through the area of the former Tallac mansions. Accessible from the Kiva Picnic Area, or the Lake of the Sky Trail from the Lake Tahoe Visitor Center.

Echo Lakes Trail. A moderate trail that reaches deep into the wilderness to Lower and Upper Echo Lakes and several other alpine waterways, including Tamarack, Lucille, Margery, and Aloha. In the summer, a water taxi offers a shortcut across Upper Echo Lake.

The trail is reached from Echo Lakes Road, off Highway 50 at Echo Summit. Bear left on Echo Lakes Road to a parking area. Upper Echo lies about two-and-a-half miles up the trail with other lakes farther on, several miles apart.

West Shore Trails

Desolation Wilderness. Permits are required to enter the 63,475 acres of woods and lakes, and travel is by foot or horseback only. Open campfires are prohibited and overnight camping permits are strictly limited in the heart of the season, from June 15 to Labor Day.

A quota system allows reservation of half of each day's permits up to ninety days in advance, with the remainder available only on the day of entrance.

Hiking permits are available year-round at the Forest Service office in South Lake Tahoe and in summer at the Forest Service Visitor Center off Highway 89 and at some of the trailheads.

Among the most spectacular trails in all of the Lake Tahoe region is the path up Mount Tallac, which leads from near the northwestern end of Fallen Leaf Lake some six miles along and 3,400 feet up to a spectacular vista overlooking Lake Tahoe.

For information on wilderness areas, contact the Lake Tahoe Basin Management Unit in South Lake Tahoe at (530) 573-2600.

Rubicon Trail. A 7.5-mile trail of moderate difficulty along the shoreline of Lake Tahoe, passing through a number of secluded coves and beaches and reaching three miles to Emerald Point and ending at Vikingsholm Castle. The trail is reached from D. L. Bliss State Park, about ten miles north of South Lake Tahoe on Highway 89.

Vikingsholm Trail. An easy one-mile descent to Lower Eagle Falls and Vikingsholm Castle with views of Emerald Bay and Fannette Island. The trail leaves from the parking lot off Highway 89, about nine miles north of South Lake Tahoe.

Cascade Creek Trail Head. Several spectacular trails lead off from this trailhead, including an easy jaunt to Cascade Falls and a difficult climb to three hidden high lakes. Located about eight miles north of South Lake Tahoe on Highway 89 at the Bayview Campground across the road from Inspiration Point.

Cascade Creek Fall Trail. An easy, nearly flat, one-mile hike to the 200-

foot Cascade Falls at Cascade Lake. The falls are at their most spectacular in the spring as winter snows melt on the slopes above.

Bayview Trail. A difficult trail up Maggie's Peak one mile to Granite Lake; from there it continues on to Dicks Lake, intersecting the Eagle Falls Trail along the way.

Eagle Falls Trail. A steep and difficult ten-mile plunge deep into the Desolation Wilderness, passing Eagle Lake and then Velma, Middle Velma, and Upper Velma Lakes and ending at Fontanillis Lake. The trailhead is at the Eagle Falls Picnic Area off Highway 89, eight miles north of South Lake Tahoe.

Granite Chief. A hiking area on the back sides of the Alpine Meadows and Squaw Valley USA ski areas, south toward Twin Peaks and Barker Pass.

Golf Courses
South Shore Golf Courses

Bijou Municipal Golf Course. 1180 Rufus Allen Boulevard, South Lake Tahoe, CA; (530) 542-6097. 9 holes. 2,064 yards. $15 for 9 holes. Open daily 7:30 A.M. to 7 P.M.

Edgewood Tahoe Golf Course. (775) 588-3566. Lake Parkway, Stateline. Adjacent to the Horizon Casino Resort. 18 holes. 7,491 yards. Rated as one of the top courses in the country. Open May through October. $150, with cart.

Lake Tahoe Golf Course. Highway 50, Meyers, CA; (530) 577-0788. 18 holes, 6,685 yards. $64 with cart.

Tahoe Paradise Golf Course. Highway 50, Meyers, CA; (530) 577-2121. 18 holes. 9-hole executive course. $32 for 18 holes. Driving range. Cart $13.

North Shore Golf Courses

Brockway Golf Course. 7900 North Lake Boulevard, Kings Beach; (530) 546-9909. Rated as one of the top 9-hole courses in northern California and home of the first Crosby Tournament in 1934. 3,314 yards. $30.

Carson Valley Golf Course. 18 holes. 5,759 yards. Gardnerville, NV; (775) 265-3181. $20 walking.

Incline Village Championship Golf Course. Incline Village, NV; (775) 832-1146. 18 holes. 7,138 yards. Designed by Robert Trent Jones Jr. Open May 1 to October 15. $115 with cart.

Incline Village Executive Golf Course. Incline Village, NV; (530) 832-1150. 18 holes. 3,200 yards. May 15 to September 30. $50 with cart.

Northstar-at-Tahoe Resort Golf Course. Highway 267 between Truckee and North Lake Tahoe; (530) 562-2490. 18 holes. 6,897 yards. Driving range. May through October. $75 with cart.

Ponderosa Golf Course. 10040 Reynold Way, Truckee. (530) 587-3501. 9 holes. 3,000 yards. $30.

Tahoe Donner Golf Course. 12850 Northwoods Boulevard, Truckee; (916) 587-9440. 18 holes. 6,961 yards for championship course. Mid-May through mid-October. $96 with cart.

Bicycling

Bike trails in and around Reno and Lake Tahoe range from nearly flat tours around lakes and across valleys to steep hill climbs on the Geiger Grade, the Mount Rose Highway, and across the top of the Sierra Nevada ridge line. And there's the spectacular and sometimes challenging seventy-two-mile coastline around Lake Tahoe, North America's largest alpine lake.

Kaspian Beach and Campground is Lake Tahoe's only bicycle campground. Located on Highway 89 between Sunnyside and Homewood, the site is two-and-a-half miles from scenic Blackwood Canyon and Creek. There are only ten camp sites available, though.

The **Pope-Baldwin Beach Trail** runs through several historical and educational sites along the south shore of Lake Tahoe; the three-and-a-half-mile path passes through the Tallac Historic Site, Lake Tahoe Visitors Center, stream profile chamber, Fallen Leaf Lake, and Pope and Baldwin Beaches.

The **Tahoe City to River Ranch Path** runs approximately five miles alongside the Truckee River. Contact the U.S. Forest Service at (775) 882-2766 or (530) 265-4531 to check on trail status.

Mountain bikers are prohibited from riding in wilderness areas, developed recreation sites, and self-guided nature trails. The U.S. Forest Service recommends several area trails for mountain bike usage: Meiss/Big Meadow, Angora Ridge Road, McKinney-Rubicon OHV Trail, Mount Watson, Brockway Summit to Martis Peak, Genoa Peak, and Marlette Lake.

Like the Lake Tahoe paths, Reno's trails also border bodies of water. Here is a selection of some of the more interesting routes:

The six-and-a-half-mile **Truckee River Trail** begins at Broadhead Park, near Wells Avenue and Kuenzi Lane, and continues along the river ending near the Vista Boulevard exit on I-80.

The **Idlewild Route** also follows the Truckee River, from Riverside and First streets and continues three-and-a-half miles through Idlewild Park to Caughlin Ranch.

Bowers Mansion to Franktown is a scenic, sparsely traveled country road. This 4-mile stretch starts at Bowers Mansion about fifteen miles south of Reno and makes a right turn on Franktown Road, winding its way past farmlands, meadows, towering pines, and large estates.

Bicycling to Extremes

The **Markleeville Death Ride** attracts 1,500 avid cyclists in a race over mountain passes, pedaling as much as 128 miles. Markleeville is about eighty miles south of Reno. For information, call (530) 694-2475.

Bicycle Rental Agencies

Reno:
Truckee River Bike Rentals. 501 West First Street; (775) 786-8888.
South Lake Tahoe:

Anderson's Bicycle and Skate Rentals. 645 Emerald Bay Road, South Lake Tahoe, CA; (530) 541-0500.
Cyclepaths. 1785 Westlake Boulevard, South Lake Tahoe, CA. (530) 581-1171.
Lakeview Sports. 3131 Highway 50, South Lake Tahoe; (530) 544-0183.
Camp Richardson's Resort Bicycle Rentals. Highway 89, Camp Richardson, CA; (530) 541-1801.
Sierra Cycle Works. 3430 Highway 50, South Lake Tahoe, CA. (530) 541-7505.
Tahoe Sports Ltd. Crescent V Center, Stateline, NV; (530) 542-4000.
Tahoe Cyclery. 3552 Lake Tahoe Boulevard, South Lake Tahoe, CA. (530) 541-2726.

North Lake Tahoe:
The Backcountry. Tahoe City; (530) 581-5861.
Northstar-at-Tahoe. Truckee; (530) 562-2248. Ride chairlifts to mid-mountain trails.
Olympic Bike Shop. 620 North Lake Boulevard, Tahoe City, CA; (530) 581-2500.
Tahoe Gear. 5095 West Lake Boulevard, Homewood, CA; (530) 525-5233.
Paco's Truckee River Bicycle. 11400 Donner Pass Road, Truckee, CA; (530) 587-5561.
Porter's Ski & Sport. Tahoe City: 501 North Lake Boulevard, CA; (530) 583-2314. Truckee: (530) 587-1500. Incline Village: 885 Tahoe Boulevard, CA; (775) 831-3500.
Squaw Valley U.S.A. Olympic Valley. (530) 583-6985. Ride the cable car with your bicycle to mountain trails.

Bowling
Bowl Incline. 920 Southwood Boulevard, Incline Village, NV; (775) 831-1900.
Tahoe Bowl. 1030 Fremont Avenue, South Lake Tahoe, CA. (530) 544-3700.

Horseback Riding the Range
Make like a real cowboy on the wide-open ranges around Reno. Here are some stables that rent horses and conduct other Western activities in and around Reno. In wintertime, some areas offer sleigh rides.

North Shore
Alpine Meadows Stables. (530) 583-3905. Open daily June through October.
Northstar Stables. (530) 562-1230. South of Truckee, California, off Highway 267, Northstar offers trail rides through beautiful, forested areas all year, weather permitting.
Squaw Valley Stables. Squaw Valley, CA; (530) 583-7433. Ride the site of the 1960 Winter Olympics. Guided rides, rentals, pony rides.
Tahoe Donner Equestrian Center. (530) 587-9470. Five miles west of Truckee, the center is open May through October for trail rides; overnight pack trips are offered in the summer.

Verdi Trails West. (775) 345-7600. Trail rides and hayrides.

Winters Creek Ranch. (775) 849-3500. Located at 1201 U.S. 395 North in Washoe Valley, offering winding mountain trails through tall pines, over creeks, and through meadows. Open year-round, weather permitting.

Wolf Creek Pack Station. (775) 849-1105. Ten miles south of Markleeville, California, offering guided day rides or fully outfitted camping trips in the Carson Iceburg and Mokelumne Wilderness Area. Open from May 15 through the end of October.

South Shore

Borges Carriage & Sleigh Rides. Highway 50 and Lake Parkway. South Lake Tahoe, CA; (530) 541-2953.

Camp Richardson Corral. Emerald Bay at Fallen Leaf Road, South Lake Tahoe, CA; (530) 541-3113. Trail rides, wagon rides, sleigh rides in winter. Overnight and extended pack trips.

Sunset Ranch. Highway 50, South Lake Tahoe, CA; (530) 541-9001. Ride through the open meadows of the Upper Truckee River, with or without a guide. Children's pony rides and petting zoo. Hayrides and sleigh rides in season. Open year-round.

Zephyr Cove Stables. Zephyr Cove Resort, Highway 50, Zephyr Cove, NV; (775) 588-5664.

Balloon Rides

If you've got the nerve, we can't think of very many more thrilling ways to explore the Lake Tahoe or Carson Valley than from a hot air balloon at 5,000 feet. The rides are generally offered from spring through fall.

There are several companies offering tours; most offer a one- to two-hour trip and charge between $100 and $200 per person. The trips leave early in the morning, before the air heats up and makes things even more unpredictable. The balloon pilots, by the way, have only a limited ability to steer their bags of air and they are chased by ground crews that will retrieve the equipment and passengers and bring them back to the base.

Balloons Over Lake Tahoe. South Lake Tahoe. (530) 544-7008.

Lake Tahoe Balloons. (530) 544-1221, (800) 872-9294.

Mountain High Balloons. Truckee. (530) 587-6922, (888) 462-2683.

Soaring

Graceful, engineless gliders soar over the mountains and meadows of the Lake Tahoe region year-round in good weather, offering a spectacular view.

Soar Minden. (775) 782-7627, (800) 345-7627.

Soar Truckee, Inc. (530) 587-6702.

Hot Springs

Carson Hot Springs. Carson City; (775) 885-8844.

Steamboat Hot Springs. Steamboat; (775) 853-6600.

Wally's Hot Springs. Genoa; (775) 782-8155.

Special Offers to Econoguide Readers

Look to your left, look to your right. One of you three people on vacation is paying the regular price for airfare, hotels, meals, and shopping. One is paying premium price for a less-than-first-rate package. And one is paying a deeply discounted special rate.

Which one would you rather be?

In this book you've learned about strategies to obtain the lowest prices on airfare, the best times to take a trip, and ideas on how to negotiate just about every element of travel.

And now, we're happy to present a special section of discount coupons for Econoguide readers.

All of the offers represent real savings. Be sure to read the coupons carefully, though, because of exclusions during holiday periods and other fine print.

The author and publisher of this book do not endorse any of the businesses whose coupons appear here, and the presence of a coupon in this section does not in any way affect the author's opinions expressed in this book.

GREAT FOR THE MAMAS & THE PAPAS AND THE OFFSPRING TOO.

Corner of Paradise and Harmon,
only 3 blocks off the "Strip" and 5 minutes from McCarren International Airport

www.hardrock.com

Present this ad and receive a complimentary collectible souvenir with the purchase of Hard Rock Cafe Merchandise ($20.00 minimum purchase required).
Limit one souvenir per purchase per guest. Expires 12/31/01

Hard Rock CAFE
LAS VEGAS

©2000,
Hard Rock Cafe,
Orlando FL

TWO FOR ONE PASS

- Dinosaurs
- Sharks
- Nevada's Wildlife
- African Savanna & Rainforest
- International Wildlife

Open daily from 9 A.M. to 4 P.M.
900 Las Vegas Boulevard North
Las Vegas, NV 89101
(702) 384-DINO

LV01-27   Expires 12/31/01

Las Vegas Natural History Museum

$3 Off
All-Day Admission

Valid 2001 Season (May–September).
Call for seasonal hours
(702) 734-0088

Present at ticket window (Las Vegas Park Only) for your discount. Coupon is good for up to six people. Not to be used in conjunction with any other offer, discount or afternoon pricing. Not for sale.

PLU G#120   PLU C#121   Expires end of 2001 season
LV01-34

Wet'n Wild®

Valid for one complimentary admission when a second admission of equal or greater value is purchased.

Open daily
Call (702) 792-3766 for information
Subject to cancellation without notice. Not to be used in conjunction with any other discount offer.

**On the Las Vegas Strip
just 1/2 block north of Circus Circus**
Expires 12/31/01

LV01-26

GUINNESS WORLD OF RECORDS™ MUSEUM

$29.⁵⁰* Sun–Thurs	$41* Fri–Sat	$12 RV Park

Stay within minutes of all the great attractions of Las Vegas.

Nevada Palace
BOULDER STRIP AT HARMON

*Present ad for the above special rates. Based on availability. Not valid with other discounts. Must be 21 or older.

Nevada Palace Hotel Casino
5255 Boulder Hwy., Las Vegas
(800) 634-6283

LV01-35

Expires 12/31/01

(23)

FREE HOOVER DAM
- See Star's Homes
- Hoover Dam
- Free Lunch Buffet
- Ethel M's & More

BUY 1 GET 1 FREE
PAY $33.95–SAVE $33.95

ECONO

FREE LAUGHLIN
The Boomtown on the Colorado River

Some Restrictions May Apply. Must be at least 21 years old.

INCLUDES
- Roundtrip Transportation
- Casino Fun Book
- Lunch Buffet & More!!

ECONO

FREE STATELINE
View the 3 Mega Resorts on the NV/CA Border.

Some Restrictions May Apply. Ages 2-20-$15.00pp

INCLUDES
- Roundtrip Transportation
- Lunch Buffet • Casino Fun Book
- California Lottery Ticket Store
- National Vitamin Factory Tour (Free samples)

ECONO

FREE PAHRUMP
Some Restrictions May Apply.
Must be at least 21 years old.

BINGO AVAILABLE

INCLUDES
- Roundtrip Transportation
- Lunch Buffet Included
- National Vitamin Factory Tour (Free samples)

ECONO

B5
B2

DEATH VALLEY GRAND CANYON
(South or West) or
BRYCE CANYON NATIONAL PARK

$99.50 pp
FOR EACH TOUR

INCLUDES
- Continental Breakfast & Lunch Buffet

Some Restrictions May Apply.

SAVE $30.00 PER PERSON

ECONO

Expires 12/31/01

Call 24 Hours
for Information & Reservations
369-1000 or (800) 777-4697

GUARANTEED TOURS

Lied Discovery Children's Museum

Home of the Las Vegas Library
and Lied Discovery Children's Museum

One free adult admission ($5 value)

833 Las Vegas Blvd. North, Las Vegas, NV (702) 382-3445
Expires 12/31/01

LV01-13   ECO

Special Rental Rates

econoguide

*One day free
on 3-day minimum*

Economy $36.95
Intermediate $42.95
Standard $48.95

or 25% off regular daily rates
FREE MILEAGE!

Source: ADV
Referral: Econoguide
Expires 12/31/01.
Subject to availability

Does not apply to any other discount or special rates and excludes any discount on luxury or sport vehicles. This coupon must be presented at time of rental. Prices does not include tax.

PAYLESS CAR RENTAL

(800) 634-6186
(702) 736-6147
For worldwide reservations
call (800) PAYLESS

**Formerly
Allstate Car Rental**

Redeemable at Payless Car Rental
Las Vegas only.

LV01-32

Fleischmann Planetarium

Valid for one complimentary show admission when a second show admission of equal or greater value is purchased.

Coupon valid any time.
Not to be used in conjunction with any other coupon or discount.

FLEISCHMANN PLANETARIUM

1650 North Virginia Street, Reno, NV 89557, Show times: (775) 784-4811
Expires 12/31/01

LV01-25

Tahoe's original Paddlewheeler company brings you

Tahoe's newest & largest Paddlewheeler

Save $5 per adult couple with coupon

Brunch • Breakfast • Sightseeing • Dinner Cruises

**CRUISIN' LAKE TAHOE
M.S. DIXIE II**

Call for current schedule.
On USFS Lands, 4 miles north of Stateline, Hwy. 50—Cruisin' Year-round, (775) 588-3508
Expires 12/31/01

LV01-33

Hollywood Entertainment Museum
One complimentary admission for each admission purchased

Present this coupon at the Museum Box Office for one complimentary admission for each admission purchased.

Not valid with any other offer.

7021 Hollywood Boulevard, Hollywood, CA 90028
(323) 465-7900

LV01-02   Expires 12/31/01

All Aboard to the Grand Canyon!
Buy one Grand Canyon Railway coach class ticket and get the second ticket of equal or lesser value for half price.
Call (800) THE TRAIN!

Grand Canyon Railway departs daily from charming Williams, Arizona, arriving just steps from the rim of the Grand Canyon. Historic depots, classic train cars, strolling musicians, and authentic western characters provide for an unforgettable Grand Canyon experience.

Not valid with any other offer. Good through 12/31/01

www.thetrain.com

LV01-45

Black Canyon Raft Tours

Experience a 1-day adventure on the Colorado River by raft! You'll float by hot springs, waterfalls, wonderful geological formations, and a wide array of desert plants and wildlife.

Season runs February 1 through November 30

$5 off with this coupon. Limit 4. No cash value.

For reservations
(800) 696-7238
Authorized Concessionaire of the National Park Service
www.rafts.com

LV01-28   Expires 11/30/01

**PALM SPRINGS
EXOTIC CAR AUCTIONS**

Collector Car Show & Auction
Two for One Coupon

Buy one $10 ticket and get one FREE. Save $10.
Sale of 300 antique, classic, sports, and special interest autos.
Held at The Palm Springs Convention Center last weekend in February and end of October each year.

Local office: 602 East Sunny Dunes Road, Palm Springs, California 92264
(760) 320-3290, (760) 320-2850, Fax (760) 323-7031
Website http://www.classic-carauction.com

LV01-01   Expires 12/31/01

Rip n' Willies
Ski & Snowboard Shop

$10 Off snowboard rental

Burton, Joyride, Morrow, K2 and M3 boards
(Boots included in package)

Rip n' Willies Ski & Snowboard Shop
1144 Ski Run Blvd., So. Lake Tahoe, CA 96150, (530) 541-6366
Void 12/22/00–1/1/01 Expires 6/1/01

LV01-29

TWO FOR ONE

Buy one 1/2 day rental (value $22)

GET ONE FREE

Limit 6 tickets total (3 free, 3 purchased)

Bighorn Bicycle Adventures
302 N. Palm Canyon Drive, Palm Springs, CA 92262
(760) 325-3367

Bighorn Bicycle RENTALS & TOURS

Expires 12/31/01

LV01-44

Rip n' Willies
Ski & Snowboard Shop

1/2 off shape or parabolic ski rental on first day of rental

(Boots and poles included) Save up to $10

Rip n' Willies Ski & Snowboard Shop
1144 Ski Run Blvd., So. Lake Tahoe, CA 96150, (530) 541-6366
Void 12/22/00–1/1/01 Expires 6/1/01

LV01-30

50% OFF
regular room rate with this ad

Gas fireplace in every room

Call (800) 669-7544 for reservations

Tahoe Valley Lodge

Reservations required, limited availability.
Not valid Saturdays or holiday weeks
2241 Lake Tahoe Blvd., South Lake Tahoe, CA 96150 (530) 541-0353
on Highway 50 at Tahoe Keys Blvd. in South Lake Tahoe, CA

www.TahoeValleyLodge.com

Expires 12/31/01

LV01-24

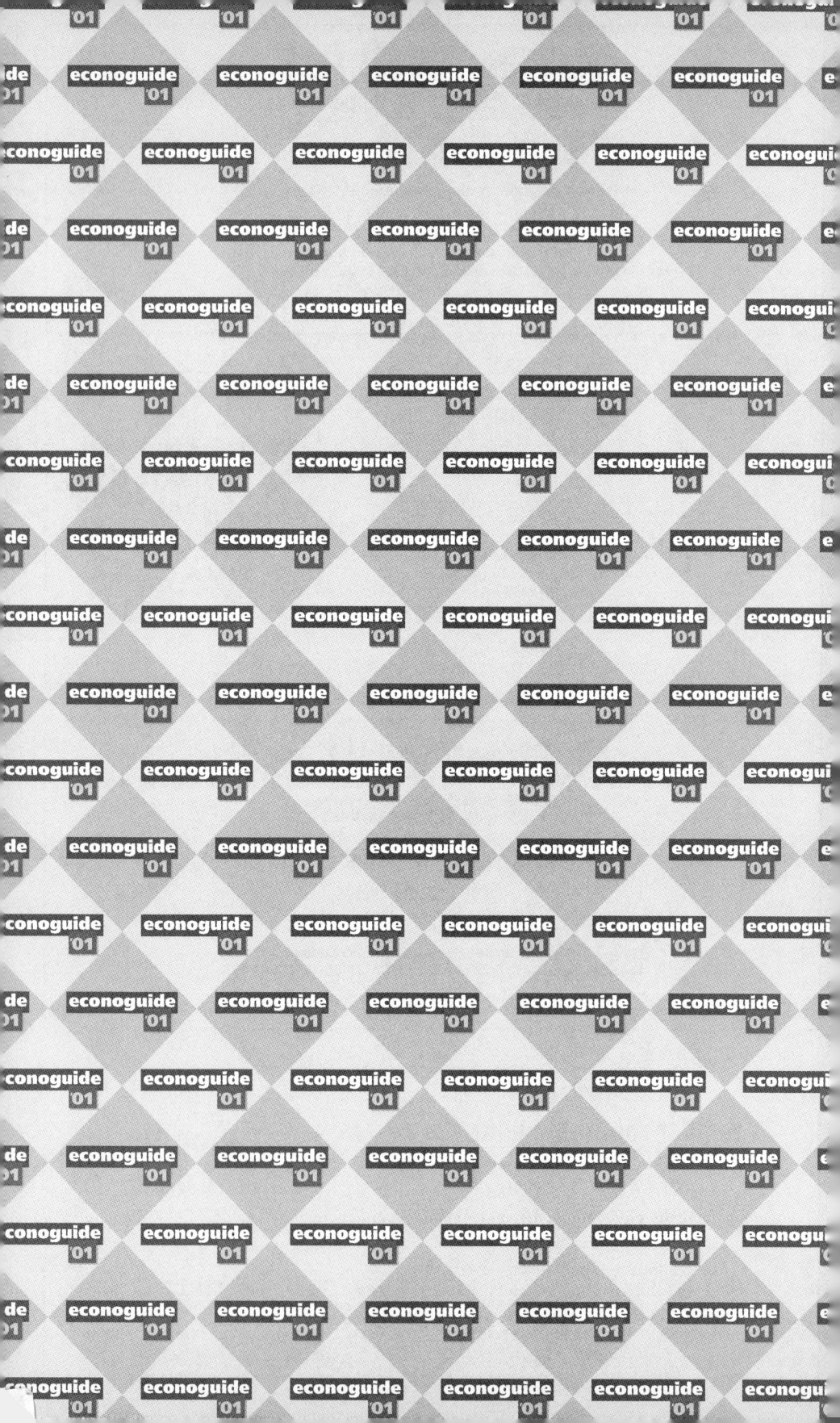

Best Western Station House Inn

Free upgrade
Based on availability and excluding holidays

901 Park Ave.
South Lake Tahoe, CA 96150
(530) 542-1101

Expires 12/31/01

Best Western
Station House Inn

LV01-43

10% Discount
Present this coupon on check-in and receive 10% off during your stay at the Best Western McCarran Inn.
Free 24-hour shuttle to airport and area attractions • Complimentary deluxe continental breakfast • Free parking • Guest laundry • Heated pool • Suites, non-smoking rooms available.
Located 1 mile east of the world-famous Strip (Las Vegas Blvd.)
4970 Paradise Rd., Las Vegas, NV 89119
(702) 798-5530 * (800) 626-7575
*Offer based on availability. Not valid with other discounts

Expires 12/31/01

Best Western
McCarran Inn

LV01-03

15% off rack rates
Microwaves, refrigerators, hairdryers • Iron and ironing board • In-room coffee • Deluxe continental breakfast • Data port phones • 27-inch remote TVs • Swimming pool • No pets
60 miles from Reno. Near Top Gun Raceway, museum, rodeo grounds, and golf
1035 West Williams Ave., Fallon, NV
Directions: 5 blocks west of Junction US 50 and US 95, on US 50 Highway
(775) 423-6005   www.bestwesternnevada.com
With coupon at check-in. Based on availability. Not valid with other discounts, during holidays or special events.

Expires 12/31/01

Best Western
Fallon Inn

LV01-06

Lake Tahoe
10% to 15% off

$$SAVE$$ ON LODGING
1–8 bedroom condos, cabins, homes.
Ski-in/out. Golfing. Mountain, lakeviews and lakefront.
Full kitchen, fireplace, hot tubs, and more.

•VACATION SPECIALISTS SINCE 1982•

Expires 12/15/01

Tahoe Management

P.O. Box 6900
209 Kingsbury
Stateline, NV 89449
www.at-tahoe.com
e-mail: tahoemagt@aol.com

(800) 624-3887

LV01-32

Golf Packages Worldwide for the Avid Golfer

This coupon is valid for 10% off your next golf vacation
CALL US TODAY — (800) 672-5620

Let our team of golf travel professionals plan your next golf vacation. We feature guaranteed tee times wherever you choose to travel.

Pacific Golf Adventures
Look for us on the web — www.pacgolf.com

LV01-36   Expires 12/31/01

HRN REBATE COUPON

(800) 964-6835
HOTEL RESERVATIONS NETWORK
www.hoteldiscount.com

Major Cities - Rooms for Soldout Dates - Special Rates

$10 REBATE with 2-Night Booking $20 REBATE with 4-Night Booking
$30 REBATE with 5-Night Booking $50 REBATE with 7-Night Booking

UP TO $50

Name: _____
Booking Number: _____
Hotel: _____
Dates of Stay: _____
See reverse side for rules.

LV01-23

VACATION TRAVEL SPECIALISTS
A DIVISION OF VTS TRAVEL ENTERPRISES, INC.

REBATE CERTIFICATE

Submit this certificate when making your reservation, and receive a **$50 Rebate** on any new three-four night air/hotel or air/cruise vacation package, or a **$100 Rebate** on any new seven night air/hotel or air/cruise vacation package booked by 12/31/01.

(800) 767-4887

LV01-10   Expires 12/31/01   Please reference #9050

UP TO $100 OFF

Save up to $100 when you buy your airline ticket from

Travel Discounters

Call (800) 355-1065 and give code ECG in order to receive the discount.

See reverse side for discount prices.
May not be used in conjunction with any other discount or promotion.
Coupon may be used more than once.

TRAVEL DISCOUNTERS
DISCOUNTING THE WORLD OF TRAVEL

LV01-07   Offer valid through 12/31/01

HRN REBATE COUPON

Coupon Rules:
1. Must return this coupon to receive rebate.
2. Coupon expires 12/31/01.
3. Rebate mailed after check-out.
4. Coupons non-combinable.
5. Not retroactive.
6. After check-out, send this coupon with self-addressed stamped envelope to: HRN 8140 Walnut Hill Lane, Suite 203, Dallas, TX 75231.
7. Rebate check mailed within 2-3 weeks.
8. One rebate per customer.

UP TO $50

VACATION TRAVEL SPECIALISTS
A DIVISION OF VTS TRAVEL ENTERPRISES, INC.

We realize that every vacation you take is a major personal investment and that you require value for your vacation dollar. Our vacation experts will offer exceptional service with no exceptions. Proficiency and knowledge of private villas, resorts, cruise lines, worldwide destinations and willingness to assist with every vacation need with one-on-one, personalized attention.

Visit Us at Our Web Site:
www.vtstraveldirect.com

TRAVEL DISCOUNTERS

Savings are subject to certain restrictions, holiday blackouts, and availability. Good for domestic and international travel that originates in the U.S. Valid for flights on most airlines worldwide. Service fees apply.

Minimum Ticket Price	Save
$200	$25
$250	$50
$350	$75
$450	$100

1-800-USA-HOTELS.com
Where cost-savings, peace of mind and superior service are guaranteed.
For All Your Hotel Needs Worldwide

EARN MORE FREQUENT FLYER MILES AND SAVE MONEY AT THE SAME TIME!

Save up to 65% on hotel rooms. (800) USA-HOTELS will find you the lowest available rates at any hotel, at any time, in any town. Earn one mile for every hotel dollar spent. **Earn 1,500 BONUS frequent flyer miles** when you make your first ONLINE reservation.

Expires 12/31/01   Please reference SC#9050

LV01-11

$100 discount

$25 per person discount on any travel package with a minimum value of $500 per person. Up to four persons per coupon. No blackout dates, no restrictions.
Does not apply to air-only bookings.

Celebration Travel & Tours

1149 South Robertson Blvd., Los Angeles, CA 90035
(310) 858-4951, (800) 272-1572

LV01-38   Expires 12/31/01

COUPON

Do you like to travel? Don't just dream about it. You've earned it.

Receive $25 or $50 off your next cruise or vacation*

*minimum purchase required. Coupon expires 12/31/01

Donna Zabel, Destination & Travel Specialist
168 Lake Terrace Drive, Munroe Falls, OH 44262
PH/Fax: (330) 686-0401   E-Mail: dz@ald.net
Web Site: www.ald.net/dreammaker/

DREAM MAKER DESTINATIONS
RESEARCH TO REALITY

LV01-09

Go-Lo Vacations
American Express Travel Service

$100 OFF any 7-night cruise or vacation
with a minimum value of $1,000 excluding air

301 Horsham Road
Horsham, PA 19044
(800) 747-0368
E-mail: info@go-lo-vacations.com   www.go-lo-vacations.com
All major credit cards accepted
Expires 12/31/01

LV01-05

1-800-USA-HOTELS.com

Where cost-savings, peace of mind and superior service are guaranteed.

For All Your Hotel Needs Worldwide

Visit Us at Our Web Site:
www.1800usahotels.com
(800) 872-4683

North Lake Tahoe's Premier Vacation Rentals
$50 OFF A 3 OR MORE NIGHT STAY

VACATION STATION has spectacular lakefronts, lakeviews, luxurious homes, condos and rustic mountain cabins. We offer our guests Tahoe's best value with competitive rates, off season discounts and your seventh night is free. No matter what your requirements, the friendly professionals at Vacation Station will take the time to make your next Tahoe holiday one you'll always remember. Call today for rates and availability.

(800) 841-7443
(775) 831-3664 • FAX (775) 832-4844
Visit our properties at www.vacationstation.net
LV00-31   Coupon not valid 12/19/00–1/05/01, 6/30–7/05/01, and 8/01–8/21/01. Expires 12/14/01

VACATION STATION
Lake Tahoe
THE HOLIDAY DESIGNERS

HOW TO PLAY FREE GOLF!
Save $10 on regular $49 membership

CALIFORNIA • OREGON • WASHINGTON • NEVADA • HAWAII • ARIZONA • BRITISH COLUMBIA

Learn how 15,000 golfers save at 500 courses.

Plus golf vacations and 50% off lodging

P.O. Box 222594, Carmel, CA 93922, Fax (831) 625-6485

LV01-20   Expires 12/31/01

Club 19
Since 1981

(800) 347-6119
Call for your free brochure

Adventure Tours USA

$50 per couple off the brochure rate on an Adventure Tours USA 4- or 7-night air and hotel ski or Las Vegas vacation package

One certificate per booking. Holiday blackouts apply. Valid on new bookings only. This certificate is not redeemable for cash; nontransferable and valid only for use on Adventure Tours USA. Not valid with any other coupon or discount.

Call (800) 522-5386 for information and reservations.
Reservations must be made by Dec. 31, 2001 for travel by Dec. 31, 2001.

Expires 12/31/01

LV01-22   Booking Code: 6096

North Lake Tahoe's Premier Vacation Rentals
$50 OFF A 3 OR MORE NIGHT STAY

VACATION STATION has spectacular lakefronts, lakeviews, luxurious homes, condos and rustic mountain cabins. We offer our guests Tahoe's best value with competitive rates, off season discounts and your seventh night is free. No matter what your requirements, the friendly professionals at Vacation Station will take the time to make your next Tahoe holiday one you'll always remember. Call today for rates and availability.

(800) 841-7443
(775) 831-3664 • FAX (775) 832-4844
Visit our properties at www.vacationstation.net
Coupon not valid 12/19/00–1/05/01, 6/30–7/05/01, and 8/01–8/21/01. Expires 12/14/01
LV00-32

VACATION STATION
Lake Tahoe
THE HOLIDAY DESIGNERS

Great Hills Travel
$100 Value

Rebate of $25 per person on any air/tour or air/cruise package with a minimum value of $475. Up to four persons per coupon. Also applies to Walt Disney World and Disneyland air/hotel packages.

(512) 795-2210
Fax (512) 345-8891 E-mail manly@texas.net

LV01-04

Expires 12/31/01

North Lake Tahoe's Premier Vacation Rentals
$50 OFF A 3 OR MORE NIGHT STAY

VACATION STATION has spectacular lakefronts, lake-views, luxurious homes, condos and rustic mountain cabins. We offer our guests Tahoe's best value with competitive rates, off season discounts and your seventh night is free. No matter what your requirements, the friendly professionals at Vacation Station will take the time to make your next Tahoe holiday one you'll always remember. Call today for rates and availability.

VACATION STATION
Lake Tahoe
THE HOLIDAY DESIGNERS

(800) 841-7443
(775) 831-3664 • FAX (775) 832-4844
Visit our properties at www.vacationstation.net
Coupon not valid 12/19/00–1/05/01, 6/30–7/05/01, and 8/01–8/21/01.
Expires 12/14/01

LV00-30

GOLF CRESTED BUTTE COLORADO!!

Home of the Award-Winning Robert Trent Jones II Championship Golf Course
Rated in the Top 1% of Mountain Golf Courses
10% Discount on Direct Bookings
Fantastic Condominium Lodging & Greens Fee Packages!

THE REMINGTON MANAGEMENT GROUP

www.crestedbutte.net
(800) 950-2133

LV01-21

Expires 10/01/01 Discount Code ECG

Samsonite®
Company Stores

10% OFF
your entire purchase

Not valid on Kodak, Hasbro, or Safety First
Not valid with any other coupon offer

Call 1-800-547-BAGS for the location nearest you or visit our website www.samsonitetravelexpo.com

LV01-12

Expires 12/31/01

Golf Shoes Plus

$5 off any pair of shoes up to $75, and $10 off any pair of shoes over $75. Also 20% off any accessories.
Golf shoes and walking shoes (Footjoy, Etonics, Nike, and Adidas) and accessories
1850 Boyscout Drive, Suite #111, Ft. Myers, FL 33907
(941) 278-3331   www.golfshoesplus.com
Expires 12/31/01

PRO'S EDGE

LV01-17

**Largest selection
Huge savings**

$5 off first order over $20

www.golfballs.com
(800) 37-BALLS

golfballs.com
1.800.37.BALLS

LV01-08

Expires 12/31/01

Promo code eg201

Golf Shoes Plus
Golf shoes, walking shoes, and street shoes

Mention ECONOGUIDE #1001 for a **10% discount**
on any one pair of shoes

www.golfshoesplus.com
Expires 12/31/01

PRO'S EDGE

LV01-15

Casio Outlet
$5 off any $30 purchase

The leading manufacturers of sport watches, keyboards, and digital technology. We also carry product lines from JVC, Olympus, Minolta, Yashica, and Maxell.

Box 134, 7400 Las Vegas Boulevard South
Las Vegas, Nevada 89123 (702) 269-9591
e-mail: vegas@casio.com

CASIO

LV01-14

Expires 12/31/01

Magnetic Therapy Sales Specialist

Discount for mail order
25% off one product

Call for brochure or information on magnetic support products (knee tube, elbow tube, back support, inner soles, head and wrist bands), magnetic bracelets, and jewelry

1850 Boyscout Dr., Suite #209, Ft. Myers, FL 33907
(888) 883-0813 or (941) 278-5503
www.magnetictherapysales.com

PRO'S EDGE

LV01-16   Expires 12/31/01

Golf Shoes Plus

Any set* of clubs in stock (cost plus 10%). *One set per coupon only. Hardgoods (Callaway, Taylor Made, Cobra, etc.) and accessories

$5 off any pair of shoes up to $75, and $10 off any pair of shoes over $75. Also 20% off any accessories.
Golf shoes and walking shoes (Footjoy, Etonics, Nike) and accessories

2704 Stickney Point Road, Sarasota, FL 34231
(941) 925-4733   www.golfshoesplus.com
Expires 12/31/01

PRO'S EDGE

LV01-18

Pro's Edge

The Big $moke Golf Clubs

Mention ECONOGUIDE #1002
for a *25% discount*
on one club *or* one complete set
of 1, 3, 5, & 7 wood, any flex available.

www.thebigsmoke.com
Expires 12/31/01

PRO'S EDGE

LV01-19

Quick-Find Index to Hotels, Attractions, and Restaurants
(See also the Contents)

LAS VEGAS

The Bests
Best Attractions in Las Vegas . . . . . xii, 111
Best Casino Buffets in Las Vegas . . . xii, 145
Best Casinos in Las Vegas . . . . xi, 29
Best Casino Shopping in Las Vegas. xii
Best Casinos in Downtown Las Vegas . . . 97
Best Places to Stay in Las Vegas. xi
Best Production Shows in Las Vegas xii, 107
Best Restaurants in Las Vegas . . . . . xi, 145
Special Mentions. xii

Maps
Lake Tahoe. 302
Las Vegas Strip 43
Laughlin. 186
McCarran International Airport 18
Nevada viii
Reno 234
Reno, Virginia City, and
  Lake Tahoe. 241

Attractions
Adventuredome, The 117–119
Bonnie Springs Ranch 124, 170
Caesars Magical Empire. 115–116
Ethel M. Chocolate Factory. 173–174
Flyaway Indoor Skydiving 119
Guiness World of Records Museum. . . . 122
Hoover Dam 174–176
Imperial Palace Antique Auto
  Collection 122
Las Vegas Art Museum 122–123
Las Vegas Natural History Museum. . . . 123
Liberace Museum 123
Lied Discovery Children's Museum. . . . 124
Lost City Museum of Archeology 124
Luxor. 117
Manhattan Express. 119–120
MGM Grand Adventures. 116–117
Nevada State Museum 124
Omnimax Theatre, Caesars Palace 124
Race for Atlantis. 120–121
Searchlight Museum 124
Secret Gardens, Mirage 124
Speedworld at the Sahara 114–115
Star Trek: The Experience 111–113
Stratosphere Tower 121
Wet 'n Wild 119
White Tiger Habitat. 124

Hotels and Casinos
Index of Las Vegas hotels 141–144
Aladdin. 29–30
Alexis Park. 81–82
Algiers Hotel. 95
Bally's 82–83
Barbary Coast 83–84
Bellagio. 30–34
Binion's Horseshoe 101–102
Buffalo Bill's Resort 182
Caesars Palace 34–40
Circus Circus. 40–41
Desert Inn. 84–85
El Cortez 106
Excalibur. 41–46
Fitzgerald's 102
Flamingo Hilton 85–86
Four Queens. 102–103
Four Seasons Hotel 59
Gold Coast 87
Golden Gate 103
Golden Nugget. 98–100
Hard Rock Hotel & Casino 46–47
Harrah's Las Vegas. 87
Holiday Inn/Boardwalk. 95–96
Imperial Palace 88–89
Jackie Gaughan's Plaza 103–104
La Bayou 106
Lady Luck. 104
Las Vegas Club. 104–105
Las Vegas Hilton 47–50
Luxor. 50–52
Main Street Station. 100–101
Mandalay Bay 57–60
Maxim's 89
Mermaids 106
MGM Grand 52–57
Mirage 60–64
Monte Carlo Resort & Casino 64–65
New Frontier. 86
New York–New York. 65–66
O'Shea's 96
Orleans Hotel & Casino 89–90
Palace Station 90–91
Paris–Las Vegas Casino Resort. 66–68
Pioneer Club. 106
Primadonna Resort. 181–182
Rio Suite Hotel & Casino 68–71
Riviera 91–92
Sahara. 92–93

353

Sam Boyd's Fremont Hotel 105
Sam's Town Hotel & Gambling Hall 96
San Remo 96
Stardust 93–94
Stratosphere Tower 71–73
Treasure Island 73–75
Tropicana 94–95
Venetian Casino Resort 75–80
Whiskey Pete's Hotel 182

Restaurants 145–160
Buffets 146–149
Casino restaurants 150–156
Non-casino restaurants 157–160
Theme restaurants 156

Signature Restaurants
Al Dente, Bally's 82–83
Alta Villa, Flamingo Hilton 85–86
Andiamo, Las Vegas Hilton 49
Andre's, Monte Carlo 64
Antonio's Ristorante, Rio Suites 70
AJ's Steakhouse, Hard Rock 46
Aqua, Bellagio 32
Asia, Harrah's 87
Aureole, Mandalay Bay 58
Bally's Steakhouse, Bally's 82
Bamboleo, Rio Suites 69
Benihana Village, Las Vegas Hilton 49
Binion's Ranch Steak House,
   Binion's 101–102
Bistro Le Montrachet, Las Vegas Hilton .. 49
Black Spot Grille, Treasure Island 74
Border Grill, Mandalay Bay 59
Broiler, Palace Station 90–91
Brown Derby, MGM Grand 55
Buccaneer Bay Club, Treasure Island ... 74
Burgundy Room, Lady Luck 104
Buzio's Seafood Restaurant, Rio Suites ... 71
California Pizza Kitchen,
   Golden Nugget 100
California Pizza Kitchen, Mirage 64
Canaletto, The Venetian 79
Canal Street Grille, Orleans 90
Center Stage, Jackie Gaughan's Plaza ... 104
Chang's, Bally's 82
China Grill, Mandalay 59
Chin Chin, New York-New York 66
Conrad's, Flamingo Hilton 86
Cortez Room, Gold Coast 87
Delmonico's Steakhouse, The Venetian .. 79
Don Miguel's, Orleans 90
Dragon Court, MGM Grand 56
Dragon Noodle Company, Monte Carlo . 64
Drai's On The Strip, Barbary Coast .. 83–84
Embers, Imperial Palace 89
Emeril's New Orleans Fish House,
   MGM Grand 56
Empress Court, Caesars Palace 37–38
Fellini's Tower of Pasta, Stratosphere ... 73
Fiore, Rio Suites 71
Fortune's, Rio Suites 69
Francesco's, Treasure Island 74
Gallagher's Steak House, New York–
   New York 66
Garden of the Dragon, Las Vegas Hilton . 49
Gatsby's, MGM Grand 55
Gee Joon, Binion's 102
Gilley's Saloon, Frontier 86
Golden Dynasty, Tropicana 95
Great Moments Room, Las Vegas Club . 105
Hilton Steakhouse, Las Vegas Hilton 49

House of Blues, Mandalay Bay 59
Ho Wan, Desert Inn 84
Hugo's, Four Queens 103
Hyakumi, Caesars Palace 38–39
Il Fornaio, New York-New York 66
Isis, Luxor 51
Jasmine, Bellagio 33
Kokomo, Mirage 64
Kristofer's, Riviera 92
La Chine, Paris–Las Vegas 67
La Rotisserie des Artistes, Paris–Las Vegas 67
La Scala, MGM Grand 55
Le Cirque, Bellagio 31
Le Provençal, Paris–Las Vegas 67
Lillie Langtry's, Golden Nugget 99–100
Limerick's Steakhouse, Fitzgeralds 102
Lutéce, The Venetian 77
Luxor Steakhouse, Luxor 51
Madame Ching's, Treasure Island 74
Magnolia's Veranda, Four Queens 103
Margarita's Mexican Cantina, Frontier .. 86
Mark Miller's Grill Room, MGM Grand .. 55
Mask, Rio Suites 70
Mediterranean Room, Gold Coast 87
Michael's, Barbary Coast 84
Mikado, Mirage 63
Mizuno's, Tropicana 95
Ming Terrace, Imperial Palace 89
Mon Ami Gabi, Paris–Las Vegas 67
Monte Carlo, Desert Inn 85
Moongate, Mirage 63
Montana's Steakhouse, Stratosphere .. 72–73
Mortoni's, Hard Rock 47
Napa Restaurant, Rio Suites 69
Neyla, MGM Grand 55
Nobu, Hard Rock 46
Olives, Bellagio 33
Onda, Mirage 63
Osteria del Circo, Bellagio 31–32
Paparazzi Grille, San Remo 93
Papyrus, Luxor 51
Pasta Remo, San Remo 93
Phil's Angus Steakhouse, Frontier 86
Picasso, Bellagio 32
Pietro's Gourmet, Tropicana 95
Pink Taco, Hard Rock 46
Pinot, The Venetian 78
Plank, The, Treasure Island 74
Portofino, Desert Inn 84
Postrio, The Venetian 79
Prime, Bellagio 33
Pullman Grille, Main Street Station ... 101
Rain Forest Café, MGM Grand 53
Range Steakhouse, The Harrah's 87
Red Square, Mandalay Bay 58
Renoir, Mirage 63
Ricardo's, MGM Grand 55
Rik'Shaw, Riviera 92
Rock Lobster, Mandalay Bay 58
Royal Star, The Venetian 79
Rumjungle, Mandalay Bay 58
Sacred Sea Room, Luxor 51
Saizen, San Rémo 93
Samba Grill, Mirage 63
Sam's American, Bellagio 33
Savanna, Tropicana 95
Seahouse, Imperial Palace 89
Seasons, Bally's 82–83
Second Street Grill, Fremont 105
Shanghai Lilly, Mandalay Bay 58
Shintaro, Bellagio 33

Index

Sir Galahad's Prime Rib House,
   Excalibur 45–46
Star Canyon, The Venetian 78
Steakhouse at Camelot, Excalibur 45
The Steak House, Circus Circus 41
Stefano's, Golden Nugget............ 99
Taqueria Canonita, The Venetian ... 79–80
Terrazza, Caesars Palace............. 38
Tony Roma's, Fremont.............. 105
Tony Roma's, Stardust 94
Top of the World, Stratosphere Tower... 72
Trés Jazz, Paris–Las Vegas............ 67
Tres Lobos, Stardust 94
Tres Visi, MGM Grand............... 55
Valentino's Italian Grill, The Venetian .. 78
Vincenzo's Italian Café, Fitzgeralds.... 102
Voo Doo Café, Rio Suite 70
WB Stage 16, The Venetian 80
WCW Nitro Grill, Excalibur.......... 45
William B's, Stardust................ 94
Wolfgang Puck's, MGM Grand 55
Wolfgang Puck's Trattoria del Lupo,
   Mandalay Bay................... 58
Zeffirino, The Venetian 79

Shopping 131–140
Bookstores, gambling supplies 134
Boulevard Mall............... 132–133
Factory outlets 133
Fashion Show Mall 131–132
Forum Shops at Caesars 135–139
Grand Canal Shoppes,
   The Venetian.............. 139–140
Las Vegas Chinatown Plaza 134
Meadows Mall................... 133
Showcase Mall................... 140

Showrooms
Celebrity shows.................. 110
Nightclubs 110
Production shows............ 107–110
   Cirque du Soleil, Bellagio 30
   Cirque du Soleil, Treasure Island 75
   EFX, MGM Grand................ 54
   Folies Bergere, Tropicana......... 95
   Tournament of Kings, Excalibur ... 42–44
   Siegfried & Roy, Mirage........... 62

Sports and Recreation
Bicycling....................... 165
Golf...................... 163–165
Horseback riding................. 162
Ice skating 162
Las Vegas Stars Baseball............ 161
Parks and scenic areas............. 165
Skiing and sledding 162–163
Tennis 165
UNLV sports 161

Touring
Boulder City 176–177
Dreamland (Area 51) 167–168
Henderson.................. 173–174
Hoover Dam 174–176
Lake Mead 177–181
   Cruises....................... 178
   Fishing....................... 178
   Swimming 179
   Boating 179
   Hiking....................... 180
Lake Mohave.................... 181
Mount Charleston 170–172
Overton 172

Primm.................... 181–182
Red Rock Canyon............ 169–170
Rhyolite....................... 172
Valley of Fire 171–172

LAUGHLIN
Area attractions 193–195
   Christmas Tree Pass 187
   Chloride...................... 197
   Colorado River Museum 194
   Davis Dam............. 184, 193–194
   Grand Canyon Railway 195
   Grapevine Canyon 187, 194
   Katherine's Landing 195
   London Bridge 195
   Oatman...................... 195
Buffets........................ 193
Hotels and casinos 187–192
   Avi Hotel..................... 192
   Colorado Belle Hotel 188–189
   Don Laughlin's Riverside 187–188
   Edgewater Hotel 189
   Flamingo Hilton Laughlin 189–190
   Golden Nugget Laughlin.......... 190
   Harrah's Laughlin............... 191
   Pioneer Hotel 191
   River Palms Resort 190
   Ramada Express............. 191–192
Outdoor activities............ 195–196

RENO, VIRGINIA CITY, AND LAKE TAHOE

The Bests
Buffets, Reno/Sparks........... 223–224
Casino-hotels in Lake Tahoe......... 283
Casino-hotels in Reno/Sparks........ 199
Casino restaurants in Reno/Sparks 223
Driving trips, Reno and
   Lake Tahoe 239–260
Non-casino restaurants in
   Reno/Sparks............... 224–225
Restaurants in Lake Tahoe 283

Attractions
Amusement Parks,
   Reno/Sparks................... 232
Carson City 277–282
   Nevada State Museum 278–279
   Nevada State Railroad Museum 280
   State Capitol 279–280
   Stewart Indian Cultural Center .. 280–281
Museums, Reno/Sparks 214–216
   Fleischmann Planetarium 231
   Great Basin Adventure............ 230
   National Automobile Museum .. 231–232
   Nevada Museum of Art 231
   Nevada State Historical Society 231
   Wilbur May Center.............. 230
   W. M. Keck Museum,
      Mackay School of Mines 231
National Bowling Stadium, Reno .. 229–230
Virginia City 261–276
   Castle, The.................... 271
   Chollar Mine 268
   Crystal Bar.................... 269
   Dayton 275
   Fourth Ward School 269
   Geiger Grade 262–263
   Gold Hill 274
   Julia Bulette Red Light Museum..... 269

Mackay Mansion. 273
Mark Twain in Virginia City. . . . 263–265
Nevada Gambling Museum 270
Piper's Opera House 272
Ponderosa Mine 267
Ponderosa Saloon 266
Silver City 274–275
Territorial Enterprise Museum. 269
Virginia and Truckee Railroad. . . 269–270
Wedding chapels,
   Reno and Sparks 237–238
Wild Island, Reno 232

Hotels
Reno/Sparks hotels. 203–222
Atlantis Casino Hotel, Reno. 203–204
Cal-Neva Club, Reno 214
Circus Circus, Reno 204–205
Comstock, Reno 205
Eldorado, Reno. 205–207
Fitzgerald's, Reno. 214
Flamingo Hilton, Reno 207–208
Harrah's, Hampton Inn, Reno . . . 208–209
John Ascuaga's Nugget, Sparks. . . . 216–218
Peppermill, Reno 209–210
Reno Hilton, Reno 210–212
Sands Regency, Reno 212
Silver Legacy 212–213

Lake Tahoe hotels
Bill's, Lake Tahoe. 288
Caesars Tahoe, Lake Tahoe 291–292
Embassy Suites, Lake Tahoe 292
Harrah's, Lake Tahoe. 289–291
Harvey's, Lake Tahoe 286–288
Horizon, Lake Tahoe 293
Ridge Tahoe Resort, Lake Tahoe 293
Hotel and condo listing,
   Lake Tahoe 297–299

Restaurants
Buffets, Reno/Sparks 223–224
Restaurants, North Lake Tahoe . . . 296–298
Restaurants, Reno/Sparks. 224–227
Restaurants, South Lake Tahoe
   and Stateline 293–294

Shopping
Factory outlets, Lake Tahoe. 236–237
Factory outlets, Reno/Sparks 235–236
Meadowood Mall, Reno 235
Park Lane Mall, Reno. 236

Sports
Cruises, Lake Tahoe. 299
Golf and tennis, Reno/Sparks 233–234
Golf courses, Lake Tahoe 322
Summer sports, Lake Tahoe. 315–325
   Balloon rides 325
   Bicycling. 323–324
   Fishing 317–318
   Heavenly aerial tram. 315
   Hiking trails 319–322
   Horseback riding. 324
   Parks. 318–319
   Water sports and cruises. 316–317
Winter sports, Lake Tahoe. 303–314
   Alpine Meadows 306
   Boreal Ridge. 306
   Cross-country ski resorts 310–312
   Diamond Peak 307
   Heavenly. 304–306
   Homewood Mountain Resort 307
   Kirkwood 307
   Mount Rose. 307–308
   Northstar-at-Tahoe 308
   Sierra-at-Tahoe 308
   Snow play areas 313–314
   Snowmobiling 312–313
   Squaw Valley USA 308–309
   Sugar Bowl 309

Touring
Bijou 255
Bowers Mansion 254–255
Cal-Neva Lodge. 246
Camp Richardson 255
Carnelian Bay 250
Crystal Bay 247
Edgewood. 244
Emerald Bay 257
Genoa 248–249
Glenbrook 242–243
Incline Village. 243
Kings Beach 250
Kingsbury Grade 249
Mount Rose 246
Pioneer Trail 259–260
Ponderosa Ranch. 245, 247–248
Pyramid Lake 239–241
Tahoe City 250–251
Tallac. 256–257
Thunderbird Lodge. 243–244
Truckee 252–254
Vikingsholm 257–258
Zephyr Cove 244